Research and Reflections on Southeast Asian American Education and Advancement

Research and Reflections on Southeast Asian American Education and Advancement

Wayne E. Wright, Vikrant Chap, Phitsamay S. Uy,
Chhany Sak-Humphry, Vichet Chhuon, and Bryan Thao Worra

Purdue University Press • West Lafayette, Indiana

Cataloging-in-Publication Data is available from the Library of Congress.
978-1-62671-100-6 (paperback)
978-1-62671-101-3 (epub)
978-1-62671-102-0 (epdf)

Cover: Amorn Setthithorn, *Pasts and Futures, Community and Dreams*, 2024.

Contents

CREATIVE WORKS

INTRODUCTION

1

Commemorating the 20th Anniversary of the *Journal of Southeast Asian American Education and Advancement* and 50 Years of Southeast Asian American Refugee Resettlement

PHITSAMAY S. UY, VICHET CHHUON,
BRYAN THAO WORRA, CHHANY SAK-HUMPHRY,
VIKRANT CHAP, AND WAYNE E. WRIGHT

RESEARCH AND REFLECTIONS ON SOUTHEAST ASIAN AMERICAN EDUCATION and Advancement is a timely collection designed to promote and commemorate some of the best work in the growing field of Southeast Asian American Studies. This volume was inspired by the 20-year anniversary of the *Journal of Southeast Asian American Education and Advancement* (JSAAEA), from which the research articles, book reviews, and creative works in this book are drawn (www.jsaaea.org). We, the editors of this book, also serve as the current JSAAEA Editorial Team.[1]

HISTORY AND CONTRIBUTIONS OF THE *JOURNAL OF SOUTHEAST ASIAN AMERICAN EDUCATION AND ADVANCEMENT*

In 2005, the Executive Board[2] of the National Association for the Education and Advancement of Cambodian, Laotian, and Vietnamese Americans (NAFEA), a national collective founded in 1978 of professionals from P–21 education and community spaces from across the United States, met in Washington, DC to discuss the educational issues of their Southeast Asian American community and wanted to make a positive impact on the educational landscape of K–21 through research and creative works. A major and consistent concern raised each year at national NAFEA conferences was the need for more research on Southeast Asian American communities and the need for a centralized outlet to disseminate this research. The *Journal of Southeast Asian American Education and Advancement* is the result of their brain trust.

Board member Wayne E. Wright was tasked with developing the journal and serving as the editor; other NAFEA board members took on important editorial roles—Chhany Sak-Humphry and KimOanh Nguyen Lam as associate editors and Leslie Turpin as book review editor. JSAAEA was launched in 2006 as a peer-reviewed academic interdisciplinary online open-access journal, with substantial material and technology support from the University of Texas at San Antonio's College of Education and Human Development, and the Department of Bicultural-Bilingual Studies. In 2015, JSAAEA transitioned to a new platform with generous support from the Purdue University College of Education and the Department of Curriculum & Instruction, and expert technical and publishing support from Purdue University Press. As recounted in the editor's introduction to the inaugural 2006 issue:

> From 1998 to 2002, NAFEA worked closely with the Office of Bilingual Education and Minority Languages Affairs (OBEMLA).[3] During this time period, NAFEA and OBEMLA co-organized and hosted a number of educational symposia, such as the National Forum on Asian and Pacific American Education, to bring together community leaders, teachers, graduate students, and researchers. A research agenda was developed and proposed to the participants. These symposia brought attention to potential Southeast Asian American doctoral candidates and the need to do more research within Southeast Asian American communities on topics of importance to the leaders and members of these communities. Since then, the number of Southeast Asian American research studies by native scholars has slowly but steadily increased. NAFEA views the creation of the *Journal of Southeast Asian American Education &*

> *Advancement* as a logical and timely next step to provide a legitimate venue for the dissemination of relevant research studies, as well as the creation of a network of concerned educators and researchers across the country. NAFEA recognizes the critical role of this journal in supporting its organizational goal of promoting Southeast Asian American educational attainment, sociocultural well-being, and community and leadership development. (Wright et al., 2006, pp. 3–4)

While NAFEA ceased operations in 2020 after over four decades of outstanding service and national advocacy for Southeast Asian American communities, its legacy lives on through the *Journal of Southeast Asian American Education and Advancement*. The journal's mission and content are encapsulated in the following overarching aims and goals (Wright et al., 2015):

1. *Research*: Provide a forum for scholars and writers conducting original research from diverse fields who share a common interest in Southeast Asian Americans and their communities.
2. *Book Reviews*: Provide a forum for readers to learn about the growing number of books being published related to Southeast Asian Americans and communities.
3. *Creative Works*: Provide a forum for creative works (e.g., poetry, essays, etc.) by native Southeast Asian American writers that provide cultural insight into the Southeast Asian American experience in ways that traditional academic research cannot address.
4. *Mentorship*: Serve as a vehicle of mentoring and support for Southeast Asian Americans pursuing doctoral degrees in fields relevant to the journal.

This book reflects this mission by highlighting a representative sample of key research articles, book reviews, and creative works published in JSAAEA over the past two decades.

At the time of the journal's launch, and now, we understand intimately that Southeast Asians in the United States are incredibly diverse and are among the least visible and understood groups in U.S. society (Chhuon, 2014; Chhuon & Hudley, 2011; Lee, 2005, 2009; Ngo, 2010, 2024; Ngo & Lee, 2007; Uy, 2018). The majority of Southeast Asians are from Vietnam, Cambodia, and Laos and came to the United States as refugees, not as voluntary immigrants (Hein, 1995; Wright & Boun, 2011). While Southeast Asian families were sometimes invoked in discussions about disparities within Asian American communities, Southeast Asian Americans were rarely the center of empirical analysis (Uy, 2016). Thus, the journal's emergence represented a timely intervention across various fields of study that examined Asian and Southeast Asian American life.

The year 2025 marks the 50th anniversary of the fall of Saigon, or what many have called the end of the "Vietnam War" (in the United States) or the American War (in Southeast Asia). The end of this particular American military involvement in Southeast Asia led to communist takeovers in Cambodia and Laos during the Killing Fields and the Secret War in Laos, respectively (Pran, 1997; Sisavath, 2019). These events, often involving horrific consequences and loss of life, would directly contribute to a mass exodus of Vietnamese, Cambodian, Laotian, and Hmong refugees from Southeast Asia (Shawcross, 1985). Over a million of these individuals eventually resettled in the United States (Kula & Paik, 2016). In the early years, few Americans knew why refugees from Southeast Asia were in the United States, and it was often challenging to secure resources to assist resettlement efforts in the 1980s. There were issues of culture shock, and many refugee assistance agencies focused on finding housing, workforce, and education assistance in addition to dealing with issues of posttraumatic stress disorder (PTSD), depression, early teen pregnancy, gang issues, gambling, and substance abuse (Chhuon, 2014; Dinh et al., 2008; Gordon, 2009; Lee, 2005; Lin et al., 2015; Ngo, 2024; Nou, 2006; Quintiliani, 2014; Smith-Hefner, 1990, 1993, 1999; Trueba et al., 1990; Xiong & Zhou, 2011). But with persistence, communities began to adapt and find solutions as they transitioned from life under the monarchies and other government styles in Southeast Asia to participation in democracies that were also undergoing the computer revolution.

For two decades, the *Journal of Southeast Asian American Education and Advancement* has been an important forum for examining the social and educational lives of these communities that have been part of U.S. society since 1975. The articles, reviews, and creative works we selected for this book are meant to highlight and bring renewed attention to many of these critical and ongoing issues.

Other journals, such as the *Journal of Asian American Studies* and the *Amerasia Journal*, have been influential in illuminating the complexities of Asian American communities. These outlets have been instrumental in challenging racism, including model minority racial stereotypes. These journals are foundational to the field of ethnic and immigration studies. Concomitantly, these publications tend to publish research on longstanding Asian American groups, including Chinese, Japanese, and Korean. Their editors and editorial boards have been primarily comprised of scholars from these communities. The arrival of the *Journal of Southeast Asian American Education and Advancement* speaks to the vital growth and heterogeneity of Asian American life.

For 20 years, JSAAEA has helped shepherd the growth of empirical and creative works that examine Southeast Asian Americans both as separate ethnic groups (i.e., Khmer, Lao, Hmong, and Vietnamese) and as a collective Southeast Asian subgroup. With continuing demographic changes in the United States, JSAAEA has expanded beyond its original focus on the refugee populations from Cambodia, Laos, and

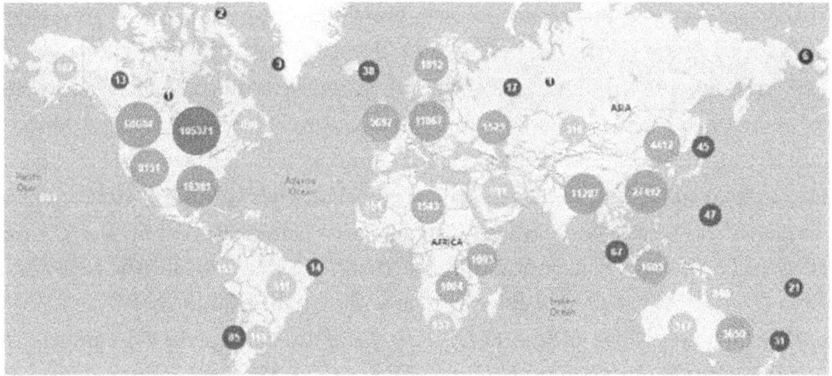

Figure 1.1. JSAAEA's global readership distribution (as of January 10, 2025).

Vietnam to be inclusive of other Southeast Asian American groups, including Thai and Filipino Americans, as well as more recent refugee groups from Burma (Myanmar).

Since its inception, JSAAEA publications have reached a broad audience across the globe, spanning more than 200 countries. The readership distribution (Figure 1.1) displays the global outreach of JSAAEA publications, including the number of views from different countries across six continents. Based on a total of 276,559 article downloads since 2015,[4] the top 10 countries are the United States (178,702), Vietnam (20,234), Canada (12,839), China (4,685), the United Kingdom (4,646), Australia (4,529), India (4,149), Germany (3,206), the Philippines (3,165), and Singapore (2,093). These numbers are distributed across nearly 8,000 institutions from a variety of sectors: education (75%), commercial (17%), organization (3%), and government (2%). By the end of 2024, JSAAEA had published 223 manuscripts.

Among the total number of publications were 84 research articles, 61 book reviews, 69 creative works, and 9 editorials, news, and reports. Most research articles are inclusive of the broader Southeast Asian American population ($n = 24$), followed by articles with a specific focus on Vietnamese Americans ($n = 18$), Hmong Americans ($n = 18$), and Cambodian Americans ($n = 16$). There are relatively fewer studies that focus on Burmese Americans ($n = 5$), Lao Americans ($n = 2$), and Filipino Americans ($n = 1$). The published book reviews highlight books that are focused on Cambodian Americans ($n = 19$), Vietnamese Americans ($n = 18$), Hmong Americans ($n = 10$), and cross-population works (Burmese, Cambodian, Filipinx, Hmong, Laotian, Vietnamese Americans) ($n = 9$)—followed by Thai Americans ($n = 3$) and Burmese Americans ($n = 2$). Creative works by Southeast Asian American writers display a broader representation of each focal population, with 20 works on Vietnamese Americans, 17 on Laotian Americans, 16 on Hmong Americans, 6 on Cambodian Americans, 5 on

Thai Americans, 3 on Burmese Americans, 1 on Filipino Americans, and 1 on collective voices.

Since its inception, JSAAEA has also been a critical mentoring and publishing space for up-and-coming Southeast Asian American scholars. For example, in 2006, Phitsamay Uy and Vichet Chhuon began with the journal as founding members of the doctoral student editorial board. Today, they are tenured faculty members who continue the journal's work as associate editor and book review editor, respectively. The coming of age of 1.5- and 2nd-generation Southeast Asian American scholars who have been part of the JSAAEA community has been essential for the field's growth. The Editorial Board and the Doctoral Student Editorial Board have some of the most influential minds and rising scholars in the field of Southeast Asian American Studies.

OVERVIEW OF CONTENTS

This book, *Research and Reflections on Southeast Asian American Education and Advancement*, is a celebration that highlights the important contributions that scholars of Southeast Asian American communities have made through publications in JSAAEA. Below we provide the context, rationale, and overview of the research articles, book reviews, and creative works selected from JSAAA for inclusion in this book.

Research Articles

The research articles reflect critical educational issues faced by the various Southeast Asian ethnic groups (i.e., language learning, academic engagement, family and community engagement, and youth issues). Chapters 2 and 3 focus on empirical research conducted with Khmer/Cambodian students. In Chapter 2, Lao and Lee examine heritage language use and maintenance among 1.5-generation Khmer college students. In Chapter 3, Chhuon, Dosalmas, and Rinthapol analyze factors that support the academic engagement of Cambodian American high school youth. Scholars Gordon and Phommasa both studied the Laotian American communities. In Chapter 4, Gordon discusses the language learning needs of the Laotian refugees, while in Chapter 7, Phommasa articulates the impact that families had on second-generation Lao American college students' aspirations. The Vietnamese American communities were the focus of Liang's and Lam's research. In Chapter 5, Lam describes the formation of a Vietnamese youth gang in Southern California. Liang highlights the experiences of Vietnamese American women public school administrators in Chapter 11. The diverse experiences of the Hmong and Hmoob communities were explored by Lee, Xiong, Pheng, M. N. Vang, and T. Vang, respectively, in Chapters 9 and 12. The health perceptions and practices of the newest Southeast Asian group, Burmese refugees, were studied by Kercood and Morita-Mullaney in Chapter 6. Some scholars examined Southeast Asian American groups as an aggregate and discussed policy recommendations for working with these communities. In Chapter 8, Uy studied the Southeast Asian American parents' and families' engagement with U.S. schools, while in Chapter 10, Nguyen discussed the role of Asian American and Native American Pacific Islander Serving Institutions (AANAPISIs) in supporting Southeast Asian American students.

Book Reviews

Since its inception, the journal has published 61 book reviews. This includes reviews of empirical research, memoirs, fiction, and children's books. Consistent with the other works in the journal, these book reviews focus on issues specific to Southeast Asian American life. The diversity of our reviewers matches the rich diversity of the books we receive. Our reviewers come from many different fields and backgrounds. Moreover, individuals who review for us range from undergraduate students to senior scholars in the field. Many individuals shared that writing for the *Journal of Southeast Asian American Education and Advancement* was their first publication opportunity and that this particular experience of reviewing helped to grow their confidence as scholars. Beyond helping the reviewer, book reviews support the scholarly community. The book reviews we have published have helped to bring attention to overlooked issues, communities, and authors. These reviews, in and of themselves, add to an important body of literature.

As was the process for research articles, selecting book reviews to publish in this book was hardly an easy task. Given space limitations, we could only select 10 reviews for inclusion. Regardless, each book review published in JSAAEA provides evaluative and compelling thoughts on important works relating to Southeast Asian American life.

In our selection process for this book, we sought a balanced representation across research, fiction, and children's literature. For example, Chapter 13 features Chang Pu's review of Stacey Lee's *Up Against Whiteness: Race, School, and Immigrant Youth*, now a seminal work on Hmong American education. Similarly, Gilbert Park's review of Bic Ngo's *Unresolved Identities* (Chapter 16) highlighted one of the best school ethnographies of Lao American youth. We sought good representation across communities (i.e., Vietnamese, Lao, Cambodian, and Hmong) and across time to reflect 20 years of the *Journal of Southeast Asian American Education and Advancement*. The book reviews of memoirs such as *The Latehomecomer* (Chapter 14 by Sarah Hansen) and *The Cambodian Family* (Chapter 22 by Jalisa Sang) help to promote tremendous Southeast Asian American writers like Kao Kalia Yang and Cathy Long. The critical analyses and insightful commentaries contained in these works demonstrate respect for the authors. Our wonderful reviewers have contributed powerfully to the journal's mission of increasing visibility of Southeast Asian American scholars and writers.

Creative Works

As the *Journal of Southeast Asian American Education and Advancement* marks this significant milestone with this volume, we have come a long way since the first issue in 2007. We did not see creative writing included until 2009 with Kay Vang's creative nonfiction piece "Do I Look Up or Do I Look Down? Reflections of a Hmong American English Learner and Educator." Poetry, creative nonfiction, and other pieces soon became a more regular part of the journal starting in 2010, when many cities were starting to observe the 35th anniversary of the beginning of the Southeast Asian diaspora.

There has always been an exciting discourse about what types of works we would include from writers, scholars, and community builders with roots in Southeast Asia. Some were U.S. citizens. Some were refugees or immigrants. A few were adopted, and several reflect diverse roots and multiple identities and geographies. The journal gave Southeast Asian artists the space to explore the possibilities of being and the types of works we shared. Many engaged with everyday life, while others were more science fiction. A few wanted to take on the traditional myths, while others wanted to discuss changing social roles and shifts in their culture and traditions.

Sometimes, it was clear what they were addressing, and in a few instances, the pieces were more opaque. But we are honored that so many talented writers opted to share their works with us and that so many were open to feedback and editorial suggestions. For many of the writers we included, it was eye-opening that contributing their creative work to academic journals could be a healthy and vibrant part of our literary reconstruction and reimagining ourselves: who we have been, who we are, and who we might yet be.

Having a consistent space for this could sometimes be taken for granted. Often, creative literary works in other journals engaged with Asian American topics have been incidental, not deliberate. But all of our cultures have ways of passing on information, data, and notions through stories, verse, songs, and expressive traditions that don't necessarily fit neatly into academic writing with its citations and formal structures. But at this delicate point in our shared conversations, it feels dangerous not to find ways to preserve these ideas.

This collection arrives with no small significance for the Hmong and Lao refugee communities, as it marks the 30th anniversary of their early literary societies and journals in diaspora, the *Paj Ntaub Voice* and the SatJaDham Lao Literary Project. Among the Cambodians, Hmong, Lao, Vietnamese, and others, cultural preservation issues became a particular concern for many elders, with an emphasis on traditional dance and music prominent in many communities. The literary arts, however, faced struggles even five decades later.

This is not to say that we have been without achievement. The Lao Canadian writer Souvankham Thammavongsa received the $20,000 Trillium Award in 2021 for her debut novel *How to Pronounce Knife* (2020). Still, she had long been noted for her poetry collections such as *Small Arguments* (2003) and *Light* (2013), which received a 2014 Trillium Book Award for Poetry. The Hmong American writer Kao Kalia Yang's (2017) memoir about her father, *The Song Poet*, was recently presented as an opera in Minnesota, and she was just awarded a 2023 John Simon Guggenheim Fellowship. The Hmong American poet Mai Der Vang received a 2016 Walt Whitman Award from the American Academy of Poets for her collection *Afterland* (2017), a finalist for the National Book Award, and received a 2024 John Simon Guggenheim Fellowship. The *Journal of Southeast Asian American Education and Advancement* published one of her works in 2010, seven years before her award-winning collection *Afterland* debuted in 2017.

It's been gratifying to see many others went on to publish their first books after publication in the *Journal of Southeast Asian American Education and Advancement* in a wide variety of genres, from children's books to poetry collections, novels, and more. And we must never take such contributions for granted.

Our creative works editor since 2008, Byran Thao Worra, is also a well-known Lao American poet and an award-winning writer, and has worked tirelessly to promote the work of other Southeast Asian American writers. His recent anthology, *Before We Remember We Dream* (2020), was published by Sahtu Press. Among many other accomplishments, Bryan received a National Endowment of the Arts Fellowship in Literature in 2009, received the Joyce Award in 2019, and was recently appointed as the chair of the Council on Asian Pacific Minnesotans.

In the mid-1990s, Southeast Asian American literary journals emerged at a time when many refugee families had begun to send their children to college. Few in this generation were majoring in English or the literary arts or the humanities, typically encouraged to pursue degrees in business, law, medicine, or computer sciences. As the internet began to become increasingly available, young Southeast Asians began to avail themselves of the opportunities this presented and began grassroots publications to share their creative writing. For the Hmong, these literary efforts have been particularly significant as they did not have a written language until the mid-20th century, even as many scholars trace their roots back to pre-dynastic China. Washington University Press published the Lao writer Outhine Bounyavong's short story collection *Mother's Beloved* in a bilingual edition in 1999, but it remains very rare to see any books involving Laos presented this way in the United States or other parts of the world.

Many writers with roots in Laos opted for self-publishing or small presses, and typically these have very small print runs, such as Mali Phonpadith's collection *A Million*

Fireflies (2011) from Synergy Press. The San Diego–based poet Krysada Panusith Phounsiri broke ground as one of the first Lue poets to publish his poetry collections *Dance Among Elephants* (2014) and *Every Passing Minute* (2020) in the United States. Thanks to social media and growing computer literacy, and increased cultural gatherings across the United States, more of these works that were made between the 1990s and the present are becoming commonly known but not necessarily easier to obtain. Older works remain difficult to find, such as the Iu Mien anthologies *Quietly Torn* (Cowy, 2000) and *Quietly reBorn* (2000), or the five anthologies printed by the SatJaDham Lao Literary Project that were distributed by the members for free but never sold in stores. Back issues of the *Paj Ntaub Voice* magazine have similarly become difficult to collect, yet they provide a distinctive snapshot of where these communities were as they became part of the American story. Geographically, California and Minnesota were among the most active states where Lao and Hmong poets emerged in the first 50 years of these Southeast Asian diasporas. Cambodian writers have been emerging from New York and Massachusetts, while Vietnamese writers are emerging from almost every state, so that it would be difficult to declare one state as a particular literary center for our diasporas.

As we look back on the last five decades, it is clear there is still much to be said and shared about the history of our diasporas in the United States, Canada, and beyond. However, there is tremendous cause for optimism that a succeeding generation of writers with roots in Southeast Asia will continue to find enervating ways to express their cultural heritage and shared experiences around the globe.

We wish we could have included all of the writers in the pages of this book who took a risk and shared their work with us in JSAAEA over the years, of course. Still, we hope you will see those represented here in this book as good advocates for their community and that you take time to seek out the others published to date and those who will appear in future issues of JSAAEA.

Concluding Thoughts

Overall, this collection highlights the need for more research, reviews, and creative works on Southeast Asian American communities. These articles, reviews, and creative works are only scratching the surface. The future of Southeast Asian American Studies is still being developed. Further studies will need to be conducted on the intersectional identities of the growingly diverse Southeast Asian American communities. For example, many newer generations are multiethnic (e.g., Lao and Khmer; Hmong and Vietnamese; Burmese and Thai, etc.) and/or multiracial (e.g., Black and Khmer; White and Lao; Latinx and Vietnamese, etc.). Their needs and experiences will differ from those of their parents and grandparents as second- and third-generation students.

Similarly, the impact of COVID on the educational and mental health needs of these students has yet to be examined. Southeast Asian Americans are still combating the controlling images of the model minority, perpetual foreigner, and gang involvement. The growing anti-immigrant and antirefugee sentiment that is pervasive in the national U.S. sociopolitical environment has impacted the availability and access to social and educational support for the newer Southeast Asian refugees like the Karen and other Burmese ethnic groups. For example, the U.S. House of Representatives recently passed a budget bill proposing to cut $11 billion from Title I and Title III funding to K–12 schools, which cuts funding for language translation and English language learner programs as well as low-income assistance programs such as free and reduced lunches. While we celebrate 20 years of scholarship, and 50 years since initial refugee resettlement, we continue to need more scholars to focus on the Southeast Asian American communities and their pressing and ongoing needs.

NOTES

1. Current JSAAEA Editorial Team—Wayne E. Wright (founding editor), Chhany Sak-Humphry (founding associate editor and past NAFEA president), Phitsamay S. Uy (associate editor, past doctoral student Editorial Board founding member, and past NAFEA president), Vichet Chhuon (book review editor and past doctoral student editorial board founding member), Bryan Thao Worra (creative works editor), and Vikrant Chap (journal manager and editorial assistant). We wish to acknowledge past JSAAEA Editorial Board members KimOanh Nguyen Lam, Leslie Turpin, and Phouang Hamilton, and past journal managers/editorial assistants James Knaack, Shereen Bhalla, Kathleen Langham, Marianna Kuhl, Sovicheth Boun, Yeng Yang, Matthew Kraft, Marshal Klassen, Fang Gao, Sungae Kim, Chen Li, and Jeffrey Sovan Wright.
2. The NAFEA Executive Board members at the time included Hiep Chu (president), KimOanh Nguyen-Lam, Chhany Sak-Humphry, Dinh Van Lo, Hongthong Niravanh, Phouang Hamilton, Leslie Turpin, and Wayne E. Wright.
3. OBEMLA was renamed the Office of English Language Acquisition (OELA) by the No Child Left Behind Act of 2001.
4. Detailed tracking of JSAAEA article views and downloads began after the move of the journal to the current Bepress platform in 2015. We estimate JSAAEA had at least 100,000 downloads between 2006 and 2014 when it was housed using the Open Journal System.

REFERENCES

Bounyavong, O. (1999). *Mother's beloved: Stories from Laos*. University of Washington Press.

Chhuon, V. (2014). "I'm Khmer and I'm not a gangster!": The problematization of Cambodian male youth in US schools. *International Journal of Qualitative Studies in Education, 27*(2), 233–250. https://doi.org/10.1080/09518398.2012.758788

Chhuon, V., & Hudley, C. (2011). Ethnic and panethnic Asian American identities: Contradictory perceptions of Cambodian students in urban schools. *Urban Review, 43*(5), 681–701. https://doi.org/10.1007/s11256-010-0172-8

Cowy, K. (Ed.). (2000). *Quietly torn*.

Dinh, K. T., Weinstein, T. L., Kim, S. Y., & Ho, I. K. (2008). Acculturative and psychological predicators of academic-related outcomes among Cambodian American high school students. *Journal of Southeast Asian American Education & Advancement, 3*, 1–25. http://jsaaea.coehd.utsa.edu/index.php/JSAAEA/article/view/30/44

Gordon, D. (2009). "She's American now, I don't like that": Gendered language ideologies in a Laotian American community. *Journal of Southeast Asian American Education & Advancement, 4*(1). https://doi.org/10.7771/2153-8999.1092

Hein, J. (1995). *From Vietnam, Laos, and Cambodia: A refugee experience in the United States*. Twayne.

Kula, S. M., & Paik, S. J. (2016). A historical analysis of Southeast Asian refugee communities: Post-war acculturation and education in the U.S. *Journal of Southeast Asian American Education & Advancement, 11*(1). https://doi.org/10.7771/2153-8999.1127

Lee, S. J. (2005). *Up against whiteness: Race, school and immigrant youth*. Teachers College Press.

Lee, S. J. (2009). *Unraveling the "model minority" stereotype: Listening to Asian American youth* (2nd ed.). Teachers College Press.

Lin, M. M., Her, P., & Gloria, A. M. (2015). Kawm Ntawv Qib Siab: Understanding the psychosociocultural educational experiences of Hmong American undergraduates. *Journal of Southeast Asian American Education & Advancement, 10*(1). https://doi.org/10.7771/2153-8999.1123

Ngo, B. (2010). *Unresolved identities: Discourse, ambivalence, and urban immigrant students*. State University of New York Press.

Ngo, B. (2024). *Re-membering culture: Erasure and renewal in Hmong American education*. University of Minnesota Press.

Ngo, B., & Lee, S. J. (2007). Complicating the image of model minority success: A review of Southeast Asian American education. *Review of Educational Research, 77*(4), 415–453. http://www.jstor.org/stable/4624907

Nou, L. (2006). A qualitative examination of the psychosocial adjustment of Khmer refugees in three Massachusetts communities. *Journal of Southeast Asian American Education & Advancement, 1*(1). https://doi.org/10.7771/2153-8999.1001

Phonpadith, M. (2011). *A million fireflies*. Synergy Press.

Phounsiri, K. P. (2014). *Dance among elephants*. Sahtu Press.

Phounsiri, K. P. (2020). *Every passing minute.* Sahtu Press.

Pran, D. (1997). *Children of Cambodia's killing fields: Memoirs by survivors.* Yale University Press.

Quietly reBorn: A literary journal by young Iu Mien American youth. (2000). Pacific News Service.

Quintiliani, K. (2014). A qualitative study of the long term impact of welfare reform on Cambodian American families. *Journal of Southeast Asian American Education & Advancement, 9*(1). https://doi.org/10.7771/2153-8999.1076

Shawcross, W. (1985). *The quality of mercy: Cambodia, holocaust, and modern conscience.* Simon and Schuster.

Sisavath, D. (2019). The US secret war in Laos: Constructing an archive from military waste. *Radical History Review,* (133), 103–116. https://doi.org/10.1215/01636545-7160089

Smith-Hefner, N. J. (1990). Language and identity in the education of Boston-area Khmer. *Anthropology & Education Quarterly, 21*, 250–268.

Smith-Hefner, N. J. (1993). Education, gender, and generational conflict among Khmer refugees. *Anthropology and Education Quarterly, 24*(2), 135–158.

Smith-Hefner, N. J. (1999). *Khmer America: Identity and moral education in a diasporic community*. University of California Press.

Thammavongsa, S. (2003). *Small arguments*. Pedlar Press.

Thammavongsa, S. (2013). *Light*. Pedlar Press.

Thammavongsa, S. (2020). *How to pronounce knife*. Little, Brown.

Trueba, H. T., Jacobs, L., & Kirton, E. (1990). *Cultural conflict and adaptation: The case of Hmong children in American society*. The Falmer Press.

Uy, P. S. (2016). Lao families' educational engagement. *Amerasian Journal, 42*(3), 69–89. https://doi.org/10.17953/aj.42.3.69-89

Uy, P. S. (2018). Unpacking racial identities: The salience of ethnicity in Southeast Asian-American youth's schooling experience. *Race, Ethnicity & Education, 21*(3), 407–421. https://doi.org/10.1080/13613324.2016.1248820

Vang, K. (2009). Do I look up or do I look down? Reflections of a Hmong American English learner and educator. *Journal of Southeast Asian American Education & Advancement, 4*(1). https://doi.org/10.7771/2153-8999.1096

Vang, M. D. (2017). *Afterland*. Graywolf Press.

Worra, B. T. (2020). *Before we remember we dream*. Sahtu Press.

Wright, W. E., & Boun, S. (2011). Southeast Asian American education 35 years after initial resettlement: Research report and policy recommendations. Conference Report of the National Association for the Education and Advancement of Cambodian, Laotian, and Vietnamese Americans. *Journal of Southeast Asian American Education and Advancement, 6*, 1–120. http://jsaaea.coehd.utsa.edu/index.php/JSAAEA/article/view/114/89

Wright, W. E., Nguyen-Lam, K., Sak-Humphry, C., Turpin, L., & Knaack, J. (2006). Editors' introduction—Fulfilling a critical need: The Journal of Southeast Asian American Education & Advancement. *Journal of Southeast Asian American Education and Advancement, 1*(1), 1–10. https://doi.org/10.7771/2153-8999.1000. https://docs.lib.purdue.edu/jsaaea/vol1/iss1/1

Wright, W., Uy, P. S., & Sak-Humphry, C. (2015). Editors' introduction to the 10th anniversary volume of the Journal of Southeast Asian American Education and Advancement. *Journal of Southeast Asian American Education and Advancement, 10*(1), 1–10. https://doi.org/10.7771/2153-8999.1119. https://docs.lib.purdue.edu/jsaaea/vol10/iss1/1

Xiong, Y. S., & Zhou, M. (2011). Ethnicity, language, and educational inequality: Challenges confronting Hmong students in American public schools. In X. L. Rong & R. Endo (Eds.), *Asian American education: Identities, racial issues, and languages* (pp. 43–58). Information Age Publishing.

Yang, K. K. (2017). *The song poet: A memoir of my father*. Picador.

RESEARCH ARTICLES

2

Heritage Language Maintenance and Use Among 1.5-Generation Khmer[1] College Students

RAVY S. LAO AND JIN SOOK LEE

ABSTRACT

Most studies of heritage language maintenance have reported a steep attrition in heritage language use among the 1.5- and 2nd-generation children of immigrants, in particular among East Asian groups. However, not much is known about the role of heritage languages and the patterns of language maintenance within refugee communities. This study focuses on heritage language use and maintenance among 1.5-generation Khmer college students. The findings show that Khmer students report a high frequency of heritage language use within the home with their parents as well as outside of the home with their co-ethnic peers. The data reveal that oral proficiency in Khmer is significantly more developed than literacy skills and is a necessity for bridging communication with parents and participating in co-ethnic peer social networks. The results of the study also indicate that these students' development of English oral and literacy skills were significantly higher than their heritage language skills, suggesting a similar trajectory of language loss similar to other immigrant groups, but perhaps at a slower rate.

> *I think language has a lot to do with it [knowing one's roots] because if you know the language, you immerse yourself in that culture . . . its past, its future, its present.*
>
> —SOUDANY (21-YEAR-OLD KHMER COLLEGE STUDENT)

For Soudany, a Khmer living in the United States, and many others like her, speaking the heritage language (HL) is the key through which x e language has been especially challenging for children of immigrants and refugees in the United States. Historically, language minority groups have experienced a three-generational language shift resulting in monolingual English speakers by the third generation (Veltman, 1988). Moreover, recent studies have documented even faster rates of heritage language loss among the 1.5- and 2nd-generation children of immigrants, particularly in East Asian groups, where the shift to English is completed by the second generation (López, 1996; Wong-Fillmore, 2000). Although there have been several studies conducted on heritage language maintenance in East Asian immigrant groups (Cho, 2000; Lee, 2002; Shin, 2005; Tse, 1998; Wong-Fillmore, 2000), research on Southeast Asian children's heritage language, with the exception of a few studies, is scarce (Portes & Rumbaut, 2001; Wright, 2003, 2004). A closer examination of Southeast Asian children's heritage language experiences is necessary not only because of the importance of understanding the central ways in which the heritage language plays a role in developing relationships within families and co-ethnic communities, but also because there are likely to be differences in heritage language maintenance patterns between immigrant and refugee groups due to the contrasts in the origins and motivations for immigration, the sociopolitical contexts of immigration, as well as cultural practices and norms[2] (Ogbu, 1987; Ogbu & Simons, 1998).

In the current educational climate, one of the top priorities is in improving English language development among children of immigrants and refugees. This study examines the HL maintenance patterns and use among the 1.5-generation Khmer college students who have successfully navigated the educational pathways to be able to enter college. This population offers a lens to understanding the role of the heritage language in the lives of linguistic minority youth who have been successful in acquiring English. In this study, the 1.5 generation is a broad category referring to children of first-generation refugees, who were born outside of the United States. We focus on the 1.5 generation in this study because this is the population of students who are among the first wave of Khmer refugee children to enter higher educational institutions in the United States. Although some scholars make finer distinctions such as the 1.25 or the 1.75 generation to capture the differences experienced by youths who arrive in the host country at different life phases,[3] for the purposes of this study, we group these individuals as the 1.5 generation to distinguish them from the 2nd generation born in the United States. Furthermore, the majority of our research participants were of Khmer descent; however, some individuals identified themselves as Chinese Khmer.[4] To better understand language use and heritage language maintenance patterns, this study addresses the following questions:

1. What are the patterns of language use in the home and outside of the home among 1.5-generation Khmer college students?
2. What are the self-perceived levels of oral and literacy skills in the heritage language and English among 1.5-generation Khmer college students?
3. Do (a) attendance of HL school, (b) language practices, and (c) perceived parental and self attitudes toward the HL affect the HL proficiency and preferences for language use among 1.5-generation Khmer college students?

THE ROLE OF HERITAGE LANGUAGE IN THE LIVES OF IMMIGRANT CHILDREN

Prior research has shown that heritage language affects the person, family, community, and educational spheres of ethnic minority children's lives in various ways (Lee & Suarez, 2009). Studies have found that proficiency in the HL supports maintenance and enhancement of family relationships and ties with members of the ethnic community (Cho, 2000; Luo & Wiseman, 2000; Portes & Hao, 2002). For instance, children who are fluent in their HL are less likely to experience frequent conflicts with parents than children of immigrants who only speak English (Portes & Hao, 2002). This is not surprising given that most first-generation immigrant and refugee parents do not acquire English proficiency at the rate that their children do. Without a common language, tensions and miscommunication within the family are inevitable. In another study, Tannenbaum and Howie (2002) examined upper elementary school–aged Chinese immigrant children living in Australia to determine the role of heritage language in immigrant families, specifically the connection between parent-child relationships and the children's heritage language maintenance. They found the children's use of their heritage language was connected to how they perceived the closeness of their family; that is, higher proficiency in the HL predicted perceptions of stronger family cohesion. Moreover, in a study by Cho (2000) on 1.5-generation adults of Korean descent, she found that those who had maintained their heritage language competence experienced better relationships with other heritage language speakers. The maintenance of their home language by immigrant children was critical because it enabled them to gain access to their parental guidance and social capital in the community. The need to have a common means of communication is particularly important for Khmer children because they have been found to experience high levels of acculturative stress resulting from parent-children conflicts at home (Ong, 2004; Um, 1999).

Furthermore, other studies have found that immigrant children who can speak their HL have a stronger sense of identity, higher self-esteem, and self-determination (Cho et al., 1997; Hinton, 1999; Phinney et al., 2001; Stalikas & Gavaki, 1995). There has been a great public concern that immigrants who maintain ties to their ethnic language and culture are resisting assimilation into the host culture (Crawford, 1999); however, on the contrary, research has found that immigrant individuals who can speak their HL are more connected with both the culture of their host country as well as their ethnic culture (Feuerverger, 1991; Imbens-Bailey, 1996; Lee, 2002; Tse, 1998). For instance, Feuerverger (1991) found that bilinguals living in Canada felt a stronger connection to both their home culture and that of Canadian culture, resulting in high levels of biculturalism. Imbens-Bailey (1996) reported similar findings for bilingual individuals living in the United States. In other words, individuals who had a stronger sense of their ethnic identity also had stronger identification with their host countries, indicating a preference for a bicultural identity.

In terms of immigrant students' academic spheres, examining Vietnamese immigrant children in New Orleans, Bankston and Zhou (1995) found that literacy in Vietnamese is positively related to academic achievement in English among this group. A study focusing on Spanish-speaking children of immigrants also found correlations between reading and writing in Spanish and achievement scores and GPA (grade point average) in English (García-Vázquez et al., 1997). In essence, García-Vásquez and her colleagues reported that students who maintained their HL, in the form of additive bilingualism, experienced greater academic outcomes on standardized tests in comparison to their English monolingual counterparts. The positive relationship between heritage language maintenance and academic achievement makes sense in that children who have high heritage language proficiency are perhaps also the ones that have high self-esteem and are able to develop stronger relationships with parents and other ethnic community members, which are all necessary conditions for positive academic experiences.

However, despite studies showing the positive relationship between HL maintenance and academic outcomes among linguistic minority students as mentioned above, we commonly witness the negative consequences of schools failing to utilize students' heritage language to assist them in their schooling. Following a group of Khmer students who attended a school district in Southern California that failed to properly comply with state and federal policies in assisting ELL students, Wright (2003, 2004) documented how the lack of home language support had negative consequences on these students in the forms of heritage language loss, low academic English skills, and negative effects on their self-identity and family communication. Scholars have widely argued for the educational benefits of tapping into and utilizing students' funds of knowledge, which are resources, skills, and knowledge bases that students bring from their home culture such as their heritage language (Moll et al., 1992). With high rates of low academic achievement among Khmer students (Reeves & Bennett, 2004; Rumbaut &

Ima, 1988), it is of urgency to explore multiple pathways that can improve Khmer students' educational outcomes. Given the positive benefits that HL proficiency is likely to bring immigrant children in their personal, social, and educational spheres (Lee & Suarez, 2009), HL development and maintenance may be one mechanism through which the overall well-being of Khmer immigrant children can be improved. Greater resources and public support are needed, for example, to assist in the development of Khmer heritage language schools and bilingual programs, particularly in areas where there is a high concentration of Khmer students. One positive model is a current program, supported by three public organizations in a local community in Southern California, which offers free Khmer literacy lessons on a weekly basis at a local public library (Lao, 2009). The significance of this program lies in the fact that it is organized and supported through a collaboration between Khmer community members and public agencies that have gained an awareness and appreciation for the need and value of heritage language support for their ethnic community members.

METHODS

Participants

The data for the present study come from a larger study that was conducted in 2001–2002 on Khmer Americans' language and educational experiences. The selection criteria for participants were that they must be: (1) 18 years or older and (2) 1.5-generation Khmer immigrants (i.e., born outside the United States) and (3) currently, enrolled in a four-year university or college. After the initial selection screening, 93 participants of whom 47 were males and 46 females were included in this study. The ages of the informants ranged from 18 to 36 years, with a mean age of 22.6. In this 1.5-generation Khmer college student sample, the majority (65.6%, $n = 61$) of them arrived in the United States before the age of 5, while only 34.4% ($n = 32$) arrived after the age of 5. Thus, most of the informants started their formal education in kindergarten in the United States. They indicated that their family immigrated to the United States between 1976 and 1990, but the majority (78%, $n = 73$) of the informants reported they had immigrated to the United States between 1980 and 1985.

Interestingly, 74% ($n = 69$) of the participants reported they came from a two-parent household, while 26% ($n = 24$) indicated they lived with a single parent. The high number of two- parent households runs counter to other studies that found most Khmer children grow up in nonintact families (Ong, 2004; Rumbaut & Ima, 1988). One reason for this finding may be that the participants were recruited on college campuses. Research has shown that children from single-parent households do not do as well in school than those from two-parent households (Sun, 2001). Thus, it is likely that having a two-parent household increased the students' chances to attend college.

In terms of ethnic identity, the majority, 74 respondents (79.6%), identified themselves as Khmer American and 19 respondents (20.4%) identified themselves as Chinese-Khmer American. As for heritage language classes, a little over half of the respondents (54.8%, $n = 51$) stated that they did not attend any heritage language classes, while 45.2% ($n = 42$) stated that they did. However, among those who attended heritage language classes, 47.6% ($n = 20$) attended the program for less than one year and 52.4% ($n = 22$) reported attending for 2 or more years. The heritage language classes that were available to the informants were generally offered by community volunteers on the weekends in local Buddhist temples (wats) or Khmer community organizations.

Instruments

The questionnaire, consisting of 59 items, was grouped into four main sections: personal background; language background; language input; and culture and identity. The questionnaire was provided in English only, because the assumption based on the selection criteria was that the informants were English proficient. The personal background section includes questions about age, gender, place of birth, and age at time of immigration to the United States. The section on language background elicits self-assessments about language proficiency in English and Khmer (e.g., "How well would you say you are able to speak Khmer?") and language use patterns at home and outside of the home (e.g., "To whom do you speak English? To whom do you speak Khmer?"). There were 28 items that asked about heritage language class attendance, attitudes toward the heritage language (e.g., "How would you rate the worth of knowing how to read and write Khmer in the U.S.?"), and living environment (e.g., "Please describe your neighbors when you were growing up"). Finally, the culture and identity section includes questions dealing with ethnic identification (e.g., "How do you identify, that is, what do you call yourself?") and cultural preferences for social conduct.

In the language input section of the survey, participants were asked to rate their perceptions of their oral (speaking and listening) and literacy (reading and writing) proficiency in three languages: Khmer, Chinese, and English. A total of 12 questions on a Likert scale (3 = very well; 2 = well; 1 = not well; and 0 = not at all) were constructed for this section. Although the majority of the informants in this study indicated Khmer as their heritage language, some informants (5 of the 93) reported Chinese to be their heritage language. Whether it was Khmer or Chinese, both were treated as the heritage language for the research participants. These assessments were based on self-reported data.

Procedures

The surveys were distributed through a paper and pencil questionnaire and an online survey. First, Khmer/Cambodian student associations on four university/college campuses located in Southern California were contacted to request participation in the study. A total of 67 surveys were hand-distributed and completed in the presence of the researcher. There were no financial incentives offered to participants.

Second, in order to reach a larger 1.5-generation Khmer immigrant population, the same questionnaire was also posted on the Internet at (http://www.angelfire.com/yt2/surveys/index.html) and then linked to the Khmer Connection website (http://www.khmer.com). Khmer Connection is an international website where mostly young Khmer adults living in diaspora engage in online communication with co-ethnic group members. The survey remained online for three months. In this period of time, a total of 57 surveys were completed by participants. However, only 26 out of the 57 were included in the study because some of the informants did not meet the three selection criteria mentioned above.

Of the survey informants that were recruited from the four campuses, volunteers were recruited to be interviewed about their heritage language maintenance and use experiences. The interview provided a more in-depth explanation of their experiences that the survey instrument was not able to capture. A total of six informants were interviewed. With the exception of one woman who identified herself as Chinese Khmer who spoke both Khmer and Teochiu[5] (or Chowjow in Mandarin) as a home language, the rest identified themselves as Khmer and spoke only Khmer as their home language. Consistent with the demographics reported on the questionnaires, the majority of the interviewees arrived in the United States before school age. With the exception of one informant, the majority of the interviewees were born in refugee camps. Although their place of birth (whether it was in a refugee camp or in their heritage country) may have a difference in their attachment or desire to connect with their heritage language, our survey results showed that there were no significant differences in the perceived HL proficiency levels between these two groups. Perhaps the reason may be due to the fact that most of the informants in our sample came to the United States at such an early age. Hence, they may not have distinct memories of their earlier experiences prior to their arrival in the United States. Table 2.1 shows the profile of the six interviewees.

The interviews were conducted in English and the protocol consisted of open-ended questions relating to language and educational backgrounds, cultural values, and identity (e.g., "What was your experience in school like while growing up?"; "When you and your parents talk about Khmer culture, what are some of the things

TABLE 2.1. PROFILE OF THE SIX INTERVIEWEES

NAME*	GENDER	AGE AT TIME OF INTERVIEW (IN YRS.)	AGE ARRIVED IN U.S. (IN YRS.)	BIRTH-PLACE	LENGTH OF U.S. RESIDENCY (IN YRS.)	YEAR FAMILY ARRIVED IN U.S.
Chhaya	M	21	1	Thailand	21	1981
Lena	F	21	2	Thailand	20	1982
Samnang	M	21	3	Thailand	19	1983
Sochinda	F	22	5	Thailand	17	1985
Soudany	F	20	7	Cambodia	13	1988
Thida	F	20	3	Thailand	18	1984

*All names are pseudonyms to ensure anonymity.

that are brought up?"; and "What do you considered your ethnic identity to be?"). Each interview ranged from two hours to two and a half hours and was audio- and video-recorded.

Analysis

Means and frequencies of the informants' Likert ratings were calculated to assess language proficiency and language use patterns. Furthermore, the means of informants' responses were also used to group the informants into different categories such as low, neutral, and high language attitudes to perform relevant statistical analyses. Chi-squares, *t*-tests, and one-way analysis of variance were conducted to examine if there were any significant differences between English and HL proficiency levels and oral and literacy proficiency in relation to heritage language class attendance, birthplace, language use, and gender. The effect sizes were also calculated to assess the strength of the relationship between the two variables being tested.

The interview data were first transcribed and coded for themes that related to the survey findings. The responses of the informants are presented to provide a deeper understanding of the statistical patterns found in the survey data.

RESULTS AND DISCUSSION

Language Proficiency

In order to examine how the informants perceived their language skills, the informants were asked to self-rate their proficiency levels in both oral and literacy skills in English

TABLE 2.2. HL AND ENGLISH PROFICIENCY SELF-ASSESSMENT

HERITAGE LANGUAGE	MEAN (SD)	ENGLISH	MEAN (SD)
Speaking and Listening	2.29 (.54)	Speaking and Listening	2.80 (.38)
Reading and Writing	0.69 (.89)	Reading and Writing	2.74 (.39)

Scale: 3 (very well); 2 (well); 1 (not well); 0 (not at all)

and their HL on a Likert scale from 0 (not at all) to 3 (very well). Although there has been much criticism about self-reported language assessments, research has shown that if there are no external benefits or consequences associated with language proficiency self-assessments, self-ratings correlate highly with standardized proficiency measures (LeBlanc & Painchaud, 1985; Oscarson, 1989; Oskarsson, 1978, 1984). Thus, for the purposes of this study, self-reported perceptions of language skills were deemed to be sufficient.

As shown in Table 2.2, not surprisingly, the means of the 1.5-generation Khmers' self- ratings for English language proficiency were higher than their HL, particularly in their literacy skills.

To ascertain whether there is a statistically significant difference between the Khmer students' English and their HL proficiency, *t*-test analyses were performed. In terms of overall proficiency (speaking, listening, reading and writing skills), the results confirmed that the informants' English is in fact significantly higher than their HL skills [$t(92) = -8.41, p = .00, d = -0.87$]. The large effect size indicates a significant difference in the proficiency levels of English and HL. Moreover, the negative correlation shows that the higher the English proficiency, the lower the HL proficiency, suggesting a subtractive bilingualism trajectory, where as English becomes more developed the heritage language will weaken. This pattern seems to be more representative of literacy skills than oral skills.

To examine whether there are specific language skills that are more developed than others, further *t*-tests were conducted to compare the perceptions of language skills in English and the HL. The results showed that there is a significant difference between reading and writing proficiency in English and the HL [$t\,(92) = -19.24, p < .001, d = -1.99$], but not in their oral skills. These students rated their abilities in reading and writing in English as "very well," but in contrast, they rated their heritage language literacy skills to be "very low." However, this difference between the informants' English and HL literacy skills is not surprising given that most of the informants have only received formal education in English. Interestingly, the interviews also revealed a common experience across the informants in that their families tended to place more priority on the learning of English. For example, Lena stated that she was taught the English alphabet in the home, but was not taught how to write in Khmer.

> My dad taught us English so that we could go to preschool like a year later. My dad taught us the ABCs but our Cambodian [Khmer] was better. We couldn't read or write [in Khmer], but we knew how to speak [it] well.

Thus, the results suggest that English is the dominant language in the lives of Khmer students, putting to rest the concerns that immigrant and refugee children are not faring well in their English language development.

The means also indicated generally stronger oral skills than literacy skills across the two languages. *T*-test results showed that there was a significant difference in the rating of their oral and literacy proficiency in English, although the effect size was not large [$t(92) = 2.25, p = .027, d = 0.23$]. Despite the fact that most of these students attended their entire schooling in the United States, they still perceived a weakness in their English literacy skills. This result supports Wright's (2004) and Souryasack and Lee's (2007) findings that showed the difficulty that Southeast Asian students faced with academic English literacy. For instance, Wright (2004) found that most of his Khmer participants had to remain at the community college for extended years or dropped out of school because they experienced great difficulties in the courses that required extensive reading and writing in English. Similar to Wright's study, Souryasack and Lee (2007) documented a lack of opportunities for Southeast Asian immigrant students to develop strong literacy skills in middle school. Because literacy skills in English play a crucial role in education and the level of literacy skills determines school outcomes, there is a need to better understand how to improve English literacy skills for Southeast Asian students, who often fall into the long-term English language learner category. Based on the body of research that has shown positive transfer between a strong basis in one language to a second language (Cummins, 2001), it is quite possible that a stronger development of heritage language literacy skills may facilitate the development of English literacy skills.

As for the heritage language, there was a greater discrepancy between their oral and literacy skills [$t(92) = 17.54, p < .001, d = 1.82$]. These youths reported their perceived speaking and listening proficiency to be between "well" and "very well." However, it was a different story when it came to reading and writing in the HL; they reported that they lack these skills. This result aligns with findings from other heritage language learners from different immigrant groups, where there is a consistent pattern of low literacy skills in the heritage language (Luo & Wiseman, 2000; Nguyen et al., 2001; Valdés, 2000). The majority (65.7%, $N = 61$) of the informants arrived in the United States prior to receiving formal education in Khmer; so it is likely that they have had no literacy instruction in the HL unless they have experience attending a HL class. However, it is surprising that despite the fact that most of the informants arrived in the United States before school age, the informants perceived their oral proficiency in the HL to be similar to English. Thus, they seem to have achieved bilingual but not biliterate competence. In sum, the Khmer 1.5 generation seems to be on a similar, but possibly slower, language shift trajectory than those of other immigrant groups. In other words, the data show that their English proficiency is stronger than their HL proficiency and their oral skills in the HL are stronger than their HL literacy skills.

Language Use Patterns

In addition to identifying patterns in these Khmer students' proficiency in English and HL, differences in patterns of language use were also examined. The results yield both expected and unexpected findings. In the home, the informants reported that their parents predominately spoke their heritage language to them 93.5% of the time and they spoke to their parents in the HL 78.5% of the time. In the interviews, Chhaya, a male participant, echoed the predominant use of Khmer with the adults in his life. He remarked, "When I was growing up, my parents, all the adults around, they spoke Cambodian [Khmer] and I responded in Cambodian [Khmer]. All the time, it was in Cambodian [Khmer], even now, it's still Cambodian [Khmer]." Similarly, Sochinda commented,

> My whole family speaks Khmer. They didn't speak English that well to speak to me in English when I was younger, even my aunts and uncles. Even right now, they still speak to me in Khmer because it's easier that way.

These two students' comments demonstrate how enduring and pervasive the use of the Khmer language has been in their lives. As Sochinda's remark reveals, an impetus for her continual use of the heritage was simply due to the fact that the adults in her life had to speak Khmer to her because of their limited proficiency in English. Hence, both in the home and community, their HL is the dominant language of communication and a necessity.

However, when communicating with their siblings, English was the main language of communication, which is consistent with prior studies. The informants reported that 61.3% of the time they spoke English with their siblings, while they only communicated 35.5% of the time in the heritage language (see Table 2.3).

TABLE 2.3. PERCENTAGE OF HL AND ENGLISH LANGUAGE USE AMONG INFORMANTS IN THE HOME

	INFORMANT TO PARENTS	PARENTS TO INFORMANT	INFORMANT TO SIBLINGS
Heritage Language	78.5%	93.5%	35.5%
English	17.2%	6.5%	61.3%

The use of English is especially prevalent with younger siblings. Thida, a female informant, explained,

> I always speak English to them [younger siblings]. I figured they're more Americanized because they have lived most of their life here. So, I speak English to them a lot. It's kind of weird to speak Khmer to your siblings when you be[6] walking around. When you're in America, you be speaking Khmer to them outside the home is just awkward.

For the younger generation of Khmer youth, their ability to linguistically assimilate completely into the English-speaking community is made possible by their older siblings' linguistic accommodations. They are able to learn English faster because of the experiences and language input from their older siblings, and they do not have to be fully proficient in their heritage language because their older siblings are able to broker the communication with Khmer speakers. This issue was brought up by Samnang who saw his role as being able to bridge the gap between his first-generation parents and second-generation younger siblings. He explained:

> Lots of times, my parents would call and tell something and right after I hung up the phone, I would call the group [his younger siblings], and tell them, kind of reiterating in the language that they could understand [laughing], that kind of things. So definitely, I take that responsibility, like a bridge.

Thus, the opportunities to develop their heritage language for the younger generation are likely to be more restricted because of their limited use of the heritage language, while for the 1.5 generation, the use of the heritage language appears to be a necessity and an expectation. It is likely that the roles, attitudes, and experiences of the younger Khmer generation will be different from the 1.5 Khmer generation discussed here. This difference warrants more research.

TABLE 2.4. FREQUENCY OF HL USE (IN PERCENTAGES) AT HOME AND OUTSIDE OF HOME BY GENDER

	HOME			OUTSIDE OF HOME		
	MALE	FEMALE	TOTAL	MALE	FEMALE	TOTAL
Heritage Lang. **Use—(Yes)**	39 (41.9%)	31 (33.3%)	75.2%	41 (44%)	32 (34.4%)	78.4%
Heritage Lang. **Use—(No)**	10 (10.8%)	11 (11.8%)	24.7%	9 (9.7%)	11 (11.8%)	21.5%

In addition, many bridge generations and bilingual users report a high use of mixing of the two languages (Zentella, 1997). Despite the fact that most of the informants reported having bilingual oral skills, interestingly, there was a very low percentage of usage of a mix of HL and English to the same interlocutor. Perhaps the reason for this is because most bilinguals generally code-switch or code-mix when speaking to other bilinguals with similar levels of proficiency in both languages, which is not the situation with the parents who have limited proficiency in English and their siblings who have limited proficiency in Khmer. In other words, the uses of the two languages appear to be in a fairly strict diglossic situation, where each language is reserved for certain people and certain situational domains.

Although heritage language practice has mainly been reserved for use in the home with family members, it was also surprising to find a regular use of the HL outside of the home. These Khmer students reported that they use HL (75.2%) in the home and (78.4%) outside of the home as well, indicating a high usage of HL. Despite the fact that they rated their English proficiency to be higher than HL language, they still reported a high frequency of interaction with co-ethnic peers and community members using the HL (see Table 2.4). Although we do not have the data to fully understand the range of reasons behind the use of the heritage language with other co- ethnic peers who also have the ability to speak English, this finding shows us that language choice is not based solely on compensatory motivations resulting from the lack of knowledge of a certain word or because of limited proficiency. We find the examination of the full range of social motivations for deliberate choices to use the HL socially, among individuals such as our informants who reported higher levels of competence in English, to be a very interesting topic for further investigation.

We were also interested in examining if there were other variables such as gender or age of arrival at the time of immigration that may have influenced HL language use patterns. Previous research has shown that females are the ones who are more likely to maintain their heritage language and pass on the HL to the next generation (Arriagada, 2005; Baral, 1979; Portes & Hao, 2002). This leads us to expect a greater use of the HL and a higher HL proficiency level among females. However, a chi-square test showed insignificant differences in the use of the heritage language in the home and outside of the home as well as in the proficiency levels between males and females. Perhaps this pattern may change in future intergenerational transmissions of the language, but for the 1.5 generation, it appears that both males and females are equally invested in the use of HL. As mentioned earlier, an explanation for this result could be that since most of the adults in their lives were limited in their English proficiency, these youths have had to use Khmer in order to communicate with them, regardless of gender.

Another factor that was predicted to make a difference in their language use patterns is the age at the time of arrival to the United States. Prior studies have shown that the children who have had some schooling in the native country have a greater likelihood of retaining the HL and that early arrival in the host country can lead to heritage language loss (Alba et al., 2002; Rumbaut & Portes, 2001; Veltman, 1988). However, among the informants, there was little difference in the patterns of heritage language use in the home and outside of the home based on their age at the time of arrival in the United States. A chi-square analysis showed that the age at the time of arrival was not a significant pattern in HL use. Yet, there was a pattern for those who arrived before school age to only use the HL in the home, while those who arrived after school age used the HL both at home and outside of the home at a greater frequency.

In sum, the opportunities to use the HL outside of the home seem to provide greater motivation and opportunities to develop their HL as well as access to more diverse domains of language use. Such opportunities are likely to be a critical factor in these individuals' ability to maintain such high levels of Khmer proficiency. This result corroborates with Luo and Wiseman's (2000) study where they found Chinese-speaking peers to be the most important factor in Chinese American children's language maintenance. These findings also suggest that regular use of the HL both in the home and outside of the home represents the significant role of the Khmer language in these students' lives. In the home, because of the lack of English language proficiency on the part of their parents, the Khmer language is the tool that enables communication with their parents and also connects their parents to the outside English- dominant world. Outside the home, the Khmer language keeps them connected with their co- ethnic peers and community members. The majority of the Khmer students who participated in the interviews stated that they lived in or near a Khmer community at one time or another while growing up. Sochinda explained, "Most of my life, I remember living near Khmer people. We moved several times but always in a Khmer neighborhood. So, I've pretty much lived with Khmer people." The access to a community of speakers offers heritage speakers opportunities to use the language, which in turn affords the opportunities to practice and increase their proficiency in the language.

Factors That Affect Heritage Language Proficiency

In order to understand which factors contributed to the development of heritage language proficiency, five factors were examined to see if they influenced the level of heritage language proficiency. They were heritage language class attendance; HL use outside the home; HL use inside the home; self-language attitudes toward HL; and perceived parental attitudes[7] toward HL.

T-test analyses showed that heritage language class attendance had a significant effect on the informants' ability to read and write in their heritage language ($t = 3.55, p < 0.001, d = 1.20$), but not on their oral ability (see Table 2.5). Based on the interviews, the informants indicated a wide range of experiences in terms of their attendance and quality of heritage language classes for themselves and other Khmer peers. Their attendance ranged from two months to three years; however, the majority indicated an average of about a year. Two of the interviewees attended informal classes taught by one of their parents or a neighbor and the rest enrolled in more formal classes held at the local Buddhist temple (wat). One of the limitations of this study was that the informants were not asked about the quality of the instruction and thus, we do not have the information to determine the extent to which the quality of the instruction makes a difference in the development of their HL literacy skills. However, what we do know is that participation in a heritage language program led to higher levels of HL literacy gains than nonparticipation. This result suggests that irrespective of the quality of the program, attendance to some degree is better than no attendance for the development of HL literacy skills.

Furthermore, heritage language use outside the home had a significant effect on informants' speaking and listening ability ($t = -4.43, p < 0.00, d = 3.32$) and reading and writing ability ($t = -2.90, p < 0.005, d = 5.26$). The large and positive effect sizes show that the more the HL is used outside the home, the greater the informant's oral and literacy proficiency. However, it is unclear whether it is the stronger language proficiency that leads to greater HL use outside the home or whether the willingness to take up HL use outside the home is leading to greater proficiency in the HL. This result may also be confounded with the age at time of arrival variable. We reported earlier that those individuals who arrived in the United States after school age reported using more HL outside the home. However, we suspect that the age at time of arrival may only have had a minimal effect, because most of the informants arrived before school age. In addition, the length of U.S. residency and the number of years in the U.S. education system are likely to have overshadowed most of the effects of schooling in the native country.

TABLE 2.5. ATTENDANCE OF HL SCHOOL AND HL USE OUTSIDE OF HOME BY HL LANGUAGE PROFICIENCY

	HL SPEAKING/ LISTENING	HL READING/ WRITING
	MEAN (SD)	MEAN (SD)
Attendance of HL School	2.31 (.51)	1.04 (.87)
No attendance of HL School	2.26 (.58)	0.41 (.82)
HL use outside of home	2.40 (.56)	2.00 (.38)
HL use in home	1.86 (.48)	0.83 (.95)

Scale: 3 (very well); 2 (well); 1 (not well); 0 (not at all)

What was most interesting was that HL use in the home with parents and siblings did not have any effect on HL proficiency (see Table 2.5), putting into question common assumptions that HL can be developed solely in the home.

The effects of language attitudes on the informants' heritage language proficiency were tested using a one-way ANOVA. Based on the means and frequencies of the informants' ratings of their HL attitudes, the informants were grouped into three categories: low/negative attitudes, neutral attitudes, and high/positive attitudes. A statistically significant difference was found for informants with differing attitudes in their heritage language literacy proficiency [$F(2, 90) = 7.24, p < .001$]. Table 2.6 shows the mean and standard deviation comparing informants' attitudes, and Table 2.7 presents the variance summary.

Not surprisingly, those that had more positive self-attitudes toward the HL significantly had greater literacy proficiency in the HL, but their attitudes did not have an effect on oral proficiency. A post-hoc Tukey test showed that there is a significant difference between those that have negative ($p < .001$) or neutral ($p < .05$) attitudes toward the heritage language versus those with positive attitudes toward the heritage language. Furthermore, the results revealed that literacy skills are better developed among those who have positive attitudes toward the language. This makes sense because the individuals with more favorable attitudes are likely to be the ones that seek out opportunities to speak the language outside the home and that make a conscious effort to attend heritage language classes. However, language attitudes did not affect the HL oral proficiency levels among the informants. Most Khmer 1.5-generation students in the sample indicated a strong level of oral proficiency in their HL. It appears that for these Khmer students speaking Khmer at home is not a choice, but a necessity for them as a means to communicate with their parents who are typically non-English speakers.

TABLE 2.6. MEANS AND STANDARD DEVIATION COMPARING INFORMANTS' ATTITUDES

INFORMANTS' ATTITUDES OF IMPORTANCE OF THEIR HERITAGE LANGUAGE	N	LISTENING AND SPEAKING	READING AND WRITING
		M (SD)	M (SD)
Low Value	35	2.26 (.46)	0.39 (.72)
Neutral	26	2.23 (.67)	0.56 (.90)
High Value	32	2.36 (.53)	1.14 (.91)
Total	93	2.28 (.54)	0.69 (.89)

TABLE 2.7. ONE-WAY ANALYSIS OF VARIANCE SUMMARY TABLE COMPARING INFORMANTS' ATTITUDES TOWARD HERITAGE LANGUAGE

SOURCE	DF	SS	MS	F	P
READING AND WRITING					
Between groups	2	10.19	5.10	7.24	.001
Within groups	90	63.32	.70		
Total	92	73.52			
SPEAKING AND LISTENING					
Between groups	2	.28	.14	.47	.627
Within groups	90	26.92	.30		
Total	92	27.20			

In terms of perceived parental attitudes, previous research has placed much emphasis on the role and attitudes of parents in the maintenance and use of heritage language among children (Shin, 2005). However, in this study, perceived parental attitudes toward the heritage language were not significantly correlated with either speaking and listening or reading and writing proficiency in the heritage language.

Interestingly, the interviews revealed another important factor that contributed to the need and desire to maintain the heritage language. The informants stated that interest in the Khmer pop culture also helps 1.5-generation youth maintain their heritage language. For Thida, watching Thai and Chinese mini soap opera shows that were dubbed in Khmer helped her maintain the language, especially her listening skills. She recalled,

As a child, it [heritage language maintenance] was because I lived around a lot of Khmer people. My neighbors were Khmers and my parents spoke to me in Khmer. In middle school and high school, it was because of the movies.

Similar to Thida, Lena also attributed her Khmer maintenance to the dubbed foreign movies. She explained,

The reason I speak Khmer and the reason that I could speak Khmer is because I watched a lot of Thai and Chinese movies that spurred my interest. That was the main reason I wanted to keep the whole Cambodian [Khmer] thing [giggling] because I wanted to watch those movies. They were interesting to me.

Besides the dubbed movies, however, for other informants like Sochinda, karaoke assisted her with Khmer literacy. That is, in order to read the lyrics to sing the songs, she had to know how to read Khmer. She mentioned,

I wanted to learn how to read [in Khmer] because of karaoke. If I sing [in Khmer], I have to memorize the whole song... but if you listen to the music and you read them, it would be easier.

In addition to the need for Khmer as a means of communication, Khmer also serves as a means to engage with popular culture to which youth can easily relate. The appeal of the Khmer pop culture to the 1.5-generation youth is that they can see a reflection of themselves in the movies and music; for example, the characters in the movies are played by people that look like them and behave like them, which is a connection not easily made in Hollywood movies. Thus, the role of ethnic pop culture serves not only as a motivating factor and opportunity for heritage language, but it also serves as a social and bonding mechanism that warrants further study.

In sum, many studies on heritage language have documented the difficulties and challenges that immigrant groups face in maintaining their home language across generations. For instance, although children are generally proficient in the heritage language before school, once they start school, they experience HL loss at accelerated rates (Hinton, 1999; Shin, 2005; Wong-Fillmore, 2000). In the case of the 1.5-generation Khmer young adults, if we consider only oral proficiency as representative of heritage language maintenance, then for this generational cohort, they are displaying evidence of HL maintenance. Given that the majority (65.6%, $N = 61$) of the informants had arrived in the United States before school age and had also lived in the United States for more than 20 years at the time of study, it is surprising that they are still maintaining their heritage language at such high levels. On the other hand, if literacy skills are included in the definition of heritage language maintenance, the results show that these 1.5-generation Khmers are following the same HL loss patterns as other immigrant groups. However, this outcome is not surprising since again the majority of them arrived in the United States prior to receiving formal education in Khmer.

CONCLUSION AND DIRECTIONS FOR FURTHER RESEARCH

This study about the 1.5-generation Khmer college students both corroborates and also extends our understanding of the heritage language maintenance process in the Khmer community. Although HL loss in this group seems to be slower in comparison to other second-generation Asian ethnic groups (López, 1996), like other immigrant groups, English proficiency appears to be headed in the direction of replacing HL proficiency. Thus, active measures need to be taken to foster an additive model of dual language development to counter the subtractive model that is currently in place. Three findings from this study suggest some measures that can be taken to support additive bilingualism in the Khmer community.

First, the findings point to the potential that heritage language programs or community schools hold. Although there have been criticisms of the effectiveness of such programs (Lee, 2002), the findings suggest that heritage language classes play an important role in the development and maintenance of HL literacy skills. Thus, more research and resources should be invested in finding ways to support and improve what such programs have to offer young ethnic minority students.

Second, HL language use opportunities outside the home in the community played a critical role in the maintenance of the HL. This suggests that the HL spoken in the home alone is not enough. For informants like Sochinda and Soudany, who grew up in various Khmer communities in Southern California, they reported that access to their community helped them to maintain their HL. For Sochinda, it helped with both her verbal and literacy skills. She explained,

> We probably lived there for ten years. So we were with other Cambodians [Khmers]. I think that what helped me with my Khmer, especially how to read and write a little bit. My friend's aunt was teaching [Khmer literacy] when I was in elementary [school], and I sat down and learned it.

Similarly for Soudany, living in a Khmer community helped her maintained her roots. She pointed out,

> It was very helpful being in an ethnic enclave because you kinda like learned to appreciate your roots and you learned to broaden your perspective. That is what I'm proud of . . . not being one thing. I lived in a Cambodian [Khmer] place. So I knew like how to speak Cambodian [Khmer language], stuff like that. I knew the Cambodian [Khmer] ways.

Although living in communities where there is a dominant presence of co-ethnics seems to be a powerful force in supporting ethnic minorities to maintain both their HL language and culture, in reality, many ethnic minorities do not live in such communities. Pyong Gap Min (2005) points out "as economic conditions and social standing improve, a significant proportion of immigrants move to more desirable residential districts" (p. 38). This seems to be a current trend among Khmer families, who after establishing financial stability tend to move out of their ethnic enclave to suburban neighborhoods. In this era of increasing mobility among immigrant groups, we need to better understand how shifts in contexts affect identity development, language use, and cultural understandings among ethnic minorities who grow up in communities where there is a low presence of co-ethnics and also explore more creative ways in which ethnic minorities in any location can gain access to communities of speakers of the heritage language. For example, advancements in technology and the internet can enable ethnic minorities to find alternative ways to gain access to cultural information, to maintain ties to the homeland, to use language, and to express their identities. However, in light of these advancements we also need to reconsider what heritage language maintenance entails, what resources and opportunities are involved, and what new challenges and barriers are formed in this process.

Finally, Khmer popular cultural activities can also provide support for heritage language maintenance among 1.5-generation youth. Interviewees indicated that pop culture, either in the forms of foreign movies dubbed in Khmer or karaoke produced and imported from Cambodia, had played a prominent role in their Khmer language maintenance, especially in their late teen years. Besides providing Khmer language maintenance, these popular media offer exposure to Asian cultures and customs as well as provide a medium where Asians are presented in positive ways. Making appropriate forms of ethnic media more readily available to youth, perhaps through public libraries, can also provide a supportive mechanism for heritage language maintenance.

The HL is not only a tie that connects these youth to their family, community, and traditional cultural practices, but it is also a tie that connects them to the changing trends, values, practices, and language use within Khmer communities. Thus, the dynamic nature and fluidity of the contexts in the lives of ethnic minorities present interesting opportunities for researchers to investigate different facets of heritage language maintenance and its value and roles in the lives of ethnic youth.

PUBLICATION NOTE

This article was published online in 2009 by the *Journal of Southeast Asian American Education and Advancement* in Volume 4, Issue 1. Minor edits have been made here. The original can be found at http://doi.org/10.7771/2153-8999.1094.

NOTES

1. The term "Khmer" is an emic (insider) word used within the Cambodian community to refer to both its people and the language. "Cambodia or Cambodian," typically used outside the Cambodian community by the general public, is the Anglicized rendering of the French word "Cambodge," the name which the country inherited when it was under the French colonial protectorate, 1863–1954 (Owen, 2005). The second-generation Khmer youths, including some of our informants, often refer to themselves as Cambodian in English to reflect the general usage in the larger public. In this paper, Khmer is used to refer to both the people and language to be consonant with the way in which members of the Khmer community use it. More recently, scholars like S. Megan Berthold (1999), Nancy Smith-Hefner (1990, 1993, 1999), and Shirley S. Tang (2006) have opted to use the term Khmer for similar reasons.
2. Ogbu (1987) argues that the educational and social trajectories of "voluntary" immigrants, who emigrated from their native country by choice for socioeconomic reasons, are different from "involuntary" immigrants such as the Khmer, Laotian, and Vietnamese refugees, who were forced to leave their native country due to fear of persecution, because of their different sociopolitical histories and status and motivations for coming to the host country.
3. First immigrant generation can be further defined according to age of arrival: 1.75 generation (ages 0–5); 1.5 generation (ages 6–12); and 1.25 generation (ages 13–17) (see Rumbaut, 2004).
4. Cambodia has a long history of Chinese settlement. During the late 1960s just prior to the occupation of the Khmer Rouge regime that was responsible for massive deaths and exodus of the country's population as political refugees, they were the largest ethnic minority in Cambodia (Willmott, 1967). Some informants in this sample referred to themselves as being both Chinese and Khmer.
5. A Chinese dialect that is spoken by Chinese who live in Southern China and by the majority of Chinese Khmers.
6. The informants' responses are presented verbatim. Deviations from what is prescribed in English grammatical rules are noted in the speech of the informants. We understood these to be characteristic of the social English used in their local communities rather than evidence of a lack of English language proficiency.

7. We use perceived parental attitudes because we only asked the informants what they think their parents' attitudes were toward the value of the heritage language. We did not interview or survey the parents directly for this study.

REFERENCES

Alba, R., Logan, J., Lutz, A., & Stults, B. (2002). Only English by the third generation? Loss and preservation of the mother tongue among the grandchildren of contemporary immigrants. *Demography, 39*(3), 467–484. https://doi.org/10.1353/dem.2002.0023

Arriagada, P. A. (2005, September). Family context and Spanish-language use: A study of Latino children in the United States. *Social Science Quarterly, 86*(3), 599–619. https://doi.org/10.1111/j.0038-4941.2005.00320.x

Bankston, C., & Zhou, M. (1995). Effects of minority-language literacy on the academic achievement of Vietnamese youths in New Orleans. *Sociology of Education, 68*(1), 1–17. https://doi.org/10.2307/2112760

Baral, D. (1979). Academic achievement of recent immigrants from Mexico. *NABE Journal, 3*(3), 1–13. https://doi.org/10.1080/08855072.1979.10668356

Berthold, S. M. (1999). The effects of exposure to community violence on Khmer refugee adolescents. *Journal of Traumatic Stress, 12*(3), 455–471. https://doi.org/10.1023/A:1024715003442

Cho, G. (2000). The role of heritage language in social interactions and relationships: Reflections from a language minority. *Bilingual Research Journal, 24*(4), 369–84. https://doi.org/10.1080/15235882.2000.10162773

Cho, G., Cho, K., & Tse, L. (1997). Why ethnic minorities need to develop their heritage language: The case of Korean-Americans. *Language, Culture and Curriculum, 10*, 106–112. https://doi.org/10.1080/07908319709525244

Crawford, J. (1999). Bilingual education: History, politics, theory and practice (4th ed.). Bilingual Education Services.

Cummins, J. (2001). *Language, power and pedagogy: Bilingual children in the crossfire*. Multilingual Matters.

Feuerverger, G. (1991). University students' perceptions of heritage language learning and ethnic identity maintenance. *Canadian Modern Language Review, 47*, 660–677. https://doi.org/10.3138/cmlr.47.4.660

García-Vázquez, E., Vázquez, L. A., López, I., & Ward, W. (1997). Language proficiency and academic success: Relationships between proficiency in two languages and achievement among Mexican-American students. *Bilingual Research Journal, 21*(4), 334–347. https://doi.org/10.1080/15235882.1997.10162712

Hinton, L. (1999). Trading tongues: Loss of heritage languages in the United States. *English Today, 15*(4), 22–30. https://doi.org/10.1017/S0266078400011226

Imbens-Bailey, A. (1996). Ancestral language acquisition: Implications for aspects of ethnic identity among Armenian American children and adolescents. *Journal of Language and Social Psychology, 15*(4), 422–443. https://doi.org/10.1177/0261927X960154002

Lao, R. S. (2009, April). Charting a new path to success: Multi-agency collaboration in the establishment of a Khmer heritage language program. Paper presented at the annual meeting of the American Educational Research Association, San Diego, CA.

LeBlanc, R., & Painchard, G. (1985). Self-assessment of a second language placement instrument. *TESOL Quarterly, 19*(4), 673–87. https://doi.org/10.2307/3586670

Lee, J. S. (2002). The Korean language in America: The role of cultural identity in heritage language learning. *Language, Culture and Curriculum, 15*, 117–133. https://doi.org/10.1080/07908310208666638

Lee, J. S., & Suarez, D. (2009). A synthesis of the roles of heritage languages in the lives of immigrant children. In T. Wiley, J. S. Lee, & R. Rumberger (Eds.), *The education of language minority students in the United States* (pp. 136–171). Multilingual Matters.

López, D. (1996). Language: Diversity and assimilation. In R. Waldinger & M. Bozorgmehr (Eds.), *Ethnic Los Angeles* (pp. 139–163). Russell Sage Foundation.

Luo, S., & Wiseman, R. (2000). Ethnic language maintenance among Chinese immigrant children in the United States. *International Journal of Intercultural Relations, 24*(3), 307–324. https://doi.org/10.1016/S0147-1767(00)00003-1

Min, P.G. (Ed.). (2005). *Asian Americans: Contemporary trends and issues* (2nd ed.). Pine Forge Press.

Moll, L., Amanti, C., Neff, D., Gonzalez, N. (1992). Funds of knowledge for teaching: Using a qualitative approach to connect homes and classrooms. *Theory into practice, 31*(2), 132–141. https://doi.org/10.1080/00405849209543534

Nguyen, A., Shin, F., & Krashen, S. (2001). Development of the first language is not a barrier to second language acquisition: Evidence from Vietnamese immigrants in the United States. *International Journal of Bilingual Education and Bilingualism, 4*(3), 159–164. https://doi.org/10.1080/13670050108667725

Ogbu, J. U. (1987). Variability in minority school performance: A problem in search of explanation. *Anthropology & Education Quarterly, 18*(4), 312–334. https://doi.org/10.1525/aeq.1987.18.4.04x0022v

Ogbu J. U., Simons H. D. (1998). Voluntary and involuntary minorities: A Cultural-ecological theory of school performance with some implications for education. *Anthropology & Education Quarterly, 29*(2), 155–188. https://www.jstor.org/stable/3196181

Ong, A. (2004). *Buddha is hiding: Refugees, citizenship, the new America*. University of California Press.

Oscarson, M. (1989). Self-assessment of language proficiency: Rationale and application. *Language Testing, 6*(1), 1–13. https://doi.org/10.1177/026553228900600103

Oskarsson, M. (1978). *Approaches to self-assessment in foreign language learning.* Pergamon.

Oskarsson, M. (1984). *Self-assessment of foreign language skills: A survey of research and development work.* Council of Europe.

Owen, N. G. (Ed.) (2005). *The emergence of modern Southeast Asia: A new history.* University of Hawaii Press.

Phinney, J., Romero, I., Nava, M., & Huang, D. (2001). The role of language, parents and peers in ethnic identity among adolescents in immigrant families. *Journal of Youth and Adolescence, 30*, 135–153. https://doi.org/10.1023/A:1010389607319

Portes, A., & Hao, L. (2002). The price of uniformity: Language, family and personality adjustment in the immigrant second generation. *Ethnic and Racial Studies, 25*(6), 889–912. https://doi.org/10.1080/0141987022000009368

Portes, A., & Rumbaut, R. G. (2001). *The story of the immigrant second generation.* University of California Press.

Reeves, T. J., & Bennett, C. E. (2004). *We the people: Asians in the United States, Census 2000 Special Reports.* U.S. Census Bureau.

Rumbaut, R. G. (2004). Ages, life stages, and generational cohorts: Decomposing the immigrant first and second generations in the United States. *The International Migration Review, 38*(3), 1160–1205. https://doi.org/10.1111/j.1747-7379.2004.tb00232.x

Rumbaut, R. G., & Ima, K. (1988). *The adaptation of Southeast Asian refugee youth.* Southeast Asian Refugee Youth Study, Department of Sociology, San Diego State University.

Rumbaut, R. G., & Portes, A. (2001). *Ethnicities: Children of immigrants in America.* Russell Sage Foundation.

Shin, S. (2005). *Developing in two languages.* Multilingual Matters.

Smith-Hefner, N. J. (1990). Language and identity in the education of Boston-area Khmer. *Anthropology and Education Quarterly, 24*(2), 135–158. https://doi.org/10.1525/aeq.1990.21.3.04x0608j

Smith-Hefner, N. J. (1993). Language, gender, and generational conflict among Khmer refugees. *Anthropology and Education Quarterly, 21*(3), 250–268. https://doi.org/10.1525/aeq.1993.24.2.05x1118z

Smith-Hefner, N. J. (1999). *Khmer American: Identity and moral education in a diasporic community.* University of California Press.

Souryasack, R., & J. S. Lee (2007). Drawing on students' experiences, cultures and languages to develop English language writing perspectives from three Lao heritage middle school students. *Heritage Language Journal, 5*(1), 79–97. Retrieved April 28, 2008, from http://www.heritagelanguages.org/

Stalikas, A., & Gavaki, E. (1995). The importance of ethnic identity: Self-esteem and academic achievement of second-generation Greeks in secondary school. *The Canadian Journal of School Psychology, 11*(1), 1–9. https://doi.org/10.1177/082957359501100102

Sun, Y. (2001). Family environment and adolescents' well-being before and after parents' martial disruption: A longitudinal analysis. *Journal of Marriage and Family, 63*(3), 697–713. https://doi.org/10.1111/j.1741-3737.2001.00697.x

Tang, S. S. (2006). Gangs, schools and what else? Educational challenges, street intervention, and cultural/community development for Khmer American youth in Revere and Lynn, Massachusetts.: Southeast Asia Resource Action Center. Retrieved on June 4, 2008, from http://www.searac.org/3-savepaper2006.pdf

Tannenbaum, M., & Howie, P. (2002). The association between language maintenance and family relations: Chinese immigrant children in Australia. *Journal of Multilingual and Multicultural Development, 23*(5), 408–424. https://doi.org/10.1080/01434630208666477

Tse, L. (1998). Affecting affect: The impact of heritage language programs on student attitudes. In S. Krashen, L. Tse, & J. McQuillan (Eds.), *Heritage language development* (pp. 51–72). Language Education Associates.

Um, K. (1999). Scars of war: Educational issues and challenges for Cambodian-American students. In C. C. Park & M. M. Chi (Eds.), *Asian American Education: Prospects and Challenges* (pp. 263–284). Bergin & Garvey.

Valdés, G. (2000). Introduction. In N. Anderson (Ed.), *AATSP Professional Development* Series *Handbook for Teachers K-16: Vol 1. Spanish for Native Speakers* (pp. 1–20). Harcourt College Publishers.

Veltman, C. (1988). Modeling the language shift process of Hispanic immigrants. *International Migration Review, 22*(4), 545–562. https://doi.org/10.1177/019791838802200401

Willmott, W. E. (1967). *The Chinese in Cambodia.* University of British Columbia Publications Centre.

Wong-Fillmore, L. (2000). Loss of family languages: Should educators be concerned? *Theory into Practice, 39*(4), 203–210. https://doi.org/10.1207/s15430421tip3904_3

Wright, W. E. (2003). The success and demise of a Khmer (Cambodian) bilingual education program: A case study. In C. C. Park, A. L. Goodwin, & S. J. Lee (Eds.), *Asian American identities, families, and schooling* (pp. 225–252). Information Age Publishing.

Wright, W. E. (2004). What English-only really means: A study of the implementation of California language policy with Cambodian-American students. *International Journal of Bilingual Education and Bilingualism, 7*(1), 1–23. https://doi.org/10.1080/13670050408667798

Zentella, A. C. (1997). *Growing up bilingual: Puerto Rican children in New York.* Blackwell Publishers.

3

Factors Supporting Academic Engagement Among Cambodian American High School Youth

VICHET CHHUON, MOZZIE DOSALMAS,
AND NIDA RINTHAPOL

ABSTRACT

This exploratory study examined the relationship between Cambodian American students' ($N = 77$) attitudes and beliefs regarding school climate and school engagement. We examined engagement through two primary constructs: academic intrinsic motivation and future educational expectations. Four specific correlates of engagement were examined to understand the quality of Cambodian American students' school engagement: sense of racial fairness; feelings of teacher support; perceptions of self-competence; and perceptions of positive classroom environment. Perceptions of self competence were positively associated with higher educational expectations. Our regression models found that students' sense of positive classroom environment in addition to teacher support was important for motivation. Motivation and future academic expectations were also associated with students' perceptions of their own academic self-competence. Implications for research and practice are discussed.

INTRODUCTION

Current data has revealed that Cambodian students in the United States, on the whole, tend to exhibit lower levels of academic achievement relative to other ethnic populations. For example, of all Cambodians 25 years and older residing in the United States, less than half (40.9%) reported attainment of a high school education and only 11.1% have earned a four-year college degree (Pfeifer, 2008). These figures are far below the national averages of 84.2% and 17.2%, respectively (Pfeifer, 2008). Research has also consistently shown that Cambodian students have poorer academic performance than their peers from other ethnic groups, including other Asian immigrant groups such as those from China, the Philippines, and Vietnam (Kim, 2002; Portes & Rumbaut, 2006; Reeves & Bennett 2004; Rumbaut & Ima, 1988). Given their school performance overall, immigration scholars have argued that Cambodian children are at risk of assimilating into the lowest social and economic segments of American society (Portes & Rumbaut, 2006; Zhou, 1997).

Most Southeast Asian students and their families, Cambodians among them, come to the United States with refugee status and many originate from lower socioeconomic statuses and experience disruption in education and family separation. Consequently, academic underperformance is not surprising when Cambodian students are compared to East Asian students whose families emigrated through starkly different contexts (Kim & Yeh, 2002). At the same time, research on Cambodian students tends to be aggregated within an Asian American collective that often falls under the model minority stereotype (Lee, 1996). As such, the present study disaggregates the experiences of Cambodian American high school students by focusing on the school experiences of this unique and understudied population.

Explanations for Cambodian American Achievement

Many studies on the challenges that Cambodians face in their school environment focus on models that place the burden of change on the very students who are experiencing inequities. For example, some research has argued that the lower achievement of Cambodian students might be associated with cultural norms that inhibit parental educational involvement and promote a fatalistic orientation to schooling (Canniff, 2001; Smith-Hefner, 1999). Other studies have maintained that Cambodian cultural norms emphasize that parents should not intervene in the formal education of their children (Garcia Coll et al., 2002; Hopkins, 1996; Um, 1999). Quantitative research has also suggested that Cambodian parents tend not to have much direct involvement in their children's formal schooling. For instance, investigations with second- and fifth-grade Cambodian, Portuguese, and Dominican immigrant students in New York City (Garcia Coll et al., 2002) and Rhode Island (Garcia Coll et al., 2005) reported that Cambodian families scored lowest on every parent involvement measure. In addition, ethnographic interviews with members of the Cambodian community in the Boston area over a two-year period argued that Cambodian parents largely preferred to defer to the teacher and that parents were essentially noninterventionists in the schooling of their children, despite expressed concerns about their children doing well (Smith-Hefner, 1993). Other explanations, concomitantly, have centered upon immigration context, low socioeconomic status, and residency in poor communities as the most likely to significantly contribute to low educational attainment (Kim, 2002; Portes & Rumbaut, 2006). While research on cultural factors is informative, we consider the school context, at a minimum, to be on par with cultural factors; and therefore we chose, for this exploratory study, to emphasize the school context in an effort to expand on previous research regarding the experiences of Cambodian American high school youth.

SCHOOL ENGAGEMENT

The present study examined the relationship between Cambodian students' attitudes and beliefs about their school climate and their school engagement. We examined engagement through two primary constructs: *academic intrinsic motivation* and *future educational expectations*. In regard to motivation, we focused on academic *intrinsic* motivation because students who are intrinsically motivated have consistently been observed to demonstrate better conceptual understanding and experience more positive feelings toward school (Grolnick & Ryan, 1987; Ryan & Deci, 2000). Intrinsic motivation is best understood as the result of an optimal fit between the student and the learning environment (Ryan & Deci, 2000). *Extrinsic* motivation, on the other hand, involves engaging in learning through an outside reinforcement (e.g., free time) and punishment (e.g., detention), rather than learning for its own sake. Students who are intrinsically motivated are more likely to persist in school, hold higher academic aspirations, and experience increased emotional well-being. Unfortunately, students' achievement motivation tends to decline as they proceed through school and into the secondary grades (Anderman & Maehr, 1994).

Our second construct, future educational expectations, has been identified as having important relationships to grades, attendance, class participation, and later achievement (Muller et al., 1999; Rumberger, 2004; Sirin & Rogers-Sirin, 2004). Essentially, students with optimistic outlooks on their educational and career trajectories are likely to be influenced by and perceive their school climate differently than those with pessimistic expectations.

Finally, we focused on four specific correlates of school engagement to understand the quality of Cambodian American students' school engagement: *sense of racial fairness, feelings of teacher support, perceptions of self-competence,* and *perceptions of positive classroom environment.*

Sense of Racial Fairness

Many ethnic minority students, including Cambodians, experience educational challenges related to low expectations, racism, and lack of teacher support in their schooling. An increasing body of research has linked students' perception of discrimination within the school environment to achievement via motivation and academic performance (Lee, 2005; Ogbu & Simons, 1998; Portes, 1999). Portes (1999), for example, explored the influence of various factors in immigrant students' (primarily Cuban, Latino, Asian, Southeast Asian and Filipino students) school achievement and found that experiences of discrimination were salient factors in school experiences of low achievers. As well, Um (2003) and Lee (2005) have shown how low- and high-achieving Cambodian American and Hmong American high school youth, respectively, reported frequent experiences with racism in their school environment. Southeast Asian youth, including Cambodians, reported being put down and ethnically stereotyped by teachers as well as by other Asian American peers (Lee, 1996; Um, 2003). Cambodian adolescent *males* in particular are often stereotyped negatively in their local communities as low achievers and/or gang members (Chhuon, 2009; Chhuon et al., 2010; Um, 2003).

Feelings of Teacher Support

Research suggests that for minority and immigrant youth, feeling a sense of support from teachers and other school staff can play a critical role in students' academic well-being (Chhuon et al., 2010; Katz, 1999; Stanton-Salazar, 2001; Suarez-Orozco et al., 2009; Valenzuela, 1999). Valenzuela's (1999) ethnography of one Texas high school argued that a sense of genuine care from teachers often led to whether or not Mexican American youth academically engaged. Other research found that youth were not only frustrated by a lack of teacher support but perceived that the teachers themselves were a major source of ethnic discrimination (Katz, 1999; Lee, 2005; Stone & Han, 2005; Um, 2003). Given that many immigrant families, including Cambodians, settle in impoverished urban neighborhoods where schools tend to be overcrowded and understaffed, developing relationships with teachers may be challenging due to high staff turnover, particularly at the secondary level (García Coll & Magnuson, 1997; Teranishi, 2004). Other research suggests that students' perceptions of high teacher support can serve as a buffer from developmental risk factors including low socioeconomic status, negative peer pressure, and underfunded schooling (Chhuon et al., 2010; Stanton-Salazar, 2001).

Perceptions of Self-Competence

Students' perception of their own self-competence represents another important variable in student motivation and achievement (Bandura, 1994; Harter, 1982; Stipek, 1996). A student's view of his/her self-competence generally refers to how the student perceives success in a broad or specific area. Some research has shown that students from immigrant households, including Southeast Asians, tend to have lower self-appraisal of their academic competence than their peers (Kao, 1999; Padilla & Duran, 1995). This finding raises some concern given that much research has shown that a feeling of self-competence generally fosters academic motivation and promotes school engagement. Perceptions of self-competence are of interest to scholars and educators because of the motivational rewards that yield from students' positive perceptions (Harter, 1982; Stipek, 1996).

Perceptions of Positive Classroom Environment

Students' perception of a positive classroom environment can significantly shape their school engagement (Brophy, 1987; Urdan et al., 1998). For instance, when material is seen as interesting or new ideas are perceived as welcoming in class, students are much more likely to be drawn into the learning process. For instance, Portes's (1999) study of ethnically diverse and immigrant adolescents suggests that for students from immigrant families, perceptions of social and cognitive support in the classroom were related to higher achievement. Thus, the observation that the successes and struggles of many Southeast Asian students, including Cambodian, can be linked to the quality of their learning environments is not surprising (Chhuon et al., 2010; Kim, 2002; Lee, 2005; Wright, 2004).

THE CURRENT STUDY

The data reported in this article are part of a larger study that examined academic motivation across other Asian American ethnic samples including Chinese and Korean youth. As mentioned, research that has focused on educational challenges for Cambodian students as a disaggregated group is glaringly scarce in the literature (Ngo & Lee, 2007; Um, 2003). Given this, we examined a number of perceived school-level factors to understand how these factors might influence Cambodian high school students' academic engagement. We hypothesized that students reporting higher levels of perceptions of teacher support, self-competence, racial awareness, and positive academic environment were more likely to have increased intrinsic motivation and higher future academic expectations and goals. Given that research has reported differing gender experiences for Southeast Asian high school youth (Chhuon et al., 2010; Lee, 2005, Ngo & Lee, 2007), we also expected these relationships to vary by gender.

METHOD

Setting and Sample

Data were collected in a large urban high school in southern California. Both the school and surrounding community were economically diverse. Forty-seven percent of the enrollment was eligible for the free or reduced lunch program. The reported school enrollment during the 2005–2006 academic year was approximately 4,500 students. The school's ethnic breakdown was as follows: 15% African American, 12% Asian (including Cambodian), 36% Latino, and 33% White.

In an effort to ensure that participants in our sample identified as ethnically Cambodian, we recruited students from a Khmer language class. As a result, all 77 high school youth that participated in this study self-identified as ethnically Cambodian or Khmer. The Khmer language course was designed for students whose first language is English but whose home language included Khmer. This class fulfills the district's language graduation requirement and the language coursework requirement to enter a University of California or California State University campus. We were informed by teachers and administrators that the students enrolled in these courses represented a cross-section of academic achievement levels at the school. A balanced number of male ($n = 39$) and female ($n = 38$) students comprised our sample. Moreover, 19.5% were reportedly in the ninth grade, 33.8% in the tenth, 27.3% in the eleventh, and 19.5% in the twelfth.

Measures and Procedures

After parental consent forms were returned, students were administered a 53-item questionnaire that measured perceived future educational expectations (e.g., "When you graduate from high school, how possible is it that you will go to a 4-year university?"), support from teachers (e.g., "My teachers encourage me to do well"), positive classroom environments (e.g., "We try new ideas in English class"), racial fairness (e.g., "I think non-Cambodians are treated better than Cambodian students in my class"), self-appraisal of academic competence (e.g., "I am very good at writing reports"), and academic intrinsic motivation (e.g., "It is more important to do a school assignment to learn about a subject, than it is to get a good grade"). Surveys were administered to participating students in each class throughout one school day and took roughly 20 minutes to complete each session.

RESULTS

We began by creating composite variables to examine our hypotheses using a principal components analysis (PCA) of our attitudinal constructs. A PCA was appropriate because of our interest in reducing our large set of measured variables to a smaller set of composite variables that retained as much information about the original variables as possible (Fabrigar et al., 1999). In addition, the variables belonging to each construct were highly correlated with one another; therefore, utilizing the composite variables based on the principal components also offered a way to manage the lack of independence between variables while still retaining much of the original information.

Correlations

In our full sample, bivariate correlations revealed that all four independent variables were related to motivation at the $p < 0.05$ level (see Table 3.1). In the overall sample, intrinsic motivation related negatively to racial fairness ($r = -0.25$), and positively to teacher support ($r = 0.36$), self-competence ($r = 0.35$), and positive classroom environments ($r = 0.35$). Overall, future educational expectation was associated significantly solely with self-competence ($r = 0.55$).

For males in our sample, motivation was significantly related to teacher support ($r = 0.41$) and positive academic environment ($r = 0.39$), whereas future educational expectation was only associated with perceptions of self-competence ($r = 0.34$). Self-competence ($r = 0.72$) was also the only measure of perception that related to future educational expectations for females in our sample while motivation was

TABLE 3.1. CORRELATIONS

	RACIAL FAIRNESS	TEACHER SUPPORT	SELF-COMPETENCE	POSITIVE CLASS ENV.
Motivation				
Overall	0.25*	0.36*	0.35*	0.35*
Male	0.28	0.41*	0.27	0.39*
Female	0.24	0.32	0.42*	0.35*
Future Educational Expectations				
Overall	0.003	0.14	0.55*	0.17
Male	0.06	-0.05	0.34*	0.09
Female	0.06	0.33	0.72*	0.26

*Significant at the 0.05 level (two-tailed).

significantly related to female students' perceptions of self- competence ($r = 0.42$) and positive classroom environments ($r = 0.35$).

Regression

Next, we conducted regression analyses for both motivation and future academic expectations (see Table 3.2). In an effort to determine which variables significantly explained the variance of our dependent variables while controlling for all other variables, we began with a regression on our full set of predictor variables (teacher support, self-competence, positive academic environment, and racial fairness). Initially, we also included gender in the regression models since we hypothesized that a relationship with either motivation or future academic expectations and any of our predictors might be mediated by gender. Although our correlations slightly varied by gender, gender was not a significant main effect or interaction in any model, thus it was subsequently dropped from this analysis. For motivation, a regression with the full set of predictors revealed self-competence as the only significant predictor at a 0.05 level ($\beta = 0.04, p = 0.04$).

The more positively students viewed their self-competence the higher their motivation, so that for every one point increase in self-competence there was a 4% increase in motivation while holding teacher support, racial formation, and positive academic environment constant. Subsequent to the full model, a stepwise hierarchical regression procedure was carried out. A model that included teacher support ($b_1 = 0.13, p = 0.009$) and positive academic environment ($b_2 = 0.08, p = 0.01$) as predictors was selected with this procedure. This model predicted a positive relationship as well, but in this model a 1 point increase in teacher support and/or positive academic environment would yield an increase in motivation between 8% and 21%.

TABLE 3.2. REGRESSION MODELS

	R^2	β
Motivation (Full)	0.26	
Self-Competence		0.04*
Motivation (Stepwise)	0.20	
Teacher Support		0.13**
Positive Classroom Environments		0.08*
Future Academic Expectations (Full/Step)	0.32	
Self-Competence		0.32*

* Significant at the 0.05 level.

** Significant at the 0.01 level.

In regard to future academic expectations, both the regression with the full set of predictors and a stepwise hierarchical regression resulted in a model where perceptions of academic self-competence was the highest predictor ($\beta = 0.32, p < 0.001$). In this model, the more positively students viewed their self-competence the higher their future educational expectations were, such that each 1 point increase in self-competence resulted in a 32% increase in future educational expectations.

DISCUSSION AND CONCLUSIONS

Cambodians in the United States represent a rapidly growing segment of society whose social and economic success will rely on the successful schooling of its school-age youth. Cambodian students, however, are often treated as a statistically marginal population and viewed within an Asian American collective that assumes all Asian-descent students are uniformly high achievers (Ngo & Lee, 2007). Moreover, much of the extant literature has focused on cultural and broad structural explanations for Cambodian American student achievement (Hopkins, 1996; Portes & Rumbaut, 2006; Smith-Hefner, 1999). Unfortunately, these explanations do not sufficiently attend to the responsibility of educational institutions and their agents (i.e., teachers, counselors, staff, etc.) but rather imply that Cambodian American families must change in order to improve the academic achievement of their children. Consequently, many Cambodian American youth fail to receive appropriate academic support and guidance.

The present study was interested in how Cambodian student perceptions of teacher support, self-competence, positive classroom environment, and racial fairness influenced their drive to learn and future educational expectations. These interests were guided by other research that argues investigation into student self-perceptions can provide fruitful data for improving academic achievement (Finn & Rock, 1997; Murdock, 1999). For Cambodian students to successfully persist through high school and beyond, their intrinsic motivation to learn and college expectations must be supported. According to our results, some ways to do this might include training teachers in support methods specific to Cambodian youth as well as creating a more positive classroom environment in diverse settings. Although gender was not a significant factor in any of our regression models, the data suggests that for male students in our sample, teacher support was most strongly correlated with their drive to learn whereas females' sense of academic self-competence was most strongly correlated with their motivation. Perceptions of self-competence were also positively associated with higher educational expectations, suggesting that for Cambodian American youth, how they view themselves is important for what they expect to be able to accomplish in the future.

In our regression models, students' sense of positive classroom environment in addition to teacher support was important for motivation. Motivation and future academic expectations were also associated with students' perceptions of their own academic self-competence. However, teacher support might be the most salient variable for potentially informing schools about how to increase the success of Cambodian children. Students in general are likely to comply with expectations of their teachers when they feel supported and respected by their teachers (Murdock, 1999; Valenzuela, 1999). Additionally, some students might disengage from school if they do not have positive bonds with their teachers. Studies on disadvantaged students have documented how students' sense of connectedness with supportive adults at school can play important protective roles in at-risk environments (Conchas, 2006; Valenzuela, 1999). Moreover, other research with Cambodian American students found that personal connections were perceived as critical factors for successful high school and college adjustment (Chhuon & Hudley, 2008; Chhuon et al., 2010; Wallitt, 2008). Cambodian American students in these studies attributed much of their high school success to teachers that genuinely cared about them.

In summary, these data resonate with other findings in the motivation literature indicating that schools must provide an educational climate that promotes a positive attitude for all students. However, we recognize the limitations of this exploratory study. For instance, these findings cannot be easily generalized to other settings given our relatively limited sample size. Future research should include more developmental (longitudinal, cross-sectional) designs to better understand how Cambodian American adolescents' attitudes and beliefs in school vary over time. Furthermore, qualitative approaches, including ethnographic methods, should be pursued to provide additional rich and textured information about those factors that support Cambodian students' academic motivation and engagement (Elliot & Bempechat, 2002). Nevertheless, we hope that these data can help direct other studies to further disaggregate the school experiences of Cambodian American students.

PUBLICATION NOTE

This article was published online in 2010 by the *Journal of Southeast Asian American Education and Advancement* in Volume 5, Issue 1. Minor edits have been made here. The original can be found at http://doi.org/10.7771/2153-8999.1330.

Mozzie DosAlmas originally published this article under their former name, Angela Dosalmas.

REFERENCES

Anderman, E., & Maehr, M. (1994). Motivation and schooling in the middle grades. *Review of Educational Research, 64*, 287–309. https://doi.org/10.3102/00346543064002287

Bandura, A. (1994). Self-efficacy. In V. S. Ramachaudran (Ed.), *Encyclopedia of human behavior* (Vol. 4, pp. 71–81). Academic Press.

Brophy, J. (1987). Synthesis of research on strategies for motivating students to learn. *Educational Leadership, 45*(2) 40–48.

Canniff, J. G. (2001). *Cambodian refugees' pathways to success: Developing a bi-cultural identity.* LFB Scholarly Publishing.

Chhuon, V. (2009). *How school structures influence ethnic and panethnic identity in Cambodian high school youth* [Unpublished Doctoral Dissertation]. University of California, Santa Barbara.

Chhuon, V., & Hudley, C. (2008). Factors supporting Cambodian American students' college adjustment. *Journal of College Student Development, 49*(1), 15–30. https://doi.org/10.1353/csd.2008.0005

Chhuon, V., Hudley, C., Brenner, M. E., & Macias, R. (2010). The multiple worlds of successful Cambodian American students. *Urban Education, 45*(1), 30–57. https://doi.org/10.1177/0042085909352583

Conchas, G. Q. (2006). *The color of success: Race and high achieving urban youth.* Teachers College Press.

Elliot, J., & Bempechat, J. (2002). The culture and context of achievement motivation. *New Directions for Child and Adolescent Development, 96,* 7–26. https://doi.org/10.1002/cd.41

Fabrigar, L. R., MacCallum, R. C., Wegener, D. T., & Strahan, E. J. (1999). Evaluating the use of exploratory factor analysis in psychological research. *Psychological Methods, (4)*3, 272–299.

Finn, J. D., & Rock, D. A. (1997). Academic success among students at risk for school failure. *Journal of Applied Psychology, 82,* 221–234. https://psycnet.apa.org/doi/10.1037/0021-9010.82.2.221

García Coll, C., Akiba, D., Palacios, N., Bailey, B., Silver, R., DiMartino, L., & Chin, C. (2002). Parent involvement in children's education: Lessons from three immigrant groups. *Parenting: Science and Practice, 2,* 303–324.

García Coll, C. T., & Magnuson, K. (1997). The psychological experience of immigration: A developmental perspective. In A. Booth (Ed.), *Immigration and the family: Research and policy on US immigrants* (pp. 91–131). Lawrence Erlbaum.

Garcia Coll, C., Szalacha, L. A., Palacios, N. (2005). Children of Dominican, Portuguese, and Cambodian immigrant families: Academic attitudes and pathways during middle childhood. In C. Cooper, C. Garcia Coll, W. Bartko, H. Davis, and C. Chatman (Eds.),

Developmental pathways through middle childhood: Rethinking contexts and diversity as resources (pp. 207–234). Lawrence Erlbaum Associates.

Grolnick, W., & Ryan, R. (1987). Autonomy in children's learning: An experimental and individual differences investigation. *Journal of Personality and Social Psychology*, *52*, 890–898. https://psycnet.apa.org/doi/10.1037/0022-3514.52.5.890

Harter, S. (1982). The perceived competence scale for children. *Child Development*, *53*, 87–97.

Hopkins, M. C. (1996). *Braving a new world: Cambodian (Khmer) refugees in an American city*. Bergin & Garvey.

Kao, G. (1999). Psychological well-being and educational achievement among immigrant youth. In D. J. Hernarder (Ed.), *Children of immigrants: Health, adjustment and public assistance* (pp. 410–77). National Academy Press.

Katz, S. R. (1999). Teaching in tensions: Latino immigrant youth, their teachers, and the structure of schooling. *Teachers College Record*, *100*, 809–840. https://doi.org/10.1177/016146819910000405

Kim, A., & Yeh, C. J. (2002). *Stereotypes of Asian American students. ERIC digest* No. EDO-UD-02-1. ERIC Clearinghouse on Urban Education.

Kim, R. Y. (2002). Ethnic differences in academic achievement between Vietnamese and Cambodian children: Cultural and structural explanations. *The Sociological Quarterly*, *43*, 213–235. https://doi.org/10.1111/j.1533-8525.2002.tb00047.x

Lee, S. J. (1996). *Unraveling the "model minority" stereotype: Listening to Asian American youth*. Teachers College Press.

Lee, S. J. (2005). *Up against whiteness: Race, school, and immigrant youth*. Teachers College Press.

Muller, C., Katz, S. R., & Dance, L. J. (1999). Investing in teaching and learning: Dynamics of the teacher-student relationship from each actor's perspective. *Urban Education*, *34*(3), 292–337. https://doi.org/10.1177/0042085999343003

Murdock, T. B. (1999). The social context of risk: Status and motivational predictors of alienation in middle school. *Journal of Educational Psychology*, *91*, 62–75. https://psycnet.apa.org/doi/10.1037/0022-0663.91.1.62

Ngo, B., & Lee, S. J. (2007). Complicating the image of model minority success: A review of Southeast Asian American education. *Review of Educational Research*, *77*(4), 415–453. https://doi.org/10.3102/0034654307309918

Ogbu, J. U., & Simons, H. D. (1998). Voluntary and involuntary minorities: A cultural-ecological theory of school performance with some implications for education. *Anthropology and Education Quarterly*, *29*, 155–188. https://www.jstor.org/stable/3196181

Padilla, A. M., & Duran, D. (1995). The psychological dimension in understanding immigrant students. In R. G. Rumbaut & W. A. Cornelius (Eds.), *California's immigrant children: Theory, research, and implications for educational policy* (pp. 131–160). Lynne Rienner Publishers.

Pfeifer, M. (2008). Cambodian, Hmong, Lao and Vietnamese Americans in the 2005 American Community Survey. *Journal of Southeast Asian American Education and Advancement, 3*(21), 1–21. https://www.jstor.org/stable/48684019

Portes, A., & Rumbaut, R. G. (2006). *Immigrant America: A portrait.* University of California Press.

Portes, P. R. (1999). Social and psychological factors in the academic achievement of children of immigrants: A cultural puzzle. *American Research Educational Journal, 36*, 489–507. https://doi.org/10.3102/00028312036003489

Reeves, T. J., & Bennett, C. E. (2004). *We the people: Asians in the United States* (Census 2000 Special Reports). U.S. Census Bureau. Retrieved from http://www.census.gov/prod/2004pubs/censr-17.pdf

Rumbaut, R. G., & Ima, K. (1988). *The adaptations of Southeast Asian refugee youth: A comparative study, final report.* U. S. Department of Human Services, Family Support Administration, Office of Refugee Settlement.

Rumberger, R. (2004). Why students drop out of school. In G. Orfied (Ed.), *Dropouts in America: Confronting the graduation rate crisis* (pp. 131–155). Harvard Education Press.

Ryan, R., & Deci, E. (2000). Intrinsic and extrinsic motivations: Classic definitions and new directions. *Contemporary Educational Psychology, 25*, 54–67. https://doi.org/10.1006/ceps.1999.1020

Sirin, S. R., & Rogers-Sirin, L. (2004). Exploring school engagement of African American adolescents. *Youth and Society, 35*, 323–340. https://doi.org/10.1177/0044118X03255006

Smith-Hefner, N. (1993). Education, gender, and generational conflict among Khmer refugees. *Anthropology and Education Quarterly, 24*(2), 135–158. https://doi.org/10.1525/aeq.1993.24.2.05x1118z

Smith-Hefner, N. (1999). *Khmer American: Identity and moral education in a diasporic community.* University of California Press.

Stanton-Salazar, R. D. (2001). *Manufacturing hope and despair: The school and kin support networks of U.S.-Mexican youth.* Teachers College Press

Stipek, D. (1996). Motivation and instruction. In D. Berliner & R. Calfee (Eds.), *Handbook of educational psychology* (pp. 85–113). Macmillan.

Stone, S., & Han, M. (2005). Perceived school environments, perceived discrimination, and school performance among children of Mexican immigrants. *Children & Youth Services Review, 27*, 57–66. https://doi.org/10.1016/j.childyouth.2004.08.011

Suarez-Orozco, C., Rhodes, J., & Milburn, M. (2009). Unraveling the immigrant paradox: Academic engagement and disengagement among recently arrived immigrant youth. *Youth & Society, 41*(2), 151–185. https://doi.org/10.1177/0044118X09333647

Teranishi, R. T. (2004). Yellow and brown: Residential segregation and emerging Asian American immigrant populations. *Equity and Excellence in Education*, *37*(3), 255–263. https://doi.org/10.1080/10665680490491551

Um, K. (1999). Scars of war: Educational issues and challenges for Cambodian-American students. In C. C. Park and M. M.-Y. Chi (Eds.), *Asian-American education prospects and challenges* (pp. 89–104). Bergin and Garvey.

Um, K. (2003). *A dream denied: Educational experiences of Southeast Asian American youth: Issues and recommendations.* Southeast Asia Resource Action Center.

Urdan, T., Midgley, C., & Anderman, E. (1998). The role of classroom goal structure in students' use of self-handicapping strategies. *American Educational Research Journal*, *35*(1), 101–122. https://doi.org/10.3102/00028312035001101

Valenzuela, A. (1999). *Subtractive schooling: U.S. Mexican youth and the politics of caring.* State University of New York Press.

Wallitt, R. (2008). Cambodian invisibility: Students lost between the "Achievement Gap" and the "Model Minority." *Multicultural Perspectives*, *10*(1), 3–9. https://doi.org/10.1080/15210960701869298

Wright, W. E. (2004). What English-only really means: A study of the implementation of California language policy with Cambodian-American students. *International Journal of Bilingual Education and Bilingualism*, *7*, 1–23. https://doi.org/10.1080/13670050408667798

Zhou, M. (1997). Growing up American: The challenge confronting immigrant children and children of immigrants. *Annual Review of Sociology*, *23*, 3–95. https://doi.org/10.1146/annurev.soc.23.1.63

4

Trauma and Second Language Learning Among Laotian Refugees

DARYL M. GORDON

ABSTRACT

Unprecedented numbers of adult refugee learners are entering ESL classes, many of whom escaped war-torn countries and endured long stays in refugee camps. Research in public health and psychology has documented high levels of depression, anxiety, and posttraumatic stress disorder in refugee populations. Drawing on ethnographic research with Laotian refugee women who experienced presettlement trauma during the Vietnam War and interviews with bilingual mental health professionals, this article examines current second language acquisition theories to consider how they elucidate the effect of trauma on second language learning. The article offers cross-cultural perspectives about the impact of trauma on learning and recommendations for working with adult refugee learners who have experienced trauma. Findings have implications for ESL instructors and second language researchers concerned with the impact of presettlement experiences on second language acquisition and implications for classroom instruction.

As an ESL teacher and researcher of Laotian refugees, many students told me of the trauma they experienced as children during the Vietnam War. Large numbers of adult ESL learners enter the United States each year as refugees, many of whom escaped violent conditions in their native countries. Refugees who have escaped armed conflict may have experienced multiple traumatic events in their native countries or in prolonged stays in refugee camps awaiting final resettlement. Nicholl and Thompson (2004) report that while the prevalence of posttraumatic stress symptoms ranges widely among different populations, studies indicate that between 30% and 86% of refugees experience trauma-related symptoms.

The concept of trauma in psychology refers to responses to dangerous and shocking events that shatter one's sense of security and overwhelm normal resilience to adversity. Traumatic events "generally involve threats to life or bodily integrity, or a close personal encounter with violence and death. They confront human beings with the extremities of helplessness and terror and evoke the responses of catastrophe" (Herman, 1997, p. 33). Symptoms of trauma range widely among individuals, with posttraumatic stress disorder (PTSD) being the most severe.

ESL teachers play a key role for refugee learners who have survived trauma as one of the first links to their new country and a main source of cultural information. When ESL students enter the classroom, they are coping with multiple stressors and may be at different stages in recovery from trauma. Instructors should not anticipate that survivors of trauma will have resolved their traumatic memories before entering the classroom (Horsman, 2000). ESL learners in particular, who need survival ESL to manage the communicative needs of daily life, often enter the classroom while still recovering from trauma. The Canadian Centre for Victims of Torture (CCVT, 2004) posits that the stability of the classroom can help trauma survivors reconnect with ordinary life and begin to acculturate to the new country. The Harvard Program in Refugee Trauma (n.d.) states that developing second language skills reduces social isolation and increases independence, while obtaining citizenship increases the "survivor's sense of security and well-being" (p. 1).

This article draws on ethnographic research with Laotian refugee women who experienced presettlement traumas during the Vietnam War and interviews with bilingual/bicultural mental health providers who worked with Southeast Asian refugees. This article examines current second language acquisition theories to consider how they elucidate the effects of trauma on second language learning and offers cross-cultural perspectives about the impact of trauma on learning. Findings have implications for ESL instructors and second language researchers concerned with the impact of presettlement experiences on second language acquisition and implications for classroom instruction.

Trauma and the Second Language Learner

Since 1975, more than 2 million refugees have settled permanently in the United States. In the 1980s, the majority of refugees entered from Latin America, Southeast Asia, and the Caribbean. In the 1990s, refugees entered the United States from war-torn countries such as Afghanistan, Bosnia, Iraq, Burundi, Sudan, and Somalia (McBrien, 2005). Psychological studies have found alarmingly high rates of depression, anxiety, substance abuse, and posttraumatic stress disorder (PTSD) among refugee populations (Jaranson et al., 2004; Mollica et al., 1987; Westermeyer & Her, 2007).

Stevens's (2001) study of Cambodians in Australia revealed that 91% of the participants experienced symptoms related to PTSD and depression. Many of the study participants experienced symptoms that directly affected learning and cognitive function, including headaches (69%), poor concentration (58%), and loss of memory (57%). A study of Vietnam veterans with combat-related PTSD indicated that they scored significantly lower on tests for short-term recall and long-term memory storage than did subjects without PTSD (Bremner et al., 1993).

Instructor and anecdotal reports have explored the impact of trauma on learning. Horsman's (2000) groundbreaking study explores the impact of violence on adult learners. Although it reveals the extent of domestic and sexual violence on women's learning, Horsman's work focuses on native speakers of English and does not expressly examine language acquisition.

A few studies have specifically examined the impact of trauma on adult ESL learners (Isserlis, 2000; Kerka, 2002; Stone, 1995). Ying (2001) provides a case study of a Vietnamese man who suffered from severe headaches, frequent nightmares, and anxiety. He was referred for treatment from his physician in part because he had complained of poor concentration, which made it difficult to attend in his ESL class. In treatment with Ying, Mr. C. revealed that he had been imprisoned in a "reeducation camp" for 13 years where he had been tortured.

Santoro (1997) documents problems of low motivation, high rates of anxiety, and reluctance to participate verbally among adult refugee learners who are trauma survivors. McDonald (2000) documented that trauma-related symptoms including inability to concentrate, dissociation, and memory problems affected cognitive function and impaired learning among adult refugees in Canada.

The most comprehensive study of trauma's impact on language acquisition is Söndergaard and Theorell's (2004) nine-month longitudinal study of Iraqi refugees in Sweden. Researchers found that refugees who reported more severe PTSD symptoms learned a second language at a significantly slower rate. In fact, the speed of language acquisition was more highly correlated with the severity of PTSD ($p = .001$) than the number of hours of language classes received ($p = .178$) or previous education level in the home country ($p = .116$). The authors note that because previous studies explored the cognitive impact of trauma among native-speaking subjects who had experienced combat trauma rather than refugee groups, trauma's impact on language acquisition may have been greatly underestimated. The authors conclude that early detection and treatment of PTSD in refugee populations could play a crucial role in minimizing post-migration stress and facilitating integration of refugees into the host society (Söndergaard & Theorell, 2004).

THEORETICAL PERSPECTIVES: THE IMPACT OF TRAUMA ON SECOND LANGUAGE ACQUISITION

Despite the importance of second language acquisition for refugee integration and the key role of ESL teachers in early refugee acculturation, the field of second language acquisition has neither developed a theory about the impact of trauma on second language learning nor offered recommendations for working with trauma survivors in the classroom. However, second language acquisition demonstrates that cognitive processing, attention, and memory, factors that are affected by traumatic experiences, are key to second language acquisition.

Schmidt's noticing hypothesis (1990, 1993; Schmidt & Frota, 1986) states that only what learners notice in input can be used as intake for second language acquisition. Ellis (2006) notes that explicit learning and consciousness, including noticing negative evidence and attending to language form in many contexts, are central to second language acquisition.

Research in cognitive psychology reveals that traumatic experiences alter neural pathways in the brain and may impact learning throughout the lifespan. The human brain is designed to sense, process, and store dangerous events. All areas of the brain and body are involved in this "fight or flight response," enabling individuals to respond quickly to threatening situations. Because so many areas of the brain are involved in this response, traumatic events impact the brain in a pervasive and profound fashion (Perry, 1999).

In individuals with PTSD, this life-saving response interferes with the ability to process information. These individuals may be triggered by a sound (fireworks) or event (a crowded room) that initiates the fear response. In turn, the brain responds to the trigger with a pervasive terror response, as if it were occurring for the first time. This flashback, or retriggering of the terror response, puts the brain in a high alert mode. However, in order to process, store, retrieve, and respond to new learning, the brain must be in a calm and attentive state. When a trauma survivor is in a state of fear, the brain, especially areas in the cerebral cortex that process language learning, is involved in the fight or flight response and not available to process new information (Perry, 2006).

Krashen's (1982, 1985) affective filter hypothesis offers promising connections for research with traumatized language learners. Krashen posited that affective factors including anxiety and self-confidence play an important role in second language acquisition. Low self- esteem and debilitating anxiety combine to raise the learners' affective filter, creating a mental barrier that prevents comprehensible input from reaching the language acquisition device.

While Krashen's theory has been criticized because of the lack of supporting empirical research, recent neurological research demonstrates that students' level of anxiety influences information transmission and storage. Neuroimaging and neurotransmitter studies demonstrate that under stress, information is blocked from entering the brain's areas of higher cognitive memory consolidation and storage. In other words, "when stress activates the brain's affective filters, information flow to the higher cognitive networks is limited and the learning process grinds to a halt" (Willis, 2007, p. 1). Because trauma survivors often deal with anxiety and eroded self-confidence, research on the neuroscience of learning and the role of the affective filter are particularly important for traumatized learners. While theories such as the affective filter and cognitive processing allude to the respective roles of anxiety and attention in language learning, these concepts have not been explored in the context of traumatized learners.

HISTORICAL BACKGROUND OF LAOTIAN REFUGEES

Laotian refugees settled in the United States as part of a massive influx of nearly one million Southeast Asians from Vietnam, Cambodia, and Laos, who sought refuge after the Vietnam War ended in 1975. Because of its border with Vietnam, Laos became the target of a "secret war" conducted by the United States to bomb supply routes to Vietnam. Between 1964 and 1973, the country was bombed continually, destroying village life as Laotian people sought refuge in caves or in the jungle. When the communist government took power in Laos in 1975, refugees fled for neighboring Thailand (Hein, 1995; Stuart-Fox, 1997).

The escape from Laos was fraught with danger. Refugees were at the mercy of Lao soldiers who would shoot escaping refugees; pirates routinely stopped refugee crafts to rob or rape passengers. Laotians endured long stays in refugee camps before final resettlement in their host country. Most camps were detention centers, holding refugees inside barbed wire compounds with minimal provisions of food and shelter. The principal participants in this study spent between two and five years in refugee camps. Many Lao refugees recounted incidents of violence, including beatings and rapes from gangs of refugees within the camp and from Thai military who oversaw the camps. Health problems were common in overcrowded conditions, where there was little access to adequate health care, food, or water (Hein, 1995). All of the women interviewed lost family members in their resettlement journey; family members were killed during the war, in the escape from Laos, or due to illnesses in the refugee camps. Upon entry into the United States, refugees were often met with mistrust and hostility by a host country healing its wounds from a controversial war that had killed many American men.

The Laotian experience of trauma is complicated by the fact that the American government played a dual role in the trauma they experienced, as both provider of refuge from the war and the party responsible for the widespread bombing of Lao villages. Branfman (1972), who worked with Lao refugees during the Vietnam War, commented that, "Most of the refugees have fled one form or another of American firepower. As a result, they tend to distrust, fear or hate Americans" (p. 12). This perception of the United States and its role in Laotian learners' trauma is part of the complex social history of these learners. While a detailed exploration of Laotian migration history and national belonging is beyond the scope of this article, I have explored this topic further in Gordon (2010).

METHODOLOGY

My involvement in the Laotian refugee community began in 1994 when I volunteered as a tutor in an ESL class for Southeast Asian adults. In 1997, I initiated a three-year ethnographic research project within the Laotian refugee community. Initial data collection took place between 1997 and 2000 in an urban, working-class Lao American community and in Laos as part of a research project focusing on women's second language socialization (Gordon, 2003, 2004, 2009). Data presented in this article were collected primarily through practitioner research in a year-long ESL class for Laotian adults in Philadelphia. This article offers vignettes of three of these students whose life and learning seemed most affected by traumatic presettlement events. The vignettes are intended to provide an ethnographic account of the multiple factors, including presettlement trauma, that affected the learning of these students. I conducted at least two formal interviews with each of these principal participants, focusing on their presettlement experiences and their process of second language learning in the United States. I also conducted intensive participant observation with the principal participants, spending time with them in their homes, at religious observances at the Lao Temple, and at their workplaces.

Pha, Ouma, and Viseth, the three female participants whose vignettes are featured in this article, lived in a low-income Philadelphia neighborhood whose residents were mainly African American, Cambodian, and Laotian. All were ethnic Lao and had entered the United States as adults after 1980, after spending between two and five years in refugee camps in Thailand and the Philippines. At the time of the study, the principal participants ranged from early thirties to early forties; all were married with children. The participants had received limited formal education in Laos; two of the participants struggled with native language literacy, which hindered acquisition of English literacy. In the United States, they worked in nonunion factory jobs, where they had little contact with native speakers of English. Their stated goals for learning English were to become U.S. citizens and to be able to use English in situations such as interactions with the doctor and their children's school.

In 2009, in preparation for this article, I conducted telephone interviews with four bilingual mental health workers who are native speakers of Lao, Khmer, and Vietnamese. Two individuals founded a Southeast Asian Mental Health Program in 1984 in order to serve the needs of large populations of refugees entering the area, and both have worked as social service coordinators in the community since the program's inception. The third individual is a social worker who works with Cambodian clients in that program. The fourth individual is a therapist with Intercultural Family Services who works primarily with Southeast Asian clients who have survived traumatic events.

VIGNETTES OF PRINCIPAL PARTICIPANTS

Students frequently told me of dangerous escapes from Laos or experiences during the war in the context of individual interviews or private conversations. As more students shared these experiences, learners began to bring up the topic in class discussions and some chose to write journal entries about experiences during the war. My participant observation in the Lao American community facilitated students' familiarity and trust, which may have made them more comfortable in sharing these experiences. While learners often related experiences during the war, I suspect that many stories of personal traumas were not disclosed. In particular, no women shared stories of sexual violence, which is well documented in the literature on Southeast Asian refugees (Hein, 1995; Sylapheth, personal communication, July 2009). While not surprising, given the stigma surrounding sexual violence in this community, teachers should be aware that learners may disclose only some of the events they experienced (see Horsman, 2000, for a discussion of learner disclosure in writing activities). Below are vignettes of the migration experiences of three Laotian women who were trauma survivors and the challenges they experienced in the ESL class.

Pha

Pha was six years old when she witnessed the bombing of her aunt's house in which her relatives were killed. To avoid the relentless bombing, Pha's family sought safety in the capital city, walking nearly two hundred miles. Soon after she married at 15, Pha's husband was imprisoned in a reeducation camp for 9 years. In 1984, when her husband escaped, they fled Laos with their four children. Because she feared that the family would be killed in the escape, Pha made the excruciating decision to leave her oldest son with her parents in Laos. Pha's family was in a refugee camp for two years, during which all her children contracted tuberculosis and one child nearly died of a parasitic infection. Describing an ESL class she took in the refugee camp, Pha told me that it was difficult to concentrate in those circumstances. She said, "Why study what? For what? Your kid crying next to you, you hear it. It's bother your mind, cannot study nothing" (Interview, October 1998).

While Pha enjoyed ESL class in the United States, studying continued to be difficult for her. She often complained of headaches and fatigue, which sometimes prevented her from attending class. She took multiple medications—both natural remedies and those prescribed by doctors. She felt that bad memories from the war contributed to the headaches. She also worried a great deal about her sons, one of whom was in jail on an aggravated assault charge connected to a drug sale. Pha's family had multiple problems with housing and faced eviction at one point during the class. These problems sometimes distracted Pha, so her level of participation and attention varied greatly in class sessions. When she was able to focus and engage in class activities, she was an inquisitive and independent student. At other times, she seemed consumed by worry and pain.

Ouma

Ouma's family lived in Southern Laos. Her family moved multiple times in an attempt to evade the bombing raids. Although she is not certain of her exact age when her family first left their village, she remembers being so young that she could only carry a small basket of rice as her family fled. Her family was displaced by the bombing for most of her childhood and adolescence, and did not return to their original home until Ouma was 18. Describing this time in which they hid in the jungle to avoid the planes that continually bombed her village, Ouma said:

> Hide from the planes, we scare they shoot us. And then the planes they go down very low and then all day all night. We go out in the jungle. . . . We go the place it's safe. And then at nighttime, we still live in the jungle. It's very big, jungle tree and mosquito bite. We want to cook, but we scared the smoke—plane could see and then shoot. A lot of people got killed. (Interview, January 1999)

Ouma escaped from Laos with her husband in 1981, using inner tubes to cross the Mekong River. After five years in a refugee camp, Ouma and her family arrived in the United States in 1986. Upon entering my ESL class, her goals were to pass the citizenship exam, to understand and complete forms more easily, and to enter a cosmetology program. However, while a good student with intermediate-level proficiency in listening and speaking, Ouma missed many classes. I began to wonder whether she was motivated to continue the class. She explained that she had been unable to find stable work and her employer called without prior notice when they needed workers. We continued our work through private tutoring lessons, which were adaptable to her shifting work schedule. However, Ouma had to stop her lessons when she fled the city because of an abusive relationship with her husband. Her plans for education have been put on hold indefinitely.

Viseth

Viseth's family lived in Southern Laos. At the age of 12, she was captured by the North Vietnamese Army. Viseth was forced at gunpoint to walk through the jungle for days to the Vietnamese border with guns and bullet rounds strapped to her chest. Two of Viseth's brothers were killed in the war. At 21, Viseth escaped from Laos, swimming across the Mekong with a group of four others. She described a treacherous trip in which two of her friends drowned. She arrived in Thailand with no clothes and no money because they had been swept away by the strong river current. After years in the refugee camp, Viseth entered the United States in 1982, finding an apartment in a poor inner city community. During her first year in the United States, she was robbed at knife-point when she was at home alone with her three-month-old baby. This was a profoundly difficult experience for Viseth, as it reactivated previous traumatic events and she did not speak enough English to communicate with the robber or with police.

Viseth enjoyed the social aspect of the ESL class and often entertained fellow students with stories told in English and Lao about events at her job and with her children. However, ESL class was often difficult for her. Despite having been in the United States for many years, she had never taken an ESL class before, as she worked long hours in a factory and had young children. She had little native language literacy in Lao, so acquiring English literacy was frustrating. She often complained of difficulty remembering English words and phrases and began to assert that she was "too old" to learn English. Complicating matters, she often came to class exhausted, so her attention was impaired.

These learners experienced many obstacles in their path to learning English. Evidence of trauma including memory and attention problems, fatigue, depression, and somatic symptoms—as well as current stress—remained significant factors in their language learning difficulties. However, during the course, I was unable to locate second language acquisition studies that helped me to understand how their traumatic experiences contributed to their language learning difficulties. The following section discusses findings from Southeast Asian Mental Health providers, in order to provide a context for student experiences.

FINDINGS FROM MENTAL HEALTH PROVIDERS

Interviews with bilingual mental health professionals who work closely with Southeast Asian trauma survivors offered insight into the cultural perspectives that influence how Southeast Asian clients conceptualize traumatic events. While the basic emotions accompanying traumatic events are universally felt, research with refugee trauma survivors from diverse cultures indicates that culture influences how suffering is conceptualized, how strong emotions are expressed, and how individuals cope with grief (Wilson & Drožđek, 2004).

Mental Health Stigma

Each of the mental health professionals interviewed stated that despite treating many clients with depression, anxiety, and PTSD, mental health problems were highly stigmatized in Southeast Asian culture. Clients worried that others in the close-knit refugee community would learn of their mental health problems, which would reflect badly on the family. In Southeast Asian culture, mental health problems are regarded as hereditary, so admission of a problem is damaging to the family reputation (Lu, personal communication, July 2009). Refugees may also fear that reports of mental illness will spread to government agencies, resulting in deportation or discontinuation of government benefits (Gong-Guy et al., 1991).

Contributing to this stigma is the belief that violent or traumatic events are the result of karma, the Buddhist belief that one's actions shape past, present, and future experiences. In this world view, particularly strong among Cambodian and Laotian followers of Theravada Buddhism, traumatic events are the result of misdeeds one committed in a former life or which one's ancestors committed (Math, personal communication, July 2009; Ying, 2001).

Somatic Symptoms

Southeast Asian survivors of trauma often present with somatic symptoms, rather than discussing depression or grief, as the culture views body and mind as more interconnected than in Western culture and does not make a clear distinction between physical and emotional pain. Bunrath Math stated that clients often visit him after having sought help for physical problems such as headaches, insomnia, and chest pain for many years. He said that clients often come with multiple prescriptions for physical problems and are frustrated that they have not cured the symptoms. Ying (2001) similarly notes that Southeast Asian trauma survivors who seek treatment in her community mental health clinic conceive of their problem as "primarily somatic" (p. 71). Gong-Guy et al. (1991) notes that the tendency to focus on physical complaints may be related to traditional backgrounds that discourage the direct expression of feelings or to more holistic views of body and mind.

Learner Communities

Traumas such as wars and natural disasters impact the entire community. Despite commonly held beliefs that communities unite in difficulty, catastrophic events "force open whatever fault lines once ran silently through the structure of the larger community, dividing it into divisive fragments" (Erikson, 1995, p. 189). This is an important consideration for ESL teachers who may assume that learners who speak the same language or are from the same area share a common experience and similar beliefs. However, this is often not the case, especially for learners in refugee communities who have fled political conflicts.

Strong divisions existed in the Laotian refugee community between community members who advocated establishing relations with the Laotian Embassy and those who refused to recognize the current communist government. Socioeconomic differences, which became heightened during the war, were important distinctions within the community. During a class activity in which students created timelines of their lives, a long discussion ensued about the ways people escaped from Laos. Some were considered fortunate enough to hire a boat, others escaped on inner tubes, and still others crossed the Mekong without any device. In a later class, as we discussed a news story about a Southeast Asian refugee, one learner reported that access to water was a major problem in the refugee camp and that fights sometimes broke out as refugees waited in long lines for water. After class, another student pointedly informed me that the woman who told the story never had that experience, because she was among the privileged who were able to pay someone to wait in line and to bring her water. She then related her personal struggles in the refugee camp.

Revealing Traumatic Events

Cultures differ widely about whether disclosure of traumatic events is considered an important step in healing from trauma. Horsman (2000) writes eloquently of the empowerment that many women survivors of abuse experience from disclosing traumatic events. This concept of breaking the silence has been an important contribution of Western feminist research and activism on domestic and sexual violence. However, the importance of relating the traumatic event as part of the healing process may not be shared by other cultures (von Peter, 2009). Cultural beliefs influence "what is seen as private and public pain . . . what should be shared with others and what must remain a secret" (Drožđek, 2007, p. 8).

Lu recounted the story of a Southeast Asian woman who had been raped in the refugee camp. The woman was in great psychological and physical distress and experiencing flashbacks. A close friend, who had been raped in the same camp, urged her not to mention the rape and to forget about the incident. While the friend's reaction may seem unsympathetic from a Western point of view, she was concerned about the impact of community gossip about the rape, which would prevent the woman from finding a husband (Lu, personal communication, July 2009). Tankink and Richters (2007) discuss silence as a coping strategy among women who were raped during war in Sudan. Because rape is perceived as shameful to the woman, maintaining silence is essential to prevent gossip within the refugee community.

The themes above demonstrate how Southeast Asian refugees may experience, understand, and respond to traumatic events differently from Americans of other cultural backgrounds. Becoming familiar with students' cultural backgrounds and the circumstances that forced them to leave their countries can help the ESL teacher work more effectively with trauma survivors.

Interaction of Past Trauma and Current Stressors

Coping with traumatic memories is one of many stressors experienced by refugees. Refugees are adapting to a new culture and language while experiencing stress related to the practical difficulties of migrating to a new country, including locating housing, employment, and education, without access to traditional social support (Adkins et al., 1999). Ongoing stress in the host country plays a major role in a refugee's recovery from trauma (Drožđek, 2007; Oorth et al., 2004).

Each of the mental health workers pointed out past traumas and current stressors as mutually reinforcing. Difficulties locating affordable housing, supporting family members on low-wage jobs, and communication difficulties were significant problems in the lives of the refugees with whom they worked. Also, intergenerational acculturation patterns within the family complicate trauma recovery, as the children of refugees may not understand or appreciate the abuses that occurred during the war (Sylapheth, personal communication, July 2009).

In understanding the experiences of refugee ESL learners, it is crucial to appreciate the complexity of stressors that may affect second language learning. Researchers acknowledge the convergence of multiple factors in the health of refugees. Nou (2006) highlights the concurrence of premigration, trauma-related stressors and ongoing stressors in the host country, writing that "most Cambodians are caught between lingering historical painful memories and the difficulties of adjusting to life in a new social environment" (p. 2). Nicholl and Thompson (2004) write of the importance of acknowledging multiple factors that affect the health of refugee populations, including prior experiences of trauma, socioeconomic deprivation factors, lack of social support, and isolation arising from living in exile. Hinton et al. (2009), in their study of family-directed anger among traumatized Cambodian refugees, point to three specific sources of postmigration stress experienced by the refugees: acculturative stress, financial stress, and stress stemming from living in neighborhoods with frequent violence and gang activity. While Laotian refugees had a very different presettlement experience than Cambodians, they share many of these current stressors as refugees struggling to acculturate in poor communities.

The intent of this article is not to posit that PTSD is the cause of all second language learning difficulties experienced by these students. Rather, it invites ESL teachers and second language researchers to consider the impact that presettlement traumatic experiences may have on language learning and the role ESL teachers may have in facilitating the second language learning of traumatized refugee learners. Toward that end, the following section details specific steps that ESL teachers may use in working with refugee learners experiencing posttraumatic stress.

IMPLICATIONS FOR TEACHING

Learners who have undergone traumatic experiences may experience symptoms such as anxiety, poor concentration, and memory problems, which have direct connections to learning difficulties (Isserlis, 2000; Kerka, 2002; McDonald, 2000). Horsman (2000) suggests that rather than focusing on identifying learners who have had traumatic experiences, educators find ways to make learning safer for all students. The recommendations that follow are designed to help ESL teachers create a safe and productive learning environment.

Classroom Configuration

Learners who have been confined or imprisoned may be sensitive to closed spaces, so keeping doors and windows open may help learners feel more comfortable. Loud noises are a trigger for some trauma survivors, so locating a quiet classroom is optimal. Because traumatized learners may have days when it is difficult to participate in class activities, creating a quiet corner in the classroom where learners can work independently may be helpful (CCVT, 2004).

Managing Concentration Difficulties

Trauma survivors commonly experience difficulties with concentration and memory loss. The Canadian Centre for Victims of Torture writes that:

> A major problem faced by survivors of torture is their inability to concentrate for long periods of time. This deficit has far-reaching implications for a survivor who is endeavoring to receive formal ESL instruction because concentration is necessary if the material presented in the class is to be absorbed. (CCVT, 2004, Concentration section, para. 1)

Because learners may struggle with concentration and memory issues, keep learning sessions short, vary group structures and activities, and include movement, music, or art activities when possible (Math, personal communication, July 2009; Oorth et al., 2004). Trauma survivors may find it difficult to discuss topics, such as family relationships, if they have lost family members. Share plans for the day's agenda before starting class, so that learners can make a decision about their ability to participate (CCVT, 2004).

Community Resources for Wellness

ESL teachers can include a focus on wellness and stress management as part of their class, with mini-lessons on tai chi, meditation, or yoga. Learners may have traditional methods of relaxation, which they can share with other class members. ESL teachers can develop lessons to help learners share and build their knowledge of community resources. Teachers can start this project with the simple question, "Where do you go for help?" (Math, personal communication, July 2009). Learners can write a resource on an index card, which could be shared on a bulletin board or in a community resource book.

Learner Investment

Many psychosocial impacts of trauma, such as dissociation, attention difficulties, missing classes, or dropping out may be interpreted as a lack of motivation (Kerka, 2002). Learners dealing with traumatic memories and adjusting to life in the United States may have difficulty sustaining investment in English learning and attending class regularly. However, the ESL class offers a source of structure and normalcy for learners who are often in a period of transition and upheaval. The CCVT (2004) offers strategies to encourage attendance and punctuality by asking learners to self-monitor their attendance on a classroom chart. Also, helping learners reflect on progress through authentic assessments at regular intervals can help learners maintain investment in language learning.

CONCLUSION

Increasing numbers of adult refugees enter the United States from war-torn countries and may have experienced presettlement trauma, which can negatively affect their learning. Therefore, it is imperative for the ESL field to recognize and investigate trauma as a factor in language learning. This is of particular importance as the United States prepares to receive large numbers of Iraqi refugees. Refugees from Iraq increased more than eightfold from 2007 to 2008 and are expected to continue rising dramatically (Office of Immigration Statistics, 2009). A study conducted among Iraqi refugees in Syria showed that all of the 754 refugees interviewed experienced at least one traumatic event, including rocket attacks, witnessing the killing of someone close to them, interrogation by militias, car bombings, and torture (United Nations High Commissioner for Refugees, 2008).

Research into how trauma impacts second language learning and cognitive processing will help the field better understand the language learning process and offer important implications for classroom instruction. The women in this study, like all trauma survivors, possess a remarkable capacity to overcome horrific events. Through acknowledging this capacity, ESL teachers can help trauma survivors draw on their indomitable strength as they adjust to their new country, so they can view their traumatic past as one aspect of their life history, rather than the defining moment.

PUBLICATION NOTE

This article was published online in 2011 by the *Journal of Southeast Asian American Education and Advancement* in Volume 6, Issue 1. Minor edits have been made here. The original can be found at http://doi.org/10.7771/2153-8999.1029.

REFERENCES

Adkins, M. A., Sample, B., & Birman, D. (1999). *Mental health and the adult refugee: The role of the ESL teacher. ERIC Digest.* National Clearinghouse for ESL Literacy Education.

Branfman, F. (1972). *Voices from the Plain of Jars: Life under an air war*. Harper & Row.

Bremner, J. D., Scott, T. M., Delaney, R. C., Southwick, S. M., Mason, J. W., Johnson, D. R., . . . & Charney, D. S. (1993). Deficits in short-term memory in posttraumatic stress disorder. *American Journal of Psychiatry*, 150, 1015–1019. https://doi.org/10.1176/ajp.150.7.1015

Canadian Centre for Victims of Torture. (2004). *Torture and second language acquisition*. Retrieved from http://www.ccvt.org/torture_esl.html

Droždek, B. (2007). The rebirth of contextual thinking in psychotraumatology. In B. Droždek & J. Wilson (Eds.), *Voices of trauma: Treating survivors across cultures* (pp. 191–210). Springer Science.

Ellis, N. (2006). Cognitive perspectives on SLA: The associative-cognitive CREED. *AILA Review*, *19*, 100–121. https://doi.org/10.1075/aila.19.08ell

Erikson, K. (1995). Notes on trauma and community. In C. Caruth (Ed.), *Trauma: Explorations in memory*. Johns Hopkins University Press.

Gong-Guy, E., Cravens, R., & Patterson, T. (1991). Clinical issues in mental health service delivery to refugees. *American Psychologist*, *46*(6), 642–648. https://doi.org/10.1037/0003-066X.46.6.642

Gordon, D. (2003). *"I'm* tired. *You clean and cook.": Shifting gender identities and language socialization in a Lao-American community* [Unpublished doctoral dissertation]. University of Pennsylvania, Pennsylvania.

Gordon, D. (2004). "I'm tired. You clean and cook.": Shifting gender identities and second language socialization. *TESOL Quarterly*, *38*(3), 437–457. https://doi.org/10.2307/3588348

Gordon, D. (2009). "She's American now, I don't like that": Gendered language ideologies in a Laotian American community. *Journal of Southeast Asian American Education & Advancement*, *4*, 1–19. https://www.jstor.org/stable/48684488

Gordon, D. (2010). Disrupting the master narrative: Global politics, historical memory, and the implications for naturalization education. *Anthropology & Education Quarterly*, *41*(1), 1–17. https://doi.org/10.1111/j.1548-1492.2010.01064.x

Harvard Program in Refugee Trauma. (n.d.). *HPRT/ Treatment Plan*. Retrieved from http://hprt- cambridge.org/?page_id=69

Hein, J. (1995). *From Vietnam, Laos and Cambodia: A refugee experience in the United States*. Twayne Publishers.

Herman, J. L. (1997). *Trauma and recovery*. Basic Books.

Hinton, D., Rasmussen, A., Nou, L., Pollack, M., & Good, M.-J. (2009). Anger, PTSD, and the nuclear family: A study of Cambodian refugees. *Social Science Medicine*, *69*(9), 1387–1394. https://doi.org/10.1016/j.socscimed.2009.08.018

Horsman, J. (2000). *Too scared to learn: Women, violence, and education*. Lawrence Erlbaum.

Isserlis, J. (2000). *Trauma and the adult English language learner*. Center for Applied Linguistics.

Jaranson, J. M., Butcher, J., Halcon, L., Johnson, D. R., Robertson, C., Savik, K., . . . & Westermeyer, J. (2004). Somali and Oromo refugees: Correlates of torture and trauma history.

American Journal of Public Health, 94(4), 591–598. https://ajph.aphapublications.org/doi/abs/10.2105/AJPH.94.4.591

Kerka, S. (2002). *Trauma and adult learning: ERIC Digest.* ERIC Clearinghouse on Adult Career and Vocational Education.

Krashen, S. (1982). *Principles and practice in second language acquisition*. Pergamon Press.

Krashen, S. (1985). *The input hypothesis: Issues and implications*. Longman.

McBrien, J. L. (2005). Educational needs and barriers for refugee students in the United States: A review of the literature. *Review of Educational Research, 75*(3), 329–364. https://doi.org/10.3102/00346543075003329

McDonald, S. (2000). Trauma and second language learning. *The Canadian Modern Language Review, 56*(4), 690–696. https://doi.org/10.3138/cmlr.56.4.690

Mollica, R. F., Wyshak, G., & Lavelle, J. (1987). The psychosocial impact of war trauma and torture on Southeast Asian refugees. *American Journal of Psychiatry, 144*, 1567–1572. https://doi.org/10.1176/ajp.144.12.1567

Nicholl, C., & Thompson, A. (2004). The psychological treatment of post traumatic stress disorder (PTSD) in adult refugees: A review of the current state of psychological therapies. *Journal of Mental Health, 13*(4), 351–362. https://doi.org/10.1080/09638230410001729807

Nou, L. (2006). *A qualitative examination of the psychosocial adjustment of Khmer refugees in three Massachusetts communities*. Institute for Asian American Studies.

Office of Immigration Statistics. (2009). *Refugees and asylees: 2008, annual flow report.* U.S. Department of Homeland Security.

Oorth, J., Doorschodt, L., Verburgt, J., & Drožđek, B. (2004). Sounds of trauma: An introduction to methodology in music therapy with traumatized refugees in clinical and outpatient settings. In J. Wilson & B. Drožđek (Eds.), *Broken spirits: The treatment of traumatized asylum seekers, refugees, war and torture victims* (pp. 443–480). Brunner-Routledge.

Perry, B. (1999). The memories of states: How the brain stores and retrieves traumatic experience. In J. Goodwin & R. Attias (Eds.), *Splintered reflections: Images of the body in trauma* (pp. 9–38). Basic Books.

Perry, B. (2006). Fear and learning: Trauma-related factors in the adult education process. *New Directions for Adult and Continuing Education, 110*, 21–27.

Santoro, N. (1997). Why won't they talk: The difficulties of engaging victims of trauma in classroom interaction. *TESOL in Context, 7*(2), 14–18.

Schmidt, R. (1990). The role of consciousness in second language learning. *Applied Linguistics, 11*(2), 129–158. https://doi.org/10.1093/applin/11.2.129

Schmidt, R. (1993). Awareness and second language acquisition. *Annual Review of Applied Linguistics, 13*, 206–226. https://doi.org/10.1017/S0267190500002476

Schmidt, R., & Frota, S. (1986). Developing basic conversational ability in a second language: A case study of an adult learner of Portuguese. In R. Day (Ed.), *Talking to learn: Conversation in second language acquisition* (pp. 237–326). Newbury House.

Söndergaard, H. P., & Theorell, T. (2004). Language acquisition in relation to cumulative posttraumatic stress disorder symptom load over time in a sample of resettled refugees. *Psychotherapy and Psychosomatics, 73*(5), 320–323. https://doi.org/10.1159/000078849

Stevens, C. A. (2001). Perspectives on the meanings of symptoms among Cambodian refugees. *Journal of Psychology, 37*(1), 81–98. https://doi.org/10.1177/144078301128756210

Stone, N. (1995). Teaching ESL to survivors of trauma. *Prospect: The Journal of the Adult Migrant Education Program, 10*(3), 49–58.

Stuart-Fox, M. (1997). *A history of Laos*. Cambridge University Press.

Tankink, M., & Richters, A. (2007). Giving voice to silence: Silence as coping strategy of refugee women from south Sudan who experienced sexual violence in the context of war. In B. Drožđek & J. Wilson (Eds.), *Voices of trauma: Treating survivors across cultures* (pp. 191–210). Springer Science.

United Nations High Commissioner for Refugees. (2008). *Iraq: Trauma survey in Syria*. Retrieved from https://reliefweb.int/report/iraq/iraq-trauma-survey-syria

von Peter, S. (2009). The concept of "mental trauma" and its transcultural application. *Anthropology & Medicine, 16*(1), 13–25. https://doi.org/10.1080/13648470802425922

Westermeyer, J., & Her, C. (2007). Western psychiatry and difficulty: Understanding and treating Hmong refugees. In J. Wilson & C. S. Tang (Eds.), *Cross-cultural assessment of psychological trauma and PTSD* (pp. 371–394). Springer Science.

Willis, J. (2007). The neuroscience of joyful learning. *Educational Leadership, 64*, 1–5.

Wilson, J., & Drožđek, B. (Eds.). (2004). *Broken spirits: The treatment of traumatized asylum seekers, refugees, war and torture victims*. Brunner-Routledge.

Ying, Y. (2001). Psychotherapy with traumatized Southeast Asian refugees. *Clinical Social Work Journal, 29*(1), 65–78. https://doi.org/10.1023/A:1005210628134

5

Racism, Schooling, and the Streets

A Critical Analysis of Vietnamese American Youth Gang Formation in Southern California

KEVIN D. LAM

ABSTRACT

This paper is an analysis of the relationship between educational experiences, street life, and gang formation for Vietnamese American youth gang members in Southern California. I use critical narrative methodology to center the life and experiences of a Los Angeles area gang member. His narrative substantiates how racism in schools and on the streets works together to impact and inform gang formation. Schools were sites of interethnic conflict and racialized tension, and streets were spaces for contentious interactions with the police. In addition, I place the Vietnamese American youth gang phenomenon in larger historical and political contexts such as California's antiyouth legislation, representations of Asian American youth, and U.S. geopolitics and imperialism—factors that have serious material and ideological implications and consequences.

INTRODUCTION

Compared to other racialized youth groups, very little is known about Asian American youth and even less about those who are gang members. This is by no means surprising, given that Asian Americans are not necessarily perceived as worthy theoretical and political subjects of inquiry, due to where they are located in the U.S. racialized hierarchy. To put it more clearly, Asian Americans are not considered "marginalized enough" in their marginal status as a minority population in the United States to warrant critical examination. In our attempts to create a truly progressive politics of difference in these times, it is fundamental that we rethink how marginalized populations are racialized and represented, in particular, urban youth of color. Although much research is needed, the available data does suggest that certain Asian American ethnic youth groups, including Vietnamese, face serious issues with poverty, school dropouts, and juvenile delinquency (Umemoto & Ong, 2006).

Not coincidentally, the emergence of Vietnamese American "street" gangs coincided with California's increasing racialization of youth and, in particular, gang members of all hues. Such criminalization is usually associated with Black and Chicano/Latino youth; as a result, discussions of youth of color impacted by the juvenile justice system often overlook Asian American and Pacific Islander youth. However, the reality is that arrest rates for Asian and Pacific Islander youth have increased dramatically while the national arrest rates for black and white youth have declined in the last 20 years (Kwon, 2006, p. 221; Le, 2002). Since Asian American youth (including Vietnamese Americans) are racialized as model minorities and presumably nonviolent, they are not necessarily given the same kind of legitimacy by their peers, policymakers, scholars, and educators when discussing gang violence and historical/personal struggles. In California's urban centers, however, they are racialized as both *model minority* and *gang-banger* because of the substantial number of Asian American youth gangs.

In this paper, I examine the ways in which Vietnamese American youth gang members in Southern California experience schooling—in particular, interethnic conflict with other youth of color. I argue that schooling needs to be understood in relation to questions of racism, migration, and class. These factors are interconnected, and they speak to why it is important to frame the subject matter within larger social, political, and economic contexts. I describe classroom experiences but also discuss the relationship between schooling and the communities in which Vietnamese American youth gang members attend school. I want to understand the connection between schools and "the streets." More specifically, I believe it is necessary to understand these two entities dialectically. I explore (a) how Vietnamese American youth gang members experience racialized schooling, (b) the dialectical relationship between schooling and "the streets," and (c) the significance of racism for Vietnamese American youth gang members.

LITERATURE REVIEW

Representation of Asian American Youth

Although this paper is on Vietnamese American youth, it is necessary to discuss the representation of Asian American youth because of the long history of racialization of Asian American subjects as a whole. The rhetoric of Asian Americans as a model minority and Vietnamese as the good refugees has been harmful in its distortion of the complex issues that take place in immigrant and racialized communities. The simplistic representation of Asian American youth as "whiz kids" (Osajima, 2000); their "over-representation" in higher education (Hune, 2002); and the ability of Asian Americans to overcome any obstacle to excel and flourish, reinforced the idea of America as the "land of opportunity" and a "refuge for democracy" (Espiritu, 2005, 2006). Such one-dimensional distortions have definitely cast a shadow over those who have not done as well, including Asian American youth who drop out of school, get caught up in the juvenile system, and struggle with adolescent life (Umemoto & Ong, 2006, p. v). Indeed, these are some of the central issues in this paper. This alone points to a long-standing need for research and analysis on Vietnamese Americans and Asian Americans that substantively examines the problems, concerns, and hardships faced by this population, especially its youth.

Asian American Youth Gangs

At the turn of the 21st century, the estimated number of youth gangs nationally was over 30,000, and the number of gang members was over 800,000. The Los Angeles area, being the "gang capital of the U.S.," tops the list with close to 8,000 gangs and 200,000 gang members (Vigil, 2002). Asian American youth gangs account for 3% to 6% of the entire gang population, as reported by the National Youth Gang Center (Vigil, 2002). Although these statistics give us a sense of gang formation numerically, it is often difficult to label given the various degrees of gang involvement. With that said, Asian American youth gangs make up a relatively small percentage of all youth gangs nationally. However, it is estimated that there are 20,000 Asian American gang members in Los Angeles County alone (Asian Gangs in Los Angeles County, 2012). The ethnic breakdown for Vietnamese is unknown, given that some youth groups tend to include other Southeast Asian Americans. Although many share similar class backgrounds and immigration histories, I make the distinction between Vietnamese/Southeast Asian youth gangs and Chinese/Taiwanese and some Filipino American youth gangs. The latter two migrated under very different contexts, as a number of these youth (certainly not all) settled in more "suburban" middle-class areas in Southern California.

Vietnamese American Youth Gangs: A Brief History

It is important to note that the emergence of Vietnamese American youth gangs coincides with the "second wave" that came from Vietnam in the late 1970s and early 1980s, which exacerbated the "boat people" crisis in their escape from Vietnam. A significant number of "boat people" (over 50%) were young children or teenagers, and some came without parents or other family members (Chan, 1994; Vigil, 2002). Unlike "first-wave" families that arrived mostly intact, a significant number of "second-wave" youth came on their own because parents did not have the resources to pay for their own escape. Often, these youth would make the journey with a relative or a family friend. The "second-wave" refugees were also comprised of more rural and working-class Vietnamese and ethnic Chinese, which made up 70% of these refugees (Chan, 1994; Takaki, 1989). As a group, they were less educated and familiar with Western ideology and values, compared to the "first wave" that migrated immediately after the fall of Saigon in 1975.

The first generation of Vietnamese youth who became involved in gangs in the early and mid-1980s are now dead, in prison, or grew out of "the game." Building on the works of James Diego Vigil and his associates (1998, 2002, 2006), I have found a prominent phenomenon of second-generation Vietnamese American youth gangs that are more street-socialized than their predecessors. By any account, they are products of U.S. youth gang culture that emerged in major cities across the United States. Historically, Black and Chicano/Mexican American gang activity has been demarcated by streets and blocks. Yet Vietnamese and Asian American gangs do not adhere to traditional conceptions of the "street," given the fact that Vietnamese in particular and Asian Americans in general have very different residential and settlement patterns when compared with other racialized populations. Vietnamese American youth gangs are not spatially bound. If anything, Vietnamese American youth gangs complicate our commonsense notions of "urban" and "street" gangs. They do not necessarily claim *turf* or territory, as it is understood (Gonzales, 2004). As a result, their businesses, both legitimate and illegitimate, are not necessarily governed by rules of the "streets."

In the context of schooling, the early arrivals from Vietnam in the early 1980s faced the negative effects of a fairly recent and highly divisive war. They were reminders of the enemy, the "yellow peril" who moved in next door, both literally and metaphorically. Invariably, they were often targets of physical and verbal attacks from other students due to their comparatively smaller stature, different physical characteristics, refugee status, limited English language proficiency, and distinct hairstyle and dress (Vigil & Yun, 1998).

Many of these youth grew up in poor and working-class neighborhoods with other Asians and Latinos, in areas where there has been a long history of gangs. Inevitably, they came into conflict because they had to share the same spaces and go to the same schools. Some Vietnamese American youth got picked on when they were younger by more established Chicano gangs in the area. As a way to protect themselves, establish their own sense of identity, and find ways to deal with their family's material conditions, these youth formed their own gangs.

Gang formation also has diasporic and national effects. Vietnamese American youth gangs become connected to the larger patterns of people moving out to other areas of California and to other parts of the United States. Given the deportation of many youth gang members to their countries of origin since the mid- to late 1990s, a transnational element is also taking place. We see this take form in countries like El Salvador and Cambodia (Chow, 2005; Guerra Vasquez, 2005). Vietnamese American gang members are very aware that they might be next in line to get deported, as the United States and Vietnam continue to normalize diplomatic relations.

THEORETICAL FRAMEWORK

This paper seeks to understand the dialectical relationship between large-scale forces like immigration, war, geopolitics, and empire and the particularities of youth gang formation (Nayak, 2003, p. 6). For this reason, I examine the Vietnamese American youth gang phenome- non in relation to experiences of gang members in the schools and "the streets." These two entities inform one another and by no means can be separated.

My theoretical framework is also informed by critical educational theorist Paulo Freire's (1970/1993) notion of humanization:

> While both humanization and dehumanization are real alternatives, only the first is the people's vocation. This vocation is constantly negated, yet it is affirmed by that very negation. It is thwarted by injustice, exploitation, oppression, and the violence of the oppressors; it is affirmed by the yearning of the oppressed for freedom and justice, and by their struggle to recover their lost humanity. (p. 26)

Freire succinctly describes the struggles that a number of Vietnamese American gang members are going through. They struggle to fully live because of the conditions surrounding them, including both real and symbolic violence, racism, and marginalization. The choices and decisions they make (arguably, perhaps they do not have a choice) cost them dearly, as a number of them are locked up, dead, or just trying to survive. This article is fundamentally a humanizing project that desires to give voice to the most marginalized in society. It seeks to give redeeming value to those that are marked most deviant in society and "the wretched of the earth," to borrow from Fanon (1963).

CRITICAL NARRATIVE METHODOLOGY

I used critical narrative methodology for the research. D. Soyini Madison (2005) outlines three key main points that were very helpful for my interviews with Vietnamese

American youth gang members. First, Madison discusses the importance of *positionality* as researchers. She suggests that it is fundamental to "acknowledge our own power, privilege, and biases just as we denounce the power structure that surround our subjects" (p. 14). I was clear with my subjects about the research goals and intentions. This is articulated through my research questions, methodology, and theoretical frameworks that drive this work. They agreed to do the interviews because of the level of trust and respect placed on the intermediary. In this manner, it was also extended to me because of my close relationship with these intermediaries. At the time of the research, I was positioned both as a "graduate student/researcher" and perhaps more significantly, as someone "from the neighborhood" who could and would respect their humanity.

Second, Madison (2005) speaks of the need to engage in a *dialogical* manner with your research subjects: "Dialogue emphasizes the living communion of a felt-sensing, embodied interplay and engagement between human beings.... It keeps the meanings between and the conversations with the researcher and the Other open and ongoing" (p. 14). There was a sense of dialogical engagement with both myself and the subjects. As much as they shared with me their life stories, I was also willing to engage them in mine—as open and honest as I possibly could. I believe that they were as open and honest as they were because we were in dialogue with one another. It is clear to me that these subjects, through their narratives, want to be in dialogue with the rest of the world. They, as Vietnamese American subjects, want to be heard and to be able to share their pain, frustration, joy, sorrow, and happiness. They expressed that no one is really hearing them, and to a greater extent, not recognizing their history and humanity. More succinctly, one interviewee expressed that "no one is looking into our shit" and that folks "don't understand the roots of it." In many ways, I am trying to do both.

Third, Madison (2005) stresses the importance of the *theory/method* nexus. Hence, critical ethnography becomes the "doing" of critical theory: "Theory, when used as a mode of interpretation, is a method, yet it can be distinguished from method when a set of concrete actions grounded by a specific scene is required to complete a task. We rely on theory... to interpret or illuminate a social action" (p. 15). In looking at the narratives and other sources, I am constantly engaged in theorizing Vietnamese American youth gangs. Much theorization, in concrete ways, is done through the grounding of the research, designing interview questions, developing themes, and coding the data (p. 15). For me, there has to be an alliance with theory and practice (method), as each drives the other.

RESEARCH DESIGN

The larger project involved three Vietnamese American gang members in Southern California in November and December 2007. This paper presents a critical narrative from one interview, P-Dog. The interview was set up through an intermediary that both the researcher and interviewee trusted. To be sure, it really helped that I knew the contexts extremely well—as I attended similar schools and grew up in the community.

The in-depth interview with P-Dog was open-ended and lasted more than two hours. Before the interview began, I explained the purposes of the research and why he was asked to participate. I made clear that criminal activity was not the focus of the research. Rather, I was interested in hearing his story. During the interview, I used a digital recorder. He consented to be audio-recorded. It was made explicit to P-Dog that he was given all rights to turn off the audio-recorder at any given moment, ask questions or request clarification, or to retract certain information once it was recorded. I decided not to take notes because I felt that it was important for me to engage him in dialogue. He was a bit apprehensive at the beginning. But once he felt comfortable, he was more than willing to share his experiences. I spent time writing out notes after the interview as well as my interpretations.

Before I proceed further, I also want to clarify the notion of "youth." Nayak (2003) problematizes the commonsense notion of youth:

> Terms such as "youth" and "young people" are used for their economical ease. These terms have been subject to critique and should not be seen as biological states (e.g. "the pubescent teen") or psychological phases (e.g. "adolescence") in an individual's development. Instead, "youth" is treated here as a social and mutable category that continues to have different meanings in different times and places. (p. 3)

I am not using youth as a biological state, but rather analyzing youth gang formation—situated in very particular social and historical contexts. A critical narrative methodology is best used here because it allows the subjects to speak, substantively, on their own terms. They are able to bring much passion and humanity to their stories. P-Dog was 30 years old at the time of the interview. He got involved as a 13-year-old and continues to be immersed in gang life. Below is a critical narrative from P-Dog.

CRITICAL NARRATIVE: P-DOG

P-Dog was born in Vietnam in 1977 and came to the United States as a 3-year-old in 1980. His family migrated by boat from Vietnam across the South China Sea to a refugee camp in Hong Kong before resettling in Seattle, Washington. His father's siblings also resettled in Seattle. After spending a couple of years in the U.S. Northwest, P-Dog's father first made the drive down Interstate 5 to Southern California. P-Dog and his mother came shortly after. Although they did not have relatives in California, his parents had some friends from their hometown who settled in the "Golden State," around the same time they moved to Seattle. P-Dog and his parents moved to Lincoln Heights, a predominantly Latino and Asian American working-class section in Los Angeles and eventually to the diverse San Gabriel Valley. His mother is ethnic Vietnamese and father ethnic Chinese from Vietnam.

P-Dog is a second-generation gang member. He is a member of the Asian Boyz. His father was an original member of Viet Ching, an ethnic Chinese youth gang whose members were from Vietnam. They were part of the first wave of Southeast Asian youth gangs in Southern California in the late 1970s and early 1980s. As P-Dog's father and his homeboys were involved in the early 1980s as young adults, P-Dog and his homeboys were "putting in work" (by ways of committing violent offenses and getting involved in other illegal activities) in the early 1990s as teenagers. P-Dog states, "So what escalated is—what the story is—[my father's generation] brought the [Vietnamese Chinese gangs] down here [to Southern California from Vietnam]." P-Dog parallels his refugee experience with that of fictional character Tony Montana, the notorious Cuban gangster from the movie *Scarface*: "I am from the refugees, man. I am from the camps. Same thing you see [with] Tony Montana in the Cuban camps... when he got sponsored to the U.S. Same thing with us. [Montana] came as a dishwasher. My dad came here chopping meat [as a butcher]." His mother has worked in the nail salon business since the early 1980s. They got off welfare five years ago and Section 8 (federal assisted housing) two years ago.

In the early 1990s, P-Dog's Asian Boyz clique was the first generation of Asian gang members in the area to break away from tradition with their dress, style, and gang protocol. They were young and trying to build a "rep" [reputation]. For P-Dog, choosing to wear Dickies [clothing brand], Nike Cortez, and shaving their heads was as much stylistic as it was a lifestyle:

> A lot of people these days... they think it's a style. But basically, it's not a style, it's a way of life. A lot of kids [are] wearing Cortez, Dickies... whatever. It's how you feel. Like, I am 30 years old, I'm still wearing Dickies. I'm still wearing the jacket representing [Asian Boyz], but I'm not part of it anymore.

Due largely to their dress and style, P-Dog and his homeboys are frequently "hit up" (harassed) by other gang members and the local police departments. As he explains:

> They [the police]... they check, "What hood are you from?... What does this number stands for on your body?" They asked for all this stuff, you know. Back when we were young, they asked for cigarette burns... like, "Why do you have the cigarette burns here?"... you know... this and that. That's how they represent themselves as Asian gangs, fuck... in '90, '91.

P-Dog further explains:

> The first thing [the police] ask you, "Who do you roll with?" They don't ask, "What's your name?" [I'll say] "I don't roll with nobody." ... They decide to check (for tattoos).... "What does this stand for?" Does it really matter, you know? Back then, I used to tell them where I was from and whatever ... this and that. But [as] I see it now, it shouldn't matter where I am from. You know, we got fucked by cops back in the day when they make the Asian [Gang] Task Force. Asian Task Force used to come and beat our ass up.

P-Dog received his education on the streets. He is a high school dropout with a 9th grade education. He has gotten straight F's on his report card since the third grade. He was in and out of Los Angeles County's youth detention facilities during his teen years and got most of his high school credits while in juvenile hall. For P-Dog, school was where he went for fun and "to meet girls and get into fights." The junior and high schools P-Dog attended in the Rosemead/San Gabriel area are predominantly Asian and Latino. At his public high school in San Gabriel, his gang would get into fights with other Asian and Chicano/Mexican American gangs.

P-Dog discusses these "race fights" between Asian and Latino students and how these youth experience schooling at his high school and in the West San Gabriel Valley area. He states, "You take any two groups ... they can be best of friends ... stuck in the hall ... stuck in a room for a whole day, they're going to start bugging each other." These "race fights" between racialized groups are by no means just gang members. The general populations at the school would also get involved:

> Just random people ... I don't know how it starts, man. I just know it starts. One day, we say "fuck the *ese* ... fuck the *beaner* ... and they would say fuck the *chino*, you know. That's how it is. We'll get into it and don't know why, to tell you the truth. People will be bringing guns to school. I see that shit all the time ... back when we were going to school.

To get away from gang life in Southern California, P-Dog moved to Seattle to live with an uncle in 1993 when he was 16. He talks about his high school experience in Seattle:

> I tripped out in school over there, man. It was like "Saved by the Bell" [TV show] or something. It's like the show with big-ass lockers. My high school in Seattle's cool. It was good experience, man. I saw, how you say ... the football field is made out of [artificial] turf, you know what I'm saying. It's pretty rich man. It's nice.

He compares his high school in Seattle with the one in Southern California: "You went to the restroom, you see mirrors. San Gabriel [High School] and stuff . . . you don't see mirrors, man. They got no lockers for us, man . . . like fucking six inches big, six inches wide, you know. It's crazy." P-Dog struggled with traditional schooling and never enjoyed being in the classroom:

> [I] never did school . . . I didn't like school. I guess I wasn't the kind of person that can sit down and just sit there, you know. It can be trade school. I tried all that trade school. I tried any kind of school that will work for me, that benefit [me] . . . not just to learn from the books, but to make a career out there. I'm not saying I'm stupid. I just can't sit in a classroom.

He sums it up: "I just can't do school. Like when I went to continuation [high school], all I got to do is cheat off the notebooks to get a diploma, I couldn't even do that."

The shuttling between different high schools, youth camps, juvenile hall, and continuation school added to P-Dog's unstable schooling experiences. He states:

> Ever since I turned 16, I'll go to Century [continuation school] until I do good and then go back to regular school. I'll go back to the regular school for a month or two until they kicked me out for getting in a fight. This is at San Gabriel [High School]. . . . Rosemead [High School]. I went to Rosemead my first year . . . got kicked out that place in two weeks. The longest I stayed in school was like, four months.

P-Dog was afforded some stability in Seattle when he stayed at his high school for a full year. Although out of state and away from his homeboys, he could not stay away from trouble: "I was busted for stealing cars and radio. I moved away from the environment that you see in Southern California . . . just couldn't get away [from] it." He eventually finished off the school year and went back to California. His one year away from California could have saved P-Dog's life. It was at a time when many of his homeboys went to prison for "putting in work" on rival gangs and were involved in other illicit activities. P-Dog states,

> Like I said, a group of 10 friends . . . like the 10 I kicked it with, like seven of them are doing life, two of them are dead. I basically lost them all of them at the age of 17. We're just like 17 years old at the time. We weren't that old.

P-Dog is a two-strike felon. He was released from prison two months ago at the time of this interview. He is doing a work release program at the sheriff's headquarters in East

Los Angeles to gain his freedom. He has three more months of work before he goes on probation. If P-Dog violates his probation, he will be sent to state prison for three years because of a joint suspension: "I'm straight . . . I ain't trying to go up-state [state penitentiary]." Due to his criminal records, P-Dog is not qualified for U.S. naturalization. He is greatly concerned that he might get deported back to Vietnam, a country he has never been to since leaving as a 3-year old. The deportation issue hits very close to home for P-Dog because he has a friend [due to his criminal records] who recently was deported to Hong Kong. P-Dog is very well aware that Vietnam and the United States are making efforts to make this a reality.

DISCUSSION

P-Dog's narrative tells the story of one gang member who has been socialized in a particular time and place. However, I believe his narrative substantiates how racism in schools and on the streets works together to impact and inform gang formation. The confluence of these two entities are tied to the fact that schools, as institutions of learning (and socialization), are part of the larger state apparatus. Schools, in essence, are an extension of the streets. We can also argue that the streets are an extension of schools. The following sections provide contexts and specificities for P-Dog, his homeboys, and the Asian American youth gang phenomenon in Southern California, especially in the San Gabriel Valley in the late 1980s and early 1990s. Their stories are part of a larger narrative that has impacted youth, but especially youth of color—marked by surveillance, criminalization, and dehumanization.

Racism in the Schools

Gang formation and schooling are intimately linked in the narrative of P-Dog. His schooling experiences are informed by class, gender, and spatial differences, which are crucial factors in their gang involvement. A significant reason why P-Dog and his friends came together as a gang is because they got tired of being bullied by older Chicano/Mexican American gang members. He tells of incidents where Lomas (an old local Mexican American gang based in the Rosemead/South San Gabriel/Monterey Park area) gang members were trying to steal his bicycle and pushed him and his friends around while they were playing basketball at the park or walking home from their junior high school. They got "hit up" and asked if they belonged to a gang.

In addition to being in conflict with Chicano youth, P-Dog's Asian Boyz gang also had to contend with rival Asian American youth groups in school and the surrounding areas. During the 1980s and 1990s, these "race fights," or rather, racialized conflicts, were common occurrences at various schools in Southern California. These conflicts are still happening in some Southern Californian schools given dramatic demographic and economic changes and shifting class relations in some areas (Darder & Torres, 2004). Some of these incidents involving Asian and Latino students occurred in Long Beach (Haldane, 1991), Los Angeles's Lincoln Heights (Quintanilla, 1995), Orange County's Little Saigon area (Gomez & Boucher, 1991; Rivera & Licthblau, 1991; Welborn, 2006), and the San Gabriel Valley (Hamilton, 1993; Tawa, 1993).

Over the years, these "race fights" between Asian and Latino students, at varying degrees, occurred at all three high schools (Mark Keppel, San Gabriel, and Alhambra) in the district. Gang members are involved, but by no means are they the only ones. One of the more memorable "race fights" occurred in February 1992 when Asian and Latino students were in conflict with each other at Mark Keppel High School in Alhambra in the West San Gabriel Valley. The tension "boiled over" in two days of fistfights as five Asian and seven Latino students were arrested (Hamilton, 1993). The school was in lockdown, as students were not allowed to leave their classrooms. The police confiscated seven knives, a piece of sharpened glass, and a loaded gun. School officials expelled 24 students and recommended that those arrested be prosecuted for hate crimes.

The 1992 conflict at Keppel High School and other incidents in racialized contexts were a sign of things to come for Vietnamese/Asian American youth in the Los Angeles area. The year P-Dog was sent to live with an uncle out of state, a number of his homeboys got locked up—many of whom are doing double life sentences with no parole for murder. Luis Rodriguez, author of *Always Running, La Vida Loca: Gang Days in L.A.* (1993) and former Lomas member from South San Gabriel, talks about racialized tension between Chicano/Mexican American and white students when he was a Mark Keppel student in the 1970s. In the early 1980s, tensions were brewing between U.S.-born and newly arrived refugee and immigrant students. Racialized conflict and gang violence went to another level in the 1990s, as it coincides with the accessibility of high-powered firearms.

Racism on the Streets

In conjunction with their experiences of racism in schools, P-Dog and his homeboys had to deal with racism and discriminatory acts by the local police department. According to P-Dog, their relationship with the police and the Asian Gang Task Force (as alluded to in his narrative), in particular, was always contentious. Invariably, the first thing the police asked them was, "Who do you roll with?" and then proceeded to ask them to lift up their shirts to check for tattoos and cigarette burns, signifiers of Asian gang affiliations back in the day. Given the rise of Asian American youth gangs in Southern California since the 1980s, some police departments created ethnic-specific task forces.

The Asian Gang Task Force was set up in multiple locations with visible Asian American gang culture, from Los Angeles to Long Beach, down to Orange County, and back to both valleys (San Gabriel and San Fernando) (Lam, 2009).

In 1987, the Law Enforcement Communication Network and the Los Angeles County Sheriff's Department began to develop a large database known as the Gang Reporting, Evaluation, and Tracking System (GREAT) to "collect, store, and analyze personal information about suspected gang members" (Pintado-Vertner & Chang, 2000). Also known as Cal-Gang, the database contained more than 300,000 names and was used across the country (p. 10). Since Asian American youth gangs are highly mobile and have satellite groups in other parts of the United States, this form of surveillance did impact them tremendously. As Pintado-Vertner and Chang (2000) state, these databases "indiscriminately" criminalize youth and identify them as suspects before any crime has been committed (p. 10). It is unfathomable to think that wearing FUBU jeans and being related to a gang member qualifies someone as a "gang member" in some states.

As Daniel Tsang (1993, 1994) and Chorswang Ngin (1996) document in their work with Vietnamese American students in Orange County, California, many of these youth unwillingly had their photos taken and are linked to gangs. Ngin (1996) articulates in her ethnographic findings that "Asian youths are racialized through a process of signification based on their fashion and who they 'hang out' with" (p. 93). She further notes that "labels such as 'gang members' and 'gang associate' and signifiers such as hair styles and clothes have become the new 'community' criteria for defining gang membership" (p. 93). A number of Vietnamese/Asian youth have been criminalized through this racializing mechanism, as their mugs and files are in the local police departments' gang database.

P-Dog talks about the criminalization of gang members in the 1990s in the contexts of antiyouth legislation which included the Street Terrorism Enforcement and Prevention (STEP) Act of 1988 and Proposition 184, also known as the "three strikes" law. Under the STEP Act, gang membership is punishable by up to three years (Gilmore, 2007). So in addition to doing time for the offense, gang members do extra time for a violent offense. The STEP Act allows for law enforcement to come up with a set of criteria to determine who is and is not a "gang member." P-Dog was very aware of laws created to criminalize his status as a "gang member" and his Asian Boyz gang, in particular: "It's not that easy. You get labeled. You're from Asian Boyz, you get labeled, man. . . . Back then, Pete Wilson [then governor of California] put the 18th Street [large Latino youth gang in Los Angeles] law for the Mexicans . . . they put the Asian Boyz law for us." Here, P-Dog is referring to gang injunctions placed on so-called high-profile gangs in California, including 18th Street and his own gang. This includes getting extra time because of one's association with the Asian Boyz.

CONCLUSION

Second-generation Vietnamese American gang formation does not happen in the vacuum of California/U.S. contemporary urban life. Their "lessons of racism" in schools and the streets are in the context of economic and political turmoil both here in the United States and abroad. As migration from Vietnam, Cambodia, and Laos reached its peak in the late 1970s and early 1980s (a consequence of the conflict in Southeast Asia), many of the youth who migrated to the United States under these horrendous conditions came of age in the early 1990s. Many started high school after arriving in the United States as toddlers. Even though immigration has subsided from Southeast Asia, we see and feel the lasting effects of war and displacement. We see this in the experiences of Vietnamese American youth who negotiated spaces in schools and communities.

This is most evident through P-Dog's narrative. His testimony suggests a number of concerns related to the education of refugee and immigrant populations. His failure, or more specifically, his unwillingness to engage school, tells us that there is a disconnect between schooling and our most marginalized populations. It is clear from his narrative that the schools and streets are highly contentious and dangerous spaces. Students live with real and imagined violence on a daily basis. Like a number of youth of color, especially the most marginalized, there are plenty of Vietnamese/Southeast/Asian American youth who fall through the cracks. In P-Dog's case, he described being disengaged from school at a very young age and never quite recovered from it. He had a very difficult time learning in traditional ways and spaces.

The fact that he was on the move did not afford him much stability. He was constantly on the run. Not surprisingly, he was "in deep" with gang involvement and was not able to get out, both socially and academically. As he mentioned, all he had to do was to copy some work from a notebook to get his high school diploma via continuation school, and he did not even want to do that. In order to be culturally and politically relevant for youth like P-Dog, critical scholars must situate family and community histories within larger discourses of geopolitics, militarization (both overseas and here at home), and class struggle. Educators interested in social justice and economic democracy must seek to understand histories of marginalized populations comparatively—and acknowledge that all students bring a certain set of knowledge to the classroom.

For example, it might be good for students to understand and recognize that racialized tensions in the schools and communities stem from major economic, political, and demographic shifts that impact poor and immigrant communities. They are inextricably tied to police brutality and suppression in various communities of color, U.S. economic imperialism, and geopolitics in their countries of origin. Interethnic tensions between Asian and Latino students, as P-Dog alluded to, are not the exception. For example, we see this happening with Black and Latino youth in South Los Angeles, and Armenian and Latino students in the San Fernando Valley, to name a few (Lam, 2009). As P-Dog makes clear, it does not matter that you put the "two best friends" in the same room; things will happen, especially if students do not and have not yet developed a language of critique and solidarity. Perhaps critical pedagogical approaches and an ethnic studies curriculum and classes might be useful at junior high and high schools. Often, "diversity" and "sensitivity" training is put in place only after racialized conflicts happen at schools and spill out onto the streets—with serious consequences.

This article attempts to fill some of the gaps that currently exist in the literature on Asian American youth and students today, in particular those youth who are involved with gangs. While there is some literature on the racialization (e.g., "ideological blackening") of Southeast Asian American youth (Lee, 2005, 2009; Ong, 2003; Reyes, 2007), it is my intent to build on this literature by examining how Vietnamese American youth gang members experience schooling and its relationship to racism, class, and migration. The material implications are real, as reflected through P-Dog's narrative, and should have an impact on our theorizing and policy- making. Hence, we cannot begin to talk about educational policy issues and their impact on Vietnamese American youth without understanding the differences and complexities of the historical, political, and economic trajectories that shape the lives and academic experiences of youth from Vietnamese and Asian American communities.

PUBLICATION NOTE

This article was published online in 2012 by the *Journal of Southeast Asian American Education and Advancement* in Volume 7, Issue 1. Minor edits have been made here. The original can be found at http://doi.org/10.7771/2153-8999.1043.

REFERENCES

Asian Gangs in Los Angeles County. (2012). Asian gangs. Retrieved from http://www.streetgangs.com/asian

Chan, S. (1994). *Asian Americans: An interpretive history*: Twayne Publishers.

Chow, G. K. (2005). Exiled once again: Consequences of the congressional expansion of deportable offenses on Southeast Asian refugee community. *Asian Law Journal, 12*, 103–136.

Darder, A., & Torres, R. (2004). *After race: Racism after multiculturalism*. New York University Press.

Espiritu, Y. L. (2005). Thirty years afterWARd: The endings that are not over. *Amerasia Journal, 31*(2), xiii–xxiii. https://doi.org/10.17953/amer.31.2.v171j838l4455118

Espiritu, Y. L. (2006). The "we-win-even-when-we-lose" syndrome: U.S. press coverage of the twenty-fifth anniversary of the "Fall of Saigon." *American Quarterly, 58*(2), 329–352. http://doi.org/10.1353/aq.2006.0042

Fanon, F. (1963). *The wretched of the earth*. Grove Press.

Freire, P. (1970/1993). *Pedagogy of the oppressed.* Continuum.

Gilmore, R. W. (2007). *Golden gulag: Prisons, surplus, crisis, and opposition in globalizing California*. University of California Press.

Gomez, J., & Boucher, G. (1991, September 30). Latinos beat 3 Asian students. *Los Angeles Times*, p. 1.

Gonzales, R. (2004, September 26). Asian gangs latest threat sweeping the neighborhood. *Pasadena Star-News*, p. 1.

Guerra Vasquez, G. A. (2005). Homies unidos: International barrio warriors waging peace on two fronts. In S. Maira & E. Soep (Eds.), *Youthscapes: The popular, the national, and the global* (pp. 103–118). University of Pennsylvania Press.

Haldane, D. (1991, April 15). Latino and Asian gangs engage in deadly warfare violence. *Los Angeles Times*, p. 1.

Hamilton, D. (1993, June 10), Tension between Asian and Latino students in the Alhambra school district has climbed to a fever pitch. *Los Angeles Times*, p. 1.

Hune, S. (2002). Demographics and diversity of Asian American college students. In M. K. McEwen, C. M. Kodama, A. N. Alvarez, S. Lee, & C. T. H. Liang (Eds.), *Working with Asian American college students: New directions for student services* (pp. 11–20). Jossey-Bass.

Kwon, S. (2006). Youth of color organizing for juvenile justice. In S. Ginwright, P. Noguera, & J. Cammarota (Eds.), *Beyond resistance!: Youth activism and community change* (pp. 215–228). Routledge.

Lam, K. (2009). *Reppin' 4 life: The formation and racialization of Vietnamese American youth gangs in Southern California* [Unpublished doctoral dissertation]. University of Illinois, Urbana Champaign, Illinois.

Le, T. (2002). Delinquency among Asian/Pacific Islanders: Review of literature and research. *Justice Professional, 15*(1), 57–70. https://doi.org/10.1080/08884310212825

Lee, S. (2005). *Up against whiteness: Race, school and immigrant youth*. Teachers College Press.

Lee, S. (2009). *Unraveling the model minority stereotype: Listening to Asian American youth*. Teachers College Press.

Madison, D. S. (2005). *Critical ethnography, method, ethics, and performance*. Sage.

Nayak, A. (2003). *Race, place and globalization: Youth cultures in a changing world.* Berg.

Ngin, C. (1996). Racism and racialized discourse on the Asian youth in Orange County. Retrieved from http://www.patbrowninstitute.org/documents/RacismandRacializedDiscourseonAsianYouthinOrangeCounty.pdf

Ong, A. (2003). *Buddha is hiding: Refugees, citizenship, the new America*. University of California Press.

Osajima, K. (2000). Asian Americans as the model minority: An analysis of the popular press image in the 1960s and 1980s. In M. Zhou & J. Gatewood (Eds.), *Contemporary Asian America: A multidisciplinary reader* (pp. 449–458). New York University Press.

Pintado-Vertner, R., & Chang, J. (2000). The war on youth. *Colorlines, 2*(4), 9–15.

Quintanilla, M. (1995, September 29). Children of hope. *Los Angeles Times*, p. 1.

Reyes, A. (2007). *Language, identity, and stereotype among Southeast Asian American youth: The other Asian*. Lawrence Erlbaum.

Rivera, C., & Licthblau, E. (1991, September 19). After-school fight blamed on ethnic tension unrest: A Westminster high student was knifed when Latino and Asian youngsters scuffled near the campus. *Los Angeles Times*, p. 1.

Rodriguez, L. (1993). *Always running, la vida loca: Gang days in L.A.* Simon & Schuster.

Takaki, R. (1989). *Strangers from a different shore*. William Morrow.

Tawa, R. (1993, December 5). Students learn about bias—their own: Race relations: Hoping to unmask stereotypes, Pitzer College students present eye-opening workshops at three local high schools. *Los Angeles Times*, p. 1.

Tsang, D. (1993). Is innocent until proven guilty a lost principle? Retrieved from https://webfiles.uci.edu/dtsang/public/lostprin.htm

Tsang, D. (1994). Asians are automatically labeled gang members. Retrieved from https://webfiles.uci.edu/dtsang/public/asiansgang.html

Umemoto, K., & Ong, P. (2006). Asian American and Pacific Islander youth: Risks, challenges, and opportunities. *AAPI Nexus, 4*(2), v–ix. https://doi.org/10.17953/appc.4.2.8106654364n53u01

Vigil, J. D. (2002). *Rainbow of gangs: Street cultures in the mega-city*. University of Texas Press.

Vigil, J. D., Nguyen, T. H., & Cheng, J. (2006). Asian Americans on the streets: Strategies for prevention and intervention. *AAPI Nexus, 4*(2), 1–11. http://doi.org/10.17953/appc.4.2.n31xu64253009701

Vigil, J. D., & Yun, S. C. (1998). Vietnamese youth gangs in the context of multiple marginality and the Los Angeles youth gang phenomenon. In K. Hazelhurst & C. Hazelhurst (Eds.), *Gangs and youth subcultures: International explorations* (pp. 117–139). Transaction Publishers.

Welborn, L. (2006, May 10). 2 reputed gang members convicted of murdering boy, 14. *Orange County Register*, p. 1.

6

Health Perceptions and Practices of Burmese Refugee Families

A Participatory Mixed Methods Study

SUNEETA KERCOOD AND
TRISH MORITA-MULLANEY

ABSTRACT

Health care providers in the United States often view the lifestyle choices made by refugees from Burma through the lenses of America's norms for healthy living. Although health care providers often recognize the role that language plays in the refugees' ability to communicate their health care needs, they often ignore the role of culture. This lack of understanding of cultural difference contributes to the marginalization of refugees in the health care system. Using a transformative mixed methods methodology, this study employed the East Asian Acculturation Measure (EAAM) to identify participants' perceived level of acculturation within health care contexts. The researchers then engaged participants in a qualitative exploration of their lifestyle choices using a Photovoice protocol. These two methods, girded by critical and ecological theories, elucidate the participants' counter-stories that provide insight into how the refugees are negotiating culturally relevant lifestyle choices in their new American contexts.

INTRODUCTION

Health care providers in the United States often view the lifestyle choices made by refugees from Burma through the lenses of America's norms for healthy living. Although health care providers often recognize the role that language plays in the refugees' ability to communicate their health care needs, the role of culture needs deeper examination. Using a transformative mixed methods methodology, this study employed the East Asian Acculturation Measure (EAAM) to identify participants' perceived level of acculturation within health care contexts. The researchers then engaged participants in a qualitative exploration of their lifestyle choices using a Photovoice protocol. These two methods, girded by critical and ecological theories, demonstrate the participants' narratives that provide insight into how Burmese refugees are negotiating culturally relevant lifestyle choices in their new American contexts.

STATEMENT OF THE PROBLEM

The institution of translators and interpreters is a common response in facilitating the health related needs of immigrant and refugee communities. Although interpretation and translation is an initial response to make a health care exchange accessible, its orientation is technical in nature and does not examine the background experiences of its patients and how they experience their health care in the United States and how healthy living is conceived by them. While research on health disparities is extensive on the refugee community, very few studies examine the experiences of the Burmese community. This study intends to address this area through its unique mixed methods design and participatory framework with and among the Burmese community of Indiana.

LITERATURE REVIEW

Health disparities are very commonly noted in the refugee population. By definition, refugees are individuals who have fled their country of origin with a well-founded fear of persecution due to their culture, religion, or political opinion (United Nations High Commission for Refugees, 2010). As a result of the migration process, refugees can have serious mental health problems, such as depression, schizophrenia, posttraumatic stress disorder (PTSD), and psychosis (Beiser, 2005; Bhui et al., 2003; Grisaru et al., 2003; Li & Browne, 2000; Lin & Cheung, 1999; Shepard, 1992; Thurston & McGrath, 1993). Refugee children and families are often in lower socioeconomic situations and many live in extreme poverty (Beiser et al., 2002), and children from refugee families have higher rates of illnesses such as tuberculosis, intestinal parasites, and other related conditions (Chambers & Ganesan, 2005). Most refugees do not participate in health screenings and experience significant barriers in accessing health care due to lack of understanding of the health care system, language, and culture. This leads to problems in continuity and consistency of care (Birman et al., 2008). Families often have different social and material resources to assist children in effectively navigating new education, health, and social service systems (DéVoretz et al., 2004). This subtractive portrayal of their health inadequacies often promotes a model of fixing or remediating their poor health.

Numerous studies have addressed the relationship of acculturation and assimilation on the health of immigrants; however, there have been fewer studies examining this relationship among refugees. High acculturation level of Somalian refugees in various locations in the United States were significantly associated with greater use of preventive dental care (Geltman et al., 2014), prenatal care (Flynn et al., 2011), and improvement in levels of food insecurity (Dharod et al., 2013) compared to similar refugees who were newer in the country.

Researchers have frequently reported that refugees struggle with mental health issues, such as posttraumatic stress disorder or depression (Fazel et al., 2005). Contrary to what might be expected, higher levels of assimilation may not necessarily lead to improvement, especially in mental health care for refugees. Among Eritrean and Sudanese refugees in Israel, it was noted that those who reported themselves to be assimilated reported higher depressive symptoms than those who considered themselves as being integrated (Nakash et al., 2012). Mental health issues were noted to be the likely cause of increased use of psychotropic drugs in refugees from Iraq, Iran, Eritrea, Ethiopia, Somalia, and Afghanistan who had had a longer duration of residence in Sweden compared to newer refugees (Brendler-Lindqvist et al., 2014). Among young women from refugee populations and their attempts to assimilate in the new country, they tend to face higher levels of family conflict and poorer psychological health resulting from parental restrictions and expectations in the new country compared to their nonrefugee counterparts (Koh et al., 2013). Among adolescent refugees from Somalia living in the United States, for girls, greater Somali acculturation was associated with better mental health, whereas among boys, greater American acculturation was associated with better mental health (Ellis et al., 2010). Refugees have also reported devolution of their nutritional habits as a result of their extended stay in their new country, with increased access to fast food, limited options for fresh produce, and fewer opportunities for physical activities (Rondinelli et al., 2011). Results of these limited numbers of studies indicate inadequacies, but also articulate that assimilation is not a panacea for health care access and healthy living.

Refugees or humanitarian entrants come to North America with sponsored and legal status. They are therefore eligible for public assistance including food stamps, housing, and Medicare (Exodus Social Services, 2014; United Nations High Commission for Refugees, 2010). Although this is a beneficial condition for refugee families, availability does not always promote culturally responsive accessibility. Agencies assist in identifying primary care physicians, but providers function within their same framework, utilizing the services of an interpreter to convey a standard health message (Johnson et al., Kumar, 2013). This technical transference limits cultural responsiveness by diminishing it to a task orientation of "language translation only," ignoring cultural differences on perspectives for healthful living. Further, language translation is often conceived monolithically and distinct dialects may not be differentiated, leading to a linguistic mismatch for Burmese patients (Vang & Mong Trieu, 2014).

In addition to language differences, the focus on refugee infectious disease prevention and treatment creates a narrow view of refugee health. Refugees tend to have a higher rate of infectious diseases such as tuberculosis, and the health arena reacts to ameliorate the spread of this infectious disease. This focus on communicable diseases can be a refugee's first experience with an American health care provider, creating immediate dissonance between provider and patient (Kumar, 2013). A medical model of tuberculosis uses the practice of surveillance, which seeks to establish methods for its eradication at the onset of immigration, but such interventions have been found to have a low impact (Kimbrough et al., 2012; Lobou & Moser, 2004; Uppaluri et al., 2002). This diagnostic or medical model focuses on the presence of disease and creates mechanisms that serve to modulate and disquiet the refugee community, potentially invoking their own self-care for resolution (Foucault, 1995; Johnson et al., 2009; Kopecky, 2011; Kumar, 2013).

BACKGROUND

Since most of the research within the refugee population in North America has been limited to Canada, we explored their health within the U.S. geographical location of the Midwest. Currently, Indiana has seen a dramatic increase in the number of Burmese refugees resettled. In Indianapolis, the focal site of this study, 11,708 Burmese refugees have made primary or secondary settlements there, and it is the largest host city in the state. The Burmese community is ethnically, linguistically, and religiously diverse, representing eight distinct groups, but the majority is Chin (Burmese American Community Institute, 2014; Vang & Mong Trieu, 2014). Among the Chin, 31 different language dialects are spoken (Lewis et al., 2015). In this site of study, Hakha Chin and Tedim from the Chin region of Burma are the most dominantly spoken. Burmese is a lingua franca, so most are multilingual (Barron & Ranard, 2007).

In 2008, the local resettlement agency sponsored more than 400 persons, in 2009 more than 500, and in 2010 more than 650 individuals and their families. Refugee resettlement agencies are projected to resettle over 800 individuals in the coming years (Exodus Social Services, 2014). Additionally, refugees who were resettled elsewhere are increasingly making secondary migrations to Indiana because the local area is now considered a major Burmese refugee resettlement site, and it is anticipated that the region will continue to experience growth (Burmese American Community Institute, 2014).

THEORETICAL FRAMEWORK

Specific to this inquiry is the integration of critical and ecological theories, which grounds the interpretation and analysis of this inquiry. Critical theory grounds itself in examining unequal power relationships within locally situated systems, and in this case, the health care system (Crotty, 1998; Morrow & Brown, 1994). As participants examine their experiences and assumptions about "normal" practices of healthful living, this reflexivity allows for an analysis of how the Burmese community is (re)defining the normalcy of healthy living. Critical theory pushes on the restrictive ways institutions interface with their clients and promotes perspectives that are multifaceted with a particular focus on those that have been marginalized by such systems. This dialectic approach recognizes the presence of multiple perspectives, which are generative and potentially empowering for the participants (Greene, 2007; Mertens, 2003, 2009).

Complementary to the systems perspective of critical theory, ecological theory focuses on how an individual is shaped by a system and how that person may inform, challenge, and transform the systems to be more responsive to their needs (Fielding et al., 2011; Mertens, 2003). While these systems include sociocultural, political, or physical environments, just to name a few of the possible contextual influences, relationships of power often govern these contextual factors (McLaren, 2005). In fixed views of relations of power, the dominant culture will exert its influence over newcomers to the culture by defining its worldview and cultural practices as natural or normal. Conversely, in dynamic or ecological views of power, power is negotiated between the dominant culture and the newcomers, with both groups shaping the system (Bourdieu, 1984; Fairclough, 2001; Fielding et al., 2011; Smith, 2003). From this dynamic perspective on power, the newcomers can shape the health care system to be more responsive and inclusive of their understandings.

Within the participatory design, we included participants in the data collection and analysis process. This approach mirrors the work of Mertens (2003, 2009), who addresses the ecological theoretical lenses within mixed methods research by attending to its focal participants at multiple stages of analysis and interpretation as they author the research. By examining how Burmese refugees are positioned by health care providers and how they situate themselves within these experiences, the theoretical paradigm is inherently participatory, emancipatory, and transformative.

METHODOLOGY

This mixed methods study used a concurrent transformative design with data from a survey measure and interviews with the Burmese community (Canales, 2013; Creswell, 2003; Mertens, 2009; Sweetman et al., 2010; Zacharadias et al., 2013). The quantitative survey tool, the East Asian Acculturation Measure (EAAM) of health perceptions (Barry, 2001), and a Photovoice protocol with semistructured interviews were employed (Wang & Burris, 2004; Wang et al., 2004; Wang et al., 1998). Photovoice invites participants to photograph their lived realities around the research topic to contextualize and story their community health realities (Wang & Burris, 2004). This qualitative portion is well suited for the question of inquiry and supports the emancipatory nature of this study. Responses from the survey were mixed with findings from participant-captured photographs and accompanying interviews to represent the multiple ways that the Burmese refugee community is conceived institutionally and how they individually interface with their health needs. The qualitative findings are weighted more heavily in collection and analysis, consistent with this methodological design (Figure 6.1).

A concurrent transformative design attends to a specific research goal that seeks to understand the needs of a marginalized community with the experiences that are relevant and meaningful to them. Participants construct meaning about their experiences individually and collectively as they develop shared meaning and a deeper understanding of their own cultural practices. In turn, they share this understanding with the researchers of the study. This focus creates opportunities for illumination and empowerment among those being studied (Mertens, 2003, 2009; Sweetman et al., 2010).

Critical and Ecological Theories

Concurrent Transformative Design

quantitative ⇔ QUALITATIVE

Demographic	Photovoice process
EAAM Survey	Individual and focus groups

Figure 6.1. Mixed methods design.

This concurrent transformative study explored the following questions:

1. What are the perceptions of Burmese refugees in receiving medical/health care services?
2. What kind of dietary, exercise, and practices do they utilize to stay healthy?
3. What are the challenges in maintaining a healthy lifestyle in their new home?

The Institutional Review Board from the respective universities of participating researchers approved all research procedures and protocols.

Participant Recruitment

Participants were recruited by the researchers as a purposive sample of those of Burmese descent who came to the United States under refugee status and were taking English classes at an after-school program in an elementary school, and classes within an apartment community guest-house. The purpose and procedures of the project were explained to the individuals in the English classes, and they were invited to participate in the study. Those who provided verbal consent were then read aloud the written consent, with concurrent translations by an interpreter. This purposive sample is referenced as typical case sampling, which is best suited for the questions of inquiry when experiences are shared (McMillan & Schumacher, 1997).

Participants

Participant recruitment procedures resulted in a sample of 10 participants, age range 25–46 years (five male and five female). Six of the 10 participants also completed the EAAM survey and completed all sections of the demographic questionnaire. Seven of the 10 participants participated in the qualitative, Photovoice portion of the study. Time of residence in the United States ranged from two months to six years, and the education level of participants in their home countries of Burma ranged from some schooling (elementary/middle school) to some level of college education (see Table 6.1). Given the low number of participants in the study, a statistical analysis was not conducted on quantitative data and was used to inform the more weighted qualitative portion. Photovoice studies of historically marginalized immigrant groups have utilized a small number of participants ranging from as few as four (Mejia et al., 2013) to as many as 62 (Wang et al., 1998).

All participants were born in Burma, but represented a variety of religious and ethnic groups, including Hakha Chin, Burmese, and Tedim, and relocated to the United

TABLE 6.1. DEMOGRAPHIC INFORMATION FROM THE PARTICIPANTS

ID	GENDER	AGE (IN YRS)	TIME IN U.S.	EDUCATION	CURRENT OCCUPATION IN THE U.S.	NUMBER LIVING IN CURRENT HOUSEHOLD	ROLE IN HOUSEHOLD	FAMILY MEMBERS LEFT IN HOME COUNTRY	CURRENT HOUSING	ANY AT HOME HAVE SPECIAL OR MEDICAL NEEDS, YES/NO (EXPLAIN)	HAVE MEDICAL INSURANCE YES/NO	FREQ. OF MEDICAL VISITS
1	Female	37	3 yrs	High school	Unemployed	5	Mother	11	APT	No	Yes	**
2	Male	43	3 yrs	10th grade	Fixes watches	4	Father	6	APT	No	Yes	Never
3	Male	46	6 yrs	Middle school	Works in factory/ production	8	Lives with Friends	5	House	No	Yes	Never
4	Female	40	5 yrs	4th grade	Unemployed	4	Mother	>10	APT	Yes Son has asthma	Yes	Every 6 months
5	Female	28	5 yrs	High school	Factory work	4	Mother	4	House	No	Yes	Every 6 months
6	Female	40	4 yrs	High school	Works in Warehouse	3	Mother	> 10	House	Son—thyroid problems	Yes	Every 6 months
7	Male	25	2 ms	8th grade	Unemployed	2	Friend	4	APT	No	Yes	Not yet
8	Male	29	2 ms	9th grade	Unemployed	2	Friend	3	APT	No	Yes	Not yet
9	Female	33	3 ms	Some schooling	Unemployed	5	**	**	APT	Yes—9 yr daughter with eye problems	Yes	Every 2 months
10	Male	38	**	High school	Unemployed	1	Lives alone	3	APT	No	Yes	1 x/yr

Note: Yrs = Years; ms = Months; APT = Apartment; ** Did not answer; Freq. = Frequency.

TABLE 6.2. LANGUAGE AND ETHNICITY OF THE PARTICIPANTS

PARTICIPANT ID	LANGUAGES	ETHNICITY
1	Not reported	Not reported
2	Chin Falam, Hakha, Mizo, Tedim, Burmese	Chin
3	Hakha Chin	Chin
4	Chin	Chin
5	Burmese, Chin	Chin
6	Burmese, Mizo	Burmese
7	Tedim, Chin	Chin
8	Zomi, Zalai	Chin
9	Tedim	Chin
10	Burmese	Burmese

States fleeing from political, economic, and religious persecution. The language representation was also diverse, most reporting that they knew some Burmese as a lingua franca, but nearly all speaking indigenous languages from the various areas in the Chin region (Table 6.2).

Materials and Data Collection Procedures

Participants met three times within three months for 60–90 minute intervals. The first session was to introduce the study, obtain informed consent, and complete demographic information. In the second session, participants completed the EAAM scale and were trained on the use of the camera and how to conceptualize images for capture. The third session involved short interviews of 10–15 minutes with each participant about their captured images. One 90-minute focus group discussion about the images they had selected as most salient in describing their health experiences followed. There were two focus groups, one having four participants and the other having three. All interviews and small group discussions were audio recorded and transcribed by the researchers. Details of each of these activities are described in the following sections. Participants were given a $25 stipend at the conclusion of the study. The two interpreters were offered $50 for their help, but they declined to accept. They were thankful that the researchers were addressing this area of need for the participants and were glad to help in the project. An unintended outcome of the study was the beneficence that the interpreters sensed as a result of the collaborative research work.

SURVEY

The East Asian Acculturation Measure (EAAM) (Barry, 2001) is a 29-item self-report questionnaire that contains four subscales (Table 6.3): assimilation (8 items; e.g., "I find that Americans understand me better than Asians do"), separation (7 items; e.g., "Asians should not date non-Asians"), integration (5 items; e.g., "I feel very comfortable around both Americans and Asians"), and marginalization (9 items; e.g., "I sometimes feel that neither Americans nor Asians like me"). Items are scored on a 7-point Likert-type response format (strongly disagree, disagree, disagree somewhat, neutral, agree somewhat, agree, agree strongly). The total score for each scale is derived by summing reverse-scored and positive-scored items. The higher the total score in each subscale, the higher the level of assimilation or separation or integration or marginalization, respectively. The scales have demonstrated adequate internal consistency (Cronbach alphas of .76, .77, .85, and .74, respectively).

Barry (2001) posits that low acculturation is associated with East Asian patients not seeking care when necessary and that language and cultural differences impact the way health needs are expressed and conceived. It can be instructive in creating more culturally responsive services and practices (Vang & Mong Trieu, 2014).

PHOTOVOICE TRAINING

The qualitative Photovoice component followed quantitative data collection. This Photovoice process invited participants to take pictures of their everyday representations of healthy living. This protocol allows participants to later discuss and interpret their current circumstances and imagine future possibilities for their healthy living in the United States. Wang and Burris (2004) and Wang et al. (2004) posit that Photovoice can inform policy and institutional practices, and empower participants in intellectualizing their healthy living. Participants were trained on the use of the digital cameras and how

TABLE 6.3. EAST ASIAN ACCULTURATION MEASURE (EAAM)

ITEM	DESCRIPTION
Assimilation	The degree to which one gives up their native culture in favor of new Western culture
Separation	Maintenance of ethnic culture and absence of relations with greater society
Integration	The degree to which one's native culture is maintained and new culture is fostered
Marginalization	No contact and/or isolation with native culture and new culture

Note: Adapted from Barry, 2001.

to view photos after capture. They were advised to take multiple pictures of images that represented content of healthy and unhealthy living in their daily lives. Participants were shown a variety of examples that represented healthy living, including a bowl of colorful fruits and vegetables from an area supermarket, a well-groomed sidewalk for walking and exercise, and a doctor's office. Most were familiar with the camera's functions and were able to assist others who were not as technically proficient. Participants were given two weeks to capture the photographs. They then met with the researchers and interpreter(s) in short individual interviews followed by focus group discussion sessions.

INDIVIDUAL AND FOCUS GROUP INTERVIEWS

Photos captured are used as a data source in individual interviews and a collaborative group discussion to illuminate questions about their health care conditions, the efforts and understanding about healthy living, and how they are situated institutionally by health care providers.

INTERPRETATION

Two interpreters proficient in English, Burmese, and a variety of Chin dialects were recruited for the study. These interpreters were selected because they were recommended by the English language program staff as they served in support roles in the instructional program and were familiar and trusted by the participants. Prior to data collection, the interpreters were trained in the EAAM survey, Photovoice strategies, and the overall scope of the study. This type of preparation with interpreters is necessary to understand the contextual and nuanced qualities of interviews involving translation and interpretation (Pochhacker, 2004). Consecutive translation was used with the primary investigators asking questions first in English followed by appropriate interpretation in the target language. Interviews and group discussions were conducted using the Photovoice protocol, and field notes were taken by the lead researchers.

Data Analysis

The data yielded from the EAAM survey provided information on the participants' perceptions about their assimilation, integration, separation, and marginalization, whereas the qualitative Photovoice portion and the follow-up individual interviews and focus group discussion demonstrated how they were experiencing and enacting healthy living.

EAAM SURVEY

The EAAM survey, an attitudinal survey, was analyzed using Barry's (2001) metric of levels and/or degree of assimilation, integration, separation, and marginalization.

Outcomes were aligned with participants' demographic characteristics to determine if there was a relationship between particular variables. Although the survey was administered concurrently with the qualitative data collection, it was not analyzed until after the collection of the qualitative data as co-analysis is central to this study's design. Discussion was held with participants to extend their explanations of their responses on the scale, mixing it with qualitative findings in the Photovoice portion.

PHOTOVOICE PROTOCOL

The participants engaged in participatory analysis of the qualitative Photovoice portion with the researchers and then their focus group. First, participants shared a selected image with the research team and offered a title or a caption for their photos and qualified it as an asset or challenge. Next, participants brought their captioned photo to the focus group, describing it in detail and providing a rationale for its selection. Focus group participants asked questions and connected the photos with their own experiences, deepening the interpretation. This process helped "identify the problem or the asset, critically discuss the roots of the situation, and develop strategies for changing the situation" (Wang et al., 1998, p. 80).

Finally, the researchers worked with participants through mixing the data from the quantitative and qualitative findings. The results from the EAAM survey were shared and compared and contrasted with Photovoice analysis. Participants identified where the quantitative survey was reflected within their stories and how the results differed from the scale. This complementary protocol of mixing quantitative and qualitative findings improves rigor (Stewart et al., 2007) and attends to the central contributions of participants (Canales, 2013). Using inductive coding with the participants, themes were then collapsed with axial coding (Creswell, 2007; Creswell & Plano Clark, 2007).

Johnson et al. (2009) used a conceptual theoretical framework as an interpretive tool throughout in a mixed methods study of Somali refugees with experiences of female genital cutting in an effort to understand their health-seeking behaviors. Although Johnson et al. (2009) did not use ecological theories, their study design was mixed methods and grounded in critical theory with an emancipatory focus for its participants. Building on Johnson et al.'s work and Mertens's (2003, 2009) avocation for theory being conceived throughout the study, the following conceptual framework was created (Figure 6.2). Although Johnson et al.'s work did not specifically address a Burmese refugee community, the participants were recent refugees with conceptions of healthy living that differed from those they experienced in the United States.

This framework represented in Figure 6.2 articulates a likely timeframe of Burmese refugees' entry into the United States and the interfaces with healthy living. The pink

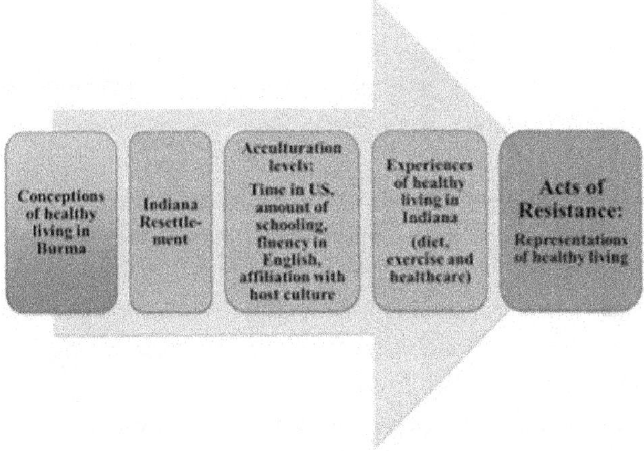

Figure 6.2. Conceptual framework of Burmese refugees and healthy living. Adapted from Johnson, Ali, & Shipp, 2009.

rectangles denote the institutional practices and processes that the Burmese refugees negotiate. The last green rectangle identifies the experiences of the Burmese refugees blending their historic health experiences within new systems and how they are embodied. This conceptual framework assists with the visualization of the units of analyses, which for this study are the EAAMS survey and Photovoice protocol.

Our Positionalities as Lead Researchers

As researchers from local universities, we inherently realize the immediate disequilibrium of power that can be sensed by the participant community. Although the instructors of the English program have told the participants to "trust in our work," we were consistently attentive to keeping their analyses central as they represented their stories. The researchers were Asian American and Eastern Indian, and this appeared to help build trust with the participants.

RESULTS

Quantitative Findings

Given the low number of participants in the study, a statistical analysis was not conducted on quantitative data and was used to inform the more weighted qualitative portion. This is consistent with an exploratory, transformative design.

EAAM SURVEY

An analysis was conducted by the research team comparing the demographic characteristics of the participants to their perceptions of the various dimensions of acculturation within the EAAM survey. Years living in the United States had the largest impact on participants' perceptions of their sense of inclusion in their new home. Four of the seven participants lived in the United States for three years or greater and had moderate levels of integration and assimilation, yet separation and marginalization was moderate to high (see Figure 6.3).

Participants 5 and 6 had been in the United States the least amount of time, ranging from three to five months, and they perceived themselves as having low levels of integration and assimilation and higher levels of separation and marginalization. These two participants were also unemployed and actively seeking work.

In comparing the survey scores with education levels, four of the 10 participants had some schooling (up to elementary/middle school), five completed high school, and one attended college but did not complete an undergraduate degree. Seven participants provided details on both their education levels as well the EAAM survey (Figure 6.4). Visual analysis of data based on years of education demonstrated that this had an impact on their level of integration and assimilation. Participants 5 and 6 had the lowest levels of education (some schooling) and demonstrated greater acculturation challenges in marginalization and separation. The remaining participants had either a high school or some college education, and most of them demonstrated higher scores in assimilation and integration (Figure 6.4).

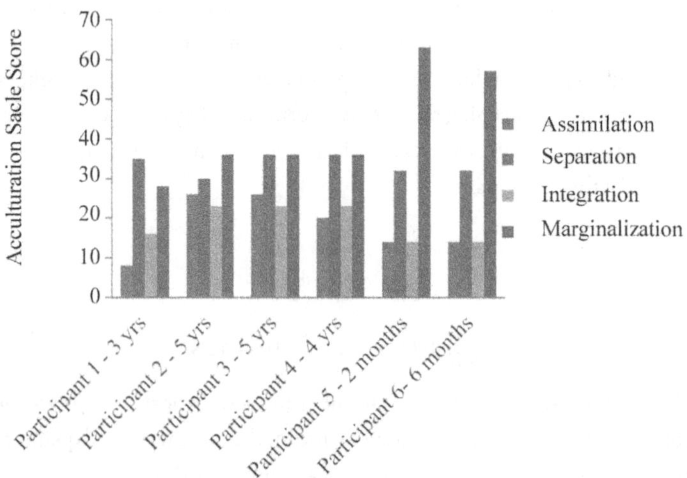

Figure 6.3. Years (yrs)/months in the United States and the participant's level of acculturation.

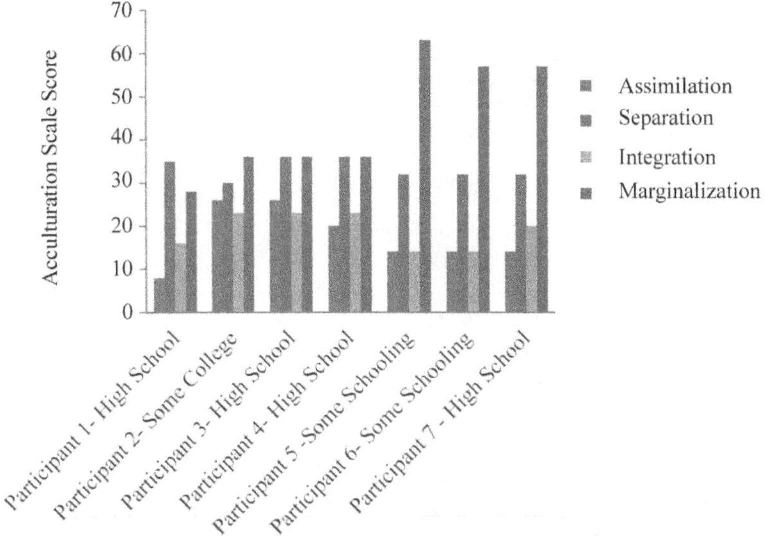

Figure 6.4. Participants' education level and their levels of acculturation.

In examination of Barry's (2001) EAAM's survey, items related to assimilation largely relied on proficiency in English, which all participants were actively seeking to master. Integration items were associated with their perceived capacity to interact with individuals from dominant institutions, specifically health care providers, and institutionally available resources through local church agencies, social services, schools, their English classes, and publicly furnished health care. Separation and marginalization items attended to reciprocal interactions with individuals whom they regarded as different from their own heritage and conditions, including health care providers. The systems and supports within the health care system available to the Burmese refugee community are instruments to realize higher levels of acculturation. However, acculturation relies heavily on the variable of time to realize a greater sense of assimilation and integration, such as acquiring English and fostering relationships from cultures other than their own. For participants living in the United States for three to five years, a level of marginalization and separation strongly persists (Table 6.4).

Participants resisted the description that amount of time in a new country and acquisition of a new language was predictive of assimilation, which could realize greater access to healthful living. Health was a daily and imminent need and as such, immediacy could not be reconciled by simply waiting for a sufficient level of acculturation to be acquired.

TABLE 6.4. SCORES ON EAST ASIAN ACCULTURATION MEASURE (EAAM)

	SCORES ON EAST ASIAN ACCULTURATION MEASURE (EAAM)				TOTAL
ID	ASSIMILATION	SEPARATION	MARGINALIZATION	INTEGRATION	SCORE
1	8	35	16	28	87
2	**	**	**	**	**
3	**	**	**	**	**
4	26	30	23	36	115
5	26	36	23	36	121
6	20	36	23	36	115
7	**	**	**	**	**
8	14	32	14	63	123
9	14	32	14	57	117
10	14	32	20	57	123

Note: Higher scores on the EAAM indicate higher participant's perception of the various dimensions of acculturation. ** Did not answer/complete the EAAM.

Qualitative Findings

Participants identified the following themes in the analysis of the individual interviews and focus group discussions using the Photovoice protocol. A discussion with the participants prior to capturing photos illustrated a tacit understanding of what they needed prior to finding healthy food to prepare and consume and realize improved comfort with health care providers. Time was identified as their major barrier to acquiring sufficient English to adequately navigate English- speaking food markets and health care systems. As time was not an adequate resolution to their expressed immediacy, qualitative findings revealed other interpretations that expanded the notions of waiting. The emergent themes are described as follows.

LOST IN TRANSLATION

Based on the reports of participants, area health centers and, in particular, primary care doctors furnished interpreters (spoken) for the Burmese community when they had appointments. In emergencies, a service was solicited and someone came to interpret. One participant took a photo of a medical form (Figure 6.5). Forms were seldom in their native language, only being explained through a medical interpreter or a family member who could potentially explain the documents. Forms were seldom translated, so the reliance on spoken interpretation was central. One example of the comment made by a participant was as follows:

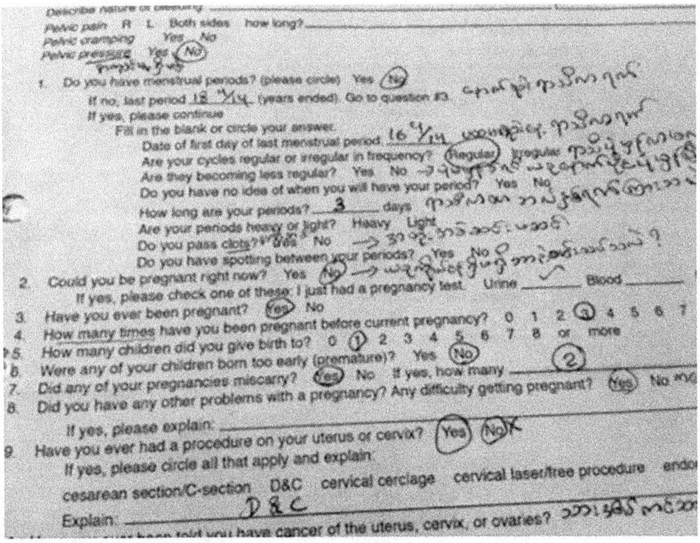

Pelvic pain R L Both sides how long?

Pelvic cramping Yes No

Pelvic pressure Yes No

1. Do you have menstrual periods? (please circle) Yes No
   If no, last period 18 ⁄14 (years ended). Go to question #3.
   If yes, please continue
   Fill in the blank or circle your answer.
   Date of first day of last menstrual period 16 ⁄14
   Are your cycles regular or irregular in frequency? Regular Irregular
   Are they becoming less regular? Yes No
   Do you have no idea of when you will have your period? Yes No
   How long are your periods? 3 days
   Are your periods heavy or light? Heavy Light
   Do you pass clots? Yes No
   Do you have spotting between your periods? Yes No
2. Could you be pregnant right now? Yes No
   If yes, please check one of these: I just had a pregnancy test. Urine ✓ Blood
3. Have you ever been pregnant? Yes No
4. How many times have you been pregnant before current pregnancy? 0 1 2 3 4 5 6 7
5. How many children did you give birth to? 0 1 2 3 4 5 6 7 8 or more
6. Were any of your children born too early (premature)? Yes No
7. Did any of your pregnancies miscarry? Yes No If yes, how many 2
8. Did you have any other problems with a pregnancy? Any difficulty getting pregnant? Yes No
   If yes, please explain:
9. Have you ever had a procedure on your uterus or cervix? Yes No
   If yes, please circle all that apply and explain:
   cesarean section/C-section D&C cervical cerclage cervical laser/free procedure
   Explain: D&C

have cancer of the uterus, cervix, or ovaries?

Figure 6.5. The "form."

> If they're [referring to the interpreter] a good person and they give it [referring to the medical forms] to me. I don't feel good if they fill it out. I should fill the form out before, so I don't get frustrated. The same day, I go and I don't speak English well, how can the interpreter know as well? They gave to me the same day.

Having to complete to a required health form ten minutes before she saw the physician was unsettling, as she felt she would be inaccurate and this could change the course of decisions made in the examination room (Figure 6.5). Having an interpreter available to her created further frustration. She recalled her historic experiences:

> Here is the problem is about the interpreter, even though they want to say something, if they want to say it, they may not. I've seen that a lot. They want to say it, by action, the patient shows by action, but the interpreter does not. If they want to say it, they will and if they don't, they won't.

As an interpreter was employed, the perception from the doctor was that his message had been received and understood by the patient. The function of the interpreter was insufficient and did not attend to the accuracy or the emotive story of her health concerns. This lack of thoroughness diminished her contribution and reduced the reciprocity that she anticipated between physician and patient. The doctor appeared oblivious to her, assured that the presence of an interpreter was adequate.

Figure 6.6. "The clock."

The participant went on to describe the interpreter having an economic incentive. He was paid for two hours regardless of the time that he spent with her. She inferred that the interpreter was motivated to conclude quickly, so he could move on to his next assignment, being paid for two hours for ten minutes of work. This created unanticipated tension where she felt betrayed by a Burmese national whom she originally conceived to be a supporter. She conceived the doctor to be the content specialist and complaining about the interpreter's accuracy was not a domain she felt the doctor could influence.

Furnishing a technical solution of "language only" support created an unequal relation of power between doctor and patient, and patient and interpreter. The participant self-identified a need for medical care and interpretation, but this promoted a transmission model of language that ignored the complexity of her health condition.

Another participant added to the translation and interpretation dilemma with his photograph of a clock (Figure 6.6). As a senior member of the Burmese community, he was frequently called upon by other Burmese to intervene in health situations of immediacy. He was regarded as a Burmese patient advocate within his community. He described the ill state of a friend that he accompanied to the emergency room. He said:

> My friend is very seriously ill. Blood sick . . . and he threw up blood. I checked at the counter and everything and he kept throwing up blood and they didn't call us. My friend almost died on that night, there were no other patients in the waiting room, but when I talk about that, whenever Burmese go to the emergency room, we wait.

The representation of the clock was a reccurring theme with the participant who frequented the emergency room. His understanding was that emergency rooms were for immediate care and an appointment was not needed. Although he did not speak English well, he conveyed that vomit and blood should be sufficient for attention, but the consistent response at the front desk was to wait longer. After having multiple experiences of long wait times, he concluded that the Burmese were the ones that had to wait. He asserted, "I want to understand how this emergency room works!" As an ambassador to his community, he felt he could not serve in his senior and esteemed role because the institution had collectively excluded him from a timely response.

This Burmese patient advocate found that his unique skill and identity in this revered role collided with what he believed was a collective inscription of him as "Burmese" and having to "always wait." He had a clear devotion to wanting to understand the system and despite the use of a hospital-furnished interpreter, more wait time persisted as the response.

NAMING AS A FORM OF RESISTANCE

Although names of places such as the doctor's office and area health clinics were translated for the Burmese refugees in three dialects with their sponsoring refugee agencies and reinforcement from their adult English program, Burmese refugee participants offered different understandings. One participant remarked on her experiences of immunizing her family upon arrival in the United States. She discussed the role and name of a comprehensive health clinic she visited upon her arrival: "They give immunizations . . . and then they check if they have the TB or anything and that kind of stuff. The doctor checks for that." This participant identified area health clinics supported by her Medicare plan as the "immunization place." The participants' first memories of receiving health care in Indianapolis were a battery of immunizations and injections. Regarding the health center as the first stopping point for health care upon their arrival, one participant described its myopic focus.

> They give me appointments for immunization appointment. On that day, my child has a fever. We had to take [child] to the doctor for the immunization and when they don't give him a shot, the doctor is supposed to see him and give him medicine, so we don't like going there a lot.

When the doctor at the clinic did not prescribe medicine for their child's fever and informed them that they would receive the required immunizations later, the participant and her spouse conceived the "immunization place" as lacking immediacy for them individually while protecting the narrow focus of vaccinations. This institutional preservation in scope and purpose led to a disdain for doctors and staff working in the "immunization place."

By naming the "immunization place" they resisted the prescribed focus of its expressed purpose and scope. They shared their concerns about the clinic with other Burmese friends and families. They created a navigation system, leading them to more individual and responsive care, seeking out their primary care physician in lieu of the area clinic.

FROM FRESH TO FROZEN

Participant-captured photos of refrigerators revealed produce that would be regarded as fresh by North American standards. Other photos captured flash frozen fruits and vegetables in the freezer section. One was a frozen durian, a Southeast Asian delicacy eaten at special times: "My employer told me that if you can eat [durian] once a day, that is very good for your body, healthy skin and everything. But, whenever we have money, we eat it." He was excited to find durian at a large-scale Asia-Mart when he arrived, but because it was frozen, it didn't have the same taste or texture of fresh durians that he previously enjoyed.

Another participant also remarked on the difference between the fresh durians of Burma and the frozen ones in the local Asia-Mart: "It's different. . . . Frozen one is not very good to suck. But, from the tree where I got right away, it's very good to suck." The participant enjoyed acquiring durian at the store and bought it more frequently than he would in Burma because of its availability and reasonable price. Even though its flavor was impacted by its frozen state, changing how he enjoyed it, he still found that it had a place on his plate as it represented a healthy purpose for good skin care and anti-aging (Figure 6.7).

Figure 6.7. Fresh and frozen.

NOT MY FOOD PYRAMID

One participant took photos of a halal[1] meat section sign at a local Asia-Mart and of a diagram of the food pyramid from the U.S. Department of Agriculture. This food pyramid provides a visual model for diets being dense in grains, fruits, and vegetables with lesser representation of fatty foods (Center for Nutrition Policy and Development, 2005). Its purpose is to promote balanced food consumption for overall health and weight management. Regarded as a compass for healthy eating, it was viewed as restrictive to a Muslim participant who ate halal prepared meats.

This participant remarked on the consistent review of the "food pyramid" when she went to her primary care physician with her children. She reflected on what she was preparing her children at home as a Muslim Burmese and felt that the "halal" preparation that she employed violated the strict food pyramid. A researcher asked if it was easy to find halal prepared meat. One participant remarked, "No. It's easy the vegetables and fruits, but chicken it's not easy. We are Muslim and we just eat the meat, the halal." Although a regional Asia-Mart has halal prepared meat, it was distant and costly. Further complicating the acquisition of halal meat was the food pyramid that was consistently shown during her doctor's visits with her children (Figure 6.8). She did not use the food pyramid, but felt pressure to impose it to meet the healthy living standards for her doctor.

Healthy consumption of food was conceived within a tight and fixed pyramid. Diets conceived within cultures other than the United States and from religions that were locally unfamiliar situated the Burmese as not being as healthy. Mere adjustments were necessary and she would meet the healthy living standard deemed proper by her doctor. Simplifying these dietary changes within the paradigm did not consider her religion, history, and identity, which she felt were conscious decisions and not mere choices. The doctor had a technical orientation of health, asserting that good

Figure 6.8. Halal and the food pyramid.

health was simply a matter of a few changes and driven by a menu of "choices" on the food pyramid.

EXERCISE AND PHYSICAL ACTIVITY

Participants reported that their physical activity was reduced since their relocation as they were limited to borrowing a car, being driven by a case worker, or taking a public bus that did not have the frequency or reliability to which they were accustomed. Also, due to inclement weather, being able to ride a bike was only available during warmer months: "So, it's not the same, not only when we work and exercise. In Burma, there's the bus that people take and then walking and bike that we ride." Two female participants also remarked that the rules for riding in a car differed as children had to sit in their own seats in the back and if young, they had to be in an appropriate car seat: "In Burma, kids can sit in the front." For these two mothers with more than two children, it was complicated to get the entire family to the store in ways that were lawful and safe. They therefore traveled less altogether and their mobility was limited to the geography surrounding their apartment community.

QUANTITATIVE AND QUALITATIVE MIXING

The use of an interactive mixing model between quantitative and qualitative data sets was employed during focus group discussions (Creswell, 2003; Creswell & Plano Clark, 2011). Participants demonstrated varying degrees of resistance with the outcomes of the EAAM survey. They clearly noted that waiting for a sufficient level of acculturation to take place was unreasonable because being healthy was imminent. The Photovoice portion illuminated other logics that resisted the fixed structure of time. The following section describes the participants' self-perceptions of their acculturation status, within the areas of assimilation, integration, separation, and marginalization, and how these areas related to their health-related behaviors and practices. The EAAM survey demonstrated low levels of acculturation in assimilation due to low proficiency in English and integration, due to low levels of interactions with the dominant culture. Presumptively, this inhibits access to healthful living, but participants articulated their efforts toward these areas of low acculturation by taking English courses and finding foods from their Burmese diet that were frozen versus fresh.

Separation and marginalization were both rated as high on the EAAM survey. In the area of separation, their lack of networks outside the Burmese community restricted their capacity to influence their healthful living, but qualitative findings

TABLE 6.5. DATA MIXING—ANALYSIS OF QUANTITATIVE AND QUALITATIVE COMPONENTS OF THE STUDY

QUANTITATIVE OUTCOMES/ EAAM SURVEY	QUALITATIVE THEMES
Assimilation is low because participants don't know language and its cultural systems well yet	Participants are all taking English courses and consistently attend Foods of home country are found and prepared well. When fresh food is absent, frozen is acquired as substitute.
Integration is low because participants do not have friends outside the Burmese community	A Burmese advocate for seriously ill patients makes integration attempts at the hospital. His attempts at integration through agency are not met with reciprocity from the hospital.
Separation is high because participants do not have friends or networks outside the Burmese community	Representing their distinct languages and religious practices, agencies and health care providers use devices to convince patients that "mere choices" will satisfy doctor's conception of healthy living.
Marginalization is high because the Burmese do not feel heard by their health care providers	Interpretation in health care settings is necessary, but advocacy is most central and should be recognized. Participants feel empowered when in settings of Burmese affinity, where experiences are shared and validated.

demonstrated that health care institutions also limited their contributions to their preexisting healthy food habits. Participants often felt misunderstood by their health care providers even with interpretation being furnished. Qualitative themes demonstrated that interpretation was at a minimum and that advocacy and a more responsive understanding of an interpreter's skills and a doctor's cross-cultural understanding needed to be addressed.

Assimilation

The outcomes on the EAAM survey for assimilation demonstrated a correlation between years in the United States and levels of assimilation. Assimilation suggested that low proficiency would create significant barriers to healthy living. Photovoice findings suggested that accessibility to healthy foods was not a limitation.

HEALTHY FOOD AVAILABLE

Despite low proficiency in English, participants found foods that were healthy and available in local Asia-Marts. Although halal prepared meats were costly, other foods were affordable and attainable. Families regularly cooked their familiar foods that met their criterion for healthy living, which extend beyond North American conceptions of protein for energy and calcium for good bone development. Specific Burmese foods were equated with healthy skin and anti-aging. Each food not only had a specific and familiar flavor, but a specific nutritional goal.

LANGUAGE AND CULTURAL AMBASSADORS

Participants were cognizant about how "more time" was imbued in them in health care and educational settings. Addressing this central concern of their sponsors and the health care settings, participants actively attended English classes unless their work schedules conflicted. They showed a central devotion to acquiring English and held high levels of communicative competence. "Understanding the system" was most central and other avenues were examined and executed to understand and acquire what they needed for healthy living.

Integration

Integration on the survey demonstrated low outcomes for all participants; yet there was a strong resolve by one participant to be a collective advocate for Burmese refugee families in hospitals. Attempts were made to understand the hospital system, so the "clock" was not an inhibiting factor. This participant's attempt to receive timely responses for his sick friends in the emergency room by knowing what questions to ask and following historic procedures was met by hospital staff with responses that were neither timely nor responsive. The participant was deeply troubled that there seemed to be such a passive denial as he met the criterion for being communicatively competent and also knowledgeable about the hospital system.

Separation

Separation on the survey demonstrated that participants did not have friends or networks outside their local Burmese community, and this became situated in a power conflict in the doctor's office. One participant was troubled by her doctor's suggestion that she follow the food pyramid. In disclosing the halal diet she provided for her two children, she felt the doctor's continued reference to the food pyramid inferred it was the best "choice" for her family. Her efforts to demonstrate how her halal diet fit within the pyramid were dismissed. Her resilience in explaining her conformity within her tradition and within the pyramid was an attempt to be "non-separate," yet the physician's persistent framework positioned her as uncooperative.

Marginalization

Interpretation was a consistent theme of concern that was shared when one participant shared her photo of the detailed health form she was to complete before of a doctor's visit (Figure 6.5). In health care settings, Burmese interpreters were presumed to be skillful and hardworking by providers, but participants were troubled that they moved too swiftly between interpretation tasks, reducing accuracy and responsiveness. This work ethic and interpretation skill sanctioned by the health care provider masqueraded for physicians as being accurate, adequate, and complete. Participants regarded interpretation as harried, inaccurate, and distant.

Physicians' trusting the interpreter's quality made participants feel marginalized when their needs were not conveyed with accuracy, emotion, and timeliness. By discussing this photo, each participant recollected a time of misunderstanding and partiality due to poorly conceived interpretation experiences in health care provider contexts. Together, the participants distilled different logics about the accuracy and responsiveness of interpretation. While in most health care patient/doctor situations an interpreter was furnished, the participants claimed interpretation was conceived as a transmission model and met the immediacy needs of the doctor, but not the patient (Freire, 1986; Pochhacker, 2004). This repositioning of agency from patient to interpreter created an expansive power division that made their care reliant on the perceptions and practices of the interpreter.

DISCUSSION

The purpose of this study was to explore health perceptions, access, and attitudes toward preventive health care and identify individual, cultural, and other environmental challenges toward health behaviors and practices among refugees from Burma who now reside in a central Midwest town in the United States. Results showed that the Burmese participants resisted normativity of health care provision, pushing on the fixed mental structures of their physicians and health care clinics. In other words, the local health care system did not reflect the health practices, needs, and concerns of the Burmese. For example, the use of an interpreter was conceived in expediency by health care providers, but foreclosed on the immediacy and accuracy of patients' needs, which was found in a similar study conducted by Kumar (2013). Health care providers presented food pyramids as universalisms, yet participants could all describe foods distinct to their diet and their related health benefits that were not taken into consideration by health care providers.

These transmission models of health care provision were hierarchical: doctor, interpreter, and patient. This particular power structure created disequilibrium that participants challenged by resisting the notion of more time needed to learn English in order to be fully acclimated and acculturated. Through their photographic representations and collaborative analysis of healthy living, they demonstrated their commitment to healthy lives.

Using critical and ecological theories, this study illuminated the disequilibrium of power that the Burmese experienced in their health care settings that are built on a normative set of standards. Participants articulated their logics for their diets and the need to be accurate in portraying their health care needs. They expanded the notions of normalcy with specific narratives and photos with distinct rationales. Theorizing through these two lenses enabled new definitions of healthy living that expand the notions of healthful living instead of restricting it to the dominant paradigm.

Limitations of the Study

There are several limitations to this study. There were limitations encountered due to the survey and the interpretation of photos. The original EAAM survey was validated with the use of Asian participants, some of whom were not East Asian. Further, the survey was developed on a university campus and as such, it represented many individuals with high levels of education. This can create interpretive concerns as the participant pool differs in the site of the study. Furthermore, the use of interpreters adds another layer of complexity to the study. Did the interpreters interpret correctly the intended meaning of the survey questions? Did the researchers understand the intended meaning of the participants? To what extent did cultural differences influence the communication of intended meaning?

The Photovoice protocol can be limiting as photos can be difficult to co-interpret and familiarity with the local context may be not be as developed with the community and the research team (Mejia et al., 2013). Efforts were made with the research team to include input of the participants at all stages to reduce these possibilities.

The small number of participants can be a concern. As stated previously, the quantitative portion was less weighted and provided descriptive data to inform the qualitative portion. As Photovoice participants listen to each other's stories, they help to identify emerging themes and develop the themes. Because of the storytelling and co-construction of meaning involved, groups need to be small. Future studies could take into consideration these limitations while exploring follow-up questions.

IMPLICATIONS AND NEXT STEPS

This study shows a cultural context in which it is evident that rather than creating spaces for culturally relevant health care practices, health care providers are more likely to interact with the Burmese newcomers through a fixed mental structure of care. Survey outcomes can place the impetus on institutions to react to levels of acculturation and accommodate based on those outcomes. These accommodations are often made by the institution and conceived in sensitivity and responsiveness, yet these changes may not be inclusive of the voices of the Burmese community. Further, these accommodations attend to incremental changes such as language interpretation, which has limited impact as indicated by this study on trustworthiness between patient and care provider. Surveys, however, coupled with interviews or focus group discussion protocol that is participatory in nature has the power to inform institutions to employ different logics about how they may subtractively conceive new Burmese sojourners in the Midwest. As a research collective with and among the Burmese community, we suggest the following.

Training and Practices in Patient Interpretation and Translation

The hierarchical model of health care provider to interpreter to patient needs to be illuminated, so the source message of the patient is central. The transmission model of translation and interpretation simplifies the very complex process of conveying health care needs. More time needs to be built into scheduled appointments requiring interpretation, so the power can be resituated to focus on the patient and not the expedience of mere message delivery.

The "pay by the job" format for translation and interpretation work needs to be reassessed. Economic incentives drive the speed by which interpreters make their income. This points to the need to have full-time interpreters with benefits in health care settings. This will create greater interpreter retention, consistency of care, and embedded professional development experiences for health care providers to learn about responsive interpretation practices.

Any necessary medical documents need to be furnished to patients prior to appointments with translation resources available to the patient, so forms are filled out comprehensively and accurately. Additionally, identifying other strategies to solicit information should be explored.

Representation and Interpretation of the Food Pyramid

In this study, a care provider used the old food pyramid, even though a newer one has been available since 2011. Called ChooseMyPlate, the new nutritional format consists of sections for proteins, grains, vegetables, fruits, and dairy ("ChooseMyPlate," 2014). While this food format is more simplified and imbued with the notion of choice for nutritional aims, it still articulates a fixed format that does not recognize current dietary practices of the Burmese. Specific representations of what can be on one's plate should be explored with and among specific communities, so Burmese patients can be empowered by their food choices instead of judged for them.

CONCLUSION

The Burmese refugees were agentic in avocation for self, family, and community when it came to healthy living. Healthy foods were accessible in Asia-Marts and preparation of their meals met their defined dietary needs and preferences. The health care system, including doctor's offices, clinics, and hospitals, were places of resistance where they troubled the fixed formulas of healthy living. Burmese refugees pushed on the traditional notions of assimilation, integration, separation, and marginalization, redefining their methods as creative, collective, and instructional to the health care system.

Follow-up studies have been established to deepen our understanding as researchers on how institutions mitigate translation and interpretation services for Burmese refugees. Specifically, work is being established to examine the implications of using interpreters and translators in identifying health promotion goals with an ultimate goal of empowering the sojourners from Burma.

PUBLICATION NOTE

This article was published online in 2015 by the *Journal of Southeast Asian American Education and Advancement* in Volume 10, Issue 1. Minor edits have been made here. The original can be found at http://doi.org/10.7771/2153-8999.1124.

NOTE

1. Halal references permitted or lawful, but is specific to the dietary customs of Muslim followers. Pork or pork products, animals that were dead prior to slaughter, or animals slaughtered improperly are considered a violation of halal preparation.

REFERENCES

Barron, S., & Ranard, D. (2007). *Refugees from Burma: Their backgrounds and refugee experiences.* Center for Applied Linguistics, Washington, DC: Cultural Orientation Resource Center.

Barry, D. T. (2001). Development of a new scale for measuring acculturation: The East Asian acculturation measure (EAAM). *Journal of Immigrant Health, 3*(4), 193–197. https://doi.org/10.1023/A:1012227611547

Beiser, M. (2005). The health of immigrants and refugees in Canada. *Canadian Journal of Public Health, 96*(2), 30–44. https://doi.org/10.1007/BF03403701

Beiser, M., Hou, F., Hyman, I., & Tousignant, M. (2002). Poverty, family process, and the mental health of immigrant children in Canada. *American Journal of Public Health, 92*(2), 220–227. https://doi.org/10.2105/AJPH.92.2.220

Bhui, K., Stansfield, S., Hull, S., Priebe, S., Mole, F., & Feder, G. (2003). Ethnic variations in pathways to and use of specialist mental health services in the UK: Systematic review. *British Journal of Psychiatry, 182*, 105–116. http://doi.org/10.1192/bjp.02.159

Birman, D., Beehler, S., Harris, E. M., Everson, M. L., Batia, K., Liautaud, J., & Cappella, E. (2008). International Family, Adult, and Child Enhancement Services (FACES): A community-based comprehensive services model for refugee children in resettlement. *American Journal of Orthopsychiatry, 78*(1), 121–132. https://doi.org/10.1037/0002-9432.78.1.121

Bourdieu, P. (1984). *Distinction: A social critique of the judgement of taste.* Harvard University Press.

Brendler-Lindqvist, M., Norredam, M., & Hjern, A. (2014). Duration of residence and psychotropic drug use in recently settled refugees in Sweden—A register-based study. *International Journal for Equity in Health, 13*(1), 116–130. http://doi.org/10.1186/s12939-014-0122-2

Burmese American Community Institute. (2014). *The Burmese population in the U.S., Indiana and Indianapolis.* Retrieved from http://www.baci-indy.org/resources/burmese-refugee-population-in-the-us

Canales, G. (2013). Transformative, mixed methods checklist for psychological research with Mexican Americans. *Journal of Mixed Methods Research, 7*(1), 6–21. http://doi.org/10.1177/1558689812446022

Center for Nutrition Policy and Development. (2005). *My pyramid—Getting started.* Retrieved from http://www.choosemyplate.gov/food-groups/downloads/MyPyramid_Getting_Started.pdf

Chambers, N., & Ganesan, S. (2005). Refugees in Canada. In N. Waxler-Morrison, J. Anderson, E. Richardson, & N. Chambers (Eds.), *Cross-cultural caring: A handbook for health professionals* (2nd ed., pp. 289–322). University of British Columbia Press.

ChooseMyPlate. (2014). Retrieved from http://www.choosemyplate.gov/about.html

Creswell, J. W. (2003). *Research design: Qualitative, quantitative, and mixed methods approaches* (2nd ed.). Sage Publications.

Creswell, J. W. (2007). *Qualitative inquiry & research design: Choosing among five approaches* (2nd ed.). Sage Publications.

Creswell, J. W., & Plano Clark, V. L. (2007). *Designing and conducting mixed methods research*. Sage Publications.

Creswell, J. W., & Plano Clark, V. L. (2011). *Designing and conducting mixed methods research* (2nd ed.). Sage Publications.

Crotty, M. (1998). *The foundations of social research: Meaning and perspective in the research process*. Sage Publications.

DéVoretz, D. J., Pivnenko, S., & Beiser, M. (2004). The economic experiences of refugees in Canada. *RIIM Working Paper Series* (Vol. No. 04–04). Vancouver Centre for Excellence.

Dharod, J. M., Croom, J. E., & Sady, C. G. (2013). Food insecurity: Its relationship to dietary intake and body weight among Somali refugee women in the United States. *Journal of nutrition education and behavior, 45*(1), 47–53. https://doi.org/10.1016/j.jneb.2012.03.006

Ellis, B. H., MacDonald, H. Z., Klunk-Gillis, J., Lincoln, A., Strunin, L., & Cabral, H. J. (2010). Discrimination and mental health among Somali refugee adolescents: The role of acculturation and gender. *American Journal of Orthopsychiatry, 80*(4), 564–575. https://doi.org/10.1111/j.1939-0025.2010.01061.x

Exodus Social Services. (2014). *The life ahead: Learn more.* Retrieved from http://www.exodusrefugee.org/news.html

Fairclough, N. (2001). *Language and power*. Longman.

Fazel, M., Wheeler, J., & Danesh, J. (2005). Prevalence of serious mental disorder in 7000 refugees resettled in western countries: A systematic review. *The Lancet, 365*(9467), 1309–1314. https://doi.org/10.1016/S0140-6736(05)61027-6

Fielding, J., Teutsch, S., & Breslow, L. (2011). A framework for public health in the United States. *Public Health Reviews, 32*(1), 174–189. https://doi.org/10.1007/BF03391597

Flynn, P. M., Foster, E. M., & Brost, B. C. (2011). Indicators of acculturation related to Somali refugee women's birth outcomes in Minnesota. *Journal of Immigrant and Minority Health, 13*(2), 224–231. https://doi.org/10.1007/s10903-009-9289-9

Foucault, M. (1995). *Discipline and punish: The birth of the prison* (2nd Vintage Books ed.). Vintage Books.

Freire, P. (1986). *Pedagogy of the oppressed.* Seabury Press.

Geltman, P. L., Adams, J. H., Penrose, K. L., Cochran, J., Rybin, D., Doros, G., & Paasche-Orlow, M. (2014). Health literacy, acculturation, and the use of preventive oral health care by Somali refugees living in Massachusetts. *Journal of Immigrant and Minority Health, 16*(4), 622–630. https://doi.org/10.1007/s10903-013-9846-0

Greene, J. (2007). *Mixed methods in social inquiry* (1st ed.). Jossey-Bass.

Grisaru, N., Irwin, M., & Kaplan, Z. (2003). Acute psychotic episodes as a reaction to severe trauma in a population of Ethiopian immigrant to Israel. *Stress and Health, 19*, 241–247. http://doi.org/10.1002/smi.976

Johnson, C. E., Ali, S., & Shipp, M. P. (2009). Building community-based participatory research partnerships with a Somali refugee community. *American Journal of Preventative Medicine, 37*(3S1), 230–236. http://doi.org/10.1016/j.amepre.2009.09.036

Kimbrough, W., Saliba, V., Dahab, M., Haskew, C., & Checchi, F. (2012). The burden of tuberculosis in crisis-affected populations: A systematic review. *The Lancet: Infectious Disease, 12*, 950–965. https://doi.org/10.1016/S1473-3099(12)70225-6

Koh, L. C., Liamputtong, P., & Walker, R. (2013). Burmese refugee young women navigating parental expectations and resettlement. *Journal of Family Studies, 19*(3), 297–305. https://doi.org/10.5172/jfs.2013.19.3.297

Kopecky, D. (2011). Foucault, governmentality, neoliberalism and adult education-perspectives on normalization of social risk. *Journal of Pedagogy/Pedagogický Casopis, 2*(2), 246–262. http://doi.org/10.2478/v10159-011-0012-2

Kumar, R. (2013). *Negotiating healthcare structures in the United States: Reassessing resettlement through Burmese refugee voices.* [Doctoral dissertation]. Purdue University. http://docs.lib.purdue.edu/dissertations/AAI3604941/

Lewis, M., Simmons, G., & Fennig, C. (2015). *Ethnologue: Languages of the World—Myanmar*. Retrieved from https://www.ethnologue.com/country/MM/languages

Li, H. Z., & Browne, A. J. (2000). Defining mental health illness and accessing mental health care services: Perspectives of Asian Canadians. *Canadian Journal of Community Mental Health, 19*, 143–159. https://doi.org/10.7870/cjcmh-2000-0008

Lin, K. M., & Cheung, F. (1999). Mental health issues for Asian Americans. *Psychiatric Services, 50*(6), 774–780. https://doi.org/10.1176/ps.50.6.774

Lobou, P. A., & Moser, K. S. (2004). Screening of immigrants and refugees for pulmonary tuberculosis in San Diego County, California. *CHEST, 126*, 1777–1782. https://doi.org/10.1378/chest.126.6.1777

McLaren, P. (2005). *Capitalists and conquerors: A critical pedagogy against empire.* Rowman & Littlefield.

McMillan, J. H., & Schumacher, S. (1997). *Research in education: A conceptual introduction* (4th ed.). Longman USA.

Mejia, P. A., Quiroz, O., Morales, Y., Ponce, R., Limon Chavez, G., & Olivera y Torre, E. (2013). From madres to mujeristas: Latinas making change with Photovoice. *Action Research, 11*(4), 301–321. http://doi.org/10.1177/1476750313502553

Mertens, D. M. (2003). Mixed methods and the politics of human research: The transformative- emancipatory approach. In A. Tashakkori & C. Teddlie (Eds.), *Handbook of mixed methods in social and behavioral sciences* (pp. 135–164). SAGE.

Mertens, D. M. (2009). *Transformative research and evaluation*. Guilford Press.

Morrow, R. A., & Brown, D. D. (1994). *Critical theory and methodology*. Sage Publications.

Nakash, O., Nagar, M., Shoshani, A., Zubida, H., & Harper, R. A. (2012). The effect of acculturation and discrimination on mental health symptoms and risk behaviors among adolescent migrants in Israel. *Cultural Diversity and Ethnic Minority Psychology, 18*(3), 228–238. https://doi.org/10.1037/a0027659

Pochhacker, F. (2004). *Introducing interpreting studies*. Routledge.

Rondinelli, A. J., Morris, M. D., Rodwell, T. C., Moser, K. S., Paida, P., Popper, S. T., & Brouwer, K. C. (2011). Under- and over-nutrition among refugees in San Diego County, California. *Journal of Immigrant and Minority Health, 13*(1), 161–168. https://doi.org/10.1007/s10903-010-9353-5

Shepard, J. (1992). Post-traumatic stress disorder in Vietnamese women. In E. Cole, O. M. Espin, & E. D. Rothblum (Eds.), *Refugee women and their mental health: Shattered societies, shattered lives* (pp. 281–296). Haworth Pub.

Smith, E. (2003). Habitus and situation for learning: An ecology. *British Journal of Sociology of Education, 24*(4), 463–470. https://doi.org/10.1080/01425690301916

Stewart, M., Makwarimba, E., Barnfather, A., Letourneau, N., & Neufeld, A. (2007). Researching reducing health disparities: Mixed-methods approaches. *Social Science and Medicine, 66*, 1406–1417. https://doi.org/10.1016/j.socscimed.2007.11.021

Sweetman, D., Badiee, M., & Creswell, J. W. (2010). Use of the transformative framework in mixed methods studies. *Qualitative Inquiry, 16*(6), 441–454. http://doi.org/10.1177/1077800410364610

Thurston, W. E. & McGrath, A. (1993). *"With two pennies in my pocket, I just feel not so helpless": A report on the mental and occupational health promotion needs of immigrants in Calgary.* University of Calgary, Department of Community Health Sciences.

United Nations High Commission for Refugees. (2010). Convention and protocol relating to the status of refugees (pp. 1–52). Geneva, Switzerland.

Uppaluri, A., Naus, M., Heywood, N., Brunton, J., Kerbel, D., & Wobeser, W. (2002). Effectiveness of the immigration medical surveillance program for tuberculosis in Ontario. *Canadian Journal of Public Health, 93*(2), 88–91. https://doi.org/10.1007/BF03404544

Vang, C. Y., & Mong Trieu, M. (2014). *Invisible newcomers: Refugees from Burma/Myanmar and Bhutan in the United States.* Asian and Pacific Islander Scholarship Fund.

Wang, C. C., & Burris, C. A. (2004). Family, maternal, and child health through Photovoice. *Maternal and Child Health Journal, 8*(2), 95–102. https://doi.org/10.1023/B:MACI.0000025732.32293.4f

Wang, C. C., Morrell-Samuels, S., Hutchison, P. A., Bell, L., & Pestronk, R. M. (2004). Flint Photovoice: Community building among youths, adults and policymakers. *American Journal of Public Health, 94*(6), 911–913. https://doi.org/10.2105/AJPH.94.6.911

Wang, C. C., Yi, W. K., Tao, Z. W., & Carovano, K. (1998). Photovoice as a participatory health promotion strategy. *Health Promotion International, 13*(1), 75–86. https://doi.org/10.1093/heapro/13.1.75

Zacharadias, M., Scott, S., & Barrett, M. (2013). Methodological implications of critical realism for mixed-methods research. *MIS Quarterly, 37*(3), 855–879. https://www.jstor.org/stable/43826004

7

Expanding Definitions of Family

Influences on Second-Generation Lao American College Students' Aspirations

MALAPHONE PHOMMASA

ABSTRACT

This research examines familial influences on the educational and occupational aspirations of second-generation Lao American college students. In-depth, individual interviews were conducted with 10 Lao American college students. Findings from this study illustrate the value of familial relationships in students' educational experiences and how these relationships are perceived to have considerable influence on students' aspirations. Consistent with previous studies on aspiration development, the data suggests that Lao parents are highly influential on students' aspirations. However, Lao American students also placed high value on the advice of extended family members, almost to the point where their influence appeared indistinguishable from that of parents. This paper also extends the research on aspiration development in immigrant populations by examining the influence of refugee migration.

INTRODUCTION

Lao American students have been placed within an educational paradox due to the stereotypes that plague Asian American and Southeast Asian American students. They are either labeled as overachieving Asian Americans due to the model minority stereotype, or they are viewed as underachieving dropouts due to the deviant minority stereotype that is associated with Southeast Asian Americans (Museus, 2014; Ngo, 2006; Ngo & Lee, 2007). In reality, census data consistently proves that Lao American students continue trailing in educational attainment in comparison to their fellow Asian American counterparts and the general U.S. population (Kouanchao, 2013; Uy, 2011). Even among Southeast Asian American groups, Lao Americans have the lowest percentage (13%) of adults aged 25 and older who have earned a bachelor's degree or higher (SEARAC, 2011). In California, where the largest population of Lao Americans has settled, scholars have observed that the children of Lao refugees experience among the most serious disadvantages in their schooling across racial and ethnic categories (Portes & Rumbaut, 2006). Disparities in opportunity and achievement pose severe problems for the Lao American community; lower educational attainment levels are positively correlated with higher rates of poverty, which could force families to rely on social services (Baum & Payea, 2005; Museus, 2013; Swail, 2002). Despite these alarming circumstances, there is a paucity of educational research examining the experiences or educational needs of Lao American students.

Although several scholars have addressed the unique educational experiences of Southeast Asian American students (e.g., Chhuon, 2013; Chhuon & Hudley, 2008; Kouanchao, 2013; Museus, 2013; Ngo, 2009; Ngo, 2010; Uy, 2011; Vue, 2013), this research is the first to focus on the educational and occupational aspirations of Lao American college students. Research has consistently found a correlation between educational aspirations, educational expectations, and academic achievement; students with higher educational aspirations and expectations are more likely to achieve (Feliciano, 2006; Hong & Ho, 2005; Sewell et al., 1969; Yamamoto & Holloway, 2010). For this study, educational aspirations refer to students' desired major and the highest educational attainment level (degree) desired, and occupational aspirations refer to students' desired career (Mau & Bikos, 2000). Additionally, I narrowed the focus of influence on students' aspirations to family. Since the family is the "strongest social unit" (Schapiro, 1988, p. 159) for Lao people, it is important to understand how families play a role in students' aspiration development. First, I set the context for understanding these experiences by discussing Lao migration to the United States.

Lao Migration to the United States

As refugees, Lao Americans endured a journey to the United States that is much different from that of other voluntary immigrants. During the Vietnam War, the United States created mass devastation by continuously bombing Laos in order to cut North Vietnamese supply chains on the Ho Chi Minh Trail. Bankston and Hidalgo (2007, p. 239) aptly noted, "War created the paths of migration between North America and Southeast Asia." Once South Vietnam fell to Communist forces in 1975, the Pathet Lao quickly took over the Royal Government of Lao, and the mass migration of Laotians to the United States began. Nearly one million refugees from Southeast Asia entered the United States between 1975 and 2000 (Zhou, 2005). Compared to other Southeast Asian groups, Laotians spent the most time in refugee camps; nearly 23% of Laotians spent more than two years in refugee camps before arriving in America (Caplan et al., 1991). The majority of Laotians who migrated as part of the third wave of Southeast Asian refugees were subsistence farmers with little or no formal education (Ngo & Lee, 2007; Portes & Rumbaut, 2006).

Recognizing the more recent immigration of Lao refugees to the United States, this study extends the aspiration development literature by considering how the circumstances of parental migration can influence their children's aspirations.

ASPIRATION FRAMEWORKS

Studies on the educational aspirations of low-income and minority youth demonstrate the value of utilizing multiple theoretical frameworks in order to capture influential factors in different aspects of Lao American students' lives (home, school, and individual experiences) that impact their aspirations.

Kao and Tienda (1998) were the first to examine the aspirations of Asian and Latino students in their study comparing the educational aspirations of white, black, Asian, and Latino youth. They combined the status-attainment model (Sewell et al., 1969; Sewell et al., 1970) and the blocked-opportunities frameworks (Fordham & Ogbu, 1986; Gibson & Ogbu, 1991; Ogbu, 1991; Sue & Okazaki, 1990) in order to appropriately capture aspiration development among minority students. The status-attainment model posits that educational aspirations are largely influenced by significant others, who are "the persons exerting the greatest influence" upon the student (Sewell et al., 1970, p. 1015). Significant others primarily refer to parents and their background characteristics, which include education, socioeconomic status, and the educational expectations for their children. However, the status-attainment model was developed on studies with white, male youth and has been found to be insufficient for understanding aspiration development among racial and ethnic minority students (Kao & Tienda, 1998). Therefore, Kao and Tienda integrated the blocked opportunities to examine the social and structural barriers that influence the aspirations of minority youth. Both frameworks were also integrated into this study to evaluate how family background (family's race/ethnicity, parents' education, family structure), family resources (immigrant mother, educational resources, outside classes), and students' own educational experiences shape their educational aspirations. I expand further on these frameworks by adding another dimension in this study—Lao parents' migration history as refugees.

ASPIRATIONS OF LAO AMERICAN YOUTH

Few studies have exclusively examined the aspirations of Lao American students, and the few that exist describe Lao American youth as having low aspirations (Baizerman & Hendricks, 1988; Park, 2001). Baizerman and Hendricks's (1988) study focused on Lao youth (age 13 through 24) in Minneapolis and St. Paul, Minnesota. These students had much lower expectations for their future than their parents had for them. Even though students reported "dreams" of obtaining college degrees and professional occupations, they were not academically qualified for scholarships nor were their families able to provide financial support. However, considering that most Lao refugees settled in the United States after the mid-1980s, Baizerman and Hendricks's study should be considered a preliminary examination into the struggles of first- and 1.5-generation Lao immigrants. In a more recent examination, Park's (2001) study comparing the educational and occupational aspirations of Southeast Asian and white high school students also found that Lao students had the lowest educational and occupational aspirations when compared to other Southeast Asian and white students.

Despite reportedly lower aspirations, some have argued that second-generation children will develop higher educational aspirations out of respect for their parents' struggles (Zhou, 2005). Zhou found that immigrant children often internalize the daily struggles they see their parents experiencing as new immigrants and develop a new level of respect for them; consequently, many children will internalize their parents' high educational aspirations. Unfortunately, parents' and children's aspirations can often be conflicting. Several scholars have found that Asian American parents tend to push their children toward what they deem to be "safe" careers, which includes medicine and engineering (e.g., Fuligni et al., 1999; Museus, 2013; Park, 2001). Due to family and ethnic community pressure to bring pride to the family, many children will forgo their own educational and career interests to pursue the safe professions their parents desire for them.

PARENTAL INFLUENCES ON STUDENTS' ASPIRATIONS

As mentioned in the prior section, parental educational expectations and aspirations can have a profound influence on children's own educational aspirations and attainment (e.g., Davies & Kandel, 1981; Feliciano, 2006; Goyette & Xie, 1999; Hong & Ho, 2005; Kim et al., 1998; Mau & Bikos, 2000; Park, 2001; Portes & Rumbaut, 2006; Schneider & Lee, 1990; Yamamoto & Holloway, 2010). Using an ecological approach with the status-attainment model, Kim, Rendon, and Valadez (1998) found that parental expectations had the largest effect on Asian American students' educational aspirations. Other scholars have argued that parental expectations are instilled in their children through a cultural context, claiming that the high value that Asian cultures place on education results in higher parental expectations of students. Thus, these expectations are "extremely powerful" in shaping their children's achievement and aspirations (Schneider & Lee, 1990, p. 374). Similarly, Museus's (2013) examination of parental influence on Southeast Asian American students' educational trajectories using a cultural mechanisms perspective found that students had a deep respect for parental sacrifice and a strong understanding that their parents viewed education as a means of socioeconomic success.

PURPOSE OF THE STUDY

The purpose of this article was to examine how family is perceived to influence the educational and occupational aspirations of second-generation Lao American college students. The questions guiding this research were: (1) What role do Lao parents play in the development of their children's educational and occupational aspirations? (2) What role does Lao parents' migration history as refugees play in the development of their children's educational and occupational aspirations? and (3) What role do other family members play in the development of Lao American students' educational and occupational aspirations? Drawing from prior research, I expected that Lao parents would play an important role in the development of their children's aspirations, but on the other hand, little is understood about the influence of extended family members. Therefore, the nuances of how these relationships were influential were explored using qualitative methods.

METHODOLOGY

The data in this article is drawn from a larger study of educational aspirations in Lao American families. This exploratory study used in-depth interviewing and grounded theory methods to guide data collection and data analysis.

Participants

Purposeful sampling techniques were used to recruit second-generation Lao American college students (Patton, 2002). I recruited my participants from across the California

TABLE 7.1. STUDENT PARTICIPANTS

NAME	AGE	YEAR IN SCHOOL	TYPE OF INSTITUTION
Southern California			
Arthur	19	2	4-year state college
Kat	20	2	4-year state college
Nathan	20	2	community college
Sara	21	2	community college
Peter	23	5	4-year state college
Central Valley			
Matthew	19	1	4-year university
Donna	19	2	community college
Maddy	19	3	4-year state college
Jack	20	2 (part-time)	community college
Derrick	22	recently graduated	4-year state college

Note: All names are pseudonyms.

Central Valley and Southern California due to the relatively substantial Lao communities near Garden Grove and Fresno, California. Using word of mouth, social networking sites, and emails, a request for participants was sent to Lao community members with whom I was connected. Students who answered the original call for participants then recommended the study to their peers. The final sample included 10 student/parent pairs; five pairs of families were from Southern California and five pairs were from the Central Valley. This study focuses on interview data collected with the students.

Student participants ranged in gender, age, and grade level in each location. Demographic information is presented in Table 7.1. Overall, the study contained four females and six males. Only one participant lived away from his home and community; all other students lived with their parents.

Data Collection

Students were asked to complete a demographic questionnaire and participate in individual, face- to-face interviews. The demographic questionnaire solicited information regarding students' age, living situation, and school information, and started an initial inquiry into students' major and career aspirations. Once students signed consent forms to participate in the study, questionnaires were filled out prior to the start of the interview. In-depth interviewing methods were used in conjunction with grounded theory methods in this exploratory study (Charmaz, 2001; Johnson, 2001). In-depth interviews are appropriate for researchers seeking depth in information and knowledge, which often involves topics that are very personal to informants. Examples of questions included: "What is the highest level of schooling you hope to achieve? And how did you make this decision?" and "What do you know about your parents' immigration story?" These semistructured student interviews generally lasted one hour in length and were digitally recorded with permission from students.

Data Analysis

Interviews were transcribed verbatim and analyzed using grounded theory methods. According to Charmaz (2001), researchers "already possess a set of 'sensitizing concepts' that inform empirical inquiry and spark the development of more refined and precise concepts" during the process of coding (p. 683). A primary sensitizing concept in this study was "aspirations." Guided by grounded theory methods of coding, open coding was first used to analyze the data. During the second round of reading, notes were made on the transcript to demarcate emerging themes arising from the data. After the second round of coding, data analysis was then guided by the conceptual framework. The emergent themes from the second round of coding were organized according to the components of the conceptual framework: family background, family resources, students' educational experiences, and parents. Parents' immigration history was a new component added by this study. The findings that are reported in this paper are the main themes that emerged from the data.

Researcher Role and Identity

My own identity as a second-generation Lao American better allowed for the establishment of rapport and trust with my participants. Rapport is an important component of an in-depth interview and often requires more personal self-disclosure on the part of the researcher (Johnson, 2001). However, this also meant extensive reflexivity was required during the process of data collection and data analyses. I am what anthropologists would consider a "halfie researcher" (Subedi, 2006). Halfie researchers' "in-between status requires that they be more accountable to how they have researched and written about the people with whom [they] affiliate" (Subedi, 2006, p. 574). As a Lao American who is familiar with the communities from which I recruited participants, I was determined, as a co-ethnic and as an educator, to conduct research that honors and advances the Lao community in an ethical manner. While I acknowledge that my identity as a Lao American helped me relate to my participants, I used rigorous reflexivity to examine my role as an educational researcher and as a Lao American in the design, data collection, data analyses, and write-up of this study in order to ensure ethical research practices.

FINDINGS

Consistent with previous studies on aspiration development, the data suggests that Lao parents were profoundly influential on students' educational and occupational aspirations. While some parents were perceived to directly influence their child's educational choices, others appeared more indirectly influential. Two subthemes emerged under parental influence: respect for parents' immigration histories and the guilt of financial dependence. The data also suggested that extended family members had significant influence on the aspirations of second-generation Lao American college students and often were as impactful as parents' opinions. Although the interview protocol did not ask about the specific roles of extended family members, it emerged across the interviews that narrow definitions of family do not apply to Lao American students. Rather, all members of one's family (e.g., parents, siblings, aunts, uncles, cousins, and grandparents) was how students conceived of the term "family."

The Role of Parents: Respecting Parents' Immigration Histories and the Guilt of Financial Dependence

Parents played an important role in the aspiration development of all 10 student participants in this study. Some parents were perceived to have directly influenced their child's choice of major, while other parents were perceived to have a more indirect role in their child's decision. The direct influence manifested in two ways: Parents pressured their child to choose the academic major that they desired, or the child internalized the pressure they perceived coming from their parents. Students who had chosen a major of their parents' desire had previously preferred career paths that were considered economically unstable for their future. Across these interviews, two main reasons were found to explain why parental influence appeared so strong: respect for parents' immigration histories and the guilt of financial dependence.

Four out of 10 students chose the major of their parents' desire. For example, Jack took the advice of his high school Regional Occupation Program (ROP) teacher and spent his first two years of community college planning to major in linguistics so he could join the FBI. However, two weeks prior to our interview, Jack changed his major to electrical engineering after intense pressure from his father and extended family members. When asked how he came to decide on electrical engineering as a major, he replied, "Well, I didn't really decide on it. [sigh] My family kind of forced me to change my major." Jack's father and extended family disregarded his aspirations to major in linguistics because they did not understand how it would translate into a stable career. This produced an enormous amount of guilt that Jack could not overcome. As his father's only son and as the eldest male cousin in the family, he felt forced to be a dutiful son and good role model for his younger cousins. Despite the time and effort he had invested into becoming a linguistics major, Jack abandoned his own aspirations for those of his family's. As seen in Jack's situation, Lao parents will tend to push their children as a result of their high educational expectations (Schapiro, 1988).

Peter's childhood dream was to be an architect; however, he never attempted to pursue this lifelong dream due to the pressure imposed by his parents to choose accounting as a major. Similar to Jack, Peter shared that the selection of his academic major was based almost solely on what his parents wanted him to do. He explained why he believed his parents pressured him into accounting:

> I think it has to do with like other people talk to them saying, like, what I should do, and, I think they also agree with them saying like, I can find accounting, like, in many places other than doing other careers, I don't know. Because I've heard them talking to like other parents, their kids who have like, sociology degrees or like, yeah. They really want me to do accounting just because I can find a job after I graduate.

Like many immigrant parents, Peter's wanted him to pursue a major that would lead to financial stability in the future, even though he stated that he had "no passion for it." Already in his fifth year at a four-year state college, Peter was struggling in the major. When asked whether he had ever considered changing his major, he responded, "If I can? Yeah . . . I would love to . . . I still want to do architecture." However, after five years, Peter just wanted to graduate. Previous research has found that many immigrant parents tend to push their children into the sciences or technological fields because these majors were known to provide "safe" professions (e.g., Kao, 2010; Kao & Tienda, 1998; Ngo, 2006; Sue & Okazaki, 1990; Um, 2003). In Peter's case, the field of business, specifically accounting, is understood as a "safe" profession within the Lao American community.

Direct pressure from parents was not the only determinant of children choosing to fulfill their parents' aspirations. Some students chose "safe" majors based on perceived parental expectations. For example, Sara selected nursing as a major because she perceived this to be her parents' desire. While she preferred to study sociology and pursue a career in social work, she felt indirect pressure from her family to choose a path that would lead to a more economically stable future. Sara's parents did not know what a sociology major is, but she was certain they would be disapproving of a major that did not immediately translate into a promising career. When asked if sociology was the major she would have wanted to pursue, she enthusiastically replied:

> Oh yeah! Definitely. A lot more than nursing at one point. . . . But I think being around an environment with my family, they kind of influenced me to do what would be more considered stable in my life and would have a better life that way.

Her final decision was to enter the medical field in hopes of guaranteeing a comfortable economic future while also appeasing her parents.

Parental pressures also led students to choose a major that was a compromise between what they desired for themselves and what their parents desired. For example, when Arthur was in high school, he began considering possible majors and became interested in sociology and psychology. Arthur described how his mother responded to his interests,

> Well, she took it in at first, and then the next day she was telling me how it's low paying and you would have to work like six years to actually get a good paying job, like get a good income.

Arthur's mother demonstrated her disapproval of his intended majors by providing him with a list of degrees and their corresponding salaries after graduation. She wanted him to be the first doctor of the family, whether it be a medical doctor or earning a PhD. In the end, Arthur chose accounting and explained his decision by saying, "I would be guaranteed like a good job, an income, and pleasing my parents." Since he knew he had no desire to pursue medicine as a career, Arthur compromised his original desires for a career path that would be satisfactory for himself and his parents.

The experiences of Jack, Peter, Sara, and Arthur mirror the experiences of Southeast Asian students in other research on parental influences on college students' educational trajectories (Museus, 2013). However, as can be seen in Peter's and Arthur's cases, Lao American parents also view accounting as a field that promises a stable economic future. In both instances, Peter and Arthur explained that they had family members who are successful accountants.

Of the 10 students interviewed, six pursued their own educational and occupational aspirations. Three students reported that their parents expressed a preference for them to pursue certain majors, yet there was no pressure to pursue these majors. Earning a doctorate and entering the medical field is what all of these parents hoped their children would aspire to, but they also understood the realities of not being able to force their children into career paths that they did not desire for themselves. There was a mutual understanding in these parent-child relationships that although parents hoped their children would become doctors, they would be satisfied with any major or career so long as their children were successful and happy. For example, Nathan shared what he perceived to be his parents' aspirations for him:

> I think the main thing would be just going to a four-year [college] and getting my degree from there. They told me to just find something that I would love to do, you know? Because my mom always says, "You don't want to wake up and hate your job."

Nathan's parents were very supportive of his decision to explore the fields of medicine and information technology. Despite not having any direct pressure placed upon them, all six students took their parents into consideration when making educational decisions due to some of the factors discussed below.

RESPECTING PARENTS' IMMIGRATION HISTORIES

The overwhelming majority of students expressed a sense of obligation to consider choosing the major of their parents' choice, even for students who pursued their own aspirations. Parents' history as refugees and their experiences as immigrants commanded a high level of respect from students, but this did not appear as a direct influence on students' major or career aspirations. Kat's statement reflected how the majority of the students felt regarding the impact their parents' histories have had on them:

> I mean, coming from a poor country to come here and to have a better life, it just pushes me to want to give them, to help them out with a better life and to help myself with a better life. That's always, that's always an influence. It's always in the back of my head. I feel like "You need to do this because you need to give yourself a better life," . . . because not even stories, just little tidbits, ya know?

All participants acknowledged the struggles their parents endured in order to provide for their family, and some felt more influenced by this experience than others. Interestingly, only one out of 10 students knew the entirety of his parents' immigration story, but this was only due to the fact that he had recently asked as a young adult. Another student, Sara, also claimed to know the majority of her parents' immigration journey, but intriguingly, her mother's interview contradicted this. She assumed that Sara was uninterested in learning about her immigration story. The majority of students knew the "basics" of their parents' story—that they escaped from Laos, lived in refugee camps, and then came to the United States very poor. Regardless of not knowing the details, all of the students expressed the utmost respect for their parents' struggles.

Stemming from the limited knowledge of their parents' immigrant experiences and students' current financial dependence on their parents, there was a clear desire for future economic stability from all students. Having internalized their parents' experiences, students desired a future that was more comfortable than their parents' arduous efforts to settle in America. As a result of their gratitude, many of these students desired to care for their parents after they established themselves in their careers.

Parents' refugee experiences and struggles motivated their children to succeed not just for themselves, but also for their parents. These findings are similar to the experiences of first-generation Latino students in Ceja's (2004) study, whose aspirations were also influenced by the internalization of their parents' lived experiences. Not only have these experiences help shape Lao American and Latino students' aspirations, they are a source of motivation for academic success.

THE GUILT OF FINANCIAL DEPENDENCE

Financial dependence was an emergent theme from the data during open coding. Although the issue of student finances and tuition was not an explicit topic in the interview guide, many students shared how they were paying for college. Seven of the 10 students had parents who were contributing to their education. Many of the students relied on both financial aid and parental assistance, but three students shared that their education was completely funded by their parents. These were also students whose parents were perceived to directly influence their choice of majors: Sara, Peter, and Jack. They openly discussed the effect that their financial dependence had on their educational decisions. While students in Zhou's study (2005) felt pressured to pursue safe professions due to family pride, these Lao American college students succumbed to the guilt of financial dependence. They felt obligated to be obedient due to their financial dependence. Sara shared:

> I definitely think that if I was not living with my family. You know if, could be, if I had my expenses, you know, be fine, and I was fairly independent with that. I definitely don't think I'd be going into nursing.... But um, I just think that the major influence was the family and the living arrangements.

For Sara, the obligation and influence she felt from her family extended beyond their support of her educational expenses, but it was also due to the fact that she was living at home and financially supported by her parents. In fact, all of the students except Matthew were living at home. Peter's educational decisions were also highly impacted by this financial guilt and he felt obligated to choose the path his parents desired. He expressed:

> Just because I would feel bad. Like I know they're paying for school so I just want to make them happy.... School's just way too expensive now, and I just want to get done so they can stop paying for it.

In Peter's situation, the financial burden he was placing on his parents was the main reason he had chosen accounting as a major. However, none of the students reported that their parents had used finances as leverage for choosing their desired majors. The guilt of financial dependence had developed within themselves. Combined with feelings of being trapped in a particular situation and the real/perceived parental pressures, Sara, Peter, and Jack felt forced to abandon their own aspirations.

The Role of (Extended) Family

Many cultures consider family as the strongest social unit. In Lao culture, this is certainly the case, but the term "family" extends far beyond the nuclear family (Schapiro, 1988). Siblings, cousins, aunts, uncles, and grandparents were all involved in the development of students' aspirations. Similar to parents, extended family members had very high expectations for students. The role of family members was seen in three main ways: encouraging students to attend a specific school, assisting in the process of getting into college and offering advice based on experience, and offering to assist students entering into a profession in which they themselves were employed. At times, the role of the extended family and the role of parents appeared indistinguishable.

Family members who attended college were valuable in offering students advice and assisting in the application process. All of the students had a family member, nuclear or extended, who had attended college before them, and half of the students had a sibling who was also in college. Maddy shared:

> I have two aunts who are very studious and they've got their bachelor's and one of my aunts got her master's. They've always really enjoyed school and told me about their experiences and to really take advantage of going to school and getting a degree.

Often, older relatives encouraged practicality in their discussions regarding students' aspirations for their desired major or career. For example, Donna discussed two of her aunts' involvement:

> I feel like they kind of like were supportive in our decisions and kind of, but then again, supportive but realistic.... My aunt, she's always been the one to say, "Can you afford this?", or like, "Can you see yourself majoring or like getting a career from anthropology?"

Although older relatives wanted students to pursue their own aspirations, they also understood the realities that students would face once they finished their degrees. Therefore, they did not discourage students from pursuing their own aspirations, but they also encouraged students to consider the career prospects of majors they intended to pursue.

Siblings and cousins were also helpful in the college application process and offered advice on which courses to enroll in. The guidance of older siblings or cousins was crucial for many of these students. Although they were going through the application process with their friends, family members often offered insider advice on things like what courses to enroll in. Peter shared how his cousin was instrumental in helping through the process of getting into college: "[My cousin] helped me a lot. Just because she was already in college and she told me what I would do, so yes, it was very, very nice having her." Unlike the experiences of older relatives, siblings and cousins were close enough in age that their experiences were similar and their advice was fresh. These younger relatives tend to be more positive about pursuing academic goals for reasons related to interests and passions rather than solely practical concerns. For example, when Peter raised the idea of becoming a culinary chef, his older cousin offered to help him secure an internship with the chef at her workplace. Younger relatives were more empathetic about students' happiness and ability to pursue their own interests. This may be due to their generational similarities, while older relatives, such as Donna's aunts, are 1.5- or first-generation immigrants who are more likely to gravitate toward safe professions. Younger relatives were likely experiencing, or had recently experienced, the same emotions as the students in this study.

Family members also encouraged students to pursue majors that would lead to the careers that they currently had. It was mentioned earlier that Jack wanted to major in linguistics, but his family wanted him to choose engineering. Aside from facing pressure from family members, Jack's sister and uncle were already engineers, and his uncle felt confident he could secure him a job after graduation. Describing the family pressure, Jack said, "My cousin—she has a son, and she said, 'You gotta set the role model for him.' Because I'm the oldest of all the boys." For Jack, the pressure from the family to choose a career path that younger family members can look up to was strong, but it was also compounded by the possibility of guaranteed employment with his uncle's help. Although the job guarantee was not the deciding factor in why Jack chose engineering, there was also a sense of relief that his future was secure. This also illustrates that although students want to pursue their own passions, they can also be doubtful of their future job security and its prestige. If Jack were certain that he would pursue a career with the FBI after earning his linguistics degree, would he have tried harder to explain this educational path to his family? Instead, he chose a major that he was pressured into by his family. Engineering has positive implications for Jack's future in two ways: it is considered a safe career and he is already guaranteed a position right out of college.

Some students had as much of a desire to fulfill the wishes of their extended family members as they would for their own parents. Donna described her family's influence on her aspirations, "The *whole* family raised us, and so I don't think I would've been here [in college] if it weren't for them." She acknowledges the family's role in helping her successfully enter college as well as being part of her motivation to succeed in college. Matthew's grandparents and aunt played important roles when he was deciding on universities. He shared:

> Once junior year came around I was like I don't want to go to UCLA, but Irvine, that sounds like a pretty cool place and it's close to like my cousins and stuff. And then I guess after [my grandparents] passed away, it's like aw man, I should probably go there because I told them I want to. It's kind of like a promise, so I kind of want to keep that promise. And also [my aunt], like she's always telling me, "You do really good in school so you should go to UCI."

Also, since Matthew planned to leave his home community due to a lack of job prospects, he was determined to find other universities near extended family members. While previous research has found that Southeast Asian American students' college choice are highly influenced by proximity of the campus to their home, this study illuminates that for Lao American students, the close proximity of the college to extended family members seemed just as important in their college decisions (Teranishi et al., 2004).

DISCUSSION

This study revealed the importance of not only parents, but also other significant relationships on students' educational and occupational aspirations (e.g., Berzin, 2010; Goyette & Xie, 1999; Kao & Tienda, 1998; Kim et al., 1998; Park, 2001; Poon & Byrd, 2013; Yamamoto & Holloway, 2010). As one of the first qualitative studies to explore the influences on students' aspirations, the results provided detailed description as to how each of these relationships were influential. Thus, it is important to understand that for Lao American students, it is likely that the concept of family influence extends beyond parents and perhaps even siblings; the influence of extended family members can sometimes be indistinguishable from the influence of parents for Lao American students. Kouanchao's (2013) study of Lao American college students' identity development found that participants "could not conceptualize an identity in which family and culture were disentangled or divorced from their experience or sense of being" (p. 138). Similarly, this paper showed that students' educational and occupational aspirations are intimately connected to the perceived desires of their family, which includes members of students' extended family. Therefore, high schools that offer college informational sessions should explicitly extend the invitation to any member of a student's family and not just parents. Parents who have limited knowledge of the English language or of the school systems may rely on other children and extended family members to translate and explain the information being disseminated about colleges and careers.

Second, the findings also provide insight into how Lao American parents' histories as refugees had a profound and indirect influence on their children's aspirations. All of the students considered their parents' histories and struggles to be influential on their educational and occupational aspirations. These students were motivated to succeed academically, not only for themselves, but also for their parents. Southeast Asian American students in previous research expressed similar sentiments; parents' hardships as new immigrants served as motivators for students' academic endeavors. Familial histories of struggles served as an important motivational tool, despite students not knowing the entirety of their parents' immigration experiences. Future studies examining the development of educational and occupational aspirations of the children of immigrants should consider the different modes of migration. Most existing theoretical models on aspiration development use quantitative measures to consider race/ethnicity, socioeconomic status, parent education, and parent immigrant status (Kao & Tienda, 1998). These studies have not delineated between more traditional immigrants and refugee migrations and adjustment. Hence, this qualitative examination provides a valuable look into how refugee experiences shape young adults' motivation and aspirations in higher education.

Third, the impact of financial dependence revealed negative consequences on students' happiness with their educational decisions. The guilt that students feel for relying on their parents can lead them to abandon their own educational aspirations for a potentially unfulfilling path. There is likely a relationship between parents' immigration histories and students' guilt of financial dependence due to the fact that the guilt had developed within the students themselves and not due to parental pressure. All of the Lao American students in this study expressed how they very much respected and honored their parents for their experienced hardships as refugees to the United States. Therefore, this respect may be compounded onto the guilt of financial dependence, leading students to succumb to the pressure of satisfying their parents. A focus for future study would be to understand the psychological effects of the financial hold parents have over their children. Although none of the students reported that their parents were using financial reliance as direct pressure to adopt their aspirations, it was also not addressed in the present study. Exploring the financial situations of students and parents may provide beneficial findings. Do students who rely on financial aid perceive/face less pressure from parents than those who pay for their child's education?

Lastly, students who were pursuing a major or career that was chosen by their parents were unhappy with their educational experience. In addition, all of these students' educational aspirations ended with a bachelor's degree, while students who were pursuing their own desired majors or careers were considering at least a master's degree.

It is important to understand the effects and consequences of students choosing their own educational pathways as opposed to students electing to follow what their parents wanted. Research concerning the role of family obligation on the education of immigrant youth found that students who felt the highest sense of family obligation earned low or lower grades than students who felt the least sense of family obligation (Fuligni et al., 1999). However, students who felt a moderate sense of family obligation tended to achieve higher academic success. Also, since educational aspirations have been found to correlate with academic achievement, what are the effects when students are not able to pursue their own aspirations?

As we can see from these findings, it was necessary to consider multiple theoretical perspectives on aspiration development in order to observe the breadth of influences on Lao American college students' aspirations (Kao & Tienda, 1998). Many of the findings in this study resonate with previous research examining parental influence on Southeast Asian American college students' educational experiences (e.g., Museus, 2013; Poon & Byrd, 2013). However, these findings shed light on the very strong influence of extended family for Lao American college students. This qualitative study has captured students' unique educational experiences and allows us to not only see how family influences Lao American students' aspirations, but also allowed us to delve deeply into seeing how these influences varied, or sometimes unvaried, by the type of relationship to the student. As well, the study calls for an extension of these conceptual frameworks to consider parents' immigration histories when examining the aspiration development of Lao American or Southeast Asian American students. It is important to mention that the findings in this study also parallel aspiration development among first-generation Latino students (Ceja, 2004). Ceja found that the perceptions of the lived experiences of their parents not only played a role in Latina students' aspiration development but also in the development of their educational resiliency. With the abundance of literature examining the crucial role that parents play in the aspiration development of Latino students (e.g., Ceja, 2004; Ceja, 2006; Delgado-Gaitan, 1990; Gandara, 1995), it would be beneficial to examine these parallels to understand how Latino students' aspirations have been successfully supported.

This research also argues that Lao American students would benefit from a relationship created between family and educators/schools. Kouanchao (2013) called for colleges to provide resources and reach out to Lao American families and communities. Educators and counselors should understand the history and background of Lao Americans in order to help them work with Lao parents to understand the different pathways their children may take for successful careers. Due to their limited understanding of the U.S. education system, Lao parents in this study conflated academic majors and careers. Therefore, some parents pressured their children out of majors such as sociology and linguistics, because they feared their children pursuing educational paths that would not lead directly to a stable profession. These stable careers have traditionally been viewed as those in the medical or technical fields, but we have begun to see that Lao parents now consider accounting as a worthy educational pursuit. These connections between family and educators/schools need to be developed throughout the PreK–16 pipeline, ensuring the success of Lao American students from the beginning of their education.

As with all research, there are limitations to this study. Although the study has provided depth into understanding the influences on the aspirations of Lao American college students, I cannot conclude that understanding these influences will affect the eventual educational attainment of these students. Also, due to the snowball sampling strategy used to recruit participants, students' demographics were quite varied. Class level, type of college institution, and whether or not students were living at home could have also affected aspirations in ways that cannot be distinguished in this study. Despite these limitations, this study sheds light on the educational experiences of an underserved and underexamined group in higher education. Certainly, my Lao American college student participants are successful in that they have made it to higher education, but we need to ensure that they maintain high aspirations and graduate. This is imperative considering nearly half of Cambodians, Laotians, and Hmong Americans aged 25 or older who have attended college left without earning an associate's or bachelor's degree (CARE, 2011). The findings in this article contrast with those of previous studies (e.g., Baizerman & Hendricks, 1988; Park, 2001) that depict low educational aspirations for Lao American youth. Lao Americans students in this study described high aspirations and that they can potentially be more academically successful if they follow their own educational and occupational aspirations. This initial understanding of the influences on Lao American college students' aspirations allows us to target key areas that require support from educators and counselors to complete their college degrees and enter careers with more potential for fulfillment.

PUBLICATION NOTE

This article was published online in 2015 by the *Journal of Southeast Asian American Education and Advancement* in Volume 10, Issue 2. Minor edits have been made here. The original can be found at http://doi.org/10.7771/2153-8999.1133.

REFERENCES

Baizerman, M., & Hendricks, G. (1988). *A study of Southeast Asian refugee youth in the twin cities of Minneapolis and St. Paul, Minnesota.* U.S. Office of Refugee Resettlement.

Bankston III, C. L., & Hidalgo, D. A. (2007). Southeast Asia. In M. C. Waters, R. Ueda, & H. B. Marrow (Eds.), *The new Americans: A guide to immigration since 1965*. Harvard University Press.

Baum, S., & Payea, K. (2005). *Education pays, 2004: The benefits of higher education for individuals and society*. College Board.

Berzin, S. C. (2010). Educational aspirations among low-income youths: Examining multiple conceptual models. *Children & Schools, 32*(2), 112–124. https://doi.org/10.1093/cs/32.2.112

Caplan, N., Choy, M. H., & Whitmore, J. K. (1991). *Children of the boat people: A study of educational success*. University of Michigan Press.

Ceja, M. (2004). Chicana college aspirations and the role of parents: Developing educational resiliency. *Journal of Hispanic Higher Education, 3*(4), 338–362. https://doi.org/10.1177/1538192704268428

Ceja, M. (2006). Understanding the role of parents and siblings as information sources in the college choice process of Chicana students. *Journal of College Student Development, 47*(1), 87–104. https://doi.org/10.1353/csd.2006.0003

Charmaz, K. (2001). Qualitative interviewing and grounded theory analysis. In J. F. Gubrium & J. A. Holstein (Eds.), *Handbook of interview research* (pp. 675–694). Sage.

Chhuon, V. (2013). "I'm Khmer and I'm not a gangster!": The problematization of Cambodian male youth in US schools. *International Journal of Qualitative Studies in Education, 27*(2), 233–250. https://doi.org/10.1080/09518398.2012.758788

Chhuon, V., & Hudley, C. (2008). Factors supporting Cambodian American students' successful adjustment into the university. *Journal of College Student Development, 49*(1), 15–30. https://doi.org/10.1353/csd.2008.0005

Davies, M., & Kandel, D. B. (1981). Parental and peer influences on adolescents' educational plans: Some further evidence. *American Journal of Sociology, 87*(2), 363–387. https://doi.org/10.1086/227462

Delgado-Gaitan, D. (1990). *Literacy for empowerment: The role of parents in children's education*. Falmer.

Feliciano, C. (2006). Beyond the family: The influence of premigration group status on the educational expectations of immigrants' children. *Sociology of Education, 79*, 281–303. https://doi.org/10.1177/003804070607900401

Fordham, S., & Ogbu, J. U. (1986). Black students' school success: Coping with the burden of "acting white." *The Urban Review, 18*(3), 176–206. https://doi.org/10.1007/BF01112192

Fuligni, A. J., Tseng, V., & Lam, M. (1999). Attitudes towards family obligations among American adolescents with Asian, Latin American, and European backgrounds. *Child Development, 70*(4), 1030–1044. https://doi.org/10.1111/1467-8624.00075

Gandara, P. (1995). *Over the ivy walls: The educational mobility of low-income Chicanos.* State University of New York Press.

Gibson, M. A. & Ogbu, J. U. (Eds.). (1991). *Minority status and schooling: A comparative study of immigrant and involuntary minorities.* Garland.

Goyette, K., & Xie, Y. (1999). Educational expectations of Asian American youths: Determinants and ethnic differences. *Sociology of Education, 72*(1), 22–36. https://doi.org/10.2307/2673184

Hong, S., & Ho, H-Z. (2005). Direct and indirect longitudinal effects of parental involvement on student achievement: Second-order latent growth modeling across ethnic groups. *Journal of Educational Psychology, 97*(1), 32–42. https://doi.org/10.1037/0022-0663.97.1.32

Johnson, J. M. (2001). In-depth interviewing. In J. F. Gubrium & J. A. Holstein (Eds.), *Handbook of interview research* (pp. 103–120). Sage.

Kao, G. (2010). Asian Americans as model minorities? A look at their academic performance. *American Journal of Education, 103*(2), 121–159. https://doi.org/10.1086/444094

Kao, G., & Tienda, M. (1998). Educational aspirations of minority youth. *American Journal of Education, 106*(3), 349–384. https://doi.org/10.1086/444188

Kim, H., Rendon, L., & Valadez, J. (1998). Student characteristics, school characteristics, and educational aspirations of six Asian American ethnic groups. *Journal of Multicultural Counseling and Development, 26*(3), 166–176. https://doi.org/10.1002/j.2161-1912.1998.tb00196.x

Kouanchao, K. (2013). *Lao American college students' holistic identity development* [Doctoral dissertation]. Retrieved from ProQuest LLC. (UMI No. 3570185).

Mau, W., & Bikos, L. H. (2000). Educational and vocational aspirations of minority and female students: A longitudinal study. *Journal of Counseling and Development, 78*, 186–194. https://doi.org/10.1002/j.1556-6676.2000.tb02577.x

Museus, S. D. (2013). Unpacking the complex and multifaceted nature of parental influences on Southeast Asian American college students' educational trajectories. *The Journal of Higher Education, 84*(5), 708–738. https://doi.org/10.1080/00221546.2013.11777306

Museus, S. D. (2014). *Asian American students in higher education.* Routledge.

National Commission on Asian American and Pacific Islander Research in Education (CARE). (2011). *The relevance of Asian Americans and Pacific Islanders in the college completion agenda.* CARE.

Ngo, B. (2006). Learning from the margins: The education of Southeast and South Asian Americans in context. *Race, Ethnicity, and Education, 9*(1), 51–65. https://doi.org/10.1080/13613320500490721

Ngo, B. (2009). Ambivalent, urban, immigrant identities: The incompleteness of Lao American student identities. *International Journal of Qualitative Studies in Education, 22*(2), 201–220. https://doi.org/10.1080/09518390701770936

Ngo, B. (2010). *Unresolved identities: Discourse, ambivalence and urban immigrant students.* SUNY Press.

Ngo, B., & Lee, S. J. (2007). Complicating the image of model minority success: A review of Southeast Asian American education. *Review of Educational Research, 77*(4), 415–453. https://doi.org/10.3102/0034654307309918

Ogbu, J. U. (1991). Minority coping responses and school experience. *Journal of Psychohistory, 18,* 433–456.

Park, C. C. (2001). Educational aspirations of Southeast Asian students. In C. Park, A. Goodwin, & S. Lee (Eds.), *Research on the education of Asian Pacific Americans* (pp. 3–20). Information Age.

Patton, M. Q. (2002). *Qualitative research and evaluation methods.* Sage.

Poon, O., & Byrd, A. (2013). Beyond tiger mom anxiety: Ethnic, gender, and generational differences in Asian American college access and choices. *Journal of College Admission,* 23–31.

Portes, A., & Rumbaut, R. G. (2006). *Immigrant America: A portrait.* University of California Press.

Schapiro, A. (1988). Adjustment and identity formation of Lao refugee adolescents. *Smith College Studies in Social Work, 58*(3), 157–180. https://doi.org/10.1080/00377318809516642

Schneider, B., & Lee, Y. (1990). A model for academic success: The school and home environment of East Asian students. *Anthropology and Education Quarterly, 21,* 358–377. https://doi.org/10.1525/aeq.1990.21.4.04x0596x

Sewell, W. H., Haller, A. O., & Ohlendorf, G. W. (1970). The educational and early occupational status-attainment process replication and revision. *American Sociological Review, 35,* 1014–1027. https://doi.org/10.2307/2093379

Sewell, W. H., Haller, A. O., & Portes, A. (1969). The educational and early occupational attainment process. *American Sociological Review, 34,* 82–92. https://doi.org/10.2307/2092789

Southeast Asia Resource Action Center (SERAC). (2011). *Southeast Asian Americans at a glance: Statistics on Southeast Asians adapted from the American Community Survey.* SEARAC.

Subedi, B. (2006). Theorizing a "halfie" researcher's identity in transnational fieldwork. *International Journal of Qualitative Studies in Education, 19*(5), 573–593. https://doi.org/10.1080/09518390600886353

Sue, S., & Okazaki, S. (1990). Asian-American educational achievements: A phenomenon in search of an explanation. *American Psychologist, 45*(8), 913–920. https://doi.org/10.1037/0003-066X.45.8.913

Swail, B. H. (2002). *The art of student retention: A handbook for practitioners and administrators.* Education Policy Institute.

Teranishi, R. T., Ceja, M., antonio, a. l., Allen, W. R., & McDonough, P. M. (2004). The college-choice process for Asian-Pacific Americans: Ethnicity and socioeconomic class in context. *The Review of Higher Education, 27*(4), 527–551. https://doi.org/10.1353/rhe.2004.0025

Um, K. (2003). *A dream denied: Educational experiences of Southeast Asian American youth, issues and recommendations.* An issue paper based on findings from the first National Southeast Asian Youth Summit, Washington, DC, Southeast Asian Resource Action Center.

Uy, P. S. (2011). *The educational experiences of Lao and Khmer high school students: The influence of families, friends, and teachers on academic achievement.* (Doctoral dissertation). Retrieved from ProQuest LLC (UMI No. 3459746).

Vue, R. (2013). Campus contexts and Hmong students' experiences negotiating identity and higher education. In S. D. Museus, D. C. Maramba, & R. T. Teranishi (Eds.), *The misrepresented minority: New insights on Asian Americans and Pacific Islanders, and the implications for higher education* (pp. 182–197). Stylus.

Yamamoto, Y., & Holloway, S. D. (2010). Parental expectations and children's academic performance in sociocultural context. *Educational Psychology Review, 22,* 189–214. https://doi.org/10.1007/s10648-010-9121-z

Zhou, M. (2005, November). *Divergent origins and destinies: Children of Asian immigrants.* Paper presented at the National Invitational Conference on Minority Children and Youth: Families, Schools, Communities, and Learning, Washington, DC.

8

Supporting Southeast Asian American Family and Community Engagement for Educational Success

PHITSAMAY S. UY

ABSTRACT

Over the past 40 years, the United States has accepted over 2.5 million refugees and immigrants from the Southeast Asian (SEA) countries of Cambodia, Laos, and Vietnam. Unfortunately after four decades of resettlement and assimilation, the SEA community has the lowest levels of educational attainment when compared to other Asian American and Pacific Islander communities: 34.3% of Laotian, 38.5% of Cambodian, and 39.6% of Hmong adults over the age of 25 do not have a high school diploma or equivalent. Moreover, 65.8% of Cambodian, 66.5% of Laotian, 63.2% of Hmong, and 51.1% of Vietnamese Americans have not attended college (SEARAC, 2011).

BACKGROUND

Research has long linked parental involvement and student engagement, indicating that a high level of parent involvement significantly increases student engagement (Epstein, 2011; Henderson et al., 2007). However, the reality of how schools engage with parents of different racial and ethnic groups is varied and often complicated. Southeast Asian parents often are misperceived as not caring enough to get involved with their children's schools. School administrators and district leaders often struggle with how to fully engage SEA parents in school activities. Many scholars and practitioners agree that collaboration and partnerships are necessary in order to tackle school engagement. The challenge for policy makers is how to integrate culturally relevant strategies with research-based knowledge about Southeast Asian communities into school programs and policies. This policy brief analyzes challenges and barriers that Southeast Asian children and families face with U.S. school systems. It provides concrete recommendations for school administrators and district leaders to address SEA student issues and ensures that SEA parents' voices are valued and included in decision-making.

WHAT WE KNOW

- Southeast Asian refugees and immigrants can be found in all 50 United States.
- Among the 4.4 million English language learners, Chinese and Vietnamese are number 2 and 3 behind Spanish as the primary language spoken at home.
- One in 3 Laotians, one in 4 Cambodians, and one in 4 Hmong adults over the age of 25 do not have a high school diploma or equivalent (U.S. Census Bureau, 2010)
- One in 6 Cambodians, Laotians, and Hmong have not attended college compared to one in 2 Vietnamese who have not attended college (American Community Survey 2006–2008).
- Many teachers and administrators lack specific knowledge of Southeast Asian cultures.
- Many SEA community members had interrupted schooling experiences in Southeast Asia due to the civil wars occurring in Cambodia, Laos, and Vietnam.
- Southeast Asian youth cite their parents as the #1 motivating factor for them to do well in school (Uy, 2011).

POLICY RECOMMENDATIONS

- Collaborate with community-based organizations that work with SEA community members to provide professional development to school staff and administrators on how to develop culturally responsive strategies in working with these families.
- Create a SEA advisory committee that can give school staff and administrators feedback on how to develop meaningful relationships with SEA parents and families.
- Increase the availability of translators and translated materials in Southeast Asian languages.
- Develop programs that help SEA parents and community members become more familiar with U.S. school systems and that encourage and train them to take on leadership roles within the school district.

Southeast Asian Demographics and Characteristics

Now totaling more than 2.5 million, Southeast Asian Americans can be found in all 50 U.S. states (see Table 8.1 for the ethnic breakdown of each SEA group). Due to the combined efforts of U.S. refugee policy and voluntary secondary migration (i.e., Southeast Asian families moved from their first resettlement city to another city that offered more job opportunities and social services), the seven states where the most Southeast Asians now reside are California, Texas, Minnesota, Washington, Massachusetts, Florida, and Pennsylvania (SEARAC, 2011).

Once resettled in the United States, the Southeast Asian community began to struggle with how to adapt to their new home. Without English language proficiency, Southeast Asian adults had difficulty finding jobs, asking for public assistance, and fully supporting their families. In fact, the Southeast Asian community has a dramatically high proportion of people who are linguistically isolated. According to the U.S. Census, a "linguistically isolated" household is one in which no member more than 14 years old (1) speaks English or (2) speaks a non-English language and speaks English "very well." Of the 9% of the U.S. population who are linguistically isolated, Cambodians, Hmong, and Laotians are three times (39%, 38%, and 38%, respectively) more likely to be linguistically isolated, and Vietnamese are five times (52%) more likely to be linguistically isolated (SEARAC, 2011). Moreover, 77% of Cambodian Americans, 89% of Hmong Americans, 78% of Laotian Americans, and 85% of Vietnamese Americans age five and over speak a language other than English in their homes, compared to 21% of the total U.S. population. Unfortunately, this means that many Southeast Asian students come from homes where their family members cannot provide educational support, such as helping with homework and teaching college and career readiness skills. Two main factors contribute to this linguistic isolation: prior educational experiences in Southeast Asia and the development of ethnic enclaves in the United States.

TABLE 8.1. SOUTHEAST ASIAN REFUGEE AND IMMIGRANT POPULATIONS IN THE UNITED STATES

COUNTRY OF ORIGIN	ESTIMATED POPULATIONS
Cambodian/Khmer	276,667
Hmong	260,073
Laotian	232,130
Vietnamese	1,737,433
Total U.S.	2,506,303

(SEARAC, 2011)

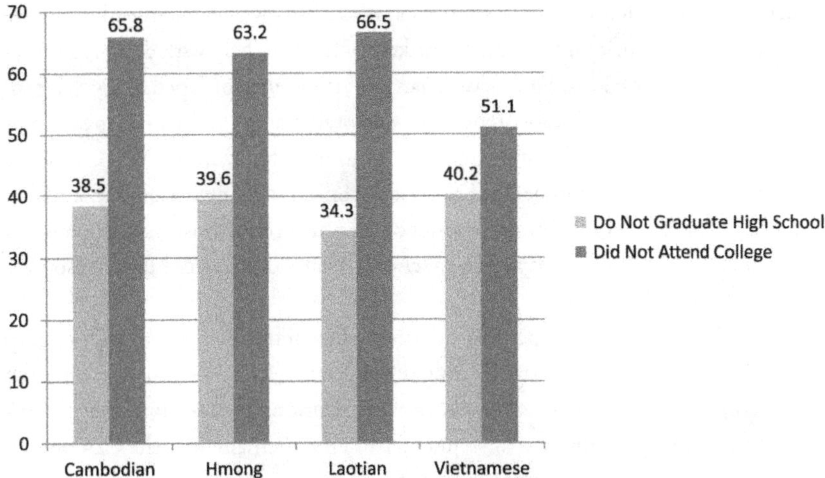

Figure 8.1. SEA Community Educational Level (SEARAC, 2011).

The demographic profile of SEA children is similar to that of other low-income immigrant and minority subgroups. Vietnamese children account for the third largest English language learner groups in U.S. schools. For SEA children under the age of 18 years old, it is estimated that 26% of Cambodians, 34% of Hmong, 21% of Laotians, and 16% of Vietnamese live in poverty. SEA children also have a large percentage of parents who are foreign-born people (i.e., more than 50%). In other words, at least one of every two SEA parents was born in Cambodia, Laos, or Vietnam.

Due to this background, as Figure 8.1 shows, SEA community members have low educational attainment (SEARAC, 2011).

Southeast Asians' Experience with Education

Many Southeast Asian refugees who entered the United States in the early 1980s had little to no formal education and limited literacy skills in their native language (Weinberg, 1997; Yang, 1981). Prior to the civil wars in Southeast Asia, the education system varied by country, geographic region, and gender (Collignon et al., 2001). For example, formal schooling for most villagers in Laos and Cambodia occurred in temples, where they learned to read and write using Buddhist doctrines (Chhim, 1981; Collignon et al., 2001; Luangpraseut, 1989). As a former colony of France, Vietnam had based its schooling on the French education system. However, comprehensive schooling was not available in most rural villages. Several villages often shared one teacher, and many students only attended school for six years at most. Boys were encouraged to pursue educational opportunities, while girls were kept at home to help with domestic duties (Luangpraseut, 1989). Most Southeast Asian educators relied on a pedagogy that centered around rote memorization, repetition, and oral fluency (Collignon, 1994; Thuy, 1976; Yang, 1981). During the civil wars, the educational opportunities were even more limited, as schools were bombed in Laos and a whole class of educators was killed in Cambodia (Te et al., 1997). Thus, as a result of the wars in Southeast Asia, generations of students lost the opportunity to go to school because of a lack of human resources and physical infrastructure.

When the United States opened its doors to these refugees in an attempt to keep promises made to their supporters during the civil wars (Robinson, 1998), Southeast Asian refugees who were fleeing the political persecution, "reeducation camps," famine, torture, and displacement that stemmed from the Vietnam War, the Cambodian "Killing Fields," and the secret bombings of Laos saw the United States as a safe haven. In their attempts to escape, many families were split up, and some family members died along the way. The "boat people" often fell victim to Thai pirates, who attacked and abused the men and raped the women. Some children died of malnutrition (Rumbaut, 2000).

Some scholars argue that many Southeast Asian adults have suffered significant political persecution and war-related trauma that compromise their ability to parent effectively (Garcia Coll et al., 2002; Han, 2006). Furthermore, some Cambodian children who lived under the Khmer Rouge were taught to see their parents as powerless and voiceless against higher authority (Te et al., 1997). These factors often have long-term implications for the familial dynamics and interactions in these people's current homes (Sack et al., 1988).

Many of these Southeast Asian refugees who suffered the lack of and/or interrupted schooling entered the United States without a strong literacy foundation in their primary language and also struggled with learning English. Without a strong first or second language, many Southeast Asians had to rely on others to help them with simple life tasks. Studies have shown that first-language development has a significant impact on the development of second-language skills (Short et al., 2008). Scholars have emphasized the importance of a strong first language in helping students learn English (August & Shanahan, 2006), and note that people who have a strong foundation in their first language become more proficient in English and at a quicker rate. Therefore, parents who lack a strong educational background and literacy skills are hard pressed to offer concrete help to their children. School administrators and district leaders need to consider this fact when creating programs to support their SEA students.

Current View of Parental Involvement

Despite over four decades of parental involvement research, no clear definition or measures of parental involvement exist (Kakli, 2010). Many scholars have documented a list of obstacles that hinder families and schools from working together on behalf of students and schools (Henderson et al., 2007; Hoover-Dempsey & Sander, 1997). They highlight educators' unwillingness or inability to work with parents (Olivos, 2006), linguistic differences (Zentella, 2005), and schools' lack of strategies to involve families in setting academic goals and expectations (Miretzky, 2004). U.S. school systems have operated under a traditional view of parental involvement, whereby parents play an accommodating role in promoting school goals (Schutz, 2006).

One scholar who has dominated the parental involvement literature is Joyce Epstein. Epstein's (2011) theory of overlapping spheres of influence identifies schools, families, and communities as major institutions that socialize and educate children. A central principle is that certain goals, such as academic success, are of interest to each of these institutions and are best achieved through cooperative action and support. She identifies six types of parental involvement, which include parenting, communicating, volunteering, learning at home, decision- making, and collaborating with community members (Epstein et al., 2002). Her first five categories focus solely on parents and collaborating with community members was added only recently, after some research (Schutz, 2006). This middle-class model of parental involvement defines activities that involve parents in supporting school interests.

U.S. schools value parental involvement as a means to promote a child's development, sense of competence, and understanding of the world (Coleman, 1988; Hao & Bonstead-Bruns, 1998). This means that schools encourage involvement by helping parents build home conditions that encourage learning, helping them understand communications from the schools, encouraging them to become productive volunteers at school and to share responsibility for their children's education in learning activities at home that are related to the curriculum, and by including parents' voices in decisions that affect the school and their children (Epstein, 2011). However, the locus of control remains with the school, which sets the priorities.

Epstein's framework lacks an analysis of the power dynamics that exist between parents and schools (Lareau & Shumar, 1996; Schutz, 2006). In some situations, particularly in low- income immigrant and minority communities, parents do not know their rights or responsibilities in terms of their children's education. In fact, Epstein's framework has no discussion of differing cultures or of accommodating the growing diversity of students and families. There is an underlying assumption in her work that there are neither cultural conflicts nor conflicting interests between schools and families. Many Southeast Asian parents living in economically depressed communities would find it difficult to fit into Epstein's parental involvement framework. For example, in some SEA families, the children may have more power due to their English language proficiency. SEA parents would often rely on their children to translate for them on household matters (i.e., utilities issues, doctor appointments, and employment questions), resulting in a sense of powerlessness. However, in Epstein's framework and in the minds of many school administrators and district leaders, it is the parents who should have the power and sense of agency to act on their children's behalf.

Despite having high expectations of parental involvement, many educators currently view immigrant and minority parents as lacking key parenting skills and knowledge that enable them to help their children (Schutz, 2006). Past research has found that teachers often have deficit views of these parents and others from economically depressed communities (Anyon, 1997; Cibulka, 1996; Lott, 2001; Miller, 1999; Villenas & Deyhle, 1999; Warren et al., 2009). While these deficit views are evident in current scholarship examining Black and Latino parents (Warren et al., 2009), it is important to note that Southeast Asian families are often found in similar urban communities and encounter similar challenges.

In a seminal comparative study of disparities in academic engagement between Southeast Asian American, African American/Black, Mexican American/Mexican, and White high school youth, fewer than half of Southeast Asian parents reported frequent discussions about school expectations with their children, compared to two-thirds of Mexican parents and three-fourths of Black and White parents (Oseguera et al., 2011). Among the four racial groups, Southeast Asians are the least likely to report having regular discussions about high school or their children's postsecondary plans; least likely to participate in family school interactions and school events; and have the lowest rate of PTA membership, nearly half that of Black and White parents. Forty percent of Southeast Asian parents perform at least one parental involvement activity, compared to 50% of Mexican and 60% of Black and White parents.

Oseguera, Conchas, and Mosqueda (2011) argue that relationships that result in opportunities for families to realize social capital—that is, the social networks and connections families can provide to support their children's educational and career aspirations—can also be created by family-school interactions. In all measures, Southeast Asian parents are somewhat less likely than Mexican parents and significantly less likely than their Black or White peers to participate in school events. Both Southeast Asians and Mexicans seem to be the least likely to be able to capitalize on potential social capital advantages. Their rate of PTA membership, attendance at PTA-sponsored activities, and volunteering at school is nearly half the rate of White and Black families. And yet, Southeast Asian parents tend to have higher educational expectations of their children than other parents in this study. By most measures, Southeast Asian students have access to fewer preconditions (i.e., circumstances in students' environment) for the realization of familial social capital than Mexican, Black, or White students, when these opportunities are measured as the frequency of interactions between parents and children, parents and school, and parents and other children's parents.

With their lack of familiarity and experience with U.S. school systems, it is no wonder that Southeast Asian parents feel less prepared to help their children academically (Adler, 2004; Ngo & Lee, 2007). Southeast Asian parents who view the teachers as their children's primary educators view their roles primarily as caretakers. In fact, like other immigrants, Southeast Asian parents consider providing moral support and motivation the parents' responsibility (Auerbach, 2007; Son, 2010; Uy, 2011). With this conception of parenting priorities, school administrators and district leaders need to look for alternative means to connect families with schools.

Alternative Conceptions of Family and Community Engagement

In recent years, community-based organizations have become engaged in educational reform generally and school, family, and community partnerships specifically, a practice founded on the community control efforts of the late 1960s. Family members in impoverished communities were frustrated with the lack of quality education their children were receiving from schools and with the lack of responsiveness and accountability of school bureaucracies (Warren, 2005). For example, some community-based groups, as "outside" organizations, have mobilized families and communities to confront educational bureaucracies and influence specific educational policies and practices (Gold et al., 2002; Hong, 2011; Jehl et al., 2001; Mediratta & Fruchter, 2001; Warren, 2001).

Using a collaborative approach to bridge the power gap between parents and schools, some community-based groups have facilitated a movement toward the partnership model. With the common goal of helping their children, these organizations have built families' capacity to work with individual schools through parent organizing, leadership development, and providing direct support and information to the families (Hong, 2011; Jasis & Ordonez-Jasis, 2004; Shirley, 1997; Warren, 2005). The key to the success of such partnerships is the willingness of schools to collaborate with families and community groups to achieve common goals. When such willingness exists, community groups have been successful in increasing family involvement and in creating more effective and responsive schools as part of a broader goal of community development (Schutz, 2006; Warren, 2005).

Collignon, Men, and Tan (2001) propose that engaging Southeast Asians through community-based organizations is possible and that it has a positive influence on their children's academic engagement. They argue that community-based organizations are "uniquely positioned to lead in brokering a relationship between the home and school" (p. 28). Their study demonstrated the capacity of Southeast Asian community-based organizations to break down barriers between home and school. The study was able to document their work on the Career Ladder Program for Southeast Asian adults interested in entering the teaching field and the Summer Academy, a summer school for Southeast Asian youth. Focus group data revealed that Southeast Asian parents value the educational opportunities provided in the United States but are confused by the parental expectations that are imposed by the schools, especially since they are not familiar with U.S. schools. They are also concerned with the lack of bicultural and bilingual school staff members who could understand the realities of their lives and help bridge cultural differences. They particularly wanted to know how to address truancy issues and how to voice their concerns to school staffs.

The community-based organization involved in the study had multiple partnerships with local, state, and higher education institutions. Through their collaborations, the community-based organization was able to make significant progress in engaging both the school officials and the Southeast Asian communities. The most notable benchmarks were creating the Southeast Asian Advisory Council, which meets regularly with the superintendent; having Southeast Asian representatives on working committees within the school districts; increasing the number of Southeast Asian credentialed teachers hired by the school district; enrolling at least 30 Southeast Asian teacher candidates in teacher education programs; building a "Family and Community Partnerships" component into the district plans; and securing continual funding of the Summer Academy.

There currently are many community-based organizations engaged in collaborations between school districts and Southeast Asian families (SEARAC, 2004). The Southeast Asian Resource Action Center (SEARAC), a national advocacy group based in Washington, D.C., works with strong grassroots community-based organizations at the local level to advocate for policy changes and support of Southeast Asian children and communities. Table 8.2 details SEA community-based organizations involved in the Southeast Asian American Action and Visibility in Education (SAVE) project. The SAVE program was created specifically to target education policy and reform. It combines capacity-building, organizing, advocacy, and action-oriented research to connect the real experiences of Southeast Asian students to the conversations of other AAPI organizations and civil rights organizations so that they can move policy at the local, state, and federal levels (Dinh, 2012).

TABLE 8.2. SEA COMMUNITY-BASED ORGANIZATIONS INVOLVED IN SAVE PROJECT

COMMUNITY-BASED ORGANIZATION	SEA POPULATION	FAMILY & COMMUNITY ENGAGEMENT ACTIVITIES
Cambodian Association of Greater Philadelphia	Cambodian	• Parent workshops through the Parent Enrichment Program • Implementing Common Core State Standards with Philadelphia School District • Disaggregating SEA Data
Hmong Women's Heritage Association	Hmong	• Capacity-building of Hmong parents and children around self-efficacy • Implementing Common Core State Standards with Sacramento School • District
Stone Soup/Fresno	Hmong	• Implementing Common Core State Standards with Fresno School District • Disaggregating SEA Data
Vietnamese American Youth Leaders Association of New Orleans	Vietnamese	• Implementing language access campaign with the Recovery School District in New Orleans, LA

CONCLUSIONS

With current policy moving toward evaluating educators on how effectively they engage families and communities, reaching out to community-based organizations may be a promising practice. Working with community-based organizations, teachers, school administrators, and district leaders can authentically engage the Southeast Asian community in a culturally relevant manner. Recommendations for policy and practice include:

1. Collaborate with community-based organizations that work with SEA community members to provide professional development to school staff and administrators on how to develop culturally responsive strategies in working with these families.

School administrators and staff should identify current community-based organizations within their school districts that partner with the Southeast Asian community. On its website, SEARAC offers a directory of mutual-assistance associations that service Southeast Asian communities nationally (http://www.searac.org/maa). This directory of Southeast Asian American community-based organizations is the most comprehensive guide to Southeast Asian American grassroots organizations yet produced. The directory includes contact and programmatic information for 180 community-based organizations managed primarily by and for Americans with roots in Cambodia, Laos, and Vietnam—communities that include more than two million resettled refugees, children of refugees, immigrants, and native-born Americans. The mutual-assistance associations listed in the directory provide culturally and linguistically appropriate services for communities nationwide and present unparalleled outreach opportunities for public agencies, funders, and others wishing to reach out to Americans from Cambodia, Laos, and Vietnam. Culturally responsive strategies should include intergenerational projects, such as community gardens and intergenerational dialogue, to promote connections across generations.

2. Create a SEA advisory committee that can give school staff and administrators feedback on how to develop meaningful relationships with SEA parents and families.

Having a Southeast Asian advisory committee will allow school staff and administrators to draw on the social capital of these community members. They can help produce ideas for outreach and provide cultural understanding of Southeast Asian parents and families.

3. Increase the availability of translators and translated materials in Southeast Asian languages.

Language access is an important tool in engaging SEA families and community members. National statistics demonstrates that Hmong and Vietnamese are the second and third largest English language learners in U.S. schools. Knowing that the majority of SEA families have limited English proficiency, school districts need to offer both written and oral translation of school materials in Hmong, Lao, Khmer, and Vietnamese.

4. Develop programs to help SEA parents and community members become more familiar with U.S. school systems and that encourage and train them to take on leadership roles within the school district

Many SEA parents are not familiar with U.S. school systems. For SEA parents and community members to be engaged, they need to understand the various roles and functions that exist in the school system. They also need to know how to meaningfully contribute and advocate for their children. SEA parents cannot do this without proper training and support.

While the recommendations offered above can help increase the engagement of SEA parents and community members, a major barrier to utilizing the assets within the community is the disconnect between the SEA families and the schools. Increased focus should be given to bridging these two disparate communities by increasing language access and communication. Community-based organizations are primed to do this work, but they will need cooperating partners and funding sources to do so.

PUBLICATION NOTE

This article was published online in 2015 by the *Journal of Southeast Asian American Education and Advancement* in Volume 10, Issue 2. Minor edits have been made here. The original can be found at http://doi.org/10.7771/2153-8999.1131.

REFERENCES

Adler, S. (2004). Home-school relations and the construction of racial and ethnic identity of Hmong elementary school students. *The School Community Journa1, 4*(2), 57–75.

Anyon, J. (1997). *Ghetto schooling.* Teachers College Press.

Auerbach, S. (2007). From moral supporters to struggling advocates: Reconceptualizing parent roles in education through the experiences of working-class families of color. *Urban Education, 42,* 250–283. https://doi.org/10.1177/0042085907300433

August, D., & Shanahan, T. (Eds.). (2006). *Developing literacy in second-language learners: A report of the National Literacy Panel on Language-Minority Children and Youth.* Erlbaum.

Chhim, S. H. (1981). *Introduction to Cambodian culture.* San Diego State University Multicultural Resource Center.

Cibulka, J. G. (1996). Toward an interpretation of school, family, and community connections: Policy challenges. In J. G. Cibulka & W. Kritek (Eds.), *Coordination among schools, families, and communities* (pp. 403–433). State University of New York Press.

Coleman, J. S. (1988). Social capital in the creation of human capital. *American Journal of Sociology, 94,* 95–120. https://doi.org/10.1086/228943

Collignon, F. F. (1994). From "paj ntaub" to paragraphs: Perspectives on Hmong processes of composition. In V. John-Steiner, C. F. Panofsky, & L. W. Smith (Eds.), *Sociocultural approaches to language and literacy: An interactionist perspective* (pp. 331–346). Cambridge University Press.

Collignon, F. F., Men, M., & Tan, S. (2001). Finding ways in: Community-based perspectives on Southeast Asian family involvement with schools in a New England state. *Journal of Education for Students Placed At Risk, 6*(1, 2), 27–44. https://doi.org/10.1207/S15327671ESPR0601-2_3

Dinh, Q. (2012). *SEARAC's education program update.* SEARAC.

Epstein, J. L. (2011). *School, family, and community partnerships: Preparing educators, and improving schools.* Westview Press.

Epstein, J. L., Sanders, M. G., Salinas, K., Simon, B., VanVoorhis, F., & Jansorn, N. (2002). *School, family and community partnerships: Your handbook for action* (2nd ed.). Corwin Press.

Garcia Coll, C. T., Akiba, D., Palacios, N., Bailey, B., Silver, R., DiMartino, L., et al. (2002). Parental involvement in children's education: Lessons from three immigrant groups. *Parenting Science and Practice, 2*, 303–324. https://doi.org/10.1207/S15327922PAR0203_05

Gold, E., Simon, E., & Brown, C. (2002). *Strong neighborhoods, strong schools: The indicators project on education organizing.* Chicago: Research for Action. Retrieved September 25, 2012, from http://www.researchforaction.org/wp-content/uploads/publication-photos/103/Gold_E_CCC_Strong_Neighborhoods_Strong_Schools.pdf

Han, M. (2006). Relationship among perceived parental trauma, attachment, and sense of coherence among Southeast Asian late adolescents. *Journal of Family Social Work, 9*, 25–45. https://doi.org/10.1300/J039v09n02_02

Hao, L., & Bonstead-Bruns, M. (1998). Parent-child difference in educational expectations and the academic achievement of immigrant and native students. *Sociology of Education, 71*, 175–198. https://doi.org/10.2307/2673201

Henderson, A. T., Mapp, K. L., Johnson, V. R., & Davies, D. (2007). *Beyond the bake sale: The essential guide to family-school partnerships.* New Press.

Hong, S. (2011). *A cord of three strands: A new approach to parent engagement in schools.* Harvard Education Press.

Hoover-Dempsey, K. V., & Sandler, H. M. (1997). Why do parents become involved in their children's education? *Review of Educational Research, 67*, 3–42. https://doi.org/10.3102/00346543067001003

Jasis, P., & Ordonez-Jasis, R. (2004). Convivencia to empowerment: Latino parent organizing at La Familia. *High School Journal, 88*(2), 32–42. https://www.jstor.org/stable/40364269

Jehl, J., Blank, M. J., & McCloud, B. (2001). *Education and community building: Connecting two worlds.* Institute for Educational Leadership.

Kakli, Z. (2010). *Creating demand parents: Approaches to parental involvement in the Miami-Dade County Public Schools* [Unpublished doctoral dissertation]. Harvard University.

Lareau, A., & Shumar, W. (1996). The problem of individualism in family-school policies. *Sociology of Education, 69*, 24–39. https://doi.org/10.2307/3108454

Lott, B. (2001). Low-income parents and the public schools. *Journal of Social Issues, 57*, 247–259. https://doi.org/10.1111/0022-4537.00211

Luangpraseut, K. (1989). *Laos culturally speaking*. San Diego State University Multicultural Resource Center.

Mediratta, K., & Fruchter, N. (2001). *Mapping the field of organizing for school improvement: A report on education organizing in Baltimore, Chicago, Los Angeles, the Mississippi Delta, New York City, Philadelphia, San Francisco, and Washington, D.C.* New York: Institute for Education and Social Policy, New York University. Retrieved September 25, 2012, from http://www.nyu.edu/steinhardt/iesp/cip/mapping/mapping_final_report.pdf

Miller, A. (1999). Squaring the triangle: Pupil behavior, teachers and parents—and psychology. *Educational Psychology in Practice, 15*, 75–80. https://doi.org/10.1080/0266736990150201

Miretzky, D. (2004). The communication requirements of democratic schools: Parent teacher perspectives on their relationships. *Teachers College Record, 106*, 814–851. https://doi.org/10.1111/j.1467-9620.2004.00359.x

Ngo, B., & Lee, S. J. (2007). Complicating the image of model minority success: A review of Southeast Asian American education. *Review of Educational Research, 77*, 415–453. https://doi.org/10.3102/0034654307309918

Olivos, E. (2006). *The power of parents: A critical perspective of bicultural parent involvement in public schools*. Peter Lang.

Oseguera, L., Conchas, G., & Mosqueda, E. (2011). Beyond family and ethnic culture: Preconditions for the potential realization of social capital. *Youth Society, 43*, 1136–1166. https://doi.org/10.1177/0044118X10382030

Robinson, W. C. (1998). *Terms of refuge: The Indochinese exodus and international response*. Zed Books.

Rumbaut, R. (2000). Laotian, Cambodian, and Vietnamese. In M. Zhou & J. V. Gatewood (Ed.), *Contemporary Asian American: A multi-disciplinary reader* (pp. 175–206). University of California Press.

Sack, W., Kinzie, D., Angell, R., Clarke, G., & Ben, R. (1988). The psychiatric effects of massive trauma on Cambodian children II: The family, the home, and the school. *Journal of American Academy of Child Psychiatry, 25*, 377–383. https://doi.org/10.1016/S0002-7138(09)60260-0

Schutz, A. (2006). Home is a prison in the global city: The tragic failure of school-based community engagement strategies. *Review of Educational Research, 76*, 691–743. https://doi.org/10.3102/00346543076004691

SEARAC. (2004). *Directory of Southeast Asian American community-based organizations: Mutual assistance associations (MAAs) and religious organizations providing social services*. SEARAC.

SEARAC. (2011). *Southeast Asians at a glance*. SEARAC.

Shirley, D. (1997). *Community organizing for urban school reform.* University of Texas Press.

Short, D., Vogt, M., & Echevarria, J. (2008) *The SIOP model for administrators*. Pearson.

Son, Y. (2010). *From high school to college: The influence of parents, peers, and teachers on Dominican students* [Unpublished doctoral dissertation]. Harvard University.

Te, B., Cordova, J. M. T, Walker-Moffat, W., & First, J. (1997). *Unfamiliar partners: Asian parents and U.S. public schools.* National Coalition of Advocates for Students.

Thuy, V. G. (1976). *Getting to know the Vietnamese and their culture*. Frederick Ungar.

Uy, P. (2011). *The educational experiences of Lao and Khmer high school students: The influence of families, friends, and teachers on academic achievement* [Unpublished doctoral dissertation]. Harvard University.

Villenas, S., & Deyhle, D. (1999). Critical race theory and ethnographies challenging the stereotypes: Latino families, schooling, resilience and resistance. *Curriculum Inquiry*, *29*, 413–445. https://doi.org/10.1111/0362-6784.00140

Warren, M. (2001). *Dry bones rattling: Community building to revitalize American democracy.* Princeton University Press.

Warren, M. R. (2005). Communities and schools: A new view of urban education reform. *Harvard Educational Review*, *75*, 133–173. https://doi.org/10.17763/haer.75.2.m718151032167438

Warren, M., Hong, S., Rubin, C., & Uy, P. (2009). Beyond the bake sale: A community-based relational approach to parent engagement in schools. *Teachers College Record*, *111*, 2209–2254. https://doi.org/10.1177/016146810911100901

Weinberg, M. (1997). *Asian-American education: Historical background and current realities*. Lawrence Erlbaum Associates.

Yang, S. K. (1981). The Hmong of Laos: 1896–1978. In *Refugee education guides: Glimpses of Hmong history and culture* (General Information Services, No. 16, pp. 3–17). Center for Applied Linguistics.

Zentella, A. C. (2005). *Building on strength: Language and literacy in Latino families and communities*. Teachers College Press.

9

The Model Minority Maze

Hmong Americans Working Within and Around Racial Discourses

STACEY J. LEE, CHOUA XIONG, LINDA MARIE PHENG, AND MAI NENG VANG

ABSTRACT

Whether framed as model minorities or used as evidence that the model minority is a myth, Hmong Americans and other Southeast Asians are constrained by the model minority stereotype. As a disciplinary tool, the model minority stereotype controls Asian American experiences and identities. This paper explores the complex and diverse ways that Hmong Americans in a community in Wisconsin are making sense of and responding to the model minority stereotype and the racial positioning of the Hmong American community. Our paper will illustrate the persistent power of the model minority stereotype to frame Asian American experiences, identities, and actions.

INTRODUCTION

Since the civil rights era, Asian Americans have been positioned as "model minorities" who have achieved economic and academic success through hard work, grit, and adherence to traditional cultural values. From the moment the stereotype emerged on the scene Asian American communities have been embroiled in debates over how to respond. Critical Asian American scholars have repeatedly argued that the model minority stereotype is a hegemonic tool that sustains the myth of meritocracy, silences charges of racial injustice, disciplines Black and Brown communities, and masks the struggles faced by Asian American communities (Hartlep, 2013; Lee, 2009; Lee & Kumashiro, 2005; Leonardo, 2009; Osajima, 1988; Poon et al., 2015). Fifty years after the model minority stereotype first came to national prominence, it continues to be used as a tool of White supremacy to justify the racial positioning and subjugation of Asian American, African American, and Latinx (Armus, 2015) students and their communities.

One strategy that scholars have used to challenge the validity of the model minority stereotype is to call for ethnically disaggregated data that uncovers the differences across various Asian American subgroups. Scholars have, for example, highlighted the high rates of poverty and academic underachievement within Southeast Asian American communities in an attempt to prove that the model minority stereotype is a myth (Lee & Kumashiro, 2005; Walker-Moffat, 1995). A significant, but unintended, consequence of this line of scholarship is that Southeast Asian Americans have come to represent an exception to the model minority or a "failed" Asian American. As Poon and her colleagues argue, the focus on ethnically disaggregated data and the educational problems faced by some Southeast Asian American communities has contributed to the reproduction of deficit thinking and the reification of the model minority stereotype (Poon et al., 2015).

Despite years of critique from Asian American scholars, the model minority stereotype continues to frame dominant understandings of who Asian Americans are and how they are doing relative to other racial groups. Whether framed as a model minority or used as evidence that the model minority is a myth, all Asian Americans are constrained by the model minority stereotype. As a disciplinary tool, the model minority stereotype controls Asian American experiences and identities. Furthermore, the stereotype contributes to how Asian Americans respond to and understand race and racialization. This paper explores the complex and diverse ways that Hmong American youth and Hmong American community leaders in a community in Wisconsin are making sense of and responding to the model minority stereotype and the racial positioning of the Hmong American community. The article will illustrate the persistent power of the model minority stereotype to frame Asian American experiences, identities, and actions.

The Hmong Experience in the United States: From Refugees to Racialized Subjects

Hmong people, often referred to as Miao or Meo in Asia, are an ethnic group that originated from China and Southeast Asia. During the Second Indochina War (Vietnam War) and the Secret War in Laos, Hmong people in Laos were recruited as guerrilla fighters to support American troops against the Communist-backed North Vietnamese Army (NVA) and Pathet Lao forces (Cha, 2010; Quincy, 2012; Vang, 2008). After the United States pulled out of Vietnam in 1975, Hmong people became targets for ethnic and political persecution (Vang, 2008). As a result of their involvement with the U.S. military, Hmong people were forced to flee from Laos to Thailand, the United States, and other European countries as refugees. After initial resettlement across the United States, many Hmong people engaged in secondary migration to California and several Midwestern states in order to maintain kinship ties and co-ethnic networks, build social and cultural capital, increase economic opportunities, and gain access to different and better educational opportunities (Chan, 1991; Office of Refugee Resettlement, 1984; Vang, 2008). Hmong Americans have experienced economic and academic challenges since their resettlement in the United States in the mid-1970s.

Race has been a central organizing principle in the United States since the formation of the nation, and research on immigrants and refugees reveals that the process of racialization is central to becoming American (Abu El-Haj, 2015; Lee, 2005; Olsen, 1997). The dominant discourse on race centers on the White and Black dichotomy that associates Whites with desirable and positive characteristics and Blacks with undesirable and negative characteristics (Feagin, 2000). Scholarship on Asian Americans has shown that the two dominant racial discourses surrounding Asian Americans are the image of Asians as "perpetual foreigners" and the image of Asian Americans as "model minorities" (Fong, 2008; Lee, 2014; Okihiro, 1994). According to the "perpetual foreigner" stereotype, Asian Americans are continuously positioned as outsiders based on binaries of profound cultural differences: Eastern versus Western, preliterate versus modern. As noted previously, the model minority stereotype suggests that Asian Americans have achieved widespread academic and economic success through hard work and adherence to traditional Asian cultural norms. While there has been a lot of attention to the academic and economic achievements associated with the model minority image, it is important to point out that the stereotype also includes significant behavioral characteristics—hard work, self-sufficiency, obedience, respect, compliance, and so on (Petersen, 1966). Like other Asian Americans, Hmong Americans are rejected for their "foreignness" through the discourse of cultural differences, yet they are accepted as "honorary Whites" when they perform model minority achievements and behavior (Tuan, 1998). These racial discourses shape (mis)understandings of Hmong Americans in educational spaces.

The educational experiences, particularly the causes of educational inequity among Hmong Americans, are often understood to be the result of cultural clashes or cultural differences between Hmong culture and mainstream U.S. culture (Donnelly, 1994; Rumbaut & Ima, 1988; Sherman, 1988). Within the cultural clash discourse, Hmong culture is depicted as homogenous, fixed, savage, and primitive in comparison to modern

Western culture (DePouw, 2012; Ngo, 2008). Hones (2002), for example, argues that due to cultural differences and limited English proficiency, parents "don't know what to expect from American schools, how to be involved, or what questions to ask regarding the schooling their children are receiving" (p. 46). Similarly, Lee and Green (2008) attribute Hmong American students' poor academic achievement to parents not being educated and not keeping track of their children's whereabouts. Xiong and Huang (2011) argue that students' low motivation level for education accounts for delinquent behaviors. As these examples demonstrate, the cultural clash discourse defaults to an individualist argument that blames parents and individuals for poor academic achievements and high truancy rates (Lee, 2015; Xiong et al., 2008). In other words, an exclusive focus on cultural differences overlooks systematic inequities (Lee, 2001).

Binary assumptions regarding Asian versus mainstream American culture and deficit perspectives on languages other than English have been identified with English as a Second Language (ESL) programs that promote English monolingualism (Xiong & Xiong, 2011). While ESL programs do provide resources for newcomers and English learners, Xiong and Zhou's (2006) study points out that Hmong Americans are tracked into ESL based on the assumption that Hmong Americans need ESL programming simply because Hmong is spoken in the home. Importantly, research demonstrates that placement in ESL classes tracks students into lower academic classes that limit academic success (Callahan, 2005; Xiong & Zhou, 2006).

As Asian Americans, the Hmong American community is also judged against the standards of the model minority stereotype. The scholarship on Hmong Americans and U.S. Census data on Hmong Americans reveal that Hmong students often struggle to achieve the levels of economic and academic achievement associated with the model minority stereotype (Ngo, 2006; Ngo & Lee, 2007). Given the Black and White discourse of race in the United States, the academic and economic struggles experienced by Hmong Americans and other Southeast Asians lead to the ideological blackening of these communities (DePouw, 2012; Lee, 2005; Ong, 1996).

Lee's (2005) study of Hmong Americans at University Heights School (UHS) reveals the ways that race and racism frame the educational experiences of Hmong Americans. In particular, Lee discovered that Hmong Americans at UHS who aspired to high academic achievement and reflected "traditional" Hmong values were viewed positively by their teachers. In contrast to the "traditional" students, many of the self-identified "Americanized" students questioned the value of education and adopted hip-hop styles of clothing and language associated with African American youth culture. As a result of the way the "Americanized" students performed their identities they were viewed negatively by their teachers. Most significantly, these "Americanized" students were compared to African American students or ideologically blackened within the school and thus excluded from opportunities.

Adding to Lee (2005), DePouw (2012) argues that colonialism and racism are embedded in the process of Hmong racialization based on the Black/White binary. Beyond statistical performances of the model minority and being ideologically blackened, DePouw's (2006, 2012) discussion of the Black/White binary suggests that the process of Hmong racialization is also tied to behavioral performances. Despite Hmong Americans' academic and economic struggles, Hmong Americans are still expected to behaviorally perform a noncomplaining citizenship. When Hmong American students help institutions recruit "diversity," promote cultural events, and graduate from their programs despite academic struggles, Hmong Americans successfully performed the behavioral aspects of the model minority. On the contrary, Hmong Americans are blackened when they engage in student activism, demand curriculum inclusivity in schools, and request meaningful inclusion in campus decision-making processes. In the performance of the model minority, Hmong Americans achieve honorary whiteness. When they engage in resistance, Hmong Americans become blackened. This process of racialization systematically silences and polices Hmong Americans to perform as the model minority.

OUR STUDY

The ethnographic data for this article is drawn from a larger, ongoing study that examines the experiences of Hmong youth in formal and informal educational spaces in Dane County, Wisconsin. This larger project is concerned with the various messages that youth are receiving from their co-ethnic communities, families, community-based organizations, and schools about their identities as Hmong youth and as students. In the tradition of in-depth ethnographic research, we are collecting data through multiple methods, including participant observation, interviews, and analysis of various site documents (e.g., websites of community organizations, etc.). Our participants include Hmong parents of middle and high school students, community leaders and youth workers at community centers, Hmong youth, and high school educators. We have conducted observations in community centers, college campuses, high schools, and other public spaces.

This article reflects preliminary findings drawn from our interviews with parents and community leaders ($N = 12$), and from our observations of youth and community leaders in community centers, school board meetings, college campuses, and other public spaces (to date, approximately 150 hours of ethnographic fieldwork). It is important to note that the term "community leader" is ambiguous and contested within co-ethnic communities. Our definition of community leaders includes those who advocate and/or organize on behalf of Hmong American communities, or those whom other members of the Hmong community look to as leaders. Therefore, we include members who encompass traditional leadership roles, middle-class professionals, community organizers, and college campus leaders. All interviews were recorded and transcribed, and pseudonyms are used for all participants.

Interviews and fieldwork were conducted by all members of our multiethnic and multi lingual research team. The research team consists of the principal investigator, a third-generation Chinese American university professor, a second-generation Khmer American doctoral student, and two Hmong American doctoral students. Both Hmong American students were born in different refugee camps in Thailand, but came to the United States as young children and have largely been socialized and educated in the United States. Because of the ethnic makeup of the research team, we recognize that some of us are positioned as cultural insiders (Peshkin, 1991). Shared language and cultural norms are important assets in our study; yet, we also recognize that there are important regional, gender, educational attainment, and class differences that influence community norms and practices. In order to increase trustworthiness, throughout data collection and interpretation, the research team regularly engages as a group in reflecting upon findings and interpretation of data to protect against potential research bias. While we are naming Dane County, Wisconsin, as the site of our research, we are using pseudonyms for all individuals and organizations to protect confidentiality and maintain anonymity of our participants. All quotes from participants are transcribed verbatim.

Finally, while we recognize that there is an ongoing debate among Hmong people in the United States regarding the terms used to describe the community (e.g., Hmong, Hmong American, or Miao/Meo), we will be using "Hmong American" to refer to our participants since this is the term most commonly used by 1.5-generation and 2nd-generation Hmong people living in the United States. We recognize that there are two main subgroups within the Hmong American communities: *Hmoob Dawb* (White Hmong) and *Moob Lees* (Blue Mong) (Lee & Tapp, 2010). While we do not want to minimize the complexity of the differences among different Hmong families and communities, for the purpose of readability, we will be using the spelling "Hmong"; this is not intended to exclude Blue Mong.

Wisconsin Context

According to the 2010 U.S. Census Bureau, Wisconsin has the third largest Hmong population (49,240) in the United States. Unlike in California (91,224) and Minnesota (66,181), the Hmong people in Wisconsin are spread throughout the state and are not concentrated in one single area. Although Dane County does not have the largest concentration of the Hmong population in the state, Dane County does possess a significant number of Hmong people (4,230) (Pfeifer et al., 2013). The Hmong American community makes up .86% of Wisconsin's population (49,240/5,686,986) and 1.8% of Dane County's population (4,230/233,209) (Pfeifer et al., 2013; U.S. Census Bureau, 2010). Forty percent of the Hmong population works in the manufacturing industry compared to 18% of the state's population. While the Hmong American community's poverty rate has decreased over time, they remain one of the poorest ethnic groups in Wisconsin and the United States (Vang, 2013). Furthermore, Hmong American communities have one of the largest youth populations in comparison to the general population and the Asian American population (44% under the age of 18) (Pfeifer et al., 2013). In addition to having one of the largest youth populations that remain in impoverished communities, Hmong Americans continue to have one of the lowest bachelor's degree attainment rates across racial and ethnic groups (Xiong, 2013b).

Dane County, Wisconsin, is an area known for its racialized achievement gap. The 2013 publication of the Race to Equity report revealed that for the 2012–2013 school year, 42% of Dane County's African American high schoolers failed to graduate on time, compared to 12.7% of White students. African American students, in other words, were 3.3 times more likely to miss this key benchmark than their White peers. This 42% rate was worse than the statewide African American failure to graduate rate of 35.2%. The Race to Equity report drew important attention to the educational injustices faced by the African American community in Dane County, but did not examine how other communities of color were faring in the region. Framed in this context, where Black/White disparities in education and well-being are among the worst in America, our ongoing study explores the experiences of Southeast Asian American youth in formal school spaces and out-of-school community-based spaces.

FINDINGS AND DISCUSSION

Recognition of Racial Discourses

U.S. Census data reveal that many Hmong Americans struggle economically, with poverty rates of 37.8% (Reeves et al., 2004; Xiong, 2013a). More recent data from the American Community Survey suggests that Hmong Americans are showing signs of economic improvement (Pfeifer, 2008). One of our first findings concerns the growing socioeconomic class diversity within the Dane County Hmong American community. Our participants include college-educated professionals who have entered the middle class and families and youth who live in poverty. In other words, our participants include those who appear to have achieved model minority success and those who represent the exception to the model minority or the "failed" Asian American. Interestingly, members of the middle-class Hmong American community have been active in raising awareness regarding the academic struggles faced by Hmong American students in local schools. One of the first things these college-educated Hmong Americans leaders did was to push the district for disaggregated data because they believed that the aggregated data on Asian American students masked the academic concerns facing Hmong students. These leaders worked with one local Dane County school district to come up with a system to disaggregate the Hmong student data within the district. The disaggregated data from the 2013–2014 academic year reveal that the vast majority of Hmong American students in the district are identified as English learners (88%) and are eligible for free or reduced lunch (79%). The data also demonstrates that while Hmong American students have relatively high graduation rates, they score low on standardized tests.

In response to the disaggregated data on Hmong American students, the previously mentioned college-educated Hmong American community leaders formed an educational advocacy group (Hmong Educational Advocates/HEA) to advocate for more services for Hmong American students in the district. Members of HEA argue that the data suggests that a large number of Hmong Americans are graduating from high school with limited academic skills, which will make them vulnerable for becoming trapped in low-wage jobs. While middle-class Hmong Americans have become increasingly focused on the educational disparities facing Hmong American students, the most economically disadvantaged members of the Hmong American community struggle to meet their basic needs, and our preliminary data suggests that their voices are largely absent in the achievement gap discussions. The leader of a Hmong American organization that represents low-income Hmong American families remarked that it is difficult for families to advocate for education when they do not have access to food and housing. While an in-depth discussion of Hmong American student achievement and community responses to the achievement gap are beyond the scope of our paper, we highlight the different responses to the achievement issues to demonstrate the growing social class diversity within the Hmong American community and to highlight the ways class informs responses to inequality.

Despite the growing social class diversity among the Dane County Hmong American community, our participants all demonstrate an awareness that Southeast Asians, and the Hmong American community specifically, are subjected to racial and ethnic stereotyping. Our participants are aware of both the overtly negative stereotypes facing the Hmong American community and the seemingly "positive" stereotypes of Asians more generally. Furthermore, there is a common understanding that stereotypes impact how the Hmong American community is seen and treated by the dominant society. With respect to the overtly "negative" stereotypes, our participants talked about the reliance on public assistance among Hmong American families, youth gangs, early marriage among girls, and Hmong boys dropping out of school. Not insignificantly, these stereotypes have been linked to the ideological blackening of Hmong American youth (DePouw, 2012; Lee, 2005). In terms of "positive" stereotypes, our participants referenced characteristics associated with the model minority—hard working, quiet, good students, family-oriented, and so on.

While many of our participants had not heard of the "model minority" stereotype per se, almost all were familiar with the idea that Asian Americans worked hard, were quiet and well- behaved, did well in school, and were family-oriented. In addition to a shared awareness of the ethnic and racial stereotypes facing the Hmong American community, our participants expressed a common concern about the relative "invisibility" of Hmong and other Southeast Asian American students. Indeed, across all of our formal semistructured interviews and in our field work, our participants expressed concerns about the lack of awareness regarding who Hmong Americans are and what concerns the community faces. Across social class backgrounds, participants regularly remarked that "people don't know who Hmong are" or "they (non-Hmong) think we are Chinese or something." The middle-class professional Hmong American participants have pointed to the exclusively Black/White discourse in the Race to Equity Report (2013) as evidence that Southeast Asian communities are largely invisible. Importantly, their awareness of racial/ethnic stereotyping and concerns regarding invisibility influence how they behave and shape their strategies for resistance.

Although all of our participants share a recognition of the relative invisibility of the Hmong American community and the simultaneous racism surrounding the Hmong American community, they did not express a common response to the racial discourses. Importantly, our preliminary findings suggest that there are heterogeneous responses to the model minority stereotype, in particular, and that the various responses are related to the social class positions and/or the social class aspirations of our participants.

Middle-Class Responses to Invisibility and the Model Minority Stereotype

Our middle-class participants were well aware that aggregated data on Asian Americans supported the idea that Asian Americans were all high-achieving students (i.e., model minorities), and that this data rendered invisible the academic concerns of Hmong American students. As noted above, middle-class Hmong American professionals worked with the school district to ethnically disaggregate student achievement. Despite their concerns about the relative invisibility of Hmong American students, however, middle-class Hmong American participants appear hesitant about expressing overt criticism of the model minority stereotype. Like the Cambodian American youth in Chhuon and Hudley's (2010) research, our middle-class participants seem to perceive the model minority stereotype to be a relatively positive representation that is preferable to the overtly negative stereotypes that the community endures.

Gao Moua, a middle-class professional who cofounded a summer program for Hmong American children and youth in Dane County, grappled with how to challenge the invisibility of Hmong American students:

> Our kids are on a double-edged sword because we teach our kids to be respectful, don't challenge teachers, don't ask too many questions, right? And then when they go [to] school they don't do that part [act out]. So they seem, when they go to school or class, and not absent— they're here, so that's good enough. They're behaving, so they don't get the substance of the material that they are learning. So with that, we continue to get high graduate rates, and that puts another edge to us, but again, we are not preparing our kids for the higher education because they don't have the deep down substance for higher education.

While Gao Moua clearly recognizes that many Hmong American students have not "achieved" model minority success, she emphasizes that Hmong American families value education and teach their children to act respectfully in school. In other words, she highlights the behavioral and cultural characteristics that are associated with the model minority stereotype. At the same time, however, Gao Moua recognizes that this model minority behavior contributes to the invisibility of Hmong American students, which leaves her wondering how she and the community can best advocate for Hmong American students.

Chou, a university staff person who works with high school students of color, expressed a similar concern about the relative invisibility of Hmong American students in Dane County:

> *Peb cov Hmoob mas niam no, uh, lawv yeej* face—I think *lawv yeej* face discrimination *tsis li ntawv los lawv yeej tsis muaj* enough support. For example, in this city, we have been big advocate for, *niam no*, more Hmong staff in the school district: teachers, uh, secretary, uh, outreach, you know, social worker, *ub no. Nws tsis yog hais tias peb tsis muaj cov neeg kawm tas na, peb muaj tab sis*, you know, for some reason *peb ho tsis muaj ntau npaum piv xam, cov mev thiab cov dub na yod*? So that's why something that *lub koos haum es, uh, cov phooj ywg lawv tau tsim lub* HEA *no nad*. Um, *lawv tau tsim no ces lawv yeej* advocate, *li uh* [lists names of people], *lawv yeej* advocate for *kom no*, uh, *thiab peb cov* personal, *peb yeej* advocate *tias kom* the school district make an effort to, uh, provide service to, um, the Hmong community.... First it's not a priority and secondly, budget cut, right. Uh, so *yog peb cov niam txiv*, the community, is not vocal about it, then it's—I mean, no news is good news, right? *Lawv tsis* need *ces cov mev thiab cov dub lawv niaj hnub qw hais tias peb cov me nyuam kawm ntawv tsis tau lau, peb poob qab no ces lawv* focus more on *cov me nyuam dub, cov me nyuam mev*.

Translation:

> Us Hmong, they do face—I think they do face discrimination and also they don't have enough support. For example, in the city, we have been big advocate for more Hmong staff in the school district: teachers, uh, secretary, uh, outreach, you know, social worker, and others. It isn't that we don't have educated people, we do, but you know, for some reason, we don't have as many as, for example, the Latinx and blacks, right? So that's why something that the organization, uh, that friends created HEA. Um, they created this organization to advocate, like, uh [list names of people], they advocate for, uh, and us personal, we also advocate for the school district to make an effort to, uh, provide service to, um, the Hmong community.... First it's not a priority and secondly, budget cut, right. Uh, so if parents, the community is not vocal about it, then it's—I mean, no news is good news, right? If they don't need then the Latinx and the blacks vocalize daily that their kids can't learn, they are falling behind, and then they will focus more on the black kids and Latinx kids.

Interestingly, Chou compares the relative invisibility of the Hmong American community with the greater visibility of the Black and Latinx communities in Dane County. While his comments suggest that he recognizes that the Hmong American, Black, and Latinx communities all face barriers to education in Dane County, he does not suggest that the groups work together. Rather, he appears to view the issues facing Hmong American students to be distinct from those facing other communities of color.

During the spring of 2016 a statewide organization for Hmong American college students in Wisconsin sponsored a conference that focused on what the model minority stereotype means for the Hmong American community, suggesting that Hmong American college student leaders recognize that the model minority stereotype is something that Hmong American communities must negotiate. At the conference, a well-respected Hmong American professor gave a historical overview of the Hmong refugee experience and proceeded to assert that the Hmong people are an ideal minority group who have been loyal and productive citizens of the United States. During his presentation he noted that the Hmong people were too often represented in the national discourse in overtly negative ways, and he cogently argued that these representations were not only damaging but incomplete. While recognizing that the model minority image was also an incomplete picture of the Hmong American community, the professor pointed to the many important achievements of Hmong Americans and argued that Hmong Americans have been good and loyal citizens. Thus, the professor drew on both discourses of achievement and behavior in his discussion of Hmong Americans as model minorities. While some audience members expressed concern about the model minority stereotype, many of the students in the audience voiced support for the idea that Hmong Americans are model minorities, and several audience members noted that being stereotyped as model minorities was better than being stereotyped in overtly negative ways.

Efforts to perform a model minority identity, however, may have unintended consequences. Tong, a member of HEA, explained that in his work at a local university he had found that many Hmong American college students were hesitant to take advantage of student services and/or to reach out to professors because they want to present an image of themselves as self-reliant and highly successful:

> What all of our students, the thing that we struggle with is where we think that asking for help is a bad thing because we think that we are too used to getting support from when we were growing up. So, we are just used to relying on the system. We are just used to relying on support, and it's a bad thing you can't help yourself. But that's how smart and wealthy kids succeed; they expect support. The minute a student of color goes and gets tutoring it's like "oh you don't know math, you are bad at math." . . . I feel like you just feel it growing up, especially if you come from communities where you rely on government support or help, you just think like dang we struggled and we needed people like this to help us. That when I get to college, I think I'm smart and I don't need tutors (students). . . . but you see all the students who go there . . . they don't need help, they just need to get better. This is problem for our students, among the Hmong students they definitely, they are not getting it.

In making sense of Hmong American students' hesitancy to seek academic support, it is important to recognize the hegemonic discourses around economic "dependence" versus economic "independence." In fact, when the model minority stereotype first came to prominence during the 1960s, Asian Americans were valorized for their economic self-sufficiency and Blacks were simultaneously criticized for their assumed over-reliance on government support (Petersen, 1966). As Tong suggests, however, Hmong American students who avoid seeking academic assistance miss out on important social capital that supports academic achievement and persistence. Thus, consistent with previous scholarship, our data suggests that efforts to conform to the model minority stereotype may lead to self-silencing and negatively impact student identity and opportunity (Lee, 2009).

Low-Income Hmong Americans and the Politics of Resistance

Like our middle-class Hmong American participants, our low-income Hmong American participants and those who work closely with these communities are deeply concerned with the invisibility of Hmong Americans in Dane County. Mee, a youth coordinator for an advocacy group that works with Southeast Asian and Black communities in Dane County (SHOUT), expressed her frustration regarding the way the model minority stereotype masks the concerns of Hmong people:

> I still think that a lot of people don't know who Hmong folks are. I think that a lot of people still think that we are East Asian, Chinese folks, right? And that we fit into the model minority myth. Yeah, I think . . . that if they do think about Hmong people they think, I think they think about the model minority folks, right. Really trying to put us into that box.

Mee goes on to assert that Hmong Americans are not model minorities:

> But I think we look at those statistics, right, and we take out SEA folks from that, when we look at it, we see that SEA folks are the complete opposite of the model minority myth. That we are not doing well at all. We are actually really poor, we are not graduating high school and college. All of that, right.

Interestingly, Mee suggests that Hmong American middle-class professionals may unintentionally confirm the model minority stereotype in the eyes of the dominant society through their advocacy work. In the following quote she argued that middle-class Hmong leaders are not the only leaders in the community:

> Hmong leadership does not only come from young people who are professionals, right. And that it's, um, that Hmong leaders comes in all shapes and forms. And that in reality at SHOUT, a lot of the Hmong leaders, a lot of folks that we think are Hmong leaders are elderly Hmong women. They are the ones that we go to, um, for like, they are the ones that we go to because they know whose family has not eaten, whose family does not have clothes, and whose families needs help, right. And yeah, I think a lot of people look at elderly Hmong women and think that they are stupid and they don't have anything to contribute and they don't know anything. Right, and that actually, they think that they are a burden to the city and the state, right. But in reality they have the most wisdom and they know the most about what the community needs.

Mee and our other low-income Hmong American participants are overtly critical of the model minority stereotype, and they also recognize that the model minority stereotype implicitly compares Asian Americans to other groups of color. Specifically, Mee argues that as Asian Americans, Hmong Americans experience relative racial privilege compared to Black people. In support of her position, she points to the disciplinary practices at schools that target Black students for behaviors that go unpunished when performed by Asian and White students.

Meng, a youth leader at SHOUT, also expressed a recognition that Whites view Hmong Americans more positively than they view Black people:

> They [Whites] see us differently from Black people, I think. They always say, "oh we have good food, you know. We behave well, we behave better than Black folks. We have good grades or, I don't know, that we're healthy."

Mee and other members of SHOUT argue that efforts to perform a model minority image represent a consent to hegemonic racial discourses that damage both the Hmong American community and the Black community (Lee, 2009). In the following quote, Mee asserted that Hmong people should not strive to become model minorities:

> It [the model minority stereotype] is just feeding into the system of White supremacy, not only that, but the model minority myth is very anti-Black. Everything about the model minority myth is being White, becoming White, and being the furthest thing from Black. We should not try to be the model minority at all. It's like we are trying to fit into the system, and the system is just using the model minority as a tool to keep us down. So that it can keep on working its magic.

Mee's critique of the model minority stereotype highlights the anti-Blackness implicit in the discourse. She recognizes that the model minority discourse is implicitly comparative in nature, and that there cannot be a model minority without a concomitant problematic minority (Lee, 2009; Poon et al., 2015). Mee and other Southeast Asian members of SHOUT have developed close relationships with low-income Black people through their work in SHOUT. Through their experiences working with SHOUT, Mee has seen firsthand the ways that race and class intersect with other identities in the lives of low-income communities, and she has come to recognize that low-income Blacks and Southeast Asians face shared forms of marginalization. Mee and other members of SHOUT argue for an intersectional approach to challenging the multiple forms of oppression faced by members of the low-income Black and Southeast Asian American communities in Dane County. Thus, Mee's critique of the model minority stereotype is based on her commitment to building cross-racial coalitions with other low-income communities of color.

CONCLUSION

Our research shows that Hmong people still struggle to be seen after over 35 years in the United States. Whether cast as model minorities or as "failed" and underachieving Asian Americans, the complex experiences of Hmong Americans are invisible. Quantitative data on Hmong American students in one school district in Dane County, Wisconsin, suggests that the academic needs of Hmong American students are going largely unaddressed. Our middle-class and low-income participants are equally concerned about the invisibility of the Hmong American community, and both groups recognize the role that the model minority stereotype plays in making the community invisible. In fact, their respective responses to the model minority stereotype are directly tied to their responses to invisibility. Although both our middle-class and our low-income participants are invested in advocating for the Hmong American communities, they take different approaches that reflect their respective class positions.

For middle-class participants, the dilemma appears to be about how to make visible the concerns facing Hmong American students without contributing to a deficit discourse. In other words, they want to draw attention to the academic challenges facing Hmong American students and build on assumptions regarding the good behavior of Hmong American students. As such, their response appears to be a partial challenge to the model minority stereotype. Their ambivalence regarding the model minority stereotype suggests that they recognize that being cast as model minorities is a form of relative racial privilege (Cheng, 2013). Their reluctance to directly challenge the stereotype, however, suggests that they may also recognize that despite their relative success, they are still constrained by the racial discourses controlled by the dominant group (i.e., Whites). Finally, it is important to point out that our middle-class Hmong American participants appear to be crafting a strategy for advocacy that involves framing the concerns of the Hmong American community as largely distinct and separate from concerns facing other communities of color. Here, they are implicitly drawing on a discourse that Asians are neither Black nor White (Ancheta, 2003; Okihiro, 1994; Wu, 2002).

In contrast, our low-income Hmong American participants are highly critical of the model minority stereotype. Their critique of the model minority stereotype is based on a larger critique of White supremacy and a commitment to cross-racial coalition building with Black communities. The differences between the ways our middle-class and our low-income participants make sense of and respond to the model minority stereotype point to the complex and important ways that race and class intersect in the lives of Hmong Americans in the United States. (Ng et al., 2007). Regardless of social class background, however, the experiences of our participants illustrate that Hmong

Americans cannot escape racialization, including racial stereotypes. Our research also demonstrates that the model minority stereotype may be a form of relative racial privilege, but it also contributes to the invisibility of Hmong American and other Southeast Asian students (Lee, 2005, 2009; Museus, 2009; Wing, 2007).

While most of the educational scholarship on the model minority stereotype has focused on issues of achievement, our research contributes to the scholarship that has pointed to the role of behavior in being cast as a model minority (Bascara, 2006; Osajima, 1988; Wu, 2002). Not insignificantly, "good" behavior is defined as obedience toward and compliance with the dominant norms and rules. Indeed, our research suggests that even in the absence of high academic achievement, Southeast Asian American students continue to be labeled as model minorities as long as the behavioral component is being performed. Future research should focus more attention on how Asian American students' behavior shapes ideas regarding the model minority stereotype. Finally, our research demonstrates that the model minority stereotype continues to shape Asian American experiences and identities in the 21st century, which highlights the fact that critically conscious educational research on the impact of the stereotype remains relevant and crucial.

PUBLICATION NOTE

This article was published online in 2017 by the *Journal of Southeast Asian American Education and Advancement* in Volume 12, Issue 2. Minor edits have been made here. The original can be found at http://doi.org/10.7771/2153-8999.1153.

REFERENCES

Abu El-Haj, T. T. (2015). *Unsettled belonging: Educating Palestinian American youth after 9/11*. University of Chicago Press.

Ancheta, A. (2003). *Race, rights, and the Asian American experience.* Rutgers University Press.

Armus, T. (2015). Student groups shift toward use of Latinx to include all gender identities. *Columbia Daily Spectator.* Retrieved from http://columbiaspectator.com/news/2015/10/07/latino-latinx

Bascara, V. (2006). *Model-minority imperialism*. Minneapolis: University of Minnesota Press.

Callahan, R. M. (2005). Tracking and high school English learners: Limiting opportunity to learn. *American Educational Research Journal, 42*(2), 305–328.

Cha, Y. P. (2010). *An introduction to Hmong culture*. McFarland.

Chan, S. (1991). *Asian Americans: An interpretive history.* Twayne.

Cheng, W. (2013). *The Changs next door to the Diazes: Remapping race in suburban California.* University of Minnesota Press.

Chhuon, V., & Hudley, C. (2010). Asian American ethnic options: How Cambodian students negotiate ethnic identities in a U.S. urban school. *Anthropology & Education Quarterly, 41*(4), 341–359. https://doi.org/10.1111/j.1548-1492.2010.01096.x

DePouw, C. (2006). *Negotiating race, navigating school: Situating Hmong American university student experiences* [Doctoral dissertation]. University of Illinois at Urbana Champaign.

DePouw, C. (2012). When culture implies deficit: Placing race at the center of Hmong American education. *Race Ethnicity and Education, 15*(2), 223–239. https://doi.org/10.1080/13613324.2011.624505

Donnelly, N. D. (1994). *Changing lives of refugee Hmong women.* University of Washington Press.

Feagin, J. R. (2000). *Racist America: Roots, current realities, and future reparations.* Routledge.

Fong, T. P. (2008). *The contemporary Asian American experience: Beyond the model minority.* Pearson College Division.

Hartlep, N. D. (2013). *The model minority stereotype: Demystifying Asian American success.* Information Age Publishing.

Hones, D. (2002). *American dreams, global visions: Dialogic teacher research with refugee and immigrant families.* Routledge.

Lee, G. Y., & Tapp, N. (2010). *Culture and customs of the Hmong.* ABC CLIO.

Lee, J. K., & Green, K. (2008). Hmong parental involvement and support: A comparison between families of high and low achieving high school seniors. *Hmong Studies Journal, 9*, 1–27.

Lee, S. J. (2001). More than "model minorities" or "delinquents": A look at Hmong American high school students. *Harvard Educational Review, 71*(3), 505–529. https://doi.org/10.17763/haer.71.3.k055628l18wp51v6

Lee, S. J. (2005). *Up against whiteness: Race, school, and immigrant youth.* Teachers College Press.

Lee, S. J. (2009). *Unraveling the "model minority" stereotype: Listening to Asian American youth.* Teachers College Press.

Lee, S., & Kumashiro, K. (2005). *A report on the status of Asian Americans and Pacific Islanders in education: Beyond the model minority stereotype.* National Education Association Human and Civil Rights.

Lee, S. S. H. (2014). *A new history of Asian America.* Routledge.

Lee, X. (2015). *The lack of motivation to pursue postsecondary education among Hmong students: A grounded theory study* [Doctoral dissertation]. University of Phoenix.

Leonardo, Z. (2009). The color of supremacy: Beyond discourse of "white privilege." In E. Taylor, D. Gillborn, & G. Ladson-Billings (Eds.), *Foundations of critical race theory in education* (pp. 261–276). Routledge.

Museus, S. D. (2009). A critical analysis of the invisibility of Southeast Asian American students in higher education research and discourse. In L. Zhan (Ed.), *Asian voices: Engaging, empowering, and enabling* (pp. 59–76). NLN Press.

Ng, J. C., Lee S. S., & Pak, Y. K. (2007). Contesting the model minority and perpetual foreigner stereotypes: A critical review of literature on Asian Americans in education: *Review of Research in Education, 31*(1), 95–130. https://doi.org/10.3102/0091732X07300046095

Ngo, B. (2006). Learning from the margins: The education of Southeast and South Asian Americans in context. *Race Ethnicity and Education, 9*(1), 51–65. https://doi.org/10.1080/13613320500490721

Ngo, B. (2008). Beyond "culture clash" understandings of immigrant experiences. *Theory into Practice, 47*(1), 4–11. https://doi.org/10.1080/00405840701764656

Ngo, B., & Lee, S. J. (2007). Complicating the image of model minority success: A review of Southeast Asian American education. *Review of Educational Research, 77*(4), 415–453. https://doi.org/10.3102/0034654307309918

Office of Refugee Resettlement. (1984). *The Hmong resettlement study: Executive summary.* U.S. Government Printing Office.

Okihiro, G. Y. (1994). *Margins and mainstreams: Asians in American history and culture.* University of Washington Press.

Olsen, L. (1997). *Made in America: Immigrant students in our public schools.* The New Press.

Omi, M., & Winant, H. (2014). *Racial formation in the United States.* Routledge.

Ong, A. (1996). Cultural citizenship as subject making: Immigrants negotiate racial and cultural boundaries in the United States. *Current Anthropology, 37*(5), 737–762.

Osajima, K. (1988). Asian Americans as the model minority: An analysis of the popular press images of the 1960s and 1980s. In G. Y. Okihiro, S. Hune, A. A. Hansen, & J. M. Liu (Eds.), *Reflections on shattered windows* (pp. 165–174). Washington State University Press.

Peshkin, A. (1991). In search of subjectivity—one's own. In C. F. Conrad, J. G. Haworth, & L. R. Lattuca (Eds.), *Qualitative research in higher education: Expanding perspectives* (pp. 455–461). Pearson Custom.

Petersen, W. (1966). "Success Story, Japanese-American Style." *The New York Times Magazine, 6*, 20–43.

Pfeifer, M. (2008). "Cambodian, Hmong, Lao and Vietnamese Americans in the 2005 American Community Survey." *Journal of Southeast Asian American Education and Advancement, 3*, 1–21. http://doi.org/10.7771/2153-8999.1104

Pfeifer, M. E., Sullivan, J., Yang, K., & Yang, W. (2013). Hmong population and demographic trends in the 2010 Census and 2010 American Community Survey. In M. E. Pfeifer & B. K. Thao (Eds.), *State of the Hmong American community* (pp. 8–9). Hmong National Development.

Poon, O. A., Squire, D., Kodama, C., Byrd, A., Chan, J., Manzano, L., Furr, S., & Bishundat, D. (2015). A critical review of the model minority myth in selected literature on Asian Americans and Pacific Islanders in higher education. *Review of Educational Research, 86*(2), 469–502. https://doi.org/10.3102/0034654315612205

Quincy, K. (2012). From war to resettlement: How Hmong have become Americans. In V. Her, & M. L. Buley-Meissner (Eds.), *Hmong and American: From refugees to citizens* (pp. 59– 80). Minnesota Historical Society Press.

Race to Equity Project Team. (2013). *Race to equity: Baseline report on the state of racial disparities in Dane County*. Wisconsin Council on Children and Families.

Reeves, T., Bennett, C. E., & U.S. Census Bureau. (2004). *We the people: Asians in the United States*. U.S. Dept. of Commerce, Economic and Statistics Administration, U.S. Census Bureau.

Rumbaut, R. G., & Ima, K. (1988). *The adaptation of Southeast Asian refugee youth: A comparative study*. U.S. Office of Refugee Resettlement.

Sherman, S. (1988). "The Hmong in America: Laotian refugees in the 'land of the giants.'" *National Geographic, 174*, 586–610.

Tuan, M. (1998). *Forever foreigners or honorary Whites?: The Asian ethnic experience today*. Rutgers University Press.

U.S. Census Bureau. (2010). *2010 U.S. Census interactive population search–Wisconsin* Washington, DC: Government Printing Office. U.S. Census Bureau. Retrieved from http://www.census.gov/2010census/popmap/ipmtext.php?fl=55

Vang, C. Y. (2008). *Hmong in Minnesota*. Minneapolis, MN: Minnesota Historical Society.

Vang, C. Y. (2013). Hmong socioeconomic trends in the U.S. In M. E. Pfeifer & B. K. Thao (Eds.), *State of the Hmong American community* (pp. 21–28). Hmong National Development.

Walker-Moffat, W. (1995). *The other side of the Asian American success story*. Jossey-Bass.

Wing, J. Y. (2007). Beyond black and white: The model minority myth and the invisibility of Asian American students. *The Urban Review, 39*(4), 455–487. https://doi.org/10.1007/s11256-007-0058-6

Wu, F. H. (2002). *Yellow: Race in America beyond black and white*. Basic Books.

Xiong, Y. S. (2013a). An analysis of poverty in Hmong American communities. In M. Pfeifer, M. Chiu, & K. Yang (Eds.), *Diversity in diaspora: Hmong Americans in the twenty-first* century (pp. 66–105). University of Hawaii Press.

Xiong, Y. S. (2013b). Recent changes and remaining challenges in Hmong Americans' educational attainment. In M. E. Pfeifer & B. K. Thao (Eds.), *State of the Hmong American community*. Hmong National Development.

Xiong, Y. S., & Xiong, N. (2011). The prevalence of English monolingualism and its association with generational status among Hmong Americans, 2005–2009. *Hmong Studies Journal, 12*(1), 1–22.

Xiong, Y. S., & Zhou, M. (2006). Six: Structuring inequality: How California selectively tests, classifies, and tracks language minority students. *UCLA School of Public Affairs*. Retrieved from: http://escholarship.org/uc/item/98d66346

Xiong, Z. B, & Huang, J. (2011). Predicting Hmong male and female youth's delinquent behavior: An exploratory study. *Hmong Studies Journal, 12*, 1–34.

Xiong, Z. B., Tuicomepee, A., & Rettig, K. D. (2008). Adolescents' problem behaviors and parent-adolescent conflicts in Hmong immigrant families. *Hmong Studies Journal, 9*, 1–21.

10

Asian American and Native American Pacific Islander Serving Institutions (AANAPISIs)

Serving and Advocating for the Educational Needs of Southeast Asian American Students

MIKE HOA NGUYEN

ABSTRACT

The purpose of this article is to highlight how AANAPISI programs can intentionally design their programming to support Southeast Asian American (SEAA) students, and their responsibility in effectively advocating for them at the policy level. In this effort, this article will first provide a background and an overview of the AANAPISI landscape over the past decade. Then it will focus on one exemplary AANAPISI, providing examples of programmatic mechanisms and efforts used to serve SEAA students. This article concludes by providing recommendations and discussing the implications regarding the role of AANAPISIs in effectively serving and advocating for their SEAA students at the policy level.

INTRODUCTION

In 2007, the College Cost Reduction and Access Act was signed into law, creating the Asian American and Native American Pacific Islander Serving Institutions (AANAPISIs) program. Since then, 35 institutions have received federal funding from the U.S. Department of Education to provide academic and co-curricular programming for Asian American and Pacific Islander (AAPI) students, staff, and faculty (Nguyen, 2019). Perhaps less understood is the intentional focus on the educational experiences and outcomes of Southeast Asian American (SEAA) students at AANAPISIs (Nguyen, 2019; Nguyen et al., 2018). Indeed, the rationale and policy arguments used to advance AANAPISI-based legislative efforts through Congress sought to dispel harmful myths by shedding light on the diversity of the AAPI community and the real educational needs of SEAA students (Park & Chang, 2009). Thus, the creation and inclusion of AANAPISIs among other Minority Serving Institutions (MSI) (e.g., Historically Black Colleges and Universities, Tribal Colleges and Universities, Hispanic Serving Institutions, etc.) is significant for several reasons. First, AANAPISIs demonstrate the federal government's commitment to AAPIs and recognition that they have educational needs (Park & Teranishi, 2008). Furthermore, it acknowledges the diversity and complexity within the AAPI community, rather than being viewed as a static "monolithic monotone" (Lee, 1996). Extending this argument further, the existence of AANAPISIs demonstrates the federal government's commitment to Southeast Asian Americans and their educational needs. However, policy makers still maintain a limited understanding of SEAAs (CARE, 2013a), and possess a limited understanding of the potential for AANAPISIs to support the needs of SEAA students (Park & Chang, 2009; Pimentel & Horikoshi, 2016).

Given that one of the primary arguments used to ensure the passage of AANAPISI legislation focused on dispelling myths about AAPI students and providing resources for these underserved students (i.e., Southeast Asian Americans), what is or should be the role of AANAPISI programs with respect to SEAA students, at both the institutional and policy levels? Thus, the purpose of this article is to highlight how AANAPISI programs can intentionally design their programming to support SEAA students, and their responsibility in effectively advocating for them at the policy level. In this effort, this article will first provide a background and an overview of the AANAPISI landscape over the past decade. Then it will focus on one exemplary AANAPISI, providing examples of programmatic mechanisms and efforts used to serve SEAA students. This article concludes by providing recommendations and discussing the implications regarding the role of AANAPISIs in effectively serving and advocating for their SEAA students at the policy level.[1]

BACKGROUND ON AANAPISIs

Housed and administered by the U.S. Department of Education, the AANAPISI program is a competitive grant that provides federal funding for eligible colleges and universities. Under Title III, Sections 320 and 371 of the Higher Education Act (HEA), colleges and universities, excluding for-profit institutions, are able to apply for and receive the AANAPISI grant under two primary criteria: (a) if 10% of the undergraduate student enrollment identifies as Asian American and Native American and Pacific Islander, and (b) if the institution meets the Section 312(b) basic eligibility criteria of Title III and V programs. To meet the Section 312(b) basic eligibility requirements, the college or university must:

- be an institution of higher education (IHE), as defined in section 101 of the HEA;
- have lower than average educational and general (E&G) expenditures per full-time equivalent (FTE) undergraduate student compared to institutions that offer similar instruction;
- have a requisite enrollment of needy students;
- be legally authorized within its respective state to award bachelor's degrees; be a community college; or be the College of the Marshall Islands, the College of Micronesia/Federated States of Micronesia, or Palau Community College;
- be accredited or making progress toward accreditation by a nationally recognized accrediting agency or association recognized by the Secretary of Education (the Secretary); and
- be located in one of the 50 states, the Commonwealth of Puerto Rico, the District of Columbia, Guam, American Samoa, the United States Virgin Islands, the Commonwealth of the Northern Mariana Islands, or the freely associated states. (Congressional Research Service, 2014, p. 2)

These requirements are often summarized as having an undergraduate student population that is at least 10% Asian American and Pacific Islander, and maintaining a significant proportion of students who are from low socioeconomic backgrounds.

Since 2007, approximately 190 institutions have been eligible to become funded AANAPISIs (Nguyen, 2019). This number has shifted over time, given that eligibility may fluctuate due to dynamic student enrollment patterns and institutional expenditures. Of those 190 colleges and universities, 35 have been awarded the AANAPISI grant and created AANAPISI programs on their campuses (Nguyen, 2019).

Analysis of data from the Integrated Postsecondary Education Data System (IPEDS) indicates that AANAPISIs educate a large proportion of all AAPI undergraduates throughout the country. Nearly 40% of eligible AANAPISIs maintain an AAPI student population over 20%. That figure increases to 57% for funded AANAPISIs. In fall 2017, over one million AAPI undergraduates were enrolled at two-year and four-year institutions across the United States. Eligible and funded AANAPISIs, while comprising only 4.4% of the over 4,000 colleges and universities in the United States, enrolled 37.9% of all AAPI undergraduates, or 412,639 students, in the nation. In other words, over one-third of all current AAPI college students are attending one of the 190 AANAPISIs.

With regard to institutional type, public two-year eligible AANAPISIs enroll the majority of AAPI college students, compared to four-year institutions. However, over the past decade, the proportion of AAPI undergraduate enrollment at four-year eligible AANAPISIs has steadily risen. Additionally, eligible and funded AANAPISIs have played an increasingly critical role in conferring degrees for AAPI students. Of all associate's degrees that were conferred on AAPI college students across the country in 2013, 43.5% of those degrees were conferred at eligible or funded AANAPISIs. Today, that figure has increased to 47.5%. Similarly, in 2013, 28.8% of all baccalaureate degrees conferred at AAPIs were at eligible or funded four-year AANAPISIs. That figure has increased slightly to 29.4% as of 2018. In other words, AANAPISIs are of crucial importance for AAPI college students, as they are enrolling and conferring degrees on large proportions of AAPI students throughout the United States.

However, given that the federal government does not collect or require reporting of disaggregated data from institutions, there is no precise mechanism to determine the percentage of SEAA students that AANAPISIs serve nationally. Nonetheless, researchers have begun to document how AANAPISIs are serving SEAA students at both two-year and four-year institutions (see CARE, 2013b; Nguyen, 2019; Nguyen et al., 2014; Nguyen et al., 2018).

SOUTHEAST ASIAN AMERICANS AND AANAPISIs

The U.S. Department of Education (2016) states that federal funding for AANAPISIs can be used to create or support a large variety of new or existing academic and co-curricular programming, some of which includes:

- Increasing student retention and progression through college level courses by re-engineering student support services and supplemental instruction and providing enhanced faculty professional development;
- Developing a summer bridge program to bridge the gap between two-year and four-year colleges and universities;
- Strengthening assessment and integrating academic advising, academic support, and academic enrichment under a new center;
- Developing faculty development, including workshops in high-impact pedagogies, technology, and instructional methods for teaching under-prepared students;

- Developing an endowment fund to meet ongoing costs for maintenance and upgrades to technology;
- Developing smart classrooms and improvement and technological enhancements to classrooms

Given that this broad mandate does not explicitly dictate or suggest initiatives intended for SEAA students, several AANAPISIs, as previous noted, maintain an explicit focus on SEAA students. AANAPISIs are spread across the United States but can be clustered in regions such as California, Massachusetts, Minnesota, Texas, and Washington, and located near large concentrations of SEAA populations due to refugee resettlement policies and patterns (Kula & Paik, 2016; Nguyen, 2019). One such AANAPISI program, Initiatives to Maximize Positive Academic Achievement and Cultural Thriving, focusing on Asian American and Pacific Islander students (IMPACT AAPI), is located at De Anza College. IMPACT AAPI maintains several distinct initiatives that are specifically geared toward enhancing the educational experiences of SEAA students. The following section will provide greater context and background on De Anza College, as well as detail four specific initiatives (i.e., academic programming, student support services, co-curricular activities, and professional development) for SEAA students that are housed within the AANAPISI program.

INSTITUTIONAL BACKGROUND

De Anza College is located in Santa Clara County, California. According to the U.S. Census Bureau,[2] nearly 750,000 Asian American and Pacific Islanders reside in Santa Clara County, comprising approximately 40% of the county's entire population. Santa Clara County is also home to a large population of Southeast Asian Americans (i.e., Cambodian, Hmong, Laotian, and Vietnamese), who make up a large percentage of the county's AAPI population, 20.7%. Indeed, one in five AAPIs who reside in Santa Clara County identify as Southeast Asian American.

In 2008, De Anza College was awarded AANAPISI funding, making it among the first cohort of institutions to receive the grant. De Anza markets itself as the premier community college in the region and state, with high transfer rates to selective and prestigious four-year universities on the West Coast, while also providing a robust vocational education program. De Anza College maintains a very large student enrollment, nearly 23,000 students, with 800 part-time and full-time faculty members. The college offers 63 different associate's degree programs and 97 certificate programs, and also has an Ethnic Studies program, where several Asian American Studies courses are offered. In fall 2019, AAPI enrollment accounted for over 48% of the total campus population or 9,127 students. Ironically, even with a heavy emphasis on SEAA students through IMPACT AAPI, De Anza College, as a whole, does not publicly report disaggregated enrollment figures. Interestingly, De Anza College does collect disaggregated data from students during the admissions process, but only publicly releases AAPI data in three groups on its website: Asian American (n = 7,723), Filipinx (n = 1,257) and Pacific Islander (n = 147). However, disaggregated data was used within the AANAPISI program to guide programmatic efforts.

INITIATIVES FOR SOUTHEAST ASIAN AMERICANS

De Anza College's AANAPISI program was specifically designed with Southeast Asian American students in mind. Publicly available documents detail IMPACT AAPI's mission to serve Southeast Asian American students. This message permeates throughout the entire AANAPISI and can be found in its physical spaces, course syllabi, and on the website, to name a few. Furthermore, this approach to serving Southeast Asian American students is embedded in the mindset of the faculty and staff who manage the AANAPISI's primary initiatives.

With respect to academic programming, IMPACT AAPI created several new courses that focused on the experiences of Southeast Asians in the United States. These classes were housed within the institution's Asian American Studies program, where readings examined Western colonization and the legacy of the wars in Southeast Asia, as well as contemporary issues for Southeast Asian American communities, both nationally and locally. Furthermore, these classes followed the tradition of ethnic studies and were taught through an interdisciplinary lens that interrogated dominant narratives through critical readings and class discussions about history, literature, public policy, and politics.

IMPACT AAPI's second component was their multipronged student services. Although De Anza already maintains highly robust counseling and student success programs, IMPACT AAPI worked to expand these services specifically for Southeast Asian American students. The student support services were operationalized through embedded counseling, where several AANAPISI staff worked in conjunction with faculty in the Asian American Studies courses to provide real-time counseling and student advising. These staff members, who identify as Southeast Asian American, also taught student success courses that provided SEAA students with culturally relevant academic and life skills, while delivering tutoring services and creating workshops focused on college transfer, applying to scholarships, and career planning.

Some of the AANAPISI program's co-curricular activities were housed at De Anza College's Asian Pacific American Leadership Institute (APALI). Founded prior to receiving the AANAPISI grant, APALI augments the academic work of IMPACT AAPI to provide civic engagement–based programming for students. APALI served as an incubator for AAPI community leaders and public officials within Santa Clara County to network and build community. For students, APALI provided direct opportunities to engage with these leaders through a series of formal and informal co-curricular events, including speaker panels, community visits and trips, internships, and volunteering, among many others. APALI specifically curated these events to ensure that Southeast Asian American leaders and communities were present and represented, in order for SEAA students to see themselves in public service, as elected officials, judges, directors of nonprofit organizations, educators, artists, activist, and community organizers.

IMPACT AAPI's fourth initiative included campus-wide faculty and staff development as well as regional AANAPISI convenings. This programming offered several curriculum-based modules that were focused on underserved and underrepresented AAPI groups, including one module on SEAA students and another on the model minority myth. The modules and workshops were open to all faculty and staff at De Anza College, with the intention to educate the entire faculty and staff corps on the Southeast Asian American refugee experience and its implications for students' educational trajectories. In addition to large format trainings, the modules were also available electronically for faculty and staff to learn about their SEAA students on their own time or remotely. External to De Anza College, IMPACT AAPI also hosted regional convenings with other AANAPISIs in order to share knowledge, resources, and best practices.

As discussed, De Anza College offers an opportunity to examine how institutions can build and direct their AANAPISI programs to develop and educate Southeast Asian American students in holistic ways. Beyond simply providing traditional academic resources or augmenting existing support services for students, IMPACT AAPI relies on several existing institutional mechanisms to create new programming designed intentionally to benefit their Southeast Asian American students. However, achieving these results is no easy task and requires multiple levels of engagement and a real commitment toward SEAA students, especially given the varied institutional and policy barriers that limit an AANAPISI program's ability to engage in this multipronged and interconnected approach.

Effectively Serving and Advocating for SEAA Students at the Policy Level

There is an institutional responsibility to serve and advocate for Southeast Asian American students at the institutional and policy levels. As noted by Park and

Teranishi (2008), AANAPISIs were created for several important reasons. First, AANAPISIs are a *racial project* that "reposition how AAPIs are viewed by carving out a unique space for AAPIs in the American racial landscape" (Park & Teranishi, 2008, pp. 117–118). In other words, the creation of this MSI designation commits to a greater understanding that AAPIs are a highly diverse and distinct racialized minority group. In demonstrating this, and in order to show that AAPIs have unique academic needs, educational data on SEAAs (and NHPIs) was used in policy arguments to sway members of Congress to support AANAPISI legislation (Park & Chang, 2009). Second, and equally important, was that the creation of AANAPISIs works toward the disruption of harmful stereotypes about Asian American and Southeast Asian American students, while providing federal resources to address these issues (Park & Teranishi, 2008).

Given these intended outcomes, there is reasonable justification for AANAPISIs to not only serve, but also to advocate on behalf of SEAA students, ensuring that this federal program lives up to the standard in which it was created. Thus, based upon the institutional and ongoing work at De Anza College, this section extends the efforts of IMPACT AAPI and offers three areas where AANAPISIs can engage policy makers, in order to advance educational opportunities for SEAA students.

First, AANAPISI must disaggregate their data and use these data points to lobby policy makers on the need to require all institutions to collect and disaggregate their data. Most institutions that maintain AANAPISI programs do not collect disaggregated data, and if they do, they often do not report disaggregated AAPI data. Thus, it is incumbent upon AANAPISI programs to do this work. While collecting internal disaggregated data for reporting and accountability purposes (from academic, student services, co-curricular, and professional development), AANAPISI programs should merge their data with institutional-wide datasets from institutional research units. Doing so would provide a more accurate and robust picture of the AAPI students who are served by the AANAPISI program.

Second, AANAPISIs should present this data to policy makers, in order to demonstrate the vast diversity that is unique to AAPI communities, as well as the positive benefits of their program for SEAA students. The mere existence of data on SEAA students may also provide an avenue to secure meetings with relevant policy makers at federal, state, and local jurisdictions. Since AANAPISIs are a federal initiative, it is self-evident that engagement with federal legislators is necessary. However, given that higher education is primarily governed by the state (McGuiness, 2005), and in the case of California community colleges at the local level (Knoell, 1997), AANAPISIs should not limit themselves to just one tier of government. State and local policy makers must also be informed about the important work that AANAPSIs are engaged in, especially with respect to SEAA students. Additionally, this provides an opportunity for state and local policy makers to become champions of AANAPISI programs and collaborate with AANAPISIs when advocating at the federal level.

Finally, AANAPISIs must coalesce in order to develop an advocacy organization that is similar to what already exists for their counterpart MSIs. Indeed, there are existing associations and organizations that are engaging in this work on behalf of AANAPISIs, yet none have emerged as the primary organization committed to this work. Although many of these associations and organizations may be the ideal vehicle for these efforts, leadership and governance must flow from the 35 funded AANAPISIs in order to create an advocacy arm that can then be housed at one of the existing associations or organizations. Only then will there be a sophisticated apparatus that can adequately advocate for the necessary resources that will ensure that AANAPISIs can live up to their historical mission of serving underrepresented and underresourced AAPI students, especially those who identify as SEAA.

As AANAPISIs celebrate and surpass their 10-year anniversary, recommitting to their true purpose would greatly strengthen the ability of those who shape academic and co-curricular programming at these colleges and universities. This approach would also create the opportunity to advance new advocacy efforts that would inform the work of those charged with overseeing AANAPISIs at the federal, state, and local levels. Doing so will provide new tools for AANAPISIs to better serve and support the educational experiences and trajectories of Southeast Asian American students in higher education and beyond.

PUBLICATION NOTE

This article was published online in 2020 by the *Journal of Southeast Asian American Education and Advancement* in Volume 15, Issue 2. Minor edits have been made here. The original can be found at http://doi.org/10.7771/2153-8999.1205.

NOTES

1. It is important to note that AANAPISIs, both as a policy and as an institutional program, were also created to serve Native Hawaiian and Pacific Islander (NHPI) students. This cannot be understated. However, given the scope of this journal, this article will focus on the role of AANAPISIs in serving Southeast Asian American students.
2. 2013–2017, American Community Survey, 5-year estimates.

REFERENCES

Congressional Research Service (2014). *Programs for minority-serving institutions under the Higher Education Act*. Washington, DC: Author.

Knoell, D. M. (1997). California community colleges. *Community College Journal of Research and Practice, 21*(2), 121–136. https://doi.org/10.1080/1066892970210204

Kula, S. M., & Paik, S. J. (2016). A historical analysis of Southeast Asian refugee communities: Post-war acculturation and education in the United States. *Journal of Southeast Asian American Education and Advancement, 11*(1), 1–27. http://doi.org/10.7771/2153-8999.1127

Lee, S. J. (1996). *Unraveling the "model minority" stereotype: Listening to Asian American youth*. Teachers College Press.

McGuiness, A. (2005). The states and higher education. In P. G. Altbach, R. O. Berdahl, & P. J. Gumport (Eds.), *American higher education in the twenty-first century: Social, political, and economic challenges* (pp. 198–225). Johns Hopkins University Press.

National Commission on Asian American and Pacific Islander Research in Education (CARE). (2013a). *iCount: A data quality movement for Asian Americans and Pacific Islanders in higher education.*

National Commission on Asian American and Pacific Islander Research in Education (CARE). (2013b). *Partnership for Equity in Education through Research (PEER): Findings from the first year of research on AANAPISIs.*

Nguyen, B. M. D., Nguyen, M. H., & Nguyen, T. L. K. (2014). Advancing the Asian American and Pacific Islander data quality campaign: Data disaggregation practice and policy. *Harvard Asian American Policy Review, 24*, 55–67.

Nguyen, M. H. (2019). *Building capacity at Asian American and Native American Pacific Islander serving institutions (AANAPISI): Cultivating leaders and civic engagement through federal policy* [Unpublished doctoral dissertation]. University of California, Los Angeles.

Nguyen, T. H., Nguyen, M. H., Nguyen, B. M. D., Gasman, M., & Conrad, C. (2018). From marginalized to validated: An in-depth case study of an Asian American, Native American and Pacific Islander serving institution. *The Review of Higher Education, 41*(3), 327–363. https://doi.org/10.1353/rhe.2018.0011

Park, J. J., & Chang, M. J. (2009). AAPI serving institutions: The motivations and challenges behind seeking a federal designation. *AAPI Nexus: Asian Americans & Pacific Islanders Policy Practice and Community, 7*(2), 107–125. https://doi.org/10.36650/nexus7.2_107-128_ParkChang

Park, J. J., & Teranishi, R. T. (2008). Asian American and Pacific Islander serving institutions: Historical perspectives and future prospects. In M. Gasman, B. Baez, & C. S. V.

Turner (Eds.), *Understanding minority-serving institutions* (pp. 111–126). State University of New York Press.

Pimentel, L. M., & Horikoshi, N. (2016). Educational opportunity and the missing minority in higher education: Changing the national narrative of Asian Americans and Pacific Islanders by 2040. *Asian American and Pacific Islanders Nexus: Policy, Practice and Community, 14*(1), 66–77. https://doi.org/10.17953/nx.014.01.66

U.S. Department of Education. (2016). *Asian American and Native American Pacific Islander-Serving Institutions program: 11. What are a few concrete examples of allowable activities?* Retrieved from: https://www2.ed.gov/programs/aanapi/faq.html#q11

11

Vietnamese American Women Public School Administrators Leading for Social Justice and Equity

JIA GRACE LIANG

ABSTRACT

In the field of educational leadership, little is known about Southeast Asian American women's perspectives and experiences as school leaders. Studies that explore the roles of Southeast Asian American women school administrators in leading for social justice are virtually nonexistent. The current study was guided by the paradigm of transnational feminism. This qualitative multicase study draws on retrospective accounts of two Vietnamese American women school administrators in a Southern state and a Midwestern state to understand the ways in which they navigate intersectional stereotypes in their leadership context to advocate for and create conditions for educational equity for their socioculturally and linguistically diverse students and families.

INTRODUCTION

Despite being the fastest growing population in the United States with a projected 200% growth rate by the year 2050 (USCB, 2011), Asian Americans continue to represent a small segment of the teaching force, unable to keep pace with the growing rates of Asian American students in the K–12 educational pipeline (Chong, 2002). The limited literature on Asian Americans in the teaching force and educational leadership has focused on the Chinese, Japanese, and South Korean ethnic groups (Endo, 2015; Goodwin et al., 2005; Pacis, 2005; Park, 2009). Furthermore, almost all the literature on discrimination toward Asian Americans and associated with race, gender, and nation/immigration status in the field of education has focused on students or education of the pan-ethnic group (Fan, 2009; Lew, 2006; Uy, 2008; Wright & Boun, 2011); there are a few exceptions that specifically attend to Southeast Asian Americans (e.g., Ngo & Lee, 2007) or Pacific Islanders (e.g., Pang & Cheng, 1998; Pang et al., 2011). In this paper, while it is not my intention to take lightly the reality that Asian Americans continue to be marginalized or excluded in policy discussions to diversify the teaching and leading forces (Museus, 2009; Wu, 2014), it is my intention to argue that it is equally critical to recognize and honor the unique and complex history, experience, culture, agency, and contributions of Southeast Asian Americans—one that is often rendered invisible under the pan-ethnic category of Asian Americans or essentialized as one-dimensionally and pathologically "at risk," as portrayed in the dominant refugee discourse about the group.

In the field of educational leadership, little is known about Southeast Asian American women's perspectives and experiences as school leaders. Studies that explore the roles of Southeast Asian American women school administrators in leading for social justice are virtually nonexistent. The sparse literature available on Asian American educators in general and Southeast Asian Americans in particular has been a case in which researchers have situated their work in the long cultural history of experiences of close-knit immigrant communities in regions such as the coastal states in the United States (Nguyen, 2008; Pang, 2009). The study reported here drew on retrospective accounts of two Vietnamese American women school administrators in a Southern state and a Midwestern state to understand the ways in which they have navigated intersectional stereotypes in their leadership context to advocate for and create conditions for educational equity for their socioculturally and linguistically diverse students and families. In contrast to a locale such as California, the two women have assumed leadership in a context where even the presence of the general Asian American communities is limited, affecting the likely supplies of social capital and conditions for access to, advancement in, and enactment of leadership in educational systems.

SOUTHEAST ASIAN AMERICANS AND VIETNAMESE AMERICANS

Under the banner of Southeast Asian Americans are ethnically diverse groups comprised of Vietnamese, Chinese, Thai, Khmer (Cambodian), Laotians, Hmong, Mien, and other ethnic minority tribes. Each group has their rich and distinct sociocultural and linguistic backgrounds, and other traditions and histories. Nonetheless, the majority of Southeast Asian Americans shares a common immigration history, which is known as the Vietnam War (1954–1975). The U.S. government's military and political attempts to control the perceived spread of communism in the region produced a massive refugee population (Grewal, 2005). As a result, between 1975 and 1994, the United States received over 1,250,000 refugees from Southeast Asia. The Geneva Convention defines a refugee as "someone who is unable or unwilling to return to their country of origin owing to a well-founded fear of being persecuted for reasons of race, religion, nationality, membership of a particular social group, or political opinion" (UNHCR, 1951).

According to Takaki (1989), there were only several hundred people of Vietnamese descent living in the United States about half century ago. Since the end of the Vietnam War in 1975 when 130,000 Vietnamese entered the United States as refugees, the Vietnamese immigrant population has increased from 20,000 a year to 29,000 a year (Yamane, 2012). Today, Vietnamese Americans are the fourth largest Asian American ethnic group behind the Chinese, Asian Indians, and Filipinos. In examining 2000 Census data, Yamane (2012) found that Vietnamese immigrants, male and female, are significantly much less likely to hold managerial and supervisory positions than comparable East European immigrants. The glass ceiling for Vietnamese Americans is not restricted to any part of the country (Yamane, 2012). Foreign-born Vietnamese women face even more wage discrimination than Vietnamese men (Yamane, 2012). Furthermore, research on Southeast Asians residing in the United States is limited and predominantly casts this population as "problems," noting high poverty, lack of education, drug and/or alcohol issues, high youth pregnancy rate, youth delinquency, gang activities and violence, and economic instability (Lee, 1994; Morrow, 1989). Such phenomena have been critiqued by critical refugee studies scholars as not only partial but also pathological representations of the populations and their traditions/cultures (Espiritu, 2014; Espiritu & Duong, 2018; Um, 2012). Moreover, such portrayals of Southeast Asian American refugees are racialized and gendered, where girls and women are biopolitically articulated as subjects of violence needing the protection of the Westerners, and boys are cast as prone to acting on violence and as such posing a potential risk or threat to themselves and others—leading to manufactured justifications for harsh disciplinary actions such as incarceration (Grewal, 2005).

The current study was informed by the paradigm of transnational feminism, an anchoring epistemological point, albeit not necessarily in the exact vocabularies/terminologies, from which the two women administrators in the study have approached their work at their schools. Built upon postcolonial feminist theories, transnational feminism further complicates global capitalism and neoliberalism by taking an intersectional approach to understand gender, the state, race, class, and sexuality and their roles in problematizing and resisting the ideologies, structures, and practices of patriarchal and capitalist power (Alexander & Mohanty, 1997, 2010; Grewal & Kaplan, 1994; Mohanty, 2003). The present article aims to extend our collective understanding of leadership of Southeast Asian American women in education. As such, I explore the complexities of the two Vietnamese American women administrators' being and leading in the mainstream classroom, namely, (a) the women's negotiation of racialized and gendered expectations across administrative roles, (b) the women's orientation to leadership and its development, and (c) the interplay between (a) and (b) in the women's actualization of social justice in leading.

RESEARCH METHODOLOGY AND CONTEXT

The current study draws upon existing data from a larger study that examined the experience of Asian American women administrators of K–12 public schools in multiple states. Purposive sampling (Patton, 2002) was used for participant selection in the larger study to recruit Asian American women school administrators who are able and willing to share with the research team their development of, orientation to, and experiences of leading in schools. Intentional effort was made to maximize the variation in geographic location, immigrant generational status, and ethnicity. Due to the lack of public information available on the group, the research team had to rely on personal and professional connections with multiple agencies and professional networks to conduct the initial recruitment and purposive sampling procedure. In the end, the larger study included three states (one Southern state and two Midwestern states) and participants from seven Asian ethnic groups (Chinese, Korean, Japanese, Thai, Vietnamese, Indian, and Filipino). During the data collection and preliminary data analysis stage, it became apparent that the two women administrators included in this paper not only self-identified as Southeast Asian Americans but also were very articulate about refugee experiences, specifically how such identification and "transnational journeys" have shaped their orientation to, development of, and enactment of leadership in relation to their refugee and other minoritized students and their families. Further, these two women administrators' self-reported commitment to social justice and equity were supported by the verification and recommendation the research team received from their colleagues. As such, for the purposes of this study, the

TABLE 11.1. PARTICIPANT DEMOGRAPHICS

	LINH	PUONG
Grade Level	Middle	High
Years of Experience in Education	> 20	> 20
Years of Experience in Administration*	> 5 but < 10	> 10
Years in Current Position	about 6	about 10
Highest Educational Level	Master's	Doctoral
Immigrant Generational Status	1.5 Generation	1st Generation
Age	50+	late 40s

Note: *Administrative experiences include the women's years as department chair, program coordinator, and curriculum coach, to name a few. The term 1.5-generation immigrants refers to those who migrated to the United States between the ages of 6 and 13, and the first generation refers to those who migrated as adults (Rumbaut & Rumbaut, 1976; Zhou, 1997).

two Vietnamese American women assistant principals served as instrumental cases to gain deeper knowledge of a particular event or context (Stake, 2006), that is, Southeast Asian American women leading for social justice in urban schools. A case, defined as a bounded system, is to provide a deeper understanding not only of the context but also of the issues that define the context (Stake, 2006). Each woman assistant principal represents a case.

The two women, Linh and Puong (pseudonyms), though they shared a strong commitment to leadership for social justice as evident in the data, represented much contextualized understanding of and distinct paths to leadership for social justice. They had certain commonalities and variations in their demographic and professional backgrounds (see Table 11.1). The two schools they served as assistant principal shared certain characteristics but differed in others (see Table 11.2).

Semistructured in-depth interviews (Rubin & Rubin, 2005) and field observations were conducted. Also collected were archival data on schools. I developed reflective memos throughout the fieldwork and analysis. Data analysis was ongoing. In the first cycle of coding, an "initial coding" method, incorporated with in vivo and process coding, was used to develop categories and subcategories from codes and iteratively revised codes or categories (Saldaña, 2016). In the second cycle, a "pattern coded" method was used to develop initial themes (Saldaña, 2016). Furthermore, an adapted constant comparative method (Strauss & Corbin, 1990) was used to generate themes within and across each case and to compare data with the literature and theoretical frameworks to look for consistencies and discrepancies. Trustworthiness of the research was addressed by the use of multiple sources of evidence, use of extensive analytic memos, and member check (Lincoln & Guba, 1985).

TABLE 11.2. SCHOOL CHARACTERISTICS

		SCHOOL	STUDENTS				TEACHERS
ENTITY NAME	ENROLLMENT	TITLE I?	% ENGLISH LEARNERS	% FR/R LUNCHES	LARGEST ETHNIC GROUP	% MINORITY	NUMBER OF TEACHERS
Linh's School	568	Yes	2.0	60.0	White	30.0	36
District A	29K		20.1	59.0	White	45.0	2.1K
Southern State	1,634K		8.1	57.0	White	56.0	115K
Puong's School	574	Yes	7.7	100	Black	100	38
District B	28.9K		11.0	75.0	Black	89.0	2.2K
Midwest State	918K		3.2	51.3	White	26.3	66.2K

Note: For parsimony reasons, numbers are rounded up by thousands, when applicable. Fr/R: Free and reduced priced.

FINDINGS

Two prominent themes emerged from the data. The first theme speaks to the impactful effects of displacement that the women and their families have experienced as they migrated into the United States as refugees on the women's perspectives on identity, education, and leadership.

Both women spoke about the years of struggles that their families as a whole had faced once they "landed" in the United States. Despite their credentials and successful careers in the past, the women's parents were no longer recognized as highly skilled professionals in "this new land called the United States." "Everything seemed to be stripped away from us except for that we were known as refugees," Linh commented. Similarly, Puong remembered seeing her parents working multiple part-time jobs just to barely make ends meet. The fact was that, before the war, Puong's father was a flight attendant in Vietnam and was fluent in French and English; her mother was a French teacher. "They [her parents] just did not have the time and energy; I mean, they would have wanted to, like attending school events, checking on us about our school work," Puong shared; she and her other five siblings learned to rely on one another. Puong further noted, "And we were the only few Asian kids in the school; a lot of time they [the administrators and teachers] didn't know how to deal with us." Likewise, Linh commented that her parents "really did not have the financial means for [her and her seven siblings] to explore anything else other than to go to school and go home." "We were pretty much swimming and sinking together as siblings, and we all struggled in schools," Linh said, "but all of us did make it to college." The families' encounters with discriminatory employment situations did not stop them from putting a high value on education. Both women emphasized that their parents insisted on them doing well in school and provided every bit of means they could afford to support them. Education, as the women put it, was important and had become even more important as the families regarded it as "the way out of poverty" after they were in the United States. Yet, quality education was robbed from the children like the women in this study.

Both women noted the negative and subpar experiences they had with American schools. Puong mentioned that her accent was ridiculed and she was bullied without intervention from the teachers and staff in schools:

> The teachers and adults in charge never reprimanded the teens for the harassment and the bullying that they did to me in the hallways, even though they witnessed the acts many times. Either they looked away, though at times I had eye contact with them asking for help, or they just shooed the students along to the classes.

Puong explained that at the time, she and her siblings were the only English as Second or Other Languages (ESOL) students in the school, and they did not have any programs to support their needs. Linh's experience was similar. Her teachers "did not know what to do with [her and her siblings]"; what they did was "cut down the number of problems" or "skip assignments," and "that was about it." Even today, Linh remembered vividly that she "was crying every night with [her] big fat dictionary." "I missed out a lot [of] curriculum because of how they did with us as the non-English proficient. I was struggling big time," Linh stated. "So, by the time I got to high school, it was time to pick a major. My dream was to become a teacher; it was just shattered." Not only were the English language curriculum and instruction inadequate, to say the least; the curricular in other subjects were also culturally insensitive and often a product of a colonial gaze (Grewal, 2005). For instance, Puong recalled,

> Learning about the Vietnam War was such an uncomfortable unit for me. I sat through the lessons feeling so uptight with anxiety, not knowing what the teacher and the classmates thought of me. I avoided looking at the history clips my teacher put on the screen.

The U.S. educational system was not established and operates with "all children are equal in mind" as critical scholars have pointed out the low expectations and education debt that minority students are subjected to (Ladson-Billings, 2006; Park et al., 2009).

As teenagers, the women learned what the "refugee" label meant and experienced the in- between space (Grewal, 2006; Mohanty, 2003); they had constantly to negotiate what "I" meant for themselves and how "I" was expected from them by others, the dominant group, and the sociopolitical circumstances in the state-nation arenas. At times, as a coping mechanism, the women would try to escape the negativity associated with being labeled a refugee by behaving more like a "model minority," a seemingly "positive" image of Asian Americans. Puong shared:

> The Vietnam War had left a forever mark on me. You know, people ask the where-are-you-from question; I would say, "I came from China." I chose China as a temporary homeland because I believed that most Americans associated the Vietnamese with savages from the images that were portrayed in movies and media at the time. I denied my roots because I did not want to be labeled as savage. I was *13* then.

Linh ended up choosing a STEM major, noting, "I played it safe by choosing software engineering in my undergraduate studies; you know, that was expected—model minorities . . . do well in math and science; so, no question, no hassle."

These autobiographic and schooling experiences have taught the women that they are always racialized, transnational subjects in U.S. society. That has played an undeniable role in shaping the women's aspiration for leadership. They were keenly aware that they were the few, if not the only, "of [their] kind" in a space predominantly occupied by people who do not look like them. Puong noted:

> It was almost a decade before I stepped into the entry level of educational leadership role of an instructional coach in the same district I taught. I was not surprised to learn that I was the only Asian American in [a] leadership role in the district, period. That was 2008, and our district was one of the biggest districts in the Midwest.

Linh also came to educational leadership late in age as she had a different career before, not necessarily by choice, as noted above. Nonetheless, she never gave up; once she learned that she could do so through alternative licensure, she went back and got her teaching credential. "That was my best decision; I never looked back." Linh said. For both women, becoming a school administrator was a way to make a difference and do so on a larger scale beyond their respective classrooms as a teacher. The following quote well captured Puong's reason for pursuing leadership:

> Throughout my life, especially in those teaching years, I often found myself having to pick a side, either siding with the White or the Black, but I am neither. I knew how that felt even as a child; I just did not have the language. When I was in my doctoral program, I learned about Black women, how they could and had transformed the power that was intended as a mechanism for oppression into an effective vehicle for change. "They rock the boat and stay in the boat." [Lorde, 1984] Could Asian American women, a Vietnamese American woman like me, rock the boat and stay in the boat?

What Puong referred to was the notion of "tempered radicalism" by Meyerson and Scully (1995), where people who are tempered radicals are "individuals who identify with and are committed to their organizations and also to a cause, community, or ideology that is fundamentally different from, and possibly at odds with, the dominant culture of their organization" (Meyerson & Scully, 1995, p. 586). Likewise, Linh believed that change, especially those demanding systemic shifts in mind and action, demands "dare to dream." She stressed,

> Because the existing systems are not equitable—you know the saying, "The master's tools will never dismantle the master's house" [Lorde, 1984]; we have to have hope and courage to envision something different, non-exist, and we have to be brave

> enough to act on them. This may sound cliché, but I am mother to two beautiful daughters; and my students are my children too. Am I selfish or greedy by wanting all of them to grow up knowing they can be anything they want to be?! And having quality education that allows them to do so?! Despite the obstacles that they may have?!

Both women's perspectives on leadership showed a strong orientation to social justice. When asked how she would define leadership, Linh shared, "Leadership is not about a position. For me, it is an outlet that allows me to turn my love for and commitment to the minoritized children to real actions." "To make a difference; to level the playground as much as I can." Linh further added, "Honestly, it really started simply as, 'I see myself in them.' I couldn't pretend that our educational systems treat every child the same. They are NOT." Likewise, in addition to being very intentional in choosing a social justice–oriented doctoral program to get her leadership degree, Puong was also very adamant in the type of schools where she wanted to work as a teacher and later a school administrator. "I am not saying one can't do social justice work in other types of schools, the well-resourced, the quote-and-quote 'well-performed' . . . it is just not for me. They don't need *me*. You know what I mean." Puong noted, "*My* kids, I mean the students I have taught and served, they—I want to be there *with them and for them*."

Furthermore, the women administrators believed that the experiential relatability and affective connections they had with their minoritized students and families not only played an undeniable role in first igniting their interest in leadership but more importantly became "the moral grounding," as Linh put it, over the years to sustain them through challenges and tough times. In their entrance to and advancement in leadership, the two women administrators received no mentorship. "No one really took interest in me and took me under their wings. I guess, they look at me and thought, I was *too* different," Puong said. Later in the interview, Puong also shared, "All these years, I still have to remind myself from time to time that why I am here and for whom—I am a human; I get fatigue and feel drained fighting injustice. My students give me the best reason to keep fighting." Likewise, Linh had to rely on herself: "You know that kind of feelings? Feeling so lonely and invisible even when you are surrounded by people? I didn't have those people, what you call, mentors or sponsors who wanted to help and groom me to be an administrator." Linh explained, "You just couldn't help but wonder, why is that? Can't you see that I have the passion? I want to be better for the kids." Linh credited her being very observant as an important means with which she developed her leadership capacity, besides formal education received from her credential programs. While Linh still considered herself a "shy and introvert" person, she remarked that her love for her students gave her strength to be "outspoken" and "fearless":

> There were suspicions, accusations from some parents, staff . . . I had a personal agenda. I felt so hurt; after all I have done, how could they not see that I care about the kids, the school so much and put in a lot work. . . . But, in my heart, I have never changed a bit—I am here to serve the kids. That makes it easier to accept what is going on. I mean, if fighting a lifetime battle for justice means that my career will take a hit along the way, then I am okay with it.

Moreover, often as the only or one of the few Asian Americans, not to mention Southeast Asian Americans, in their schools and districts, the two women were subjected to constant scrutiny and questioning regarding their leadership competency and their authority as an administrator. Puong mentioned that, after many years of being an administrator, she still encounters circumstances where people automatically disqualified her as a school leader because of her "darker skin" as a Southeast Asian female, speaking English with an accent, and having a "soft communicative style." For instance, she recalled attending a district meeting where the office clerk thought she worked at the cafeteria:

> She [the clerk] told me that I was in the wrong place, even when I had my name tag on. I did not react as I was shocked as in disbelief. Then she raised her voice, "Do you understand me?" Really? Supposing that I did not understand English, but I am not deaf!

Both women were aware of the stereotypes associated with Asian American women in general and Southeast Asian women specifically. For instance, Linh said,

> The stereotypes of Asian American women are that she is docile, weak, and quiet like a demure wife, or she is manipulative or an overachiever who goes to the Ivy League schools for all her education. When it comes to Southeast Asian women, people tend to associate us with limited education, ambition, and independence; they don't think of us as intelligent; they see us as speaking broken English and working in low-paying jobs such as laundromats. You know, we, Vietnamese Americans, are called "boat people" by the mainstream media. Is that ironic or what? Like we did not have a life in a country full of culture and history before war and being forced to exit and come to America!

Linh recalled that at meetings, some male colleagues would not even formally introduce themselves to her even after she had introduced herself to them. "You could say that they did not know what to make of me. This body of mine was not supposed to be in 'their space'—the space called administration." Linh stated, "It was not what they expected of a Vietnamese American woman." Both women administrators spoke about having to walk a fine line of being viewed as either "too soft" or being "too demanding"—in other words, too manly or un-womanlike. At times, they had to "be really articulate or really assertive in order to make a point and to be heard." The women administrators noted that male leaders were treated differently and certain leadership styles were valued more. For instance, Puong remembered:

> People above me thought that I was too soft or too friendly. . . . I feel like the mainstream culture depicts a different set of criteria. People tend to view an assertive leader as being authoritative or potentially an influential icon. . . . Male administrators have more permission or are more accepted, if they start to sound a little more sophisticated right off the bat. They can be direct and they are allowed to say the things that they want to say right off the bat, with no patting.

And yet, when the women administrators' approaches or styles were more forthright, they were perceived to be "unnecessarily perfectionist," "coming [on] too strong," and needed to "soften up."

The second theme relates to the two women leaders strategically breaking the silence of Southeast Asian refugee experiences to create space for collective remembering, redefining, and healing. They are able to do so because they understand such silence and are willing to be vulnerable by relying on their own personal experiences as refugees and Vietnamese American women to connect and build a community. Further, they have exerted their commitment to and actualization of social justice through critical care as manifested in *high expectations*, *nurturing resilience*, and *promoting communal/critical pedagogies*.

Linh recalled growing up her parents rarely talked about the war and all the losses they (and their extended families) had borne. As noted by critical refugee scholars (Espiritu, 2014; Espiritu & Duong, 2018), the generation that came of age postwar faced the "fractures caused by these traumas [that] live on in the forms of silences and erasures in published forms of history as well as within the families who survived these traumas" (Chuong, 2019, p. 7). Linh stated,

> That was something we, I mean myself and my siblings, just knew not to go there. We understood that as my parents tried to protect us from all the violence [that] occurred and pains could be inflicted by telling us what happened. We understood very early on that our parents have given up so much so that we could have a better life in this new land. The lost would never be recovered and has left wounds forever deep and raw.

Likewise, Puong shared such experiences of losing loved ones in the extended families. These common narratives shared by the two participants speak directly to the phenomenon of normalizing silence that is significant to the Southeast Asian American community, when members only understand the silences as trauma-filled (Chuong, 2019). And yet, more importantly, as critical refugee scholars and Southeast Asian American studies scholars highlight the tensions of remembering and existing in silence (Espiritu, 2014; Um, 2012), arguing that silences are not an absence of telling; instead, they communicate history from one generation to the next. The women had developed different ways of remembering and existing in such appeared-to-be silence. Though she could not recall what triggered it, Puong began to journal about things that happened and her thoughts after a few years in the United States. It has become what she called "a safe place for 'me-and-me' dialogues." "I guess I was trying to figure who I am; you know, as a teenager I was curious and confused," Puong stated. "Sometimes they saw me as this poor refugee kid, clueless and needed all the help they could give me; then other times, they expected me to be a math whiz, excelling [at] everything. But I was neither." For Puong, journaling was a channel for the then young her to process her racialized and transnational experiences under the dominant biopolitical and geopolitical discourses in the United States. It wasn't until about over a decade ago, when she enrolled in a doctoral seminar, that she found a language for that. "My stories reflect what underlies CRT [critical race theory]," Puong noted. "There is a part about being Asian Americans in a white dominant society; and there is a part about Southeast Asian Americans, our shared forced departure and loss, materially and psychologically, and generations of rebuilding, reidentifying, and reliving."

In Puong's school, under her leadership, "a quiet room" was established for students and their families if they would like some quiet time individually or collectively. Faculty and students (and families) knew she writes personal journals and understood that the room signals her and the school's commitment to "recognize and acknowledge one's stories and pains, one's individual and collective journey to memory, awareness, and agency." With the support from the principal, Puong made sure that they would have at least two guest speakers from the communities of color invited to the school for teachers and/or students, sharing their social justice perspectives and advocacy work. Gradually, Puong was able to change how holidays such as Black History Month or Columbus Day were celebrated in her school. The celebrations were no longer just superficial food events and/or with people dressing up in traditional clothing; rather, revisiting the history behind the holiday and addressing modern-day manifestations of such oppressive "legacies" were the focus and made into activities such as mini theaters so that the participants could have embodied experiences of remembering, reflecting, and honoring. When it comes to students, there was nothing small. Puong's own experiences of being "Other" have led her to be very conscious of such othering practices

(Kumashiro, 2000). For instance, Puong recalled the following instance that happened at a leadership team meeting:

> The accountability report was passed around. For the demographic data section, the races of students were listed as Asian, Black, Hispanic, American Indian, White, and Other. The word "Other" caught my attention immediately. . . . I had to say something. Could we stop reporting "Other" in our demographic section? How difficult is it to count for one school? We do it with Whites, Blacks, Hispanics, . . . ; we can do the same for the students who are classified as "Other." "Why? That's how the district reports . . . " an administrative staff [member] interrupted. "We need to start here at our school and now." I did not budge. It's not a good feeling knowing that you're being classified as "Other." I was one of them. Are we saying to these students that they are less a human being than the other races or ethnicities?

Informed by her own critical consciousness, Puong was able to problematize the norms and reject creating "the minoritized within the minorities"—one that is not alien to Southeast Asian Americans' experiences (Espiritu, 2014; Ngo & Lee, 2007; Um, 2012). Furthermore, though working as an assistant principal in a majority African American/Black neighborhood, rather than being handicapped by her perceived racial difference from the community, Puong's literacy in her racial self and the ways schools operate in racialized contexts enabled her to recognize their shared history at the intersections of race and immigration and use such collective memories for building alliances with the Black communities she serves.

Like Puong, Linh's leadership and advocacy for her minoritized students clearly echoed the notion of storytelling as "a feminist praxis of intimacy, [where] alternative intergenerational memories are created to break silences and simultaneously create communal intimacy/connections as a force of resilience" (Chuong, 2019, p. 13). Though she did not necessarily use the exact language of storytelling, Linh's ways of relationship building, community-based empowerment, and healing were anchored on collectivity, criticality, and self-agency. In Linh's school, the top three languages represented were English, Spanish, and Vietnamese. With a substantial refugee student population, Linh understood that many of her staff (predominantly white) were not prepared to educate, support, and empower their students with their mainstream teacher preparations. In addition, to insist on high expectations for all students, Linh had to be creative in obtaining external resources such as applying for grants to support continuous professional development for her staff—which she sort of jokingly called "reprograming," to challenge their discriminatory way of thinking and practice, be it unconsciously or seemingly well intentioned. She was able to secure partnerships with local businesses to help with scholarships so that the children whose families were underresourced could go on field trips. She was able to use a small grant secured from a nonprofit organization to send her social studies teachers to workshops that were organized by Vietnamese advocacy organizations so that they could bring back "the community's perspectives" and included and centered them in the curriculum. Recognizing that many of her students of color were also caretakers for their younger siblings and language brokers for their non-English-speaking parents, Linh, in collaboration with her principal and English language teachers primarily as well as some other staff, had secured donated appliances and volunteers from the neighboring communities and enterprises. These resources were used to create an after-school center, where the students and their families could get assistance in things like homework, laundry, document filing, and baby-sitting. Also, Linh was not afraid to challenge the status quo of knowledge production—that is, who is the legitimate knowledge producer and what is the legitimate knowledge. Over the years, she made one consistent request in her welcome-back message to all her students: "Cherish your intergenerational memory. Keep it alive and strong by talking to your parents, elders, extended families, and/or someone you look up to *in your community*." Such a practice is critical; according to Chuong (2019), for "many of the displaced and oppressed, the history of one's community is what lives on in intergenerational memory. As such, as one engages in ethnic culture and doing memory work can lead to liberation and empowerment" (p. 13).

Both Linh and Puong learned from their minority status to reject deficit thinking about their minoritized students and families; their personal awareness of and experiences with the agony of multiple injustices had helped them to appreciate diversity more. Both women displayed a genuine concern for their students' well-being and trusted their students' abilities to learn, showing sensitivity toward their students and the community's social concerns. The women had high expectations for their students. For instance, Puong would openly celebrate every accomplishment, small or big, any one of her students had, as part of her routine morning announcements. Over the years, she had used up eight thick notebooks filled with such information. "I want them [her students of color] to know they can be anything they want to be. They are much more sharper and resilient than the society, I mean, many people would give them credit for," Puong shared. The two women wanted the best for their students, especially the minoritized, and the most rewarding thing was to see their students succeed academically and in life. Ensuring their students had caring and quality teachers was noted by both women as their high priorities. While acknowledging hiring (and discharging as well) a faculty member or staff was rarely a straightforward and simple task without extraneous intervening factors, both Linh and Puong stressed the importance of one's having "right mind and heart." For instance, one of the documents shared by Linh was her notes from a teacher candidate interview. The notes did not contain any personally identifiable information, but what stood out for me was some of the questions she asked, for example, "How would you define 'hope'?" "Could you tell me what 'an ideal student' would be like for you and why?" Furthermore, the two women administrators were cognitive that they, at times, were "quiet" about the discrimination and injustice toward themselves. "That is a sacrifice, for lack of a better term, that I have decided to [bear] some years ago. I learned the lesson the hard way when I was still a teacher; I thought my passion could overcome anything." Linh shared, "Why would anyone want justice and equity for all children? Did we all say that? I was not re-hired. Now, what? I couldn't do anything for those kids I cared [about] so much and was trying to fight for." Puong had similar comments:

> I am much bolder when it comes to advocate and fight for my students and parents. Over the years, I have learned to do so very intentionally and strategically. Being an administrator gives me entry to spaces that I would not have otherwise; I am not gonna give it up easily, not for something related or about me. I am gonna use that for my kids.

The two women did so as "choosing your battle wisely" so that they could "remain [in] their seats [at] the decision-making table," as Linh put it, to advocate for their refugee and minoritized students and their families. This is not to suggest that such approach or "inaction" had no consequences, but rather, it shows the women understood the discriminatory nature of the educational systems and had to learn to negotiate and push through in actualizing their commitment to social justice leadership.

CONCLUSION

This study contributes to the larger body of research on women in educational leadership by filling the significant gap in the literature on Southeast Asian American women school leaders. The findings have high relevancy for schools today where the student populations become more and more diverse and challenges encountered become increasingly complex and with enduring impacts, in that they shed light on how these women negotiate their racial-ethnic and professional roles within the educational systems, and how they lead and navigate the landscape of school administration for educational equity. Also, the findings from this study have important implications for leadership development—the field can benefit from raising consciousness of nation, race-ethnicity, and gender in future and current school leaders; the field needs to recruit and develop leaders who embrace and exercise criticality in consciousness, exerting their leadership to establish culture and practice in schools that bring equity and justice.

To conclude, I use a poem entitled "Home We Made" to honor the bravery and resilience of these women leaders and the Vietnamese American community. The poem was inspired by the artwork by Trinh Mai, a Vietnamese American artist, the presentation by Yến Lê Espiritu,[1] a Vietnamese American critical scholar, and mostly the stories and spirit shared by my participants, aspirations for me and many.

where is home?
black hole, sucking every bit of breath, memory, life boat, floating, see no ends or land
white strips, hanging down from the ceiling,[2]
museum, covered, awing faces and fancy suits and dresses tears dried, yet scars
deep and raw
young sisters and brothers, nowhere to find, ever this Little Saigon, trapped and yet
a home made afar; "insulation", finally a memorial in public
hugs so often and tightly, my children, life honored,
guarded so cautiously and hopefully, my school, a home made afar and in-between

PUBLICATION NOTE

This article was published online in 2020 by the *Journal of Southeast Asian American Education and Advancement* in Volume 15, Issue 2. Minor edits have been made here. The original can be found at http://doi.org/10.7771/2153-8999.1204.

NOTES

1. Espiritu, Y. L. (2018, March 19). *Feminist refugee epistemology: Reading displacement in Vietnamese and Syrian refugee art*. Presented as part of the Critical Migration and Refugee Studies series by the Center for the Study of Race and Ethnicity in America (CSREA), Brown University. Retrieved from: https://youtu.be/P8uly PmX9FM
2. The exhibition "Insulation." Information gathered from video entitled "Honoring Life: The work of Trinh Mai" by The Artist Odyssey, retrieved at https://vimeo .com/155899048 and from Trinh Mai's personal website (http://trinhmai.com /curriculum-vitae), specifically the exhibition "Quiet," in the 2015 "Vietnamese Focus: Generations of Stories" project hosted by the Old Orange County Courthouse Museum, Santa Ana, CA. Images retrieved from https://www.ocregister.com /2015/08/24/generations-of-stories-artifacts-photos-and-a-tattered-map-piece-together-history-of-the-vietnamese-who-settled-here/

REFERENCES

Alexander, M. J., & Mohanty, C. T. (Eds.). (1997). *Feminist genealogies, colonial legacies, democratic futures*. Routledge.

Alexander, M. J., & Mohanty, C. T. (2010). Cartographies of knowledge and power: Transnational feminism as radical praxis. In A. L. Swarr & R. Nagar (Eds.), *Critical transnational feminist praxis* (pp. 23–45). State University of New York Press.

Chong, S. (2002). Asian American teachers and teacher candidates in California: Who are they and what are their needs? In E. Tamura, V. Chattergy, & R. Endo (Eds.), *Asian and Pacific Islander American education: Social, cultural, and historical contexts* (pp. 117–131). Pacific Asia Press.

Chuong, S. (2019). *SEA Us Rise: Feminist praxis of intimacy in Southeast Asian American youth organizing* (Master's thesis in Asian American Studies), University of California, Irvine.

Endo, R. (2015). How Asian American female teachers experience racial microaggressions from pre-service preparation to their professional careers. *The Urban Review, 47*(4), 601–625. https://doi.org/10.1007/s11256-015-0326-9

Espiritu, Y. (2014). *Body counts: The Vietnam war and militarized refuge(es).* University of California Press.

Espiritu, Y., & Duong, L. (2018). Feminist refugee epistemology: Reading displacement in Vietnamese and Syrian refugee art. *Signs, 14*(3), 587–615. https://doi.org/10.1086/695300

Fan, Y. (2009). Lost in institution: A Vietnamese immigrant student learning to write in Midwestern urban mainstream classrooms. *Journal of Southeast Asian American Education and Advancement, 4*(1), 1–17. http://doi.org/10.7771/2153-8999.1093

Goodwin, A. L., Genishi, C., Asher, N., & Woo, K. A. (2005). Voices from the margins: Asian American teachers' experiences in the profession. In C. Park, R. Endo, & A. Goodwin (Eds.), *Asian and Pacific Education: Learning, socialization, and identity* (pp. 99–117). Information Age.

Grewal, I. (2005). *Transnational America: Feminisms, diasporas, neoliberalisms.* Duke University Press.

Grewal, I., & Kaplan, C. (Eds.). (1994). *Scattered hegenominies: Postmodernity and transnational feminist practices*. University of Minnesota Press.

Kumashiro, K. K. (2000). Toward a theory of anti-oppressive education. *Review of Educational Research, 70*(1), 25–53. https://doi.org/10.3102/00346543070001025

Ladson-Billings, G. (2006). From the achievement gap to the education debt: Understanding achievement in U.S. schools. *Educational Researcher, 35*(7), 3–12. https://doi.org/10.3102/0013189X035007003

Lee, S. (1994). Behind the model-minority stereotype: Voices of high- and low-achieving Asian American students. *Anthropology & Education Quarterly, 25*, 413–429. https://doi.org/10.1525/aeq.1994.25.4.04x0530j

Lew, J. (2006). *Asian Americans in class: Charting the achievement gap among Korean American youth*. Teachers College Press.

Lincoln, Y. S., & Guba, E. G. (1985). *Naturalistic inquiry*. Sage.

Lorde, A. (1984). *Sister outsider: Essays and speeches*. Crossing Press.

Meyerson, D. E., & Scully, M. (1995). Tempered radicalism and the politics of ambivalence and change. *Organizational Science, 6*(5), 585–600. https://doi.org/10.1287/orsc.6.5.585

Mohanty, C. T. (2003). *Feminism without borders*. Duke University Press.

Morrow, R. (1989). Southeast Asian child rearing practices: Implications for child and youth care workers. *Child and Youth Care Quarterly, 18*(4), 273–287. https://doi.org/10.1007/BF01083874

Museus, S. D. (2009). A critical analysis of the exclusion of Asian American from higher education research and discourse. In L. Zhan (Ed.), *Asian American voices: Engaging, empowering, and enabling* (pp. 59–76). National League for Nursing Press.

Ngo, B., & Lee, S. J. (2007). Complicating the image of model minority success: A review of Southeast Asian American education. *Review of Educational Research, 77*(4), 415–453. https://doi.org/10.3102/0034654307309918

Nguyen, H. T. (2008). Conceptions of teaching by five Vietnamese American preservice teachers. *Journal of Language, Identity, and Education, 7*, 113–136. https://doi.org/10.1080/15348450801970654

Office of the United Nations High Commissioner for Refugees [UNHCR]. (1951). *Convention and protocol relating to the status of refugees*. Geneva, Switzerland.

Pacis, D. C. (2005). *Asian American females in educational leadership in K–12 public schools* [Doctoral dissertation]. Available from ProQuest Dissertations and Theses database. (UMI No. 305342434)

Pang, V. O. (2009). The beliefs of successful Asian American Pacific Islander teachers: How culture is embedded in their teaching. *Asian American & Pacific Islanders Nexus, 7*(1), 55–82. https://doi.org/10.36650/nexus7.1_55-82_Pang

Pang, V. O., & Cheng, L. L. (1998). *Struggling to be heard: The unmet needs of Asian Pacific American children*. State University of New York Press.

Pang, O. V., Han, P. P., & Pang, J. M. (2011). Asian American and Pacific Islander students: Equity and the achievement gap. *Educational Researcher, 40*(8), 378–389. https://doi.org/10.3102/0013189X11424222

Park, C., Endo, R., & Rong, X. L. (Eds.). (2009). *New perspectives on Asian American parents, students, and teacher recruitment* (pp. 123–136). Information Age.

Park, C. C. (2009). Korean Americans in the teaching profession. In C. Park, R. Endo, & X. L. Rong (Eds.), *New perspectives on Asian American parents, students, and teacher recruitment* (pp. 123–136). Information Age.

Patton, M. Q. (2002). *Qualitative research and evaluation methods* (3rd ed.). Sage.

Rubin, H. J., & Rubin, I. S. (2005). *Qualitative interviewing: The art of hearing data* (2nd ed.). Sage.

Rumbaut, R. D., & Rumbaut, R. G. (1976). The family in exile: Expatriates in the United States. *American Journal of Psychiatry, 133*(4), 395–399.

Saldaña, J. (2016). *The coding manual for qualitative researchers* (3rd ed.). Sage.

Stake, R. (2006). *Multiple case study analysis.* Guilford Press.

Strauss, A., & Corbin, J. M. (1990). *Basics of qualitative research: Grounded theory procedures and techniques.* Sage.

Takaki, R. (1989). *Strangers from a different shore: A history of Asian American.* Little, Brown.

Um, K. (2012). Exiled memory: History, identity, and remembering in Southeast Asia and Southeast Asian diaspora. *Positions: Asia Critique, 20*(3), 831–850.

United State Census Bureau [USCB]. (2011, April 29). Asian/Pacific American heritage month: May 2011.

Uy, P. S. (2008). [Special issue on SEA demographics] Response—K–12 education: How the American community survey informs our understanding of the Southeast Asian community: One teacher's perspective. *Journal of Southeast Asian American Education and Advancement, 3*(1), 44–50. http://doi.org/10.7771/2153-8999.1108

Wright, W. E., & Boun, S. (2011). Southeast Asian American education 35 years after initial resettlement: Research report and policy recommendations: Conference report of the National Association for the Education and Advancement of Cambodian, Laotian, and Vietnamese Americans. *Journal of Southeast Asian American Education and Advancement, 6*(1), Article 1. http://doi.org/10.7771/2153-8999.1017

Wu, E. D. (2014). *The color of success: Asian Americans and the origins of the model minority.* Princeton University Press.

Yamane, L. (2012). Labor market discrimination: Vietnamese immigrants. *Journal of Southeast Asian American Education and Advancement, 7*(1), Article 4. http://doi.org/10.7771/2153-8999.1046

Zhou, M. (1997). Growing up American: The challenge confronting immigrant children and children of immigrants. *Annual Review of Sociology, 23*, 63–95. https://doi.org/10.1146/annurev.soc.23.1.63

12

HMoob Eldership as Pedagogy

Reclaiming HMoob Knowledge as HMoob Education

THONG VANG

ABSTRACT

For centuries non-HMoob people and scholars have sought to label and define who HMoob people are, but this paper reclaims and repositions HMoob people as agentic and reinforces our people's power to define themselves as we have for centuries. This paper also addresses problematic discourse about HMoob people and HMoob education, such as "peb HMoob tsis muaj kev kawm"[1] or "peb tsis muaj kev txawj hab kev ntse le lwm paab lwm pawg."[2] Departing from such deficit discourse, this paper explores HMoob eldership as pedagogy as one way that HMoob people have valid knowledge systems. HMoob eldership as pedagogy examines who is considered an educator and how education is implemented within our community. I propose HMoob eldership as pedagogy as a form of knowledge from our community's multiple pedagogies and education methodologies, one that roots HMoob epistemologies in eldership. Eldership, in this sense, traces the ways HMoob knowledge is passed down from the older generations to the younger generations through everyday teaching and learning. Ultimately, this work aims to nuance HMoob people's understanding of HMoob epistemologies and cosmologies.

> Thaum yug tseem yau, yug saib moog rua qhov twg los muaj cov laug nyob rua qhov hov lug coj peb, qhuab qha peb, hab hlub peb. Ua caag lug moog txug rua nub nua, yug saib moog rua txuj kaab txuj ke twg los tsis pum ib tug laug nyob rua qhov twg le lawm? Lub sib hawm thaud moog rua qhov twg lawm? Cov laug tsawg zuj zug, leej

> twg yuav lug sawv puab qhov chaw? Zag nuav, yuav yog koj hab yuav yog kuv. Peb yuav tau dlhau moog ua cov laug lawm. Thaum ti teg ti taw, tsis muaj tug lug qhuab lug qha, peb yuav ncu txug tej laug. Yog vim le nuav, koj hab kuv, peb suav dlawg yuav tsum kawm hab paub txug tej laug tej kev qhuab kev qha. Peb yuav tau xyum hab ncu txug peb HMoob kev qhuab kev qha.[3] (Collective Teachings, n.d.)

This quote is a paraphrase of the frequent teachings that occur at my family gatherings. This quote is also a reminder for my generation that we are soon-to-be elders. There are specific times and moments when older HMoob adults realize they have become elders to the current and future generations of HMoob youth. However, this transitory process of becoming an elder has become less defined for HMoob people as we face different social and economic constraints in the United States. One of the major constraints is that U.S. education mainly focuses on individualism and upholds Eurocentric values. Eurocentric U.S. education positions Western white norms and ideologies at the top of the hierarchy of knowledge production and worldview (Dei et al., 2022). HMoob youth educated through the U.S. system are often removed from our community's understanding of the transitory process to become a HMoob elder. We become isolated from our people, our responsibilities, our past, and our shared futures. Thus, this quote reminds me that I am tied to this transitory eldership process. I will have responsibilities to learn and keep the knowledge of my elders because I am becoming one.

My perception of the HMoob community and my experience within our community is influenced by how my identities intersect. In Crenshaw's (1991) seminal work on identity and intersectionality, she argues that race and gender are among many critical identities overlooked and underexamined in law and research that further marginalizes people. As a HMoob cisgender male scholar who does research within my own community, my intersectionality grants me access to certain aspects while excluding me from other community knowledge and experiences, such as those shared among HMoob women. Moreover, as a son, an able-bodied person, and being HMoob leeg,[4] these identities also intersect and influence how I understand, interact with, and analyze my understanding of HMoob teaching and learning. My identities as the eldest son and my relationship with my community as ib tug tub, ib tug kwj tij los sis nug[5] and how they intersect allow me to better understand and situate the transitory process toward becoming an elder. Although I am in my early 30s, I had already begun my transition into an elder when I became ib tug txiv ntxawm hab ib tug laug[6] to my cousin's children. This process changed once more when I became ib leej yawm[7] for future generations within my clan. I am also ib tug txiv tsev hab ib leej txiv[8] to my partner and three children. Being the eldest son is critical for my understanding of HMoob knowledge and identity, and this understanding has strengthened as I became a father.

Moving from the discussion of intersectionality to the broader context of the HMoob communities, it is important to acknowledge the impact of historical oppression and deficit discourses on our community's self-perception and internalized beliefs. HMoob people have faced oppression for many centuries that led to discourses that characterized HMoob as premodern people (Lee, 2015; Vang, 2021). The characterization of HMoob people as premodern often implies that we must relinquish our culture and language in order to navigate the modern world. This narrative that the HMoob culture and community need "fixing" to conform to modern standards is a troubling implicit message challenged by Mouavangsou (2020) in her exploration of the impact of U.S. education on her understanding of the HMoob community and her own family. Such deficit discourses enter our consciousness, resulting in ideologies such as "peb HMoob tsis muaj kev kawm" or "peb tsis muaj kev txawj hab kev ntse le lwm paab lwm pawg." While there is a recent rise in efforts to sustain HMoob culture and language in schools (Ngo, 2015; Spycher et al., 2020) and community-based organizations (Ngo & Chandara, 2021), we must consider the continual gaps within HMoob scholarship and curricula. For instance, Yang (2012) wrote:

> Publications on Hmong and Hmong Americans, many of which are intended as teaching materials for Kindergarten to the Twelfth Grade, have grown substantially. But this body of literature also has inadvertently included information about Hmong culture, identity, history and religion that can be misleading. In my view, if steps are not taken to assess and correct this information, there is a potential for a mass mis-education of American children about the lives and background of the Hmong. (p. 2)

As seen in Yang, information about HMoob people becomes legitimized through U.S. schools; however, he noted that such teachings, despite being labeled as "H[Moob]," are inaccurate representations of the HMoob American community. Moreover, Mouavangsou (2018, 2020) suggested that implicit messages provided in schools miseducate HMoob students about who their people are and their cultural practices. Yang (2012) and Mouavangsou (2018, 2020) touch on aspects of the miseducation of HMoob Americans. Yet, Mouavangsou (2020) goes further by highlighting the complex dynamic of miseducation perpetuated by HMoob Americans and calling for critical self-reflection to disrupt the narratives of miseducation. Together these studies highlight how education misrepresents and flattens narratives of HMoob people, which influences how HMoob youth understand their community and negotiate "between the Hmong and American world" (Mouavangsou, 2018, p. 9).

As my parents became grandparents, I realized I was aging with them and had gained new responsibilities. This moment of transition also means that I have responsibilities as a father to young children and a HMoob scholar to the future generations of HMoob youth to ensure that they have access to their community's knowledge and it is made available to them. Borrowing from Indigenous scholar Chris Pexa (2019), I write this paper as my love letter to HMoob descendants "to ensure that [our] children's children would someday be able to receive those letters and make themselves stronger through the reading of them" (p. 9). This letter adds to the ongoing growth of HMoob communities and benefits our future generations so they can continue to learn through our knowledge systems.

In this paper, I argue that HMoob people have kev kawm hab kev txawj ntse le lwm paab lwm pawg[9] through our elders' everyday teaching and learning. I began by briefly sharing my journey and motivation in learning about HMoob knowledge systems. By engaging with literature written by Black, Indigenous, and People of Color (BIPOC) scholars, I gained a deeper understanding of the significance of HMoob knowledge. Next, I offer a theoretical conceptualization of HMoob knowledge systems through HMoob elders as a form of HMoob epistemology. Then, I unpack how HMoob elders are knowledge keepers and how that eldership knowledge is kept within our HMoob community. I reflect on the teachings of kuv puj[10] to explore how I understood *HMoob eldership as pedagogy*. In positioning HMoob elders and eldership as pivotal to HMoob education, this conceptual paper brings attention to the words of the collective teaching cited above. These words are a love letter, reminding us that as time passes, we will assume the role of elders.

REVEALING HMOOB EDUCATION

Growing up in the 1990s, I was captivated by the conversations and narratives shared by my elders, recounting their experiences of migrating across Southeast Asia and the United States. These moments of listening and observing HMoob elders became integral to my early learning process. Unfortunately, I realized that informal education and the wisdom of racialized elders were not adequately valued or integrated within the U.S. school system. Despite this, I was fortunate to be immersed in HMoob teachings taught by my family and extended relatives in our language. HMoob teachings, deeply rooted in our cultural fabric, extend beyond the confines of traditional classroom settings. The teachings permeate our everyday lives, unfolding within the intimate spaces of our living rooms and backyards, during sacred rituals and ceremonies, and within the vibrant community spaces of HMoob markets and community-based organizations. HMoob teaching and learning go beyond traditional classroom instruction, expanding knowledge exchange beyond the conventional "teacher-student" dynamic, where an adult in a classroom assumes the role of knowledge instructor and the youth as the recipient of knowledge (Lozenski, 2017; Milner, 2015; Tillett & Cushing-Leubnmer, 2021). In the HMoob community, learning is deeply intertwined with our community, embedded within our shared activities and experiences. Moreover, it is important to recognize that similar dynamics exist in other Indigenous communities, such as Black/African communities, where elders play a significant role in transmitting cultural knowledge to younger generations (Dei et al., 2022). This dynamic highlights the importance of elders as custodians of cultural wisdom, traditions, and values, who impart their knowledge to younger members of their communities.

While U.S. schools provided few opportunities to learn HMoob knowledge, I found outlets to sustain HMoob knowledge systems through school clubs, community spaces, and at home. For as long as I can remember, my elders have encouraged me to attend school and do well because it will allow me to succeed in the United States. While this perception may be accurate because the United States has a global influence, I became more aware of how U.S. schools are Eurocentric. Dei et al. (2022) explain that Eurocentric education is rooted in white colonial history that alienates BIPOC youth "from their homelands, languages, histories, and cultures" (p. 63). Implicitly, Eurocentric schooling is a tool of erasure that minimizes other ways of thinking and being (e.g., Mouavangsou, 2020). Eurocentric U.S. education continues to be underexamined and colonial pedagogies have become normalized in education (Dei et al., 2022). English-only education is a prime example of how U.S. education upholds colonial pedagogy, molding English as the center of knowledge production within schools. Macedo (1991) alluded to how English-only education in the classroom "denies [mulitilingual speakers] the fundamental tools for reflection, critical thinking, and social interaction" (p. 19). A U.S. education pressures students, especially BIPOC students, to speak English to legitimize their thoughts and intellectual thinking, even when speaking in their native languages offers the same or higher level of critical thinking and reflection.

In my community, I have witnessed the long-term impact of English-only practices, and its influence on my HMoob friends' sense of belonging. It was clear that the education I received in formal schooling failed to acknowledge the value of my HMoob community as a rich and diverse community with knowledge systems and complex understandings of the world. One of the reasons I could hold on to my HMoob culture and language in spaces like student clubs, community spaces, and home is because of the educational practices in these spaces. The educational practices in these spaces embrace my heritage and include educators and peers who share the common goal of sustaining our culture and language. Consequently, U.S. education failed to provide me with the education our community deserves.

As a HMoob education scholar researching within my HMoob community, I benefit from scholarships written by BIPOC scholars who challenge racist and Eurocentric education. In doing so, their work shows me that there are multiple truths and realities in which people can and do ground themselves. With their gifts, BIPOC education scholars move the field of education with culturally responsive pedagogy (Gay, 2000), culturally relevant pedagogy (Ladson-Billings, 2014), culturally sustaining pedagogy (Paris, 2012), and culturally sustaining/revitalizing pedagogy (McCarty & Lee, 2014). They highlight the importance of including students' ethnic and racial identities, along with youth culture, as part of the learning in schools. Specifically, I found McCarty and Lee's (2014) study on Indigenous youth's linguistic knowledge use within and outside of school most relevant in conceptualizing HMoob education. Since HMoob communities are multiple displaced people, we have continued to struggle for recognition of our language, culture, and self-determination. Culturally sustaining/revitalizing pedagogy demands that we hold colonialism accountable for the continual erasures of BIPOC knowledge and histories. This culturally sustaining/revitalizing pedagogy principle recognizes the need to scrutinize the Eurocentric U.S. education system thoroughly. Their work supported me in seeing HMoob language and culture as vital for HMoob youth identity development in the United States and how it is interwoven within systems of power.

Furthermore, I draw inspiration from Lozenski's (2017) work within the Black community to recognize that within my own community, HMoob elders serve as intergenerational contacts, offering valuable insights into the experiences of HMoob people in terms of racialization, life, and discrimination, both within and outside the United States. As Milner (2015) and Lozenski (2017) note, education for minoritized communities does not have to exist only in classrooms and schools. In fact, Hermes and colleagues (2021) have demonstrated that Indigenous elders play a crucial role in supporting youth to understand the connection between their language, life, and the land through activities such as forest walks. The studies mentioned in this section inform this article by shedding light on the significance of BIPOC elders and scholars in fostering intergenerational critical-thinking young people. Similarly, this article disrupts Eurocentric schooling by recentering HMoob elders in knowledge creation and reimagining education for our community to challenge the Eurocentric foundations that have historically marginalized and devalued other ways of knowing. Such an approach contributes to this body of literature by showcasing the value and complexity of HMoob elders' knowledge, thus enriching the ongoing scholarly discourse surrounding BIPOC education.

HMOOB KNOWLEDGE SYSTEMS

HMoob knowledge is multifaceted, expanding as HMoob people are socialized in different societies (Vue & Mouavangsou, 2021). Vue and Mouavangsou (2021) imply that there is no single source of HMoob knowledge, nor is one particular source better. Thus, HMoob youth raised by their parents and elders, including distant relatives, already access a specific form of HMoob knowledge production. As such, there are differences in HMoob ways of being and knowing, and as a community, we are allowed to embrace these differences. For example, HMoob knowledge is also granted to individuals based on their gender identification and/or experience. HMoob knowledge production and sustainment of our knowledge for the last century have been viewed as a patriarchal knowledge system. I am afforded access to this patriarchal knowledge system as a cisgender HMoob man. However, I urge us to examine HMoob knowledge from a place of multiplicity that decenters patriarchal knowledge. Specifically, I recognize that the sustainment and practices of HMoob knowledge are not exclusive only to men, but HMoob knowledge has been sustained and cultivated by women and children (Vang, 2023). Thus, the survival of HMoob knowledge must also include these narratives.

I have realized in observing HMoob elders over time that HMoob people possess the necessary tools for self-determination and shaping our futures. As demonstrated in Harjo (2019), Indigenous community knowledge and rationality are tools of futurity that bind together past, present, and future. Thus, HMoob relationality is rooted in how our elders hold knowledge and maintain relationships that connect us to the present and our past. Through us, we connect our elders to the future, holding together the reality of HMoob space and time—the fabric that binds us to our ancestors, the places they lived, and our shared futures. Like Harjo (2019) sharing about relationality and community knowledge, tuning in to our HMoob knowledge systems is how we can "find [our] way back to practices of relationality and kinship making and operationalize these practices into autonomy and self-determination" (p. 45). Within HMoob knowledge systems, our elders resist the ongoing erasure of our community's knowledge. Simultaneously, they embed these knowledge systems into our everyday lives, our songs, their acts of care, in their breath, and in every movement they make.

WHO ARE KNOWLEDGE KEEPERS?

This conceptual article contributes scholarship on HMoob elders by moving beyond their categorization as simply aged members of society and toward a deeper understanding of them as knowledge keepers. In many BIPOC communities, elders are well respected and play critical roles in the daily lives of BIPOC communities (Dei et al., 2022). Elders embody ancestral teachings and profoundly understand how the world functions through their community's lens (Sandoval et al., 2016). HMoob elders' knowledge aligns with what Solórzano and Yosso (2001) articulate as counterstories that challenge discourse taught in schools about BIPOC. The narratives shared by elders serve as valuable sources of knowledge, and their lived experiences and presence embody a curriculum that sustains HMoob-centric teachings (Lee, personal communication, March 2020; Thao, 2002). Similar to the formation of Indigenous knowledge systems over time, as explored by Brayboy and Maughan (2009), the HMoob knowledge systems are culminations of the lived experiences of our elders and ancestors. HMoob elders are indispensable to HMoob communities worldwide as they serve as living archives and a collective repository of culture, language, spirituality, and customs that have endured displacement spanning several centuries (Lee, 1998; Thao, 2002).

WHO IS AN ELDER?

HMoob people's conceptualization of "who is an elder" is complex. In a conversation with kuv yawm,[11] he stated: "ua qoob ua loo lug npaaj tshaib, tu tub tu kiv lug npaaj laug. . . Mej cov miv nyuas yuav lug ua nam ua txiv rua peb cov laug" (Yang, personal communication, February 18, 2021). Through his paaj lug,[12] it is evident that he understood his role as an elder. He emphasizes the interconnectedness of caring for young children and elderly parents as they age. His statement reflects teachings on generational care and reciprocity, where HMoob youth become elders as their own elders reach old age and return to the ancestral land to be reborn in future generations (Her, 2018). According to HMoob beliefs, our children are our ancestors, reflecting our profound understanding of the life cycle as described in Symonds's (2003) book, in which she detailed HMoob's cosmology, spirits, and spirituality. It is important to note that age does not determine one's elder status; however, this discussion on age and eldership is beyond the scope of this article. Therefore, the elders that I focus on are my parents, grandparents, and ancestors. *HMoob eldership as pedagogy* comes from this understanding that teaching and learning are passed from the older generation to the younger generation.

WHAT IS HMOOB ELDERSHIP AS PEDAGOGY?

The learning process of how HMoob elders pass knowledge to future generations is a pedagogy rooted in HMoob epistemologies and cosmologies. I focus on elders' daily life and activities as acts of teaching and learning opportunities to conceptualize *HMoob eldership as pedagogy*. It focuses on knowledge production, identity, language, culture, and place as a pedagogy. *HMoob eldership as pedagogy* is situated within lived experiences, the everyday life of HMoob people, and the activities that bind and bond us.

HMoob eldership as pedagogy counters deficit discourses about HMoob education by moving away from a preservationist approach often found in Eurocentric U.S. education. Instead of portraying HMoob people as relics of the past and reducing our community to one homogenous group, I explore *HMoob eldership as pedagogy* to envision HMoob people beyond the imaginations of others (Her, 2018). Since we are a community with rich histories and futures, we deserve an education that reflects our values and practices. *HMoob eldership as pedagogy* is a teaching approach that calls out and challenges deficit narratives about our people. Through the conversations, stories, and everyday actions of HMoob elders, we engage in acts of teaching and learning, carrying forward the wisdom of our ancestors and resisting the oppression perpetuated by dominant societies.

As HMoob people have existed for centuries, HMoob knowledge is facilitated through our orality. Orality, as introduced by Mahuika (2019), is more than just spoken communication; instead, orality can be seen, heard, and felt. Orality encompasses performances, storytelling, and ceremonies infused with our people's lived experiences. *HMoob eldership as pedagogy* as part of an oral community is acquired through the teachings of elders and close relatives. HMoob children learn about our knowledge by being immersed in the presence of loved ones and community members. This transmission of knowledge occurs intentionally through apprenticeship or spontaneously in various social activities. Similar to how Indigenous children learn about their communities, as suggested by Mahuika (2019), HMoob youth are exposed to HMoob language and culture through play, interactions with other HMoob children, and listening to lug nruag hab neej neeg[13] in our public spaces such as during community gatherings, in our homes,[14] through ceremonies, and in markets. In these public spaces are our elders and relatives, who may be considered uneducated and nonliterate by U.S. society (Duffy, 2007); however, they hold immense significance because they are our first educators. Their teachings ensure youth understand their connections and relationships to others, things, and places.

ELDERSHIP WITHIN THE EVERYDAY

One of my first educators was kuv puj, who taught me about the world through her everyday teachings. I remember kuv puj would stare out the window, where she frequently whispered to the birds and the insects that came by. She would say, "Miv noog koj has rua [my aunt's name] tas kuv ncu ncu nwg. Caag nwg tsis tuaj le?" She asked the birds and insects to deliver messages to her children and grandchildren who lived in different cities, urging them to visit or questioning why they had not come to see her. I did not fully understand it then, but upon reflection, I realized this was an example of *HMoob eldership as pedagogy*.

My everyday observations of how kuv puj interacted with the world helped me comprehend her teachings. Through her conversations with the birds and insects, I learned about our connection to nature, the significance of our loved ones, and the interconnectedness of the world. HMoob people have an intricate understanding of spirituality, one that considers all things as having spirits. Her actions and teachings showed her yearning for the people she loves and demonstrated the agency of animals and insects. At times, the presence of our more-than-human relatives—the animals and insects—could be interpreted as messages from our departed or living loved ones. Kuv puj recognized the mobility of birds and insects and implored them to carry her messages to her daughter, encouraging her to visit. In observing kuv puj's final moments, it finally dawned on me that her teachings, her *HMoob eldership as pedagogy*, were a repository of knowledge developed over centuries through her lineage. It was not something kuv puj invented as she aged, but rather practices shared among HMoob elders of her generation and those before.

As shared in the introduction, my intersecting positionality informed my understanding of *HMoob eldership as pedagogy* as I was exposed to HMoob culture and cultural repertoires throughout my life. *HMoob eldership as pedagogy* encompasses knowledge accumulated over centuries and evolves according to our community's time and place. Grounded in HMoob ways of being and knowing, it requires a deep understanding of HMoob people, our spiritualities, and the places we call home. Although kuv puj has departed from the physical world, her teachings persist in her children's and grandchildren's memories and manifest in our behavior and everyday actions. As an adult, whenever a meal is prepared in our home that evokes memories of kuv puj, I call out to her and leave some food outside as an offering. Like the insects and birds, her presence visits and watches over us.

CONCLUSION

In this article, I have argued that HMoob people have kev kawm hab kev txawj ntse le lwm paab lwm pawg by observing a HMoob knowledge system and how knowledge is passed from generation to generation. Despite being continuously displaced, HMoob elders have been instrumental in sustaining our knowledge over time. Drawing on Lozenski's (2017) conceptualization of Black elders as critical educators for Black youth researchers, my proposal of the concept *HMoob eldership as pedagogy* honors my elders' knowledge and teachings. Based on my observations of HMoob elders in my own life, I see their everyday teaching and learning as HMoob kev kawm hab kev txawj kev ntse[15] that is deeply connected to our epistemologies and spiritualities. The concept of *HMoob eldership as pedagogy* contributes to Rogoff and colleagues' (2016) calling for further exploration of learning within and beyond formal education.

Further research that centers on HMoob knowledge can provide nuanced perspectives for research and practice, particularly in academic fields such as education studies, Asian American studies, Southeast Asian studies, Indigenous studies, and community organizations. By establishing a solid interdisciplinary foundation in critical HMoob studies, we could work to address the misrepresentations of HMoob people in books and education lessons (Yang, 2012) and move toward a more comprehensive understanding of our community (Mouavangsou, 2018; Vue & Mouavangsou, 2021).

The power of *HMoob eldership as pedagogy* is undeniable, as it highlights the crucial role played by our elders in sustaining our community's invaluable knowledge through their daily teachings. Although it is not extensively covered in this article, development around HMoob dual-immersion programs and HMoob schools in the United States could benefit from this reminder that HMoob elders hold critical knowledge for HMoob communities. HMoob education professionals, along with our elders, could work together as a step forward to ensure that the HMoob school curricula reflect the values of their local HMoob community. Subsequently, having teacher educators and teacher education programs that are cognizant of how HMoob and other communities engage in education for their people brings the promise that prospective educators can embody the teachings of their community without fear of being judged. HMoob educators enacting their community's teachings in their educational practices honor our community's knowledge and elders.

Lastly, it is essential to acknowledge that, like me, HMoob youth are already on their way to becoming elders, as cited in the quote at the beginning of this article: "Zag nuav, yuav yog koj hab yuav yog kuv. Peb yuav tau dlhau moog ua cov laug lawm"[16] (Collective teachings, n.d.). "Zag nuav, yuav yog koj hab yuav yog kuv" reminds me that my time is here and that I am an elder. Additionally, the message in the more extensive collective teaching quote reminds me of the responsibility left for me to ensure the future of my community's knowledge. To fulfill this commitment, I find solace in Harjo's (2019) message that our elders have entrusted us with the knowledge and teachings to carry on that commitment for future generations. Woven into this article is my love letter to the collective oral teachings of elders and my grandmother's gift for later generations. HMoob knowledge cannot be learned within a classroom or through a single classroom lesson; it will take a lifetime to uncover, know, and sustain our knowledge.

PUBLICATION NOTE

This article was published online in 2023 by the *Journal of Southeast Asian American Education and Advancement* in Volume 18, Issue 2. Minor edits have been made here. The original can be found at http://doi.org/10.7771/2153-8999.1304.

NOTES

1. HMoob people do not have education.
2. We do not have forms of intelligence and brilliance like others.
3. When we were young, everywhere you look there were elders to lead us, teach us, and love us. Today, as you look around, there are not many elders left. Where has the time gone? There are fewer elders in our community, who will come stand in their place? This time it is going to be you and me. We are going to become elders. When there isn't anyone to teach us, we are going to remember our elders' words. That is why we must learn and know about our teachings. We must learn and remember our HMoob teachings.
4. HMoob Leeg is a part of the HMoob language. Here it is being used as a language identity.
5. A son or a brother.
6. An uncle.
7. A grandfather or elder.
8. Father and husband.
9. Intelligence and brilliance like other people.
10. Puj is in reference to my paternal grandmother.
11. Yawm is grandfather and it could be used in reference to paternal and maternal grandfather. In this passage, I was talking to my maternal grandfather.
12. Proverbs and idioms.
13. Orphan stories and lived narratives.
14. The home may be considered private spaces for many people, but the home could also become a public space and a place for community gatherings. For example, within my experience in the HMoob community, our homes become public spaces when we have community gatherings such as zuv mo, ua tshoob, hu plig, hab rooj sab laaj, to name a few.
15. HMoob intelligence and brilliance.
16. This time it is going to be you and me. We are going to become elders.

REFERENCES

Brayboy, B., & Maughan, E. (2009). Indigenous knowledges and the story of the bean. *Harvard Educational Review, 79*(1), 1–21. https://doi.org/10.17763/haer.79.1.l0u6435086352229

Collective teachings. (n.d.). *Oral teaching*. Personal communications.

Crenshaw, K. (1991). Mapping the margins: Intersectionality, identity politics, and violence against women of color. *Stanford Law Review, 43*(6), 1241–1299. https://doi.org/10.2307/1229039

Dei, G. J. S., Karanja, W., & Erger, G. (2022). *Elders' cultural knowledges and the question of Black/African indigeneity in education.* Springer Cham.

Duffy, J. M. (2007). *Writing from these roots: Literacy in a Hmong-American community.* University of Hawai'i Press.

Gay, G. (2000). *Culturally responsive teaching: Theory, research, and practice.* Teachers College Press.

Harjo, L. (2019). *Spiral to the stars: Mvskoke tools of futurity.* University of Arizona Press.

Her, V. K. (2018). Reframing Hmong religion: A reflection on emic meanings and etic labels. *Amerasia Journal, 44*(2), 23–41. https://doi.org/10.17953/aj.44.2.23-41

Hermes, M., Meixi, Engman, M. M., & McKenzie, J. (2021). Everyday stories in a forest: Multimodal meaning-making with Ojibwe elders, young people, language, and place. *International Journal of Multilingualism, 18*(3), 298–314. https://doi.org/10.18357/wj1202120289

Ladson-Billings, G. (2014). Culturally relevant pedagogy 2.0: Aka the remix. *Harvard Educational Review, 84*(1), 74–84. https://doi.org/10.17763/haer.84.1.p2rj131485484751

Lee, M. M. (1998). The thousand-year myth: Construction and the characterization of Hmong. *Hmong Studies Journal, 2*(2), 1–23.

Lee, M. M. (2020, March). *Oral teaching.* Personal communication.

Lee, M. M. (2015). *Dreams of the Hmong kingdom: The quest for legitimation in French Indochina, 1850–1960.* University of Wisconsin Press.

Lozenski, B. D. (2017). Pedagogies of Black eldership: Exploring the impact of intergenerational contact on youth research. *Multicultural Perspectives, 19*(2), 65–75. https://doi.org/10.1080/15210960.2017.1302337

Macedo, D. (1991). English only: The tongue-tying of America. *The Journal of Education, 173*(2), 9–20. https://www.jstor.org/stable/42742210

Mahuika, N. (2019). *Rethinking oral history and tradition: An Indigenous perspective.* Oxford University Press.

McCarty, T., & Lee, T. (2014). Critical culturally sustaining/revitalizing pedagogy and Indigenous education sovereignty. *Harvard Educational Review, 84*(1), 101–124. https://doi.org/10.17763/haer.84.1.q83746nl5pj34216

Milner, R. H. (2015). Black teachers as curriculum texts in urban schools. In M. Fang He, B. D. Schultz, & W. H. Schubert (Eds.), *The Sage guide to curriculum in education* (pp. 215– 223). Sage Publications.

Mouavangsou, K. N. (2018). Because I am a daughter: A Hmong woman's educational journey. *Journal of Southeast Asian American Education and Advancement, 13*(1), Article 4. https://doi.org/10.7771/2153-8999.1166

Mouavangsou, K. N. (2020). Hmong does not mean free: The miseducation of and by Hmong Americans. In K. L. C. Valverde & W. M. Dariotis (Eds.), *Fight the tower: Asian*

American women scholars' resistance and renewal in the academy (pp. 189–218). Rutgers University Press.

Ngo, B. (2015). Hmong culture club as a place of belonging: The cultivation of Hmong students' cultural and political identities. *Journal of Southeast Asian American Education and Advancement, 10*(2), 1–20. https://doi.org/10.7771/2153-8999.1130

Ngo, B., & Chandara, D. (2021). Nepantlera pedagogy in an immigrant youth theater project: The role of a Hmong educator in facilitating the exploration of culture and identity. *Teachers College Record, 123*(9), 87–111. https://doi.org/10.1177/01614681211051979

Paris, D. (2012). Culturally sustaining pedagogy: A needed change in stance, terminology, and practice. *Educational Researcher, 41*(3), 93–97. https://doi.org/10.3102/0013189X12441244

Pexa, C. (2019). *Translated nation: Rewriting the Dakhota Oyate.* University of Minnesota Press.

Rogoff, B., Callanan, M., Gutiérrez, K. D., & Erickson, F. (2016). The organization of informal learning. *Review of Research in Education, 40*(1), 356–401. https://doi.org/10.3102/0091732X16680994

Sandoval, C. D. M., Lagunas, R. M., Montelongo, L. T., & Díaz, M. J. (2016). Ancestral knowledge systems: A conceptual framework for decolonizing research in social science. *AlterNative: An International Journal of Indigenous Peoples, 12*(1), 18–31. https://doi.org/10.20507/AlterNative.2016.12.1.2

Solórzano, D. G., & Yosso, T. J. (2001). Critical race and LatCrit theory and method: Counter storytelling. *International Journal of Qualitative Studies in Education, 14*(4), 471–495. https://doi.org/10.1080/09518390110063365

Spycher, P., Girard, V., & Moua, B. (2020). Culturally sustaining disciplinary language and literacy instruction for Hmong-American children. *Theory into Practice, 59*(1), 89–98. https://doi.org/10.1080/00405841.2019.1665410

Symonds, P. V. (2003). *Calling in the soul: Gender and cycle of life in a Hmong village.* University of Washington Press.

Thao, Y. J. (2002). *The voices of Mong elders: Living, knowing, teaching, and learning within an oral tradition* [Unpublished doctoral dissertation]. Claremont Graduate University.

Tillett, W., & Cushing-Leubner, J. (2021). Hidden, null, lived, material, and transgressive curricula. In W. H. Schubert & M. Fang He (Eds.), *Oxford encyclopedia of curriculum studies.* Oxford University Press. https://doi.org/10.1093/acref/9780190887988.001.0001

Vang, K. (2023). Notes to my dad. *Journal of Southeast Asian American Education and Advancement, 18*(1), 1–8. https://doi.org/10.7771/2153-8999.1269

Vang, M. (2021). *History on the run: Secrecy, fugitivity, Hmong refugee epistemology.* Duke University Press.

Vue, R., & Mouavangsou, K. N. (2021). Calling our souls home: A HMong epistemology for creating new narratives. *Asian American Journal of Psychology*, *12*(4), 265–275. https://doi.org/10.1037/aap0000273

Yang, C. (2021, February 18). *Oral teaching*. Personal communication.

Yang, K. (2012). Commentary: Mis-education in K–12 teaching about Hmong culture, identity, history and religion. *Hmong Studies Journal*, *13*(1), 1–21.

Yang, P. C. (2021, February 18). *Oral teaching*. Personal communication.

REVIEWS

13

Book Review

Stacey Lee's (2005) *Up Against Whiteness: Race, School, and Immigrant Youth*

Lee, S. J. (2005). *Up against whiteness: Race, school, and immigrant youth.* New York: Teachers College Press. 151 pp. $21.95 (Paperback) ISBN 0-8077-4574-X

REVIEWED BY CHANG PU

Issues of race, social class, and gender become critical in the field of education, as the number of linguistically and culturally diverse students increases dramatically in the U.S. school system. The changing demographics in schools bring up questions about how to provide appropriate educational services. Given the dearth of research critically analyzing Asian American students' schooling experience in the United States, Stacey Lee's book *Up Against Whiteness* is important and timely. Published in 2005, this book helps educators contest stereotypes of Asian American students.

Through the use of an ethnographic approach, Lee explores the experiences of 1.5- and second-generation Hmong American students in University Heights High School (UHS) in the state of Wisconsin, a school well known for its excellent academic reputation across the state. Lee's research aims to investigate how Hmong American students negotiate and react to dominant messages from the school and the larger society regarding race while the students are in the process of forming their identities in the context of the school and in response to their school experiences. In other words, Lee's primary goal is "to demonstrate the way racism informs and constrains identity options" for Hmong American students at UHS (p. 21). She argues that "race occupies the central role in Hmong American student experiences and significantly affects their understanding of what it means to be Hmong in the United States" (p. 1). Lee does not lump all Hmong American students of different generations into one category and treat them as one homogeneous group. She uncovers the complex and various coping strategies adopted by Hmong American students to respond to the racial barriers they encounter on a daily basis, making this study unique and instrumental to educators who work with ethnic minority students. Lee contributes to Asian American studies by focusing on the Hmong ethnic minority group, which is usually "invisible" among Southeast Asian ethnic groups because Hmong history is relatively unknown in the United States.

Chapter 1 provides an overview of the study, introducing the central concern of the study (i.e., identity formation), research questions, data collection methods (i.e., participant observation, semistructured interviews, and artifact collection), and major arguments in the book. In order to help readers understand the backdrop of the study, Lee provides a thorough overview of the immigration history of Hmong people in the United States as political refugees and their status as Asian Americans as well as how they are perceived in the larger U.S. society. This overview fills the gap of limited understanding about Hmong immigrants in multicultural education in the United States. In addition, Lee reviews different assimilation theories, which provide lenses to view and understand Hmong American students' different coping strategies, which are discussed in the later chapters. Lee devotes the last part of Chapter 1 to describing her research site, the participants, and the research process.

In Chapter 2 Lee explores White privilege and White culture at UHS. She uncovers the way that the culture of "Whiteness" at UHS shapes the teachers' definitions of "a good student" and "a good parent" and the way this culture "marks Hmong American students as racialized outsiders" (p. 24). For example, "good students are defined as those who are enrolled in college preparatory classes and involved in school-sponsored sports or other [high-status] extracurricular activities" (p. 28). Based on classroom observations and interviews with faculty at UHS, Lee argues that teachers reinforce the U.S. mainstream cultural norms (i.e., middle class, White culture), by using these norms to evaluate students from different cultural backgrounds. Lee also observes that multicultural education is not central to the school's curriculum, reflecting the inferior status of students of color at UHS. Lee reports that teachers and White students at UHS have limited knowledge of multiculturalism and diversity. They did not see the necessity of teaching and learning multicultural education because "the high achievement of many White middle-class students confirmed that the schools were doing their jobs; students of color who fail are doing so because of their families' shortcomings and their own lack of effort" (p. 41).

According to Lee, many UHS educators used this explanation to free themselves of any responsibility for serving and educating Hmong American students. Such a blaming-the-victim view reflects institutional racism and encourages stereotypes about students of color. Lee further argues that racism is not limited to overt verbal or physical hostility, but also includes institutional racism, which is implicit and invisible within education.

Chapter 3 focuses on illustrating the intragroup differences among Hmong American students as well as their individual academic needs. Within the Hmong community, traditional students are usually members of the 1.5 generation or are first-generation immigrants; these students are close to their Hmong communities and they are usually placed in ESL classes at UHS. Traditional youth at UHS typically hold an optimistic attitude about life in the United States because of their previous bitter experiences in their home country, while maintaining and valuing their heritage culture. The American schooling system provides them more educational opportunities compared to their homeland, thus further validating their positive attitudes toward education. The ESL program at UHS also provides traditional Hmong students a comfortable learning environment because of the caring and culturally sensitive ESL teachers, despite the fact that it socially segregates ESL students from mainstream students. The traditional Hmong students resist the dominant group's characterization of their culture as backward by presenting the model minority identity.

Americanized Hmong students, on the other hand, are usually American-born with poor school performance. They typically challenge the authority of their parents, dress like "gang members" (in the teachers' eyes), and also estrange themselves from their ethnic communities. As Lee reports, "traditional and Americanized youth defined themselves against each other" (p. 53). Traditional youth see the Americanized Hmong students as "bad kids" because they are too Americanized, while the Americanized youth view maintaining traditional Hmong culture as problematic in the United States. However, as Lee points out, all of the Hmong American students are aware of their "foreign" and invisible status, the racial hierarchy, and power relations between Whites and students of color both at UHS and in the larger society. Lee explains that traditional youth view such social distance as the result of language differences; however, Americanized youth view it as issues of race and culture. Lee elucidates that in negotiating their identities, Americanized youth have been "blackened" in the dominant imagination (p. 65) in terms of their dress style and counter-school attitude, but they regard this style as a form of resistance to race and class exclusion (p. 69).

Chapter 4 discusses how issues of gender interplayed with race complicate the identity construction for both traditional and Americanized Hmong youth. Lee focuses on exploring the gendered messages Hmong American students receive from their families and the larger society, and how they construct and perform their gendered identities in response to these messages. As Lee explains, Hmong American male students fail to demonstrate the forms of masculinity valued by the dominant American society because they are physically shorter, quieter in class, and not involved in school activities related to sports and music. Responding to this stereotype, Hmong American male students have developed or reconstructed a hyper-masculine identity, emphasizing toughness to gain social status and resisting the image of lack of masculinity. However, this image is perceived as a sign of "bad Americanization" and is misinterpreted as possible "gang involvement" (p. 84) by the faculty at UHS. Traditional Hmong American males need to negotiate the messages about masculinity at home such as being responsible to support the family economically. These messages may conflict with dominant mainstream views of masculinity as family duties interfere with school activities. In a milieu of conflicts, Lee observed a new ideal Hmong American masculinity that has also been developed and adopted by some Hmong men who combine and reinterpret aspects of the hegemonic masculinity valued by the dominant society with aspects of the masculinity valued by Hmong culture (p. 114).

Hmong American female students, who typically are seen as sexism victims of early marriage, perform femininity differently; some of them outperformed Hmong boys academically because for girls "education is a way to gain independence" (p. 101). Americanized Hmong girls are typically viewed as being in one of two groups: "good girls" and "bad girls." Lee further explains that "good girls" respect parental authority and accept gender norms represented in popular culture, while "bad girls" resist both. Lee concludes that "the Hmong American youth at UHS are negotiating new ways of expressing and performing their gendered identities in response to the multiple, complex, and often contradictory messages about gender they receive at home, school, and the larger United States society" (p. 121). Lee provides new insight to understanding identity construction by depicting the multi-layered influences on Hmong American students' school performance and their identity construction. Particularly, Hmong male students are twice as challenged in that the first layer is their lack of manliness according to the White hegemonic masculinity; the second layer is the impossibility of being real "Americans" because they are viewed by members of the dominant society as being culturally different.

In the fifth and final chapter, Lee revisits segmented assimilation theories. Lee's findings confirm the importance of the selective acculturation strategy that helps Hmong American students maintain their home culture, identity, and intergenerational relations. Additionally, she questions the definition of "good" schools. UHS has a reputation for academic success, which is measured by high-stakes testing (e.g., SAT), teachers' education levels, and number of students who plan to attend colleges/universities following graduation; yet, UHS fails to accommodate the needs of Hmong American students in mainstream classes socially, academically, and culturally. Lee argues that the priority of schools like UHS is a focus on preparing elite middle-class students. She calls for integrating multicultural education into the school curriculum and increasing faculties' cultural sensitivity to gain immigrant students' trust and to create a caring and equitable learning environment. Finally, Lee urges UHS teachers to reflect and examine White privilege in the school to raise their awareness of the existence of racial hierarchy and inequality.

Up Against Whiteness demonstrates how U.S. schooling as a cultural and racial process affects Hmong American students' academic engagement and performance as well as their identity construction. The book explicitly addresses how some school faculty and personnel consciously or subconsciously transmit mainstream cultural ideologies to minority students and evaluate them based on mainstream norms. Lee's book highlights the importance of educational ethnographies on language minority youth in U.S. schools. *Up Against Whiteness* is a powerful and instrumental book for educators and administrators who work with language minority students. It raises awareness of racial issues beyond overt insult, and it suggests ways to better serve language minority students in mainstream schools by valuing all students for who they are, adopting culturally relevant teaching pedagogy, and recruiting culturally competent teachers. Finally, as a data-driven research study, Lee's book provides insights on data collection methodology such as what data should be collected in order to gain a comprehensible understanding of students' schooling experiences, which provides an excellent model for graduate students and scholars who are interested in educational ethnographic research in school or community settings.

PUBLICATION NOTE

This review was published online in 2007 by the *Journal of Southeast Asian American Education and Advancement* in Volume 2, Issue 1. Minor edits have been made here. The original can be found at http://doi.org/10.7771/2153-8999.1086.

14

Book Review

Kao Kalia Yang's (2008) *The Latehomecomer: A Hmong Family Memoir*

Yang, K. K. (2008). *The latehomecomer: A Hmong family memoir.* Minneapolis, MN: Coffee House Press. 277 pp. $14.95 (Paperback). ISBN: 978-1-56689-208-7.

REVIEWED BY SARAH HANSEN

> *Before babies are born they live in the sky where they fly among the clouds. The sky is a happy place and calling babies down to earth is not an easy thing to do. From the sky, babies can see the course of human lives. This is what the Hmong children of my generation are told by our mothers and fathers, by our grandmothers and grandfathers. They teach us that we have chosen our lives. . . . From the sky, I would come again.*
>
> —KAO KALIA YANG, *THE LATEHOMECOMER*

Yang situates readers in the clouds. *The Latehomecomer*, a memoir, invites us to peer down, to trace the course of many Hmong lives through the story of one family. It gives voice to memories of soul-sheltering mountains, fear-riddled jungles, body-swallowing rivers, vast oceans, and far-from-each-other states in a new homeland. It is a testimony of survival, transition, and loss. But more than that, it is a story about love. Love between parents who "stick together in a hard life when they might each have an easier one apart" (p. 199). Love between aunts and uncles, brothers, sisters, and cousins. And love between Yang and her grandmother, the woman who first welcomed her from the sky. Through these relationships, Yang narrates the story of Hmong people before, during, and after the Secret War in Laos.

The book is organized into a prologue, four sections (each with three to four chapters), and an epilogue. The prologue outlines, in broad strokes, the places marking the course of Yang's life. We glimpse her as an infant and then as a child in the Ban Vinai Refugee Camp and the Phanat Nikhom Transition Camp in Thailand, and as child and later a young adult in Saint Paul, Minnesota. At the epicenter of each space is a question or a feeling about what it means to be Hmong. In Ban Vinai, Yang "learned that *Hmong* meant *contained*" (p. 1). In Phanat Nikhom, saying goodbye to family members and familiar landscapes recalled centuries of Hmong people leaving their homelands in search of freedom. Saint Paul, Minnesota, brought questions from others: "What is Hmong? Where is your country? What are you doing here in America? Are you ever going home again?" (p. 3). To readers looking over Yang's shoulder as she surveys U.S. books for chronicles of the Hmong experience, these questions begin to make sense, as we realize along with Yang that accounts of Hmong people fighting alongside U.S. soldiers during the Vietnam War—and the atrocities that Hmong men, women, and children faced in Laos after the Americans departed—have largely gone untold. *The Latehomecomer* is, in part, a response to this historical omission. Indeed, a major contribution of this book is the work it does to reposition the lived experiences of Hmong people more centrally within the U.S. historical narrative.

Part I, "People of the Sky," takes readers to Laos in 1975. We see Yang's mother and father meet for the first time in the thickness of the jungle, both hiding with their families from Lao soldiers charged with exterminating the Hmong people. Shortly after marrying Yang's father, Yang's mother parts with her own mother for the last time. We see families torn asunder in ambush, life in an enemy camp, and the harrowing journey across the Mekong River. *We see* is not the best way to explain what readers experience in "People of the Sky"; however, *we feel* is better. When, for instance, Yang's mother secures her own mother's embroidery close to her heart before entering the Mekong so that she might find her way back to her mother after death, the reader (at least this reader) responds not *academically*, but emotionally. I cried when Yang's grandmother chose to cross the river with Yang's father—even though he did not have a raft like his brothers—because she wanted to die with her youngest son if he should not survive. When, after crossing the river, Yang's grandmother learns that one of her sons and his children have not made it to the shores of Thailand, I felt her visceral grief. My body shook with hers. Pain like this is intimate. *The Latehomecomer*, in an unprecedented way, allows readers in, invites us to feel the heaviness of the choices Yang's family—and countless other Hmong families—made in order to survive and love one another in a time of war. Some people will argue that vicariously experiencing memories of pain through reading texts produces temporary, fleeting, and superficial empathy. While readers, particularly readers who have not shared the experience of being a refugee, may never feel Yang's story to the depths that she does, the images and emotions she invokes are not fleeting. *The Latehomecomer* takes hold, burrows into hearts. It is a book that allows those of us who are not

Hmong to grieve the fact that we have not known this story sooner and to share the weight of these memories now.

Rarely are the memories we are invited to share solely centered on sadness or fear. Rather, Yang does an excellent job of conveying the complexity of the human experience. For example, we feel vulnerability mixed with bravery and pride when Yang's mother resists the efforts of a Vietnamese soldier to carry her heavy pack on the way to an enemy camp. Even in a moment of heightened vulnerability, her mother protects her character. Many years later, Yang witnesses the vulnerability of her father when he tries to communicate in English to help find a restroom for his child in a busy airport. Yang notices that his voice loses its strength in English, but she is nonetheless extremely proud of the way he protects her. Similarly, in the Ban Vinai Refugee camp, there is hardship, but also joy. In fact, for Yang and her grandmother, "the life we had in the camp was ideal. We were surrounded by people who loved us" (p. 67). Without being didactic, *The Latehomecomer* reminds us that the human spirit is never one-dimensional, that people draw on their strengths even (especially) in trying times, and that caring relationships have the capacity to nurture us in powerful ways—to help us grow—even when forces beyond our control threaten our well-being.

Yang comes down from the clouds in Part II, "The Little Girl with the Dimples." In this section of the book, readers encounter the details of daily life first in Ban Vinai Refugee Camp and later in the Phanat Nikhom Transition Camp. We breathe in "green Parrot soap that smelled like Irish Spring with lots of flowers" (p. 83), "touch the muddy, black dirt, which was always waiting to take the clean away" (p. 64), and eat from the "white enamel-covered bowls, with little cracks where the metal peeked through" (p. 61). With poetic attention to particulars such as these, "The Little Girl with the Dimples" is a prime example of Yang's literary prowess. The *style* with which she examines the small details of her memories is also noteworthy. Sentences speak themselves in quiet tones that resemble human talk—the language of living stories. The effect feels effortless and beautiful. *The Latehomecomer* is worth reading for the aesthetic experience alone.

Part III describes "The American Years." Yang observes that being in the United States necessitates new ways of being in and moving through the world. She no longer skips; instead, adults hold her hand protectively, slowing her gait to a measured walk. In many ways, the United States feels constraining. Money (and its scarcity) becomes a central issue for the Yang family. Yang witnesses the adults in her life struggle to make ends meet. Significantly, finances create a barrier between Yang and her grandmother, who is resettled in California—a long distance from Minnesota. In Yang's words:

> Money was like a person I had never known or a wall I had never breached before: it kept me away from my grandma. I saw no way to climb this wall. Sometimes I thought

> so much about money that I couldn't sleep. Money was not bills and coins or a check from welfare. In my imagination, it was much more: it was the nightmare that kept love apart in America. (p. 135)

Although Yang's family tries to focus on the positive aspects of living in the United States, Yang notices that the American life her family had envisioned in the refugee camp fell far short of their expectations. In this way, *The Latehomecomer* speaks to a larger question that critical education scholar Rita Verma (2008) has explored through her research with working-class South Asian youth: What happens when globalized discursive flows create expectations about life in the United States that do not align with the socioeconomic realities of day to day survival? What are the affective consequences of living a dream that disappoints? What are the implications for understanding the experiences of immigrant and refugee students in socioeconomically diverse communities? These are becoming increasingly important issues for educational researchers working with youth in transnational contexts.

Indeed, *The Latehomecomer* raises important questions about how educational communities teach and learn with immigrant and refugee students in U.S. schools. Throughout her memoir, Yang's family persists in viewing school as a vehicle for socioeconomic mobility. Although readers sense the urgency with which Yang's parents encouraged their children to do well in school, less prominent in the text is an account of her parents' experiences helping their children to navigate the U.S. educational system. In a recent study illuminating newcomer Hmong parents' perceptions of their children's schooling experiences, Ngo, Bigelow, and Wahlstrom (2007) suggest participants often felt unable to fully advocate for their children in schools. They note, "A perceived major obstacle to parents' involvement was their lack of knowledge about the mechanisms of school and education in the U.S." (p. 27). Did Yang's parents feel frustrated by a similar lack of firsthand experience with U.S. schooling systems? Or did the social network they cultivated with their extended family members—several of whom had successfully completed their education in the United States—serve to mitigate this frustration? Research on Hmong parents' experiences in U.S. schools is still relatively limited (Ngo et al., 2007). *The Latehomecomer* suggests we need to know more.

This call is all the more urgent given that Hmong American communities highly value education (e.g., Adler, 2004; Lamborn & Moua, 2008; Lee, 2005), but nonetheless tend to fare less well academically than other Asian American groups (Lee & Kumashiro, 2005; Ngo, 2006). Scholars contextualize this disparity by pointing to factors such as poverty and limited formal schooling opportunities that have tended to mark the Hmong refugee experience and their subsequent resettlement in the United States (Ngo, 2006, 2008). Hmong newcomer parents with limited experience navigating formal schooling institutions face barriers in partnering with teachers to promote their children's academic success (Lee, 2005; Ngo, 2008). Given the link researchers perceive between parental involvement and students' academic success (Arnold et al., 2008; Jeynes, 2007), Hmong parents' restricted participation as educational partners in schools is problematic and may partially explain the achievement gap between Hmong students and other Asian and Pacific Islander groups who do not share similar refugee experiences. For researchers concerned with educational equity, this is deeply troubling. By contributing in-depth empirical accounts of Hmong parents' and students' schooling experiences, qualitative researchers have an essential role to play in addressing these inequities. And as Yang suggests, via *The Latehomecomer*, so does memoir.

Here's why. Through memoir, authors speak their own stories. Scholar and social activist bell hooks has implored researchers to stop "talking *about* the 'Other'" (cited in Fine, 1994, p. 70, emphasis added). Through *The Latehomecomer*, Yang articulates, explains, and interprets her own experiences. Listening (instead of speaking), researcher-readers learn:

> My cousin took Dawb and me to register [for school], but they didn't want us because we couldn't speak English well enough, and they didn't have the special teachers we would need. This is my first memory of feeling embarrassed. (pp. 140–141)

Attending even more closely, we learn that "the life in school that opened before me made me feel old in a world that was struggling to be young. A silence grew inside of me because I couldn't say that it was sometimes sad to be Hmong, even in America" (p. 151). Bitter embarrassment. Unspeakable sadness. These visceral insights are powerful because they represent what episodes were salient—not for an outside observer—but for Yang herself. In words *she* chooses, we learn what school was like as a Hmong newcomer in the United States. We see education through her eyes. By privileging the voices of immigrant and refugee writers who share their experiences through arts and literature, and by positioning these texts as important sources of information for understanding the lives of students, educational researchers have an opportunity to unsettle "colonizing discourse[s]" through our scholarship (Fine, 1994, p. 70). *The Latehomecomer* reminds us that our academic community needs more voices, more memoirs. It reminds us that creative work offers a different way to trace lives, a different way to listen.

Story takes center stage in Part IV ("The Latehomecomer") of Yang's memoir. In this section of the book, Yang describes how, as a young woman, she grew into a writer consumed by the need to share the stories held close to her family. She notes:

> I began to realize how our lives in America would be our stories. I started to understand one of the many truths that governed life: by documenting our deaths, we were

> documenting our lives. The Hmong had died too many times, and each time, their deaths had gone unwritten. There were no testimonies. The witnesses grew old, and they died, and life continued, as they had never lived. I didn't want this to happen to my grandma, to this woman I adored, whom I could not imagine not loving forever. I wanted the world to know how it was to be Hmong long ago, how it was to be Hmong in America, how it was to die Hmong in America—because I knew our lives would not happen again. (p. 215)

This final section of Yang's memoir recounts stories Yang's grandmother tells about her own youth and also chronicles her spirit's journey back to her birthplace in Laos. In recounting the life journey of her grandmother, Yang bears witness to the life journeys of many Hmong men, women, and children. It is at once a family memoir and the memoir of a people. The Epilogue emphasizes the collective nature of the work. The memoir, as a whole, invites readers to share these memories, to consider the stories that have shaped so many lives. It is a literary work that rearticulates the American experience. Even more than this, however, *The Latehomecomer* urges educational research forward in important new directions. It deserves a prominent place on the bookshelves of scholars and activists committed to better understanding Hmong families' experiences in U.S. schools.

PUBLICATION NOTE

This review was published online in 2010 by the *Journal of Southeast Asian American Education and Advancement* in Volume 5, Issue 1. Minor edits have been made here. The original can be found at http://doi.org/10.7771/2153-8999.1010.

REFERENCES

Adler, S. M. (2004). Home-school relations and the construction of racial and ethnic identity of Hmong elementary students. *School Community Journal, 14*(2), 57–75.

Arnold, D. H., Zeljo, A., Doctoroff, G. L., & Ortiz, C. (2008). Parent involvement in preschool: Predictors and the relation of involvement to preliteracy development. *School Psychology Review, 37*(1), 74–90. https://doi.org/10.1080/02796015.2008.12087910

Fine, M. (1994). Working the hyphens: Reinventing self and other in qualitative research. In N. R. Denzin & Y. S. Lincoln (Eds.), *Handbook of qualitative research* (pp. 70–82). Sage.

Jeynes, W. H. (2007). The relationship between parental involvement and urban secondary school student academic achievement: A meta-analysis. *Urban Education, 42*(1), 82–110. https://doi.org/10.1177/0042085906293818

Lamborn, S. D., & Moua, M. (2008). Normative family interactions: Hmong American adolescents' perceptions of their parents. *Journal of Adolescent Research, 23*(4), 411–437. https://doi.org/10.1177/0743558407310772

Lee, S. J. (2005). *Up against whiteness: Race, school, and immigrant youth.* Teachers College Press.

Lee, S. J., & Kumashiro, K. (2005). *A report on the status of Asian Americans and Pacific Islanders in education: Beyond the "model minority" stereotype.* National Education Association.

Ngo, B. (2006). Learning from the margins: The education of Southeast and South Asian Americans in context. *Race, Ethnicity and Education, 9*(1), 51–65. https://doi.org/10.1080/13613320500490721

Ngo, B. (2008). The affective consequences of cultural capital: Feelings of powerlessness, gratitude and faith among Hmong refugee parents. *Journal of Southeast Asian American Education & Advancement, 3*, 1–16. http://doi.org/10.7771/2153-8999.1100

Ngo, B., Bigelow, M., & Wahlstrom, K. L. (2007). The transition of Wat Tham Krabok Hmong children to Saint Paul Public Schools: Perspectives of teachers, principals, and Hmong parents. *Hmong Studies Journal*, 8, 1–35.

Verma, R. (2008). *Backlash: South Asian immigrant voices on the margins.* Sense Publishers.

15

Book Review

Lac Su's (2009) *I Love Yous Are for White People*

Su, Lac. (2009). *I love yous are for white people.* New York, NY: Harper Perennial. 249 pp. $14.99 (Paperback). ISBN: 978-0-06-154366-1.

REVIEWED BY QUAN MANH HA

I Love Yous Are for White People recounts chronologically the childhood memories of the Vietnamese American narrator Lac Su (a.k.a. Big Head) and his traumatic relationship with Pa, Lac's "embarrassingly proud father" (p. 3). The opening of the book briefly summarizes Lac's family background in Vietnam before the unification of Vietnam in 1975. During the Vietnam War, Pa rose from orphanage and poverty to stability and prosperity by running a warehouse business, which made him the "embodiment of capitalism" (p. 40). He had served as a commander fighting the communists from the North militarily and supporting the former Saigon government politically. After the war ended, Lac's family fled Vietnam on a small, crowded fishing boat with other escapees and reached Hong Kong, before they relocated as refugees in California.

The narrative then focuses most specifically on Lac's and his family's life experience in the United States. The four members of his family—Lac, Pa, Ma (Lac's mother), and Quy (Lac's younger sister)—live in a small apartment in an old, squalid, and dilapidated brick building in Hollywood, and the five-year-old narrator witnesses various social ills in his neighborhood, where drug dealers, pimps, prostitutes, thieves, and gangs coexist. Thus, Pa does not allow his wife and children to leave the apartment while he is away looking for work, which makes Lac feel "suffocated and claustrophobic" (p. 28). The family's initial resettlement is fraught with misfortunes, language barriers, cultural misunderstandings, and discrimination. Despite the tribulations of life in exile, his parents emphasize the importance of education, the passport to a better life "in this white man's land" (p. 37). Lac studies at an American school, and he feels alienated from and rejected by his peers because of his lack of English proficiency and his Asian background.

His parents become upset and frustrated at Lac's unsatisfactory academic work when they compare his performance to that of other Vietnamese children. Henceforth, Lac suffers from Pa's daily beatings and relentless criticism for being intellectually retarded and stupid. His parents superstitiously pray to their ancestors to elicit their blessings, and they force Lac to eat cow brain cooked with herbs, believing that the "vitamins" in this "medicine" will make their son smarter (pp. 66–67).

After the death of his infant brother, Zeal, the family moves to a new apartment, and they later are joined by Lac's cousin, named Crazy, who often harasses Lac sexually. Ma knows about Crazy's pedophilic behavior, but she hides it from Pa, afraid that Pa will fly into a rage and kill Crazy. In the new neighborhood, Lac feels more welcome and comfortable because "people show interest in me and treat me kindly," but Pa insists that Lac socializes only with Asian kids (p. 81); Pa "doesn't trust whites, which to him means anyone who isn't Asian" (p. 82). Lac starts to hang out with a group of Chicano boys in the Kingsley Street Gang who try to convert Lac from an obedient child into a gang member. Pa becomes sick for a long time, which gives Lac complete freedom. Lac befriends Javi, a gang member. As Javi's "cash whore," or procurer of money, Lac steals his mother's food stamps and $500 from his college fund to strengthen his camaraderie with Javi, thus supporting Javi's addiction to the arcade game *Spy Hunter* (p. 108). Later, when Pa discovers the financial losses, Lac is punished severely.

After this incident, Pa buys a used car and moves his family to Alhambra, east of Chinatown, "where other Asians dwell—a place where [Lac]'ll be protected from the white people" (p. 122). While his parents feel secure and inapprehensive about their new neighborhood, Lac does not enjoy being surrounded by Asian people because Asians "remind me of the ugliness of my own" (p. 123). Lac later states, "I've always associated the Vietnamese with the ugliness of my family and my embarrassment over my culture" (p. 139). Lac enrolls in a new junior high school but chooses to socialize with Mexican peers. The memoir and Chapter 9 have the same title. In this chapter, Lac is intrigued by his friends' celebration of Christmas, and when he talks to Pa about Christmas and present-giving, Pa ridicules his son for "getting influenced by the whites" because "boat people" have nothing to do with Christmas (pp. 145–146). Lac is invited by his Mexican friend, Art, to his house for a Christmas party, and Lac is impressed by the way Art and his parents embrace the language of endearment. He contrasts the happy, affectionate atmosphere in Art's family with the suffocating, violent atmosphere in his own family, and Lac envies Art and his parents for their verbal communication characterized by such loving phrases as "I love you" and "Thank you." He does not understand why this kind of warm communication never occurs in his family. When Lac returns home, he imitates the way Art talks to his parents by saying "I love you" to Pa, who rebuts:

> What the fuck? Pa leaps up from the creeper and kicks it back against the garage door with his heel. He gets right in my face. *Motherfuck!* What did you just say? Who the fuck do you think you are? Who do you think *I* am? Are you trying to imitate those *white* people by telling me those fucking words? *Stop that shit!* Don't you ever say those weak words to me ever again, you hear me? (p. 150)

Pa then sardonically calls Lac humiliating names and emphasizes to his son that love must be shown "through action" and not through words: "Words are useless—they do nothing but piss me [Pa] off" (p. 151).

Lac then befriends Dragon Head and joins the Street Ratz Gang. While he enjoys living his adolescent life of debauchery outside his home, beyond the control of Pa, he continues to suffer from the domestic violence and turbulence within his family, primarily due to Pa's disability and paranoia. Pa is an abusive husband and tiger father who runs the family like a tyrant. Lac's mother and siblings are victims of Pa's bad temper and unpredicted rage, and the atmosphere in the family is always tense. Lac does not live up to his parents' expectations—that is, to remain Asian and become educated but obedient; rather, he lives a "thug life" (p. 167). Dragon Head and Snooky exercise extremely negative peer-influence upon Lac, teaching him to steal, drink, smoke, bully, lie, and devote his time to sex and truancy. Lac also becomes less fearful of Pa, probably because he has become inured to Pa's beatings and criticism.

Lac's parents then sponsor the emigration of Uncles Five and Nine to the United States, and the two uncles join the family. Lac often is included in the family's carousing parties. At school, Lac's grades do not improve, and after Lac is beaten by a girlfriend's brother in an alley on his way back from school, Pa decides to enroll his children in a new magnet school to avoid the troubles caused by thugs.

The epilogue focuses on Lac's eventual visit to Vietnam and his adult reflections upon his childhood memories and relationship with Pa. Lac travels to Vietnam to find and reclaim his Vietnamese roots, without informing Pa of the trip, because Pa will not allow Lac to make the journey. Due to the psychological wounds inflicted upon him, Lac decides to pursue a PhD in industrial-organizational psychology at UC-Irvine, and later he gets married. He hopes that writing his memoirs will help him become a better father through coming to terms with the bittersweet, loving-abusive relationship between him and Pa.

Su's *I Love Yous Are for White People* can be best categorized under the rubric of the literature of trauma, which focuses on the victim's painful experience and his/her writing down the traumatic memories in an attempt to make sense of the unpleasant past. Normally, it may take a victim 10 to 15 years to process the experience, and writing is an effective means to alleviate the psychological wounds. In an interview with Lac Su printed at the back of the book, the author states, "Even though this book was painful to write, it helped me to heal" ("At Last," p. 10). Su's memoir also can be categorized under the rubric of the literature of domestic realism, which generally focuses on relationships among family members and familial issues.

The memoir is a significant contribution to the corpus of Vietnamese American literature. The most important theme treated in the memoir is domestic violence. Within the Asian American community, domestic violence and child abuse are not uncommon, but they do not gain substantial public attention because generally Asian Americans consider parental discipline of children a private problem to be solved within the family. In the Introduction to *Where Are You From? An Anthology of Asian American Writing*, the editors Byron Wong, Larry Yu, and Valarie Katagiri (2012) observe, "It is a sad fact that Asian American women between the ages of fifteen and twenty-four have the highest suicide rates of any ethnicity. It is telling that Asian American males have fallen into a depressing cycle of violence" (p. 14). Patriarchy and Confucian values place the husband/father as the authority figure in the household, and thus his voice wields absolute power, while the voices of other family members are silenced. *I Love Yous Are for White People* stands as a literary testimony of domestic violence, as the narrator, his mother, and siblings are victimized by Pa's tyranny. It should be noted that Pa's abusive behavior also results from the specific conditions of poverty and traumatic displacement that impact the arrival of many Southeast Asian refugees after the end of the Vietnam War. Thus, the memoir is a critique of structural inequalities, urban poverty, and the intersection between class, gender, and race in the contexts of war and its aftermath.

Gender relations is another theme that directly derives from aspects of Asian patriarchal culture. Throughout the memoir, Ma is submissive, docile, and stoic. Her opinions are not valued by Pa because he considers them to be intellectually inferior to his own. For instance, he arrogantly ascribes Lac's poor grades to Ma's lack of intelligence: "We know he got this from you. There's no way my genes produced such a stupid child" (p. 64). Although the narrator does not say that Ma is unhappy and resents Pa, he has seen her crying, after being beaten by Pa, several times. However, she seems to accept her role as a subservient woman without accusing her husband of his wrongdoings.

Su's portrayal of Pa substantiates several negative, biased stereotypes of Asian men: They are portrayed as asexual, stoic, emotionless, unromantic, and abusive. For instance, Mary Yu Danico and Franklin Ng (2004) observe that the U.S. media often present Asian men as "having no emotions" (p. 121). Derek Kenji Iwamoto and William Minh Liu (2009) further add that Asian men who are portrayed as manifesting high emotion sometimes are depicted as "wife beater[s]" or even as "deviant sexual aggressors" (p. 218). As mentioned above, Pa believes that Asians should not use affectionate expressions because they are meaningless. There is no romance in his marriage. His personality is complex: on the one hand, he works very hard for the well-being of his family and protects his children from dangers; on the other hand, he curses, scolds, and beats his children mercilessly. The image of *home* throughout the memoir does not symbolize warmth, protection, love; rather, *home* is an archive of trauma, danger, and violence.

Another prominent theme is the loss of innocence. Very early in his childhood in Vietnam, Lac already had seen such social ills as adultery, drinking, corruption, and blackmailing. He has also witnessed the cruelty of war: the sounds of firing, the explosion of grenades, and shootings. His perilous escape from Vietnam at the age of four is so haunting that he has "recurring nightmares" about the journey (p. 61). After the family's relocation in the United States, Lac experiences sexual molestation, mistreatment, and Southern California's urban gang culture.

CNN interviewed the author about his book in 2011, and they discussed his father's tiger parenting with Amy Chua, author of the controversial Chinese American memoir *Battle Hymn of the Tiger Mother.*[1] *I Love Yous Are for White People* is Lac Su's personal journey from domestic violence and "thug life" to self-healing and higher-education success.

Su's memoir addresses some of the many themes commonly found in ethnic American life-narratives, such as survival, alienation, loneliness, the desire to belong, cultural clash, displacement, generational conflict, and racial prejudice. Once they reach American soil, the United States is not the Promised Land that many refugees and immigrants had wished for and expected. The narrative tone is honest, sincere, and sometimes humorous, despite the narrator's sorrowful past. The heart-wrenching memoir represents Su's successful debut in writing, and it has attracted the attention of a wide and varied audience. It breaks new ground in Vietnamese American literature.

PUBLICATION NOTE

This review was published online in 2013 by the *Journal of Southeast Asian American Education and Advancement* in Volume 8, Issue 1. Minor edits have been made here. The original can be found at http://doi.org/10.7771/2153-8999.1060.

NOTE

1. This interview can be accessed at http://www.cnn.com/2011/OPINION/01/20/lac.su.tiger.mother.scars/index.html

REFERENCES

Danico, M. Y., & Ng, F. (2004). *Asian American issues*. Greenwood.

Iwamoto, D. K., & Liu, W. M. (2009). Asian American men and Asianized attribution: Intersections of masculinity and sexuality. In N. Tewari & A. N. Alvarez (Eds.), *Asian American psychology: Current perspectives* (pp. 211–232). Psychology Press.

Wong, B., Yu, L., & Katagiri, V. (2012). Introduction. In L. Yu & V. Katagiri (Eds.), *Where are you from? An anthology of Asian American writing* (pp. 11–15). Thymos.

16

Book Review

Bic Ngo's (2010) *Unresolved Identities: Discourse, Ambivalence, and Urban Immigrant Students*

Ngo, Bic. (2010). *Unresolved identities: Discourses, ambivalence and urban immigrant students.* Albany, NY: SUNY Press. 146 pp. $19.95 (Paperback). ISBN: 978-1-4384-3058-4.

REVIEWED BY GILBERT C. PARK

COMPLICATING SOUTHEAST ASIAN IMMIGRANT IDENTITIES IN AN URBAN SCHOOL

While the number of immigrant students from Southeast Asia in our urban schools has been on the rise over the past few decades, their school experiences have received relatively little attention from educational researchers and policy makers. When discussed, the literature often highlights the difficulties as a result of the cultural differences between school, home, and ethnic community (Bankston & Hidalgo, 2006; Souryasak & Lee, 2007; Vang, 2005). Others explore the students' struggles to embrace or resist the pressures of assimilation (Manke & Keller, 2006; Townsend & Fu, 2001; Ying & Han, 2008). Additionally, some seek to promote understanding of Southeast Asian Americans by describing their cultures (Go & Le, 2005; Han, 2008; Yang, 2004). These works, however, seem to fall short in effectively challenging the public image of Southeast Asian American students as poor, violent, and underprivileged immigrant inner-city youth of color with a heroic few overcoming cultural, economic, and social hindrances. To this end, Bic Ngo's *Unresolved Identities* is a timely study that illuminates the complexities and contradictions in the identities and lives of today's Southeast Asian immigrant students in an urban school.

Unresolved Identities consists of six chapters and a methodological discussion. The first chapter presents the argument in the relevant literature and the next four chapters deal with the ethnographic findings. Specifically, Chapters 2 and 3 explore the discourses of urban and immigrant youth at a school she calls Dynamic High. The next two chapters highlight the "meaning-makings" of the immigrant students' individual identities within these discourses. The final chapter includes both theoretical and practical implications of the study. These are followed by the author's positionality to the researched, descriptions of the site, data collection, and analytical procedures. Overall, I found the book to be of great value in expanding the knowledge of the school experiences of Southeast Asian American students in particular and of urban immigrants in general. It includes well-supported arguments, rich ethnographic findings, and meaningful educational implications for educators to better serve today's urban immigrant students.

Ngo starts the book by contextualizing the topic within the larger literature on urban and immigrant school experiences. In the process, the findings are situated to stretch our current understanding on identity and urban immigrants in general and Southeast Asian American students in particular. This is accomplished as she locates her argument within the two conflicting discourses regarding immigrant students in an urban setting. Regarding urban schools, there are images of "ghetto" schools and communities that are responsible for their own academic difficulties while, on the other hand, showcasing the resilience of a few who overcame the related challenges. Similarly, the immigrants are also reduced to the dualistic and often dichotomous positions as traditional versus Americanized or mono- versus bicultural. In resisting these, Ngo argues the immigrant school experiences in an urban setting are "more messier and contradictory" where their identities are beyond "binary," "multiple," "hybrid," or "situated" as discussed by other researchers (p. 3). Rather, she argues the students' understanding of themselves is complex and ongoing where the "subject position of a person shifts with each speaking from one moment to the next" (p. 9).

Rich ethnographic data in the next four chapters explicates the argument. Aiming to "unsettle the hegemony of discourse that frame identities within discrete and binary categories" (p. 5), the author employs ethnographic tools like interviews and observations of Southeast Asian American students and their teachers at Dynamic High over a one academic year period. Guided by poststructural and postcolonial frameworks, the data collection and analysis focused on the moments of contradictions, uncertainty, and fractures. For instance, chapters 2 and 3 unravel the complex relationships of two seemingly contradictory discourses: the school as a *war zone* and the students as *comeback kids*.

The discourses of what Ngo calls *urban dysfunction* were voiced by teachers' own and others' perceptions of Dynamic High in Chapter 2 with discourses such as a *war zone* with *metal detectors, poverty*, and a *different kind of American kids*. These are consistent with the discourse that reduces an inner-city school to being a less desirable place to learn and work. While many of these terms no longer, if ever, accurately portray the school and its community because of the changes that have taken place under the leadership of previous administrators, the discourse still shaped how the teachers viewed the students and themselves. In Chapter 3, we hear the teachers highlighting the resilience of some successful inner-city students. Continuing the discourse of the school and the community as a *war zone*, these teachers understood their students' school experiences and challenges using the framework of "culture of poverty" (as explained by Moynihan, 1965). Speaking from this perspective, some teachers portrayed the school as a *safe haven* for their students who came from dangerous homes and neighbors in turmoil. Put differently, the students who appreciated and took advantage of the *safe haven* are positioned to succeed.

The attention shifts to the students in Chapters 4 and 5 as the author examines the discourses facing the Southeast Asian American youth. One of the discourses positions Lao students as Chinese; this describes non–Southeast Asian students' ignorance of, or unwillingness to affirm, the diversity within the Asian American community. The other is the resistance of the Hmong American students to accept the reductionist discourse mentioned above by affirming their own ethnicity, which, in turn, created another discourse that failed to account for Lao identity. In the process, the discourse and the counter-discourse worked to further marginalize Lao American students. The author further complicates our understanding of identity by illuminating subjective positions of individual students' sense of selves. This is accomplished through the collisions and negotiations of multiple constructs of the Lao identity of different students. This chapter is followed by in-depth analysis of three Lao American students to demonstrate the ambivalence of culture and identity via change and negotiation in Chapter 5. A student called Kett, for instance, showed both traces of the "good" student who was dedicated to school success and the "bad" student who dressed like a gangster. Another student, Vonechai, defied social boundaries as a preppy Lao girl who dressed like a middle-class white person and talked like a "loud" black girl. Similarly, Chintana refused to choose between being a "good" student who did well in school and a "bad" student involved in a "gang." Instead, she chose to be a successful schoolgirl from the "hood."

Ngo argues in the final chapter that identities and school experiences of Southeast Asian American students must be approached and understood holistically and in individual cases. Put differently, the binary and dichotomous discourses fail to capture the multiplicity, variability, and inconsistency of the students' identities. Consequently, Ngo calls for attention to the ways that "the experiences of the immigrant students in U.S. schools and society intersect with their experiences as adolescents, urban students and racial and ethnic minorities, among others" (p. 95). With this, she argues that attempts to understand the cultural differences are counterproductive since the students themselves were uncertain of who they were. Instead, Ngo calls for understanding how different identities intersect to produce moments of relative privilege and disadvantages, which include situating the selves as teachers and students in these contradictory positions. These require critical self-examinations beyond celebration of cultural others.

The ambivalence of identity as shown in these chapters exposes the limitations of notions that identities are multiple, situational, or even hybrid. Instead, identities are what she calls temporary where they can change from one moment to the next given the context. The findings are clearly linked to the discourses of larger society and the parallel representations of Dynamic High as an inner-city school and her students as troubled inner-city youth. Also, the seemingly consistent relationships between the school as a war zone and the students as war babies are complicated as the teachers stressed representing their workplace as a decent place to work and some of their students as good students who overcame odds. Moreover, the binary framework that situated both school and the students as good or bad was challenged and expanded as Ngo reveals its limitations and implications. As a result, the author successfully "unsettle(s) what we know about urban schools and immigrant students" (p. 5). Overall, I felt that this book adds to the current literature on identity and urban education. Also, it will appeal to researchers and educators who are interested in these topics in addition to multicultural education and the school experiences of immigrants, Southeast Asian Americans, and Asian Americans in general.

PUBLICATION NOTE

This review was published online in 2010 by the Journal of Southeast Asian American Education and Advancement in Volume 5, Issue 1. Minor edits have been made here. The original can be found at http://doi.org/10.7771/2153-8999.1009.

REFERENCES

Bankston, C. L., & Hidalgo, D. A. (2006). Respect in Southeast Asian American children and adolescents: Cultural and contextual influences. *New Directions for Child and Adolescent Development, 114*, 25–38. https://doi.org/10.1002/cd.173

Go, C. G., & Le, T. N. (2005). Gender differences in Cambodian delinquency: The role of ethnic identity, parental discipline, and peer delinquency. *Crime & Delinquency, 51*(2), 220–237. https://doi.org/10.1177/0011128704273466

Han, W. (2008). The academic trajectories of children of immigrants and their school environments. *Developmental Psychology*, *44*(6), 1572–1590. https://psycnet.apa.org/doi/10.1037/a0013886

Manke, M., & Keller, K. (2006). Lao newcomers and Mennonite settlers: A case study of local cultural and language interaction. *Journal of Language, Identity & Education*, *5*(2), 123–141. https://doi.org/10.1207/s15327701jlie0502_2

Moynihan, D. P. (1965). *The Negro family: The case for national action*. Brookings Institute.

Souryasak, R., & Lee, J. S. (2007). Drawing on students' experiences, cultures and languages to develop English language writing: Perspectives from three Lao heritage middle school students. *Heritage Language Journal*, *5*(1), 79–97. https://doi.org/10.46538/hlj.5.1.4

Townsend, J., & Fu, D. (2001). Paw's story: A Laotian refugee's lonely entry into American literacy. *Journal of Adolescent and Adult Literacy*, *45*(2), 104–114. https://www.jstor.org/stable/40014716

Vang, C. T. (2005). Hmong-American students still face multiple challenges in public schools. *Multicultural Education*, *12*(1), 27–54.

Yang, K. (2004). Southeast Asian American children: Not the "model minority." *Future of Children*, *14*(2), 127–133.

Ying, Y., & Han, M. (2008). Parental contributions to Southeast Asian American adolescents' well-being. *Youth & Society*, *40*(2), 289–306. https://doi.org/10.1177/0044118X08315506

17

Book Review

Chia Youyee Vang's (2010) *Hmong America: Reconstructing Community in Diaspora*

Vang, C. Y. (2010). *Hmong America: Reconstructing community in diaspora.* Urbana: University of Illinois Press. 192 pp. $25.00 (Paperback). ISBN: 978-0- 252-07759-3.

REVIEWED BY YANG SAO XIONG

Since the 1980s, an increasing number of researchers have documented Hmong former refugees' cultural and economic adaptation in the United States. Vang's *Hmong America* provides a recent depiction of the Hmong's historical experiences with colonialism and imperialism, their struggles for basic survival during the wars in Laos, their forced displacement, and their attempts to rebuild ethnic communities in Minnesota's Twin Cities. By taking account of the Hmong's pre-migration experiences, *Hmong America* helps clarify the dynamically evolving adaptation of Hmong former refugees and their children, especially their adaptation to new communities, institutions, and governments. By describing Hmong Americans' ongoing trans-state activities, Vang's book also sheds light on the decades-long social, economic, and political relationships between Hmong in the United States and their Southeast Asian compatriots.

Displaying vigilance and sensitivity to the consequences of group stereotypes, Vang reminds her readers that "the Hmong American community" is neither a monolithic nor homogeneous ethnic community. Rather, Vang points out, immense internal diversity of identities and interests exist in Hmong American communities. This diversity is manifested in the great variety of subcategories such as dialects, clans, subclans or lineages, voluntary associations, political organizations, ethnic churches, and other categories. From discussing the intraethnic divisions created by French colonial cooptation following indigenous revolts in Laos (pp. 20–22) to discussing Hmong Americans' contemporary "politics of representation" (pp. 88–96), each of Vang's chapters invites readers to think about what internal diversity could mean for ethnic members' ability to construct instrumental ethnicity and maintain meaningful cultural traditions.

In my view, it is in Chapters 4 and 5 that *Hmong America* provides the most lively discussions of Hmong Americans' forms of cultural adaptation and ethnic-political agency. In Chapter 4, "Continuity and Reinvention of Traditions," Vang describes the Hmong New Year celebration in Minnesota and examines its role in "affirming established Hmong cultural identities and creating new ones" (p. 98). Vang's discussion of Hmong individuals' varied interpretations of the Hmong New Year celebration evokes some of the most interesting, albeit understudied, processes of the Hmong's cultural and ideological change.

One such process involves Hmong individuals' anxiety over what they perceive to be the increasing "commercialization" of the traditionally celebrated Hmong New Year event. Arguing that "Hmong Americanization [*sic*] has come to signify increasing American cultural and economic influence," Vang points out that "many Hmong Americans contend that New Year celebrations have become too commercialized" (p. 105). Ten pages later, Vang briefly revisits this general idea. Vang cites a written passage by an individual who expressed discontent with the New Year event because, according to him/her, it has come to contain "strange and odd" programs and be "full [of] business booths . . . [that] only [benefit] business folks and the organizers" (p. 116). Vang interprets the writer's discontent to mean that s/he was "argu[ing] against the commodification of New Year celebrations" (p. 116). This interpretation is provocative. However, I wish Vang had clarified her usage of these Marx-formulated concepts, examined how and in what ways the Hmong New Year has been commodified, and discussed what consequences processes of commodification have had for other social domains of Hmong American life. If by commodification Vang means the transformation of formerly noncommercial relationships into exchange relations, then it would seem important to also address questions such as the following: In the Hmong American context, who or what is doing the commodification, to whom, and under what conditions? And what consequences have commodification of certain practices and their attendant social relationships had, if any, for the maintenance of particular cultural traditions or for the maintenance of ethnic solidarity?

Chapter 5 contains several examples of political activism within Hmong American communities. These examples not only illustrate individual and collective agency, but also help clarify the very important fact that Hmong Americans, despite their relative political invisibility, have never been social isolates. Instead, Hmong Americans frequently engage with people and governments around them and, in doing so, create tangible changes for their communities. Highlighting Hmong Americans' active role in pursuing rights, resources, and representation in the U.S. context, Vang points out that especially in recent years, Hmong Americans have engaged in political coalition building and sought political offices at school boards and state legislatures. Furthermore, Vang points out, segments of the Hmong American population continue to participate in contentious "homeland politics," including "long-distance nationalism" (p. 136), which maintains not only the imagined community but also the often ambivalent relationship between Hmong exiles and their former homelands.

Vang contends that through their participation in these forms of U.S. and foreign political activism, "Hmong Americans have been partially responsible for the maintenance of their perpetual refugee identity" (p. 122). To be sure, several factors, including the Hmong's involuntary refugee status, make their relationship with the U.S. government a perpetually fluctuating one. That is, Hmong former refugees and their U.S.-born children have, at times, been treated as U.S. allies, but at other times, as aliens ineligible for public benefits, as second-class citizens, as perpetually unassimilable foreigners, or, even worse, as former terrorists or indicted terrorism plotters. Furthermore, it is often the case that Hmong Americans must construct and evoke a military-service frame during most social movements in order to seek political recognition or resources from state and federal government departments. However, in my view, the claim that Hmong Americans are responsible for maintaining an imposed label (i.e., perpetual refugees) demands more substantiation and debate.

Although not "the first scholarly work . . . from inside the Hmong community"[1] to examine the Hmong's experiences in Laos or their ongoing struggles in America, Vang's book serves as an invaluable introduction to contemporary Hmong American society. One of its strengths is in the breadth of issues in Hmong American communities that it covers. Another is in its careful attention to the Hmong's pre-migration experiences, their internal group diversity, and how these complicate and condition the remaking of ethnic communities. Students interested in the processes of refugee adaptation, cultural change, and race-ethnic relations in the United States should read Vang's *Hmong America*.

PUBLICATION NOTE

This review was published online in 2011 by the *Journal of Southeast Asian American Education and Advancement* in Volume 6, Issue 1. Minor edits have been made here. The original can be found at http://doi.org/10.7771/2153-8999.1033.

NOTE

1. This claim appeared on the back cover of the book under review.

18

Book Review

Thanhha Lai's (2011) *Inside Out & Back Again*

Lai, Thanhha. (2011). *Inside out & back again*. New York: Harper. 262 pp. $15.99 (Hardcover). ISBN: 978-0-06-196278-3.

REVIEWED BY QUAN MANH HA

Inside Out & Back Again, by Thanhha Lai, is the first Vietnamese American memoir of childhood written *in free verse*, and it chronicles the narrator's memories of Vietnam prior to the Communist takeover in April 1975, and of her family's initial resettlement in Alabama after their escape from Vietnam just before the fall of Saigon. Although the publisher categorizes the book as a novel in verse, *Inside Out & Back Again* in most respects is a memoir in verse, formatted as a journal with entries for specific dates. In the author's note to the readers, Lai writes, "Much of what happened to Ha, the main character in *Inside Out & Back Again*, also happened to me," and "So many details in this story were inspired by my own memories" (p. 261). She dedicates her book to "the millions of refugees in the world," hoping that they will "find a home." This dedication establishes the book's themes of displacement and resettlement in diasporic communities.

Lai divides her book into four parts: "Saigon," "At Sea," "Alabama," and "From Now On," respectively. Part I, "Saigon," starts with her memories of the 1975 Tet—Vietnamese Lunar New Year—the Year of the Cat. Her father is a Navy officer in the Army Republic of Vietnam (ARVN), who has spent a few years training in the United States. He is mentioned in the book, but due to his Navy mission he is never present. The narrator, Ha, lives with her mother and three older brothers: Quang, Vu, and Khoi. The most significant image that she remembers from her childhood is of a papaya tree that she planted in her back garden—an image recurring throughout the narrative. War causes separation, fear, and a feeling of uncertainty, and the family experiences these misfortunes, intensified by the father's "missing-in-action" status. Dutifully, they pray for his safety. In March 1975, a month prior to the collapse of South Vietnam, the narrator experienced political turmoil, shortage of food, insecurity, sounds of gunfire and bomb explosions, and confusion, as "American soldiers left [Vietnam]" and the Communists approached Saigon (p. 18). On April 8, 1975, her brother Quang runs from school to bring the family the news of his father's capture by the Communists. This horrific revelation is followed by a flashback of Lai's parents' arranged marriage years earlier in the North: After their wedding, they moved south, believing that "it would be / easier to breathe / away from Communism" (p. 28); thereafter, in 1954, Vietnam then was divided, and communication between family members in the two parts of the country was forbidden. This turn of events represents her family's first exile. She recalls the moments she accompanied Mother to President Thieu's "ceremony of comfort" to widows of ARVN soldiers, in which he "cries actual tears," but the narrator "know[s] that to mean / fake tears of a crocodile" (pp. 32–36).

Amid the chaos and turbulence of Saigon, Uncle Son—Father's best friend and also a Navy officer—visits the narrator's home and urges her family to flee Vietnam with him on a ship arranged for Navy families. Mother prepares items necessary for her children, and on April 29, they clandestinely board the ship. Part I ends with the official announcement of the fall of Saigon, when the narrator already is at sea.

Part II, "At Sea," recounts the narrator's memories of the family's escape to Thailand, which is not as perilous as that experienced by thousands of "boat people" who fled Vietnam on small fishing boats, because her family fortunately had obtained seats on a Navy ship. Nevertheless, they encounter certain hardships: inadequate food rations, cramped space, thirst, and primitive sanitary conditions. On the ship, the narrator observes the apprehensions of other escapees: One woman is desperate because "without a country / she cannot live"; others feel guilt for abandoning their homeland and loved ones (p. 85). Three weeks after their departure, they are rescued by a "gigantic ship / with an American flag," (p. 91), and the narrator, for the first time, sees American men, and she becomes curious about their appearance (most specifically, about their facial and arm hair). The Americans offer the escapees abundant food and water and take them to Guam, where they stay in a refugee camp, study English, and watch American movies. Mother then decides to choose America for their resettlement destination, where her sons "*must first go to college*" (p. 106). The family eventually arrives in Florida and awaits an American sponsor-family. Mother has to write down "Christians" on the application forms in order to attract the attention of potential religious sponsors. A "cowboy-like" car dealer then brings the entire family to his home state, Alabama.

In Part III, "Alabama," the family begins its arduous process of assimilation into American culture as it adjusts to life in exile. The family first lives in the sponsor's house. Although the husband is friendly and kind, his wife impresses them as "mean" and unwelcoming (p. 119). Later, the family moves into a two-bedroom apartment provided by the U.S. government to "ease the guilt / of losing the war" (p. 124). Mother eventually writes a letter to Father's brother in Northern Vietnam, inquiring about her husband. A response does not come immediately. In the meantime, Quang focuses on mastering English and acts as the family's translator. He works as a mechanic, and Mother works at a sewing factory. The other members of the family "must go to school, / repeating the last grade, / left unfinished" (p. 136). Scattered throughout Part III are the narrator's memories of her efforts to learn English and of her confusion over complex English grammar rules. At school, she feels alienated, and she is teased by her peers because she is the only Asian student and a Buddhist. Her elementary school experience is quite unpleasant, as she faces bullying classmates and condescending teachers who erroneously equate her faulty English with poor cognitive abilities. At home, her brother Vu teaches her self-defense techniques, after which a subsequent confrontation with a bully named Pink Boy after school is comical. In the neighborhood, the family is befriended by Miss Washington, a widow and retired teacher, who kindly tutors the narrator in English and comforts her whenever necessary. Miss Washington had a son who died in the Vietnam War, and she gives the narrator a book about Vietnam that her son had sent her. Part III also gives notes to a few incidents in which the family feels embarrassed due to their limited knowledge of U.S. culture and their unfamiliarity with American food. Life in exile is fraught with many false starts and misunderstandings.

In order to help the family gain greater acceptance in the community, the sponsor takes them to the Del Ray Southern Baptist Church, where they are baptized and become Christians. Nevertheless, at home, Mother continues to chant the names of the Buddha and the Bodhisattvas. The sponsor becomes kinder and more generous after their baptism. The narrator enjoys learning about such American holidays as Halloween, Thanksgiving, and Christmas. Thus, the process of adjustment and assimilation is a mixture of positive and negative elements.

Part IV, which takes place during Christmas of 1975, opens with a letter that Mother receives from Father's brother, informing her of his death. Respectfully, she sets up a shrine for him and asks all members of the family to pray for his eternal peace. As career paths, Quang wants to become an engineer, Vu a chef, Khoi a vet, and the narrator a poet. *Inside Out & Back Again* concludes with the image of Tet, the family's first Lunar New Year celebrated in exile. The image is powerful because it recapitulates the status of the family as Vietnamese Americans: members of an ethnic community that must connect the positive values of two distinct cultures.

Thematically, *Inside Out & Back Again* does not present anything new to the corpus of Vietnamese American literature. The narrator's childhood memories resemble those described in several previous Vietnamese American works, such as Nguyen Qui Duc's *Where the Ashes Are* (1994) and Le Thi Diem Thuy's *The Gangster We Are All Looking For* (2003). The themes of loss, separation, nostalgia, homesickness, alienation, invisibility, life in exile, cultural differences, language barriers, and the mother-daughter relationship present in Lai's *Inside Out & Back Again* are common to most Vietnamese American literature. However, her book is innovative in its narrative style and form, as she chronicles her memories in verse, instead of in prose.

The book's tone and point of view are those of an innocent girl who narrates events in simple vocabulary, but readers can appreciate the beauty, charm, and emotion conveyed in such simplicity, as they are enhanced by the poetic mode. The stylistic naiveté evidenced, for example, in her choice of vocabulary is innocently charming: She does not use the word *baptize* to describe the family's baptism, but "Each of my brothers / gets dipped" (p. 171) at the Baptist church; she uses the words "pretend day" to describe Halloween (p. 196). Despite the various adversities and obstacles that the family encounters, the narrator maintains a sense of humor. For instance, not understanding why English has so many /s/ sounds and "squeezing hisses," she observes: "Whoever invented / English / must have loved / snakes" (p. 118), and not comprehending many of the seemingly illogical grammar rules, she notes: "Whoever invented English / should be bitten / by a snake" (p. 128). Lai, in these instances and elsewhere, employs descriptions of sounds and images that evoke strong emotions and memories of the past, a sense of wonder in a new country, and a Vietnamese poetic spirit that adversity challenges but does not subdue. Readers can smell and taste the papaya fruit that she describes, and they can sense the frequent tears trailing down from her mother's eyes. The author's choice of verse instead of prose permits such poetic enhancement of the narrative, and in this case it is a refreshing and satisfying choice.

Inside Out & Back Again, with its childhood perspective and lyrical language, is accessible for children and young adult readers who want to learn about the Vietnam War, the Vietnamese Americans, and the hardships one faces as the "alienated Other" in U.S. culture.

PUBLICATION NOTE

This review was published online in 2013 by the *Journal of Southeast Asian American Education and Advancement* in Volume 8, Issue 1. Minor edits have been made here. The original can be found at http://doi.org/10.7771/2153-8999.1064.

19

Book Review

Cathy J. Schlund-Vials's (2012) *War, Genocide, and Justice: Cambodian American Memory Work*

Schlund-Vials, Cathy J. (2012). *War, genocide, and justice: Cambodian American memory work*. Minneapolis, MN: University of Minnesota Press. 264 pp. $22.50 (Paperback). ISBN 978-0-8166-7097-0.

REVIEWED BY QUAN TUE TRAN

Nearly four decades after the Khmer Rouge seized control of Phnom Penh and executed the genocidal policy that killed an estimated 1.7 million Cambodians (1975–1979), it is timely to ask: How and why do Cambodians and Cambodian Americans remember and forget the genocide? What is at stake in their diverse engagement with this genocidal past? Cathy Schlund-Vials tackles these questions with depth, urgency, and theoretical nuance in *War, Genocide, and Justice: Cambodian American Memory Work*. Through an effective comparative approach, the author juxtaposes dominant cultural narratives about the Cambodian genocide with the multilayer "memory work" of 1.5-generation Cambodian American cultural producers. She convincingly argues that in light of inadequate and amnesiac state-sanctioned narratives about the Khmer Rouge era, Cambodian American filmmakers, writers, musicians, and performance artists generate alternative sites for justice, healing, and reclamation through their labor. More specifically, she shows that by engaging the genocidal past through documenting survivor testimonials, personalized narratives, and familial genealogies, Cambodian American "remembrance activists" assert cultural citizenship claims in both Cambodia and the United States. Their politicized, intergenerational, and transnational efforts offer rich platforms to explore the agency of survivors, questions of war and genocidal justice, and the politics of memory.

Comprising four engaging chapters, an introduction, and an epilogue, *War, Genocide, and Justice* draws on an impressive and unexamined archive of Cambodian

American cultural production that privileges the perspectives of genocide survivors. The book begins by confronting the "Cambodian Syndrome," which Schlund-Vials defines as "a transnational set of amnesiac politics" that "encompasses the paradoxical nonadmission of U.S. culpability before, during, and after the Democratic Kampuchean era" (p. 13). The current Cambodian government's selective remembering and strategic forgetting of the crimes committed by the Khmer Rouge also exacerbates this syndrome. For example, the author argues in Chapter 1 that because the Vietnamese occupying army (1979–1989) rehabilitated and curated sites like Toul Sleng Genocide Museum and Ek Center for Genocide Crimes for the purpose of legitimizing Vietnamese military presence in the nascent People's Republic of Kampuchea, these iconic places essentially reproduce a master narrative of Vietnamese liberation rather than providing meaningful spaces for collective remembrance and reconciliation on Cambodian terms. Such sites are additionally problematic because they emphasize the perpetrators' atrocities at the expense of the victims, whose skeletal remains are displayed indefinitely as criminal evidence and deprived of proper and culturally sensitive burials. Moreover, as these sites become renowned international atrocity tourism destinations, they perpetuate and commodify the victims' miseries.

Moving beyond the built memorials in Cambodia, Schlund-Vials turns to cinematic memory of the Khmer Rouge era by analyzing the historical drama *The Killing Fields* (directed by Roland Joffé, 1984) alongside Socheata Poeuv's autobiographical documentary *New Year Baby* (2006) in Chapter 2. Interpreting *The Killing Fields*, which is based on American journalist Sydney Schanberg's *The Death and Life of Dith Pran*, as an apologetic and redemptive narrative, she points out that the film's preoccupation with American moral qualms associated with U.S. foreign policies in Southeast Asia serves the pursuit of American atonement rather than genocide survivors' search for justice and reconciliation. In contrast, Schlund-Vials asserts that *New Year Baby*—an autobiographical film that documents the filmmaker's and her family's quest for truth and closure—engenders a powerful and intimate remembrance effort that privileges survivors' desire for justice, reconciliation, and reclamation. As the intergenerational, affective, and familial registers of remembrance that permeate *New Year Baby* confront family secrets and connect family members, they also illuminate the impacts of Khmer Rouge–era biopolitics and necropolitics. Such dimensions of Khmer Rouge violence are often overlooked in dominant narratives about this era.

Further exploring survivor remembrance through literary production, Schlund-Vials examines the memoirs of Cambodian Americans Loung Ung and Chanrithy Him in Chapter 3. Published in 2000, Loung's *First They Killed My Father* and Him's *When Broken Glass Floats* both focus on the female writers' childhood memories of life in Cambodia before and during the Khmer Rouge reign. Schlund-Vials reads these narratives not as a kind of bildungsroman that the memoir genre often beckons to, but as "evidentiary texts." She argues that they both embody a collective juridical agenda of survivors who saw their responsibility as bearing witness not only to the Khmer Rouge crimes, but also to the destructive impacts of U.S. military involvement in Cambodia during the Vietnam War era. Furthermore, by attending to class, ethnic, and gender tensions apparent in these memoirs, Schlund-Vials also shows both the similarity and diversity of these texts' remembrance agendas. Ending the chapter with the controversies over issues of authorship in *When Broken Glass Floats* and veracity in *First They Killed My Father*, Schlund- Vials maintains that although Loung's and Him's memoirs may be "less stable authentic narratives," these works are still valuable "as qualified memorials to the Cambodian genocide and as conflicted monuments to a still-forming Cambodian American selfhood" (p. 147).

The articulation of Cambodian American selfhood and genocide remembrance also manifests through music, which is the site of inquiry in the fourth chapter. Analyzing rapper praCh Ly's provocative *Dalama* trilogy, Schlund-Vials attends to both the cultural and political interventions that the Southern California–based Cambodian American musician generates. Closely examining the content and hybrid musical forms that make up praCh's multivolume and bilingual "hip hop memoir," the author argues that the *Dalama* trilogy delivers a distinct Cambodian American critique against the matrix of forgetting that Killing Fields survivors have to navigate and confront both in the United States and in Cambodia. She shows that by combining collected survivor oral histories, traditional Cambodian music forms (e.g., pin peat), and the socially conscious American hip hop genre, praCh produces a hybrid site of genocidal remembrance that resonates with both old and young Cambodians/Cambodian Americans. Such resonance exemplifies the transnational and intergenerational significance of his multivalent memory labor. In addition, praCh's "capacious" and "interdisciplinary" music also reveals the deep-seated connections between past and present U.S. foreign policies in Cambodia, Khmer Rouge authoritarianism, refugee experiences, elusive genocide justice, contemporary Cambodian politics, and present-day Cambodian American deportations.

War, Genocide, and Justice concludes with close readings of poet/performer/visual artist Anida Yoeu Ali's work. Focusing specifically on Ali's poem *Visiting Loss* and her bodily installation *Palimpsest for Generation 1.5*, Schlund-Vials highlights the lyrical and embodied memory labor of the self-described 1.5 Cambodian American Muslim transnational. As the author puts it, Ali's poetic and bodily articulations of loss simultaneously "memorialize the passing of family members, homelands, and childhoods to instantiate juridical claims of profound communal injury in need of recognition and justice" and "monumentalize survivor remembrance and recuperates refugee selfhood" (pp. 186–187). The same assessment could be extended to the Cambodian American memory work that the book previously mentioned.

The juridical stake and the resistance against state-authorized forgetting that *War, Genocide, and Justice* foregrounds renders this book a timely and substantial contribution to multiple fields of inquiry. In particular, students of Cambodian studies, Asian American/Cambodian American studies, American studies, Southeast Asian diasporic studies, genocide studies, and memory studies have much to gain from the author's deep and sustained theoretical engagement with the politics of genocide memory, transnational identity formation, and Cambodian American cultural production. The diverse forms, sites, and actors of genocide remembrance also enliven this book. The clarity of the arguments further makes this accessible to both undergraduate and graduate audiences.

War, Genocide, and Justice and the memory work that it examines prove more relevant than ever in light of the recent death of Khmer Rouge leader Ieng Sary in the midst of the ongoing UN-backed genocide tribunal in Cambodia in 2013. While the termination of the trial against Ieng Sary upon his death reveals yet again the limits of state-authorized juridical engagements with the genocide past, the cultural works that Schlund-Vials documents and analyzes powerfully remind readers that survivors and subsequent generations continue to demand justice and reconciliation beyond state-sanctioned parameters. Like the compelling Cambodian American cultural works that it investigates, this book confronts the Cambodian Syndrome and refuses to yield the final say on the questions of genocide justice and survival to the nation-state, international power, and dominant narratives that privilege the nation-state's agendas and the perpetrators.

PUBLICATION NOTE

This review was published online in 2013 by the *Journal of Southeast Asian American Education and Advancement* in Volume 8, Issue 1. Minor edits have been made here. The original can be found at http://doi.org/10.7771/2153-8999.1061.

20

Book Review

Kevin Lam's (2015) *Youth Gangs, Racism, and Schooling: Vietnamese American Youth in a Postcolonial Context*

Lam, K. D. (2015). *Youth gangs, racism, and schooling: Vietnamese American youth in a postcolonial context*. New York, NY: Springer. 179 pp. $47.45 (Hardcover). ISBN: 978-1-137- 47558-9.

REVIEWED BY EZEKIEL JOUBERT III

In *Youth, Gangs, Racism, and Schooling: Vietnamese American Youth in a Postcolonial Context*, Kevin Lam outlines the history of the Vietnamese American youth gang phenomenon as it relates to U.S. imperialism and state-sanctioned violence within the backdrop of the U.S. occupation in Vietnam and American racism. He describes the formation of Vietnamese American youth gangs in Southern California from 1979 to 2009, focusing particularly on those involved during the 1990s, as a way to examine how factors such as class, race, citizenship, migration, and laws affect youth Vietnamese refugees. In particular, Lam's project theorizes, through a materialist cultural studies lens, a way to understand youth subcultures, racialized identities, and urban schooling.

His study is based on the life narratives from three gang members collected in 2007. Using critical narrative methodology, he engages dialogically in interviews with two Vietnamese/Asian American men (P-Dog and Melo) and one woman (Linh) who at the time of the interviews were in their late 20s and early 30s. He observes how these "subjects want to be in dialogue with the rest of the world." One of Lam's subjects states, "No one is looking into our shit!" And "don't understand the roots of it" (p. 85). Thus, his research "looks into" and understands the roots of gang formation through the collective voices of these young Vietnamese. P-Dog, Melo, and Linh were involved when they were between 13 and 19 years old. Considering their ages, which would categorize them as youth or young people, Lam challenges the notion of youth as a "biological state" and borrows Nayak's use of the term where youth is viewed as more of a social and mutable category (p. 85). Additionally, he gives a full view (avoids just participant observation) of youth gangs by including the politics of imperialism, globalization of capital and labor, and theorizing of racialization.

Lam places his study in colonial and postcolonial contexts and traces U.S. involvement in the migrations of Vietnamese from 1975 to 1977 (the first wave) and 1977 to 1985 (the second wave, i.e., the boat people). In Chapter 1, he discusses resettlement and racialization as it relates to the lives of the refugees. The lasting effects of war can be linked to the economical, physical, and psychological damages accumulated over three decades (1945–1975). However, U.S. involvement did not end there. Currently, the United States, which ended its embargo in 1994, has greatly influenced Vietnam's participation in global "free market" economies. Lam suggests that the relationship—imperial or allied—has maintained a great influence on Vietnamese and American relations, particularly in the context of the United States.

For many of the first wave refugees, the transition was easier because many of them were a part of a more educated class. As Lam notes, "Western assimilation had begun well before they arrived on U.S. soil." On the other hand, the second wave of refugees, predominantly rural and working class, many of whom identified as Chinese Vietnamese, received international support due to the dreadful experiences attributed to traveling on crowded boats. Yet, these refugees were met with distrust by many Americans who were not in favor of Vietnamese resettlement in the United States. Such antagonisms fed the racialization process of Vietnamese refugees. Within the Vietnamese diaspora, individuals are racialized in two ways: the subaltern or emblematic victim (p. 37). In combination with the political economy of Southern California and class formations in Los Angeles, Vietnamese refugees were viewed as "good refugees," those who were willing to participate in minimum wage, unskilled or low skilled, part-time jobs and act as model minorities willing to "pull themselves up by their bootstraps." Conversely, due to Southern California's highly stratified economy, alternate economies, including gang and underground economies, emerged and reinforced the notion that these were unworthy and possibly dangerous immigrants. Further, Latino and Asian immigrants were racialized against each other as a way to "divide and conquer" (p. 44).

Lam strives to dismantle the dehumanizing effects of racism by examining how race is shaped as a problem in terms of sociology and education, and also critique how it is placed in binary relationships. For example, he reminds us that race is a part of a structure of power rather than individual qualities, which are reinforced by the categorization of race and racial identity. For Asian Americans, the model minority myth acts as a hegemonic device that ignores Asian Americans who are poor and working class as well as those who experience violence. More recently, there has been a lumping of identities related to Asians in U.S. communities. Lam is concerned that panethnic identities are used to turn Asians into a monolith. Using a materialist critique to examine race, he asserts that the racialization of Asian Americans must include an analysis of class formation and political economy as a way to decenter success and look closer at how American imperialism and state-sanctioned racism has shaped and informed physical and psychic violence. We learn in this book that in California's San Gabriel Valley, youth gang members interrupt the racial myths of "good refugee" and "model minority." Lam borrows Boal's "theater of the oppressed" to describe the violence performed by youth gang members within their communities and schools during a time when increased forms of legislation were designed to take on youth and violence. These laws help propel the criminalization of Asian American youth who were racialized through the images of public violence, and diminished further the chance for many youth of color to achieve social and educational success.

To make the links between youth gang culture and U.S. imperialism, Lam examines three themes developed from his interviews: "One, the politics of Migration and resettlement; two, space, labor, and street conflict; and three, racialization, racism and representation" (p. 113). Across these discussions, he works through the personal stories of P-Dog, Melo, and Linh to articulate how their communities became a hotbed for violence. The author connects the logics of turf with the formations of refugee spaces in Southern California and argues that central to the struggles for these young people were local responses and tensions tied to competition for space and capital mapped on interracial and intraracial terrains.

In closing, Lam's project, which he describes as a "recovery of our history," bridges the worlds of youth, violence, and racism while honoring the personal stories and histories of Vietnamese Americans. In Fanonian fashion, Lam reminds us that the subaltern not only speaks but writes back, talks back, and researches back in order to humanize the struggle for liberation associated with the U.S. foreign policies and criminalization of youth. Challenging the racist notion that all Asian Americans are high achievers, Lam forces the reader to examine the material realities of individuals whose experiences tell a counterstory and a counterhistory. To conclude, Lam initiates an important dialogue about the idea of "global responsibility." By bringing this to the front door of education, educators, scholars, and activists must account for how we view globalization and humanization. In many ways, there is a deep connectedness that is missing in our approaches to critical work. So, if we want to attend to how and what it means to do the antiracist, anticolonial, anticapitalist, and anti-imperialist work that he refers to, we must not only acknowledge that we are not alone in this world but confront, critique, and build on those connections in order to transform the present and future.

PUBLICATION NOTE

This review was published online in 2016 by the *Journal of Southeast Asian American Education and Advancement* in Volume 11, Issue 2. Minor edits have been made here. The original can be found at http://doi.org/10.7771/2153-8999.1152.

21

Book Review

Children's Books by Kao Kalia Yang: *The Shared Room* (2020) and *The Most Beautiful Thing* (2020)

Yang, K. K. (2020). *The shared room*. University of Minnesota Press. 32 pp. ISBN 978-1517907945.

Yang, K. K. (2020). *The most beautiful thing*. Carolrhoda Books. 32 pp. ISBN 978-1541561915

REVIEWED BY BAO DIEP

Grief and loss are often seen as taboo subjects to discuss openly in many cultures. However, grief is universal, perpetual, and complex. Grief can take many forms and depend on the nature of the attachment between the survivor and the dead (people, animals, living things). When loss happens, the survivor's attachment will influence the shape and level of grief. Kao Kalia Yang (2020) has brought the topic of attachment, grief, and loss to her children's books, *The Shared Room* and *The Most Beautiful Thing*, to initiate this difficult conversation.

The Shared Room brings the human emotions of grief and loss through the story of a Hmong American living on the East Side of St. Paul, Minnesota. Kao Kalia Yang reveals the loss of the fourth child due to accidental drowning in the swimming lake. She guides readers through different stages of grief for both the parents and the children. The impact of grief and loss depends on the attachment length between the subjects. Holinger (2020) discusses how the early child–parent relationship and vice-versa shape adult attachment. We all learn attachments from our first interaction within our families and later in social spaces (school, work, etc.). Kao's blunt but honest writing reflects the deep emotions that are often neglected and hidden by the cultural norm.

Hmong immigrants to the United States began arriving in the wake of the Vietnam War in 1975. The Hmong are family-oriented, a subtype of collectivism, in which the interests of the family come before those of the individual (Helsel et al., 2020, p. 69). The funeral is one of the most important rituals in the Hmong community, regardless of gender or religious background (Falk, 1992; Pfeifer & Lee, 2005; Yang, 2012).

Death can be an indefinite or unexpected event. We meet our death with fear and despair because of anticipated pain and hopelessness of the unknown. Eastern and Western attitudes toward death can be very different. While many Eastern societies are associated with collective values, Western societies emphasize individualistic values. This fundamental difference in perception of existence as deeply embedded in the family instead of individualist existence is significant for understanding how East Asian people cope with grief in death and dying.

Xee Reiters's illustrations really help highlight the storyline. The artist allows the reader to explore Asian American values through different characters in the story. Readers can see the functionality and structure of the Asian American family through different illustrations. Readers can relate to the characters as a son, daughter, or as parents as the illustration allows them to imagine in the storyline. As an Asian American, I am thrilled to see the book represents part of my identity and cultural values. *The Shared Room* has demonstrated that grief is universal, and it impacts every culture. While this is a children's book, the writing is tailored to older children. This book is a great contribution to the subject of Asian American literatures.

The Most Beautiful Thing brings back the memories of being newcomers in a new place. The books provide young readers with the opportunity to integrate into Hmong culture and language. The book showcases the relationship between the main character and her Hmong grandmother. In Hmong culture, children are taught to listen and respect the elders. The illustrations in the book are colorful and eye-catching. As the young girl describes, "My grandma came from a time and a place where creatures lurked in the jungles waiting to chase unwary children. She told us that she once looked into the gleaming eyes of a tiger and felt its hot breath on her face." A picture of a fearsome tiger represents her grandmother's dream. The story was moving, highlighting how family love, as symbolized by the grandmother's smile, can hold people together during tough times and bring beauty and joy to all.

Her authentic writing grabs the reader's attention and allows them to imagine being in a village in Southeast Asia. This book helps us understand more of their points of view, with both respect for the harsh history lesson and joy for the hope of the future. This book can be enjoyed by children of all ages.

Both books touch on delicate subjects. Does grief have a language? How can parents explain grief and loss to their children? When we deal with unpredictable and uncontrollable things such as grief and loss, how we allow these feelings to be felt and expressed can be significant. Unfortunately, there is no correct way to respond to grief and loss. However, Kao Kalia Yang has provided parents with some starting points for such difficult conversations.

PUBLICATION NOTE

This review was published online in 2023 by the *Journal of Southeast Asian American Education and Advancement* in Volume 18, Issue 1. Minor edits have been made here. The original can be found at http://doi.org/10.7771/2153-8999.1281.

REFERENCES

Falk, C. (1992). Hmong funeral in Australia in 1992. *Making multicultural Australia*, 1–9.

Helsel, D., Thao, K. S., & Whitney, R. (2020). Their last breath: Death and dying in a Hmong American community. *Journal of Hospice & Palliative Nursing*, *22*(1), 68–74. http://doi.org/10.1097/NJH.0000000000000616

Holinger, D. (2020). *The anatomy of grief.* Yale University Press.

Pfeifer, M. E., & Lee, T. (2005, August 11). Hmong religion. *Hmong Today*, *2*(16), 24.

Yang, Y. (2012). An introduction to Hmong culture. *Hmong Studies Journal*, *13*(1), 1–6.

22

Book Review

Cathy Long's (2023) *The Cambodian Family: Holocaust Survival*

Long, C. (2023). *The Cambodian family: Holocaust survival.* 141 pp. Excel Book Writing. ISBN: 979-8890753687.

REVIEWED BY JALISA SANG

The Cambodian Family: Holocaust Survival, by Cathy Long, is a powerful memoir that recounts the darkest days or "Year Zero" in Cambodian history. It captures the story of how the author survived the harsh regime under the Khmer Rouge as a wife, mother, and caregiver. Long's memoir also touches on the horror, trauma, grief, family separation, and loss that occurred from 1975 to 1979 that was experienced by so many, shedding a light on the atrocities inflicted on the Cambodian people during this era. Through the hardships, Long instilled a pillar of hope, resilience, and faith for a better future for her and her family. She still believed that Cambodia could still become a good country and valued democracy, diversity, and equality.

From the Introduction to Chapter 1: "Life Before Pol Pot Regime," Long described the strong and close connection between her and her mother. Long's father passed away when she was an infant, so her mother had to raise all of her siblings by herself, with the help of a few people in the village. At times, Long's mother had to leave for certain time periods for work to help support her family and to be able to give her children the education they deserved. Long was proud of her mother for working hard and making sacrifices to provide for her education. As Cathy would describe it, life as a teenager before the Khmer Rouge was happy, normal, and filled with contentment. Cathy had lots of friends, went to school Monday to Wednesday, rode bikes, picked lotus flowers with her peers, and generally enjoyed going to school every day.

Eventually she met and married her husband, Sambo, in January 1969. They relocated to Prey Romeat, Kampong Speu, which was a small village filled with mountains and difficult roads to travel on. Food and water were also hard to obtain, making it difficult to live there. Adjusting was difficult because she was homesick and had quit school and work, but it was a sacrifice she made to be with her husband. During this time, a war had started between the Khmer Rouge and the Lon Nol military. One night, Cathy heard gunshots all around the village, which scared residents into hiding from the Khmer Rouge. It was no longer safe for Cathy's family to live in Prey Romeat, so she, her husband, and her six-month-old child escaped to Phnom Penh where Sambo completed his military training and became a police officer.

In Chapter 2: "Khmer Rouge Took Over Cambodia," life was completely changed on April 17, 1975, sparking a new era in Cambodia's history. The night before, Cathy could barely sleep because of all the gunshots in the city. She knew that black-uniformed soldiers were killing the Lon Nol military, and if she had gone outside, she would have seen multiple dead bodies. Her family had no choice but to prepare to escape and leave for the unknown. In the early morning, Khmer Rouge soldiers took over Phnom Penh and evacuated everyone out of the city and into the countryside. People were scared and listened to the soldiers who had guns in their hands. Crowds of families marched in the heat, and regardless of whether they were rich or poor, they were all walking together on the same path to their unknown destiny. Children and babies were crying for food, and the elderly and those who had disabilities had trouble following along. Sick patients who were carrying all sorts of illnesses and diseases in hospitals were also evacuated or were killed on the spot.

A week into the regime, there was no money in the new world, Angka, so people traded gold or clothes for food. People starved and became very ill with the limited food that was passed around. Then, tragedy struck when Cathy's six-month-old daughter, Srey Touch, became sick with measles and passed away. A week later, more tragedy followed. Her son Pin had become constipated with a swollen stomach and passed the same day. Cathy's mind was "filled with misery and the tragedy of a broken heart because of separating [from] the loved one forever." She deeply misses her children.

The working conditions under Pol Pot were horrible, unsanitary, and scary. People of all ages, no matter if they were old or young, worked in the fields day and night, through rain and heat. Young children during this time were brainwashed or reeducated. Cathy prayed that she could live another day; everything was up to chance. In the early days of the regime in 1975, Kampream village had about a hundred families, but after a year passed, only about fifty were left. Many families eventually had a single member left, and most of the children and men had died from disease and starvation. Even through hard days, Cathy maintained high self-esteem and still found positivity in the darkness to keep her head up. This became a motivating factor for Cathy, and she was determined to get food to help her family survive.

As conditions worsened, with famine on the horizon, Cathy and her family knew it was time to escape Kampream if they wanted a shot at living. They moved to Phoom Sleng and lived in a tiny buffalo barn where Cathy gave birth to her son. Life in Phoom Sleng was no better than it was at Kampream. The family continued to live in hunger, starvation, and severe famine so her hope started to dwindle again. Sambo, her husband, was called by the Khmer Rouge to leave for another camp, leaving behind her three-week-old baby, and her mother had fallen very sick. The passing of her mother wrecked her. Cathy couldn't even see where her mother was going to be buried because she was sick herself and had just had a baby, so she prayed to her mom and dedicated a poem to her. Once Cathy got better, she was on a mission to find more food for her family. Her attitude and strength to still have hope through the worst of conditions is extremely inspiring to me. How can one person believe that there could be a better future under those conditions?

In Chapter 5: "Escaped from Khmer Rouge to Vietnamese Liberation," it was January 1979 and Vietnam had invaded Cambodia and seized Pol Pot's brutal regime. Cathy heard many gunshots and mortars throughout the village and was unsure how she and her family were going to escape. She cared more about finding food for her children than anything else. In the middle of the night, Cathy's family and another family escaped the area, and along their trek, they heard more gunshots and rockets, and that's when she knew that the Khmer Rouge had attacked Vietnamese troops. Finally, they reached the Vietnamese base and were welcomed into the area. Still, she couldn't just "relax" and feared that the Khmer Rouge soldiers would attack their base. Suddenly, the soldiers attacked, and Cathy hid herself with her children and continued their long journey through the cold and freezing morning—having to cross a river five times for her children and belongings. The unimaginable happened: Cathy and Sambo were reunited. She never thought they would see each other again, and now their family had become whole again. As they kept walking, they came across a bad smell with millions of flies around it. It was a scene of dead bodies who were either killed by the Khmer Rouge soldiers or were bombed from the mines. They stopped and Cathy reflected on how so many families never had the chance for freedom.

In Chapter 6: "Life under the Vietnamese Regime and in the Camps (1979–1980)," Cathy moved to Monkal Borey and was reunited with her sister-in-law, brother, nieces, and nephews. Cathy heard about the United Nations, Red Cross, World Relief, and UNICEF joining together to build refugee camps for Khmer survivors. Cathy and her family made their way to Chamromp Tmey Camp, then to Kok Kyoung Camp, but they did not stay for long at Kok Kyoung Camp due to rockets being dropped by the Khmer Rouge. Cathy felt reluctant to leave behind Cambodia; her home country and the only place she knew, but she knew that she wouldn't be able to return to Cambodia with all that had happened. Saying goodbye was going to be difficult. It was a sacrifice she made for her family's safety, so they made their way to a refugee camp called Khao I Dang Camp in Thailand. From there, Cathy's family flew to the Philippines to prepare for their final destination, the United States.

Once on U.S. soil, Cathy was eternally grateful that she could be in a safe place with shelter, money, and food. She describes how comfortable she became in the United States and that life was "gorgeous," and she slowly integrated herself into the American lifestyle. Although she loved America, there were difficulties adjusting to this new lifestyle. This meant new norms, expectations, routines, and assimilation into the dominant culture. She struggled during her first few years in America, but with hard work, her determination for a better future, and her positive, high self-esteem, she believed she could be successful. She wants to share her story and a sentiment that through the struggles, barriers, and hardships, you can still be successful. With that, her journey has inspired her commitment to becoming a teacher. She spent numerous years working as a paraeducator and substitute teacher in Long Beach, California. Even in semi-retirement in Texas, Long believes that educators and learning play a big role in better understanding our complex world and other cultures that are different from our own.

In all, *The Cambodian Family* by Cathy Long is a compelling memoir of how she and her family survived the Khmer Rouge regime in Cambodia. To be able to tell a story, one that is traumatic, sobering, and dark in detail with so much loss, grief, and near-death experiences is remarkable. Stories like Long's should be uplifted, heard, and acknowledged. Her bravery, dedication, and hope speak volumes about how she and so many other Cambodians survived. Long's writing is part of a larger collection of memoirs written by survivors of the Cambodian "holocaust" and should be read by anyone interested in history and the strength of the human condition. Her book is honest and without much agenda other than sharing her truth about one of the darkest periods in human history. As a daughter of Cambodian refugees and immigrants who survived the Khmer Rouge, I heard many stories from my parents, relatives, and family friends about their lived experiences during these very difficult years. The Khmer Rouge destroyed the education and economic systems, forcing the people to work under cruel conditions at communal farms, which in all claimed the innocent lives of two million people. However, I've only heard bits and pieces of my family's story because of how hard it is to retell it: the trauma, unpleasant memories, and uncomfortable conversations. I imagine that this memoir would be helpful for other Cambodians who also only know about the Khmer Rouge period through stories and history books. Long's memoir painted a vivid picture of life during this time and provided me with additional perspective on my own family and identity. It has inspired me to do more research on my family history, historical events in Cambodia, and the long-lasting impacts of the Khmer Rouge on my community today.

PUBLICATION NOTE

This review was published online in 2024 by the *Journal of Southeast Asian American Education and Advancement* in Volume 19, Issue 1. Minor edits have been made here. The original can be found at http://doi.org/10.7771/2153-8999.1320.

CREATIVE WORKS

23

To Make a Return

MAI DER VANG

In a way, we are nothing more—or less—than an encoded memory of our heritage.

—*EVA HOFFMAN,* LETTERS IN TRANSIT

You are born here,
some place alien to your ancestral tongue.
Cars replace your two feet on a spiraling superhighway.
Tract housing becomes a destination
on dizzy roads that look too much alike. Your father. Your mother.
A young couple far from home and anything familiar. Stretched
beyond sanity like hitting walls in a maze.

You go to public school,
where you are taught how pilgrims and
Indians ate together, how to pledge allegiance,
and become invisible by turning off your voice
like taking off a jacket.
Never getting the one you want
because of the jobs your parents do not
have. And what you learn on back-to-school
night, when your mother does not know how
to write your name on the chalkboard
of your fourth grade class.

You become jaded by senior year,
swallowed by the language you can

hardly speak, and the assignments that
swarm inside your backpack.
In the midst of eight kids, you feel alone
because they will not let you be.

You wake at 6AM on a Saturday morning
to move couches before the shaman arrives.
There are chickens fussing in the backyard, and
the neighbors might hear.
The night you come home late,
your father burns his words
into the cracks of the narrow driveway.

You move away from home,
chart your course in a crowded landscape.
The cup of freewill flowing to the rim,
like the expensive red wine in your kitchen pantry.
You pour wax from the candles next to the tub
where you soak. No one to bang on the door
while you sink in salts and yesterday's
edition of The New York Times.
On the subway, you watch the high rises
shield your sight beyond the city walls.

You wander the streets,
yearning for the recognizable. How you
almost cry at the sight of lemongrass
in a stranger's yard. The old woman
a few doors down whose embroidery
looks like the neon cross-stitched fabric
collecting dust in your mother's closet.
Even the homeless vet who
says he knows of your people
because he fought in 'Nam.

You comb through books, magazines, journals
to uncover scabs, peeling from the wounds
left by a war your parents did not explain,
except to say they had to run.

You shrug it off, and now, years after,
you know the reason why your mother
feared fireworks on Fourth of July.
Why she keeps an old piece of clothing
locked in a suitcase, the same one she
wore the night they left Laos.
And your father, a man of tangled emotions
who says he was only showing love
the day he cursed you from the house.
When all along you think the only war
is the one inside you.

You return home.
To loathe something, but to need it.
Like the twisted red string your mother tied
around your left wrist.
Its tainted mildew scent sometimes polluting,
your skin, but never taking over its purpose.
Never forgetting to bring you back.

PUBLICATION NOTE

This work was published online in 2010 by the *Journal of Southeast Asian American Education and Advancement* in Volume 5, Issue 1. Minor edits have been made here. The original can be found at http://doi.org/10.7771/2153-8999.1007.

24

the peace generation; the iron chain; and a poem for Con

TRANGDAI GLASSEY-TRANGUYEN

THE PEACE GENERATION

the world called us
"the peace generation"
those born after the fifteen centuries of war-torn Vietnam
after April 1975
an ending
of many beginnings
undecided

the end of a war without history
the end of an Asian tiger, of the Pearl of the Far East
the instigation of an era in exile
the instigation of humanity on trial

1975–1994
a nineteen-year fiasco
i discern the hues and chords of peace
mixed and matched

the peace my friend knows
fighting the smoldering sun

biking to school day in day out
two hours each way
taking in engine smoke, inhaling street dust

cohorts in my maternal hometown
walk three hours straight yet arriving at school
when the tide brims, it takes some away
they float in the river
no stiff in sight
kids in my town
read life, but not a half letter,
take charge of their daily excursion to catch miniature crabs
half is cooked for the family's meals
half is sold to feed to ducks

competing political convictions still unrest
warring ideologies at our backs
we dash, out of breath
only to be seized
in the noose drawing tight
the amorphous lariat

my friend
hay roof, mud wall
works the deep field, the low patch
her mother works the bike to teach in the other village
two hours through the soil path, one hour bobbing the rock road
now laid off
her father was in the "bộ đội" reserved army
where he once got lost in the soil, unearthed thereafter
half mad half dead, a terrorist at home
the day she graduated high school
the mother found a match
to marry her off to an Australian expatriate
in hope of her better future
leaving her first love
my friend filed the immigration paper
till she can no longer bear it
and turns lunatic

the farmers in my town
plow and plant
a life of toil, poverty-struck
i mind not their backbreaking work
but the absurdity of their barren stomach
breaks my heart

life
- angst-ridden
when temples
turn commune's work place
shrines and tombs
serve as local headquarters
- troubled
when the domestic authority
seize the house of worship
during the canonization of 117 Vietnamese martyrs
keeping out church members, barricading them from visiting and praying
and at each solemn mass
plain-clothed cops mingle in the only church in town
to single out the faces of teachers and government workers
to execute elimination

my friends in Vietnam these days
still fight each other for the green dollar
still at odd with the rice pot everyday
my friends, the outstanding students of the whole province,
are occupied with earning enough to send Mom-home the monthly rice
a generation negotiating peace with bread and dress

how poverty lives well
since the French colonization
now evermore impecunious
farmers renting land,
farmers taxing life
lush rice fields
withered souls
they suffer in solitude
to give my generation an era of silenced peace

our peace is the rice seed
choked in the forestry of thorns
stunted,
putrefied
huffing

who said we have peace?
who said we have peace?
who said we have peace?

oh, peace, how do Thee define thyself?
would Thee ever reify my life . . . ?

"no justice, no peace!
no justice, no peace!
no justice, no peace!"

THE IRON CHAIN[1]

"combating poverty, eliminating hunger"[2]
he left Vietnam in haste
minding not the abysmal forests in Ukraine
gorging his life into car trunks to Poland

tattered at dawn
sun-scorched with hard toil
hope jumped the fence
one day, his family would be together again . . .

his heart thinned for thoughts of his kids
his womb pained for his wife
their union has been distanced
is her love still obliged?

he endured his lot
the State[3] loves its people
in spite of his squalor
he wouldn't hate the State

the pair of callous hands
 the pair of addle eyes
the pair of withered legs
some words of blood and flesh

the noose has closed in on his neck
the fate has engulfed his life
his hair, knowing yet youth strength,
has now turned bitter-white

A POEM FOR CON[4]

A seed at summer's end
An autumn home in the womb
Warm winter, filial karma
Blooming at spring's start

PUBLICATION NOTE

This work was published online in 2010 by the *Journal of Southeast Asian American Education and Advancement* in Volume 5, Issue 1. Minor edits have been made here. The original can be found at http://doi.org/10.7771/2153-8999.1006.

NOTES

1. "The iron chain" was inspired from the struggles of the undocumented Vietnamese immigrants at the Stadium in the Polish capital city, Warsaw. The poem came to me when I was on the train going from the port of Nynäshamn en route to the center of Stockholm, Sweden, having arrived via ferry from Gdansk, Poland.
2. A slogan by the Vietnamese government, urging the people to combat poverty without making the right conditions possible.
3. The Vietnamese government.
4. "Con" is "child" in Vietnamese.

25

When The Mountain Spirit Spoke

ANCHALEE PANIGABUTRA-ROBERTS

Spirits roam to protect the valleys, the mountains, and the forests
Jao Khao, the Mountain Spirits reign and haunt the valleys
Whisper their messages into your psyche.

I didn't believe in the sixth sense
But Mae Kham's death called this into question.
One day we visited a potential house to rent
There's a noisy rice mill next door, but it seemed safer,
Not quite as isolated as the current house we rented at the edge of the village.
An uneasy and strong feeling grasped me—
"Don't rent this house," was the decoded message.
After the visit, I saw the same message in my husband's eyes.
"You felt it too?" I asked. He nodded.
A few weeks passed.
It rained so hard that week in March, with constant downpours.
Ruined all the shallot crops my village sisters and friends hoped to sell to pay for their vicious never-ending debt and life cycles.

I just returned to the village from the city,
Only to find frowns, un-smiling, sunken faces greeting me.
Like some dark force took a grip on this valley district
"Mae Kham is dead," I was told.
Her husband took seven meth pills

He's gone mad and stabbed her with a machete.
I could not remember the number of the wounds,
Certainly, one was fatal.
Her painful wail could be heard throughout the village.
Had I rented that other house, my husband, my four-year-old daughter and
  I would have heard,
or witnessed, and would be haunted by the sight
and sound her daughter and neighbors still had recurring nightmares
about.
The mountain spirit spoke, and I listened.
I wonder what it said to Mae Kham, when her husband beat her.

"I thought it was just like one of their 'normal' fights," the neighbor told
me.
"I didn't know it would kill her."
No wife-beating is normal.
I wondered what the mountain spirit might have whispered into the ears
of the villagers and her family, who turned their blind eyes to the
"normal" fights.
I wondered if the whole village listened, what could have been.

PUBLICATION NOTE

This work was published online in 2011 by the *Journal of Southeast Asian American Education and Advancement* in Volume 6, Issue 1. Minor edits have been made here. The original can be found at http://doi.org/10.7771/2153-8999.1041.

26

To Own My Own; and The Last of Her Generation

PACYINZ LYFOUNG

TO OWN MY OWN

I filled all the holes, cracks and dents in your walls
I coated you in virgin first skin and second skin
Healed all your octogenarian scars
Reborn into the blank canvas where I could explore
All the shades of my dreams

Underwater ocean waters caught between the blue of the sky above
And the glow of golden treasures sleeping in the deep
For one night you were aquatic green, so intense, the light sank
In a violent embrace, never to resurface

Then, I made you lacy cream, foaming with a hint of coconut steam
Dripping on the island sand where my toes could spread
All the pores of your smooth ivory skin like the tusks of an elephant scream
The reminder of my Southeast Asian jungle fever
Melting in this Minnesotan Norwegian winter

All those years I never dared to drive a nail in such delicate dissolution

In other places I painted you the reflection of running water, the breath of a winter morning, the seed of sunflower, the belly of a sleeping fish, the footstep of a child

This evening, I run my hands over your wooden bones, peek into the water-lily glass of your eye, and play with your crystalline tonsils teasing the roof of your buffet,

Then silently close your door . . .

THE LAST OF HER GENERATION

Fingers reaching into the universe
Patiently pull threads across
Tiny stitches sealing rents
Tearing fabric and time

Fingers reaching into the universe
Life etches from the brush
From empty space to blank paper
From shoulder to calligraphy
The chi breathes within the page

She never said she was a mountain
For a mountain stands too tall and too magnificent
Too far away on the horizon
For a mountain stands too strong and too ancient
Too brave, facing time and the elements

She never said she was lucky or smart
That was for boys, who went to school
While she bit back jealousy
Bent under the produce basket on her back
Or over her belly always growing round and ripe

She never learned the mysteries of letters
And always fingered books wistfully
Frustrated by the knowledge locked within her hands
So she became a living memory
Recording the world with her eyes and ears

She never gloried or burned under the bright light
Except for children who followed her like the sun

Starting their days and tucking them at night,
And who aimed for the stars reflecting in her eyes

PUBLICATION NOTE

This work was published online in 2013 by the *Journal of Southeast Asian American Education and Advancement* in Volume 8, Issue 1. Minor edits have been made here. The original can be found at http://doi.org/10.7771/2153-8999.1070.

27

The Two Leaders

One Wise and One Foolish

AHMAY YA

Retold in English by Ahmay Ya from a story that Moe Moe, her grandmother, had told her when Ahmay was just a small girl in Burma

Once upon a time, close to the kingdom of Bayrnathi, there was a village where one thousand carpenters lived. They had lived there happily for a very long time but now they experienced many difficulties such as not enough employment or food, and they were heavily into debt. They decided to leave their village and search for a new location where they could have a better life. So they built a big ship and sailed away, taking their families with them.

One day, far out at sea, they saw a small island. When they arrived on the shores of the small island, they explored the island and found that many different kinds of fruit trees grew there, and there was enough rice and water for everyone. As they wandered around, they met a man who had been shipwrecked on the island long before their arrival. He welcomed the carpenters and said, "Dear friends, there is plenty of food on this island, there are no dangers here, but there is something very important you all need to know about this island. It is guarded by the nats, Spirit Beings. The nats hate to see the garbage that human beings produce every day. If you want to live peacefully here, don't litter. Make deep holes in the sand, burn and bury your garbage in the holes and after that, make sure you cover the holes up with lots of sand."

The carpenters decided to settle and make their homes on this island. Among the one thousand carpenters were two leaders. One was the leader of five hundred carpenters and the other was the leader of the other five hundred. One of the leaders was wise and the other was foolish.

After they had lived on this island for some time, the foolish leader and his carpenters made alcohol from sugarcane. They were joyful, sang and danced and they kept on drinking. They became so drunk that they no longer cared about their environment. They threw garbage all over the place and they did not bother to burn and bury it.

The irresponsible behavior of these human beings made the nats very angry. The nats agreed on a plan together. "In fifteen days we will cause a tsunami and let the high waves clean the beaches and get rid of these irresponsible people as well." However, among the nats, there was a nat who was especially kind and loving. She did not want the people to die. She appeared on a cloud to warn the carpenters. She advised them to leave the island before the fifteenth day. Unfortunately, soon after she had spoken, a cruel and harmful nat came on another cloud. The cruel nat said, "Don't believe what that nat told you. She said that because she does not like human behavior or human beings. But don't worry, just keep on living and playing here as usual. Remain here, you are not in any danger."

The wise leader thought about what the two nats had said. He called for a meeting with all the carpenters and said, "Friends, I think we should build boats and get ready to leave before any danger comes our way. If the first nat spoke the truth, we will then be able to leave in our boats as soon as the water rises. And if the second nat spoke the truth, we can keep the boats in a safe place and continue to live here as before."

The foolish leader did not agree. He said, "Friend, you just want to make us do more work for nothing. The first nat hates us. We should believe the second nat because she loves us. Why should we leave this beautiful, peaceful island? There's no need to build boats!" Then the foolish leader ordered his five hundred followers not to build boats and they were happy to obey him. They just kept on feasting and drinking and enjoying themselves.

However, the wise leader helped his five hundred carpenters build boats. Then they stocked the boats with food and water. His followers listened to his advice and continued to make all the other preparations necessary for their departure. On the fifteenth day, just as the first nat had warned them, the sea level got higher and higher and the waves flooded the shore. As soon as the people were waist high in water, the wise leader told his followers to get into their boats and sail away from the island.

But the foolish leader and his followers were not disturbed. They said, "Oh, the nats are only cleaning the beach. The water will stop rising after it reaches waist level. It can't go higher than that." However, the sea level didn't stop rising. The waves rose higher and higher and soon the water was up to their shoulders, then up to their heads, then over their heads and finally even covered the tops of the tall coconut trees. The foolish leader and all his followers were drowned.

NOTES

This story was told to Ahmay by her grandmother when Ahmay was a small girl in Burma. Both Ahmay and her grandmother are from the Karen tribe. Ahmay's father is a leader in Burma trying to establish a peaceful life for the Karen. He is working to bring about a ceasefire between the military troops and the ethnic peoples such as Karen, Shan, and Kachin. Like the majority of the Karen in Burma, Ahmay and Moe Moe are Buddhist. The story shows how Karen Buddhist traditions were a strong influence in shaping their values. There are deep meanings in this story. The story cautions us to learn the lessons from wise leaders just as the five hundred carpenters listened to their wise leader. Good people pay attention to those who are wise. The story illustrates that one should associate with the wise and not with the foolish. There is also a deep meaning about living in balance and harmony with the earth in a respectful way and not spoiling the environment with our garbage.

Bayrnathi: In this story Bayrnathi refers to a kingdom that may have existed in the time of Buddha over two thousand years ago, Buddha died in about 400 BCE.

Karen: The Karen are one of many ethnic minorities in Burma. There are now over ten thousand Karen in Minnesota. The Karen suffered decades of persecution from the Burmese military.

Nat (spirit): Nats are spirits in Burmese Buddhist beliefs. There are the great nats and there are the lesser spirits of trees, water, mountain, island, ocean, house, school, and buildings. Almost all of the 37 Great Nats were human beings who met violent deaths.

PUBLICATION NOTE

This work was published online in 2014 by the *Journal of Southeast Asian American Education and Advancement* in Volume 9, Issue 1. Minor edits have been made here. The original can be found at http://doi.org/10.7771/2153-8999.1082.

28

Chanda Says; and Dropping Chanda Off at Nursery School

BUNKONG TUON

CHANDA SAYS

"You're the greatest daddy
in the whole wide world."

Her arms wrap tightly around my neck
as she plants

A big fat juicy kiss on my cheek.
For a minute, I almost forgive

The Khmer Rouge. Then I remember
my daughter would never know

Her *Lok-Yiey* and *Lok-Ta*.

DROPPING CHANDA OFF AT NURSERY SCHOOL

Tiny legs wrap around my waist,
tears streaming down her flushed cheeks,
and the wailing "Daddy, Daddy, Home!"
Then the door shuts behind me.
I still hear her crying as I walk by

the classroom window and carry
her cries as I get in the car,
drive to the college to teach
the American/Viet Nam War.
The wailing continues in the cries
of soldiers missing their girlfriends,
wives, and families at home, wishing to spit at their fathers
who talk about doing the things
men must do in a world of evils,
wanting to burn their town's city hall
and vandalize the draft board
because no one there knows
what they are going through.
The wailing is heard in the little girl
stripped naked by the flaming
fingers of napalm as she runs
with other villagers.
The wailing is felt in the trembling
silence of the boy in My Lai
who hides underneath the warm
bodies of his aunt, younger
sister, and mother.

PUBLICATION NOTE

This work was published online in 2019 by the *Journal of Southeast Asian American Education and Advancement* in Volume 14, Issue 1. Minor edits have been made here. The original can be found at http://doi.org/10.7771/2153-8999.1185.

29

Light

SENGARONE PETER VETSMANY

LIGHT ແສງ

My grandma rubs my chest, says bo lukkkun,
I listen to her, not rising from table, I open my eyes
to   dining room light warming my memories back,
commotion eats my ears—uncles argue, Xok cries.

Ma weeps drown   light when I look at   uncles
kneeling beneath   window with tumbling sun,
on   floor Xok screams with no legs, his hand gone.
Light is striking—silent flash, an eruption.

I drift off from agony. I recall tree branch
I held onto when Xok came running to   tree,
a cloud   diminished his smile, a land mine   stole
his laughter, a flash   brought me back down to dirt.

Eyes open to incense smoke dims   light,
roams in   shadows of   war-torn house.
Grandma starts to chant a prayer,   uncles follow
her cadence, I knew when Ma stood beside light.

My brother, who followed me around   Lao jungles,
who I promised to buy chocolate for when we reach America,
will never taste   escape. In   window, spirits comfort Xok
away, his eyes extinguish in   candlelight set beside him.

PUBLICATION NOTE

This work was published online in 2019 by the *Journal of Southeast Asian American Education and Advancement* in Volume 14, Issue 1. Minor edits have been made here. The original can be found at http://doi.org/10.7771/2153-8999.1191.

30

Charges Against a Newborn; Unanswered; and For the First Generation

DO NGUYEN MAI

CHARGES AGAINST A NEWBORN

How guiltless an infant, before she

Starved an entire nation.

Snapped soldiers' ribcages open into
blossoms of dust in the light.

Razed ten thousand acres of heartbeat.

Gutted a bloodline.

Buried her grandmother in a hospital room
like it wasn't already lined with white.

Scorched her grandfather's limp corpse
until roots ran unhindered through his skin.

Taught her mother the sound
of bullet to spine.

Cried out her first breath.

UNANSWERED

After Joshua Nguyen

Em ơi,
don't look back

when my spine snaps
against the cold click
of the trigger,

when my lungs flood
with the fullness
of the night sky,

when my body drops
                                        headfirst

when the ocean folds
its palms over my chest,

when my ribcage whistles
with the waking shore,

when the water ripples,

when the boat tips over,

when I become the sea
swelling beneath your swaying ship—

em ơi,
I will carry you

 to shore.

FOR THE FIRST GENERATION

We entered the world

gun—fire—work,
metal, burning, bleeding.

we, born screaming
keep our mouths shut
(our mothers safe)
we fear a fire
bodies scorched

to quiet rage is to die without grave
another corpse unnamed

we fear a fire
we, already alight not the soot,
but the ash:
rise, rise
afraid, a blaze.

PUBLICATION NOTE

This work was published online in 2019 by the *Journal of Southeast Asian American Education and Advancement* in Volume 14, Issue 1. Minor edits have been made here. The original can be found at http://doi.org/10.7771/2153-8999.1183.

31

Your American Songbook; and Context Clues

SOKUNTHARY SVAY

YOUR AMERICAN SONGBOOK

Ameling, Caballé, Norman, Bonney, Fleming, Battle

Arpeggios, immunizations
Successful completion for the fall, English Major code
Passport expired 04 Nov 2012
Eyebrows thin as commas hair articulates the plump
Drug-free face. A runny signature.
Naturalization certificate a partially sleepy-eyed citizen one less
boyfriend two sizes down.
I don't want to know the stars in Ashbery's "America" they feel of
asterisks beside the names of my family on the refugee pages indications of sickness, by-the-ways
Who is "your janitor"? *My* janitor is a father who gave me his name, books with titles
left for garbage pick up by NYU.
Honors and Awards skills education transcriber, flute, cum laude MS office
I run into Kimiko at the bar after she teaches. She rips pages out of a discarded book and
we do a writing exercise over martinis. Highlight words from a self-help book. I found
her found words.
Aggressively dissatisfied but
A surprising body, which is
A plant   in some way

Groups children
From homes happy and happy
Excepting for the unhappy
Blood.

John keeps mentioning this janitor and this country. I sang an Aaron Copland song for an audition:
"Long Time Ago" Ballad of lost love where "droop'd the willow" and "back
the billow

Ashbery's "Terrain / Glistening" as "her blue eyes glisten'd"
American songs are in the eyes
in what we see. Or in the luring across the waters to Europe
in the languages and songs, *o quand je dors* *morgen*

Mozartian sixteenths staccato of the immigrant at the conveyor belt
my brother assembles pistons. Pistons.
That hymn we sang in the church for the god I don't believe in exalts
"How can I keep from singing?"

CONTEXT CLUES

Nyam
Nyum
Nyim
Nom
Nawm
Nov
Ngai
Nung

No
Not
Nut
Near
Nub
Nun
Now
Naught

Nope
Next
Nip
Knot

These are the sounds and yet the words differ. I want to say "ut ey dtay" but that won't put you at ease, no more than "don't worry" does in English. The sounds float in my memory and release in situations where the sounds become relevant. Unearthed for those who pronounce the labiodental, lip-to-tongue sounds with a cluck, a glottal, a breath, aspirate, an aspiration. Here. How. Hold. Home. Help. Who? Humble. Heart. Whole.

Wear
Knear
Thear
Twear
Trey
Ey
Bey
Srey
Parey
Tmey
Sdey
Soursdey

What is translation? What do their English equivalents matter? They aspire for accuracy, but are not answers. Diphthongs and umlauts, vowels extending into different shapes of the mouth, closed or opened in the back, swallowed and regurgitated.

Bei
Bong
Baht
Borey
Bai
Badt
Baich

Butt
Bar
Boss
Bold
Bit
Bye
Buy
Bend

Twist the diction until it sounds authentic, local, regional, mistaken-for someone else. Speak to belong, speak to other, to own—whether one's or another's. Crippling crunch of consonants. Crew of long vowels crashing into the sea. This is history.

For a language with vocal stops, child and mother end with open vowels as if moaning, calling: oan, mae

My Mae is my cry. Before I have the words in the womb, in the crib, the cry elongates because duration is the key to being heard. I endure.

Even "Mak" with its vocal stops, I defy it, shout Maaaa-(k). Hold the "a" into an "ah." Does this relieve, does it sing? My voices teacher wants me to sing pure vowels in Italian opera. What is purity? What makes a language impure?

A woman answers yes with a "cha" (unaspirated) the "a" lengthened while men are cut off in "baht" the tongue stopping itself behind the upper teeth. The teeth a cage of mouth that seeks opening. What gender opens and what pricks.

I seek trust in the seed of this language // BUN DTAY (but) // it grows with uncertainty.

PUBLICATION NOTE

This work was published online in 2021 by the *Journal of Southeast Asian American Education and Advancement* in Volume 16, Issue 1. Minor edits have been made here. The original can be found at http://doi.org/10.7771/2153-8999.1236.

32

Day 785

KOUA MAI YANG

October 17, 2020

To the future HMoob/HMong identifying people,

It has been seven hundred and eighty five days since I started dressing myself in the clothing of our ancestors. Although they have experienced thousands of years with ris tsho HMoob or HMong clothing in the everyday, within the last sixty years, the HMong living in the Western hemisphere have stopped wearing HMong clothing. I started the *Hnav HMoob, Wear HMong* project because I was curious about what would happen to my life if I looked like our ancestors and over the course of two years much has happened.

In the first fifty to one hundred days, my family, especially the elderly women, my mother and grandmother were shocked that I wear ris tsho HMoob or HMong clothes everyday. They said, "ua li koj yuav nyiam ua HMoob ua luaj" or "why do you like being HMong so much?" and "tus txhais nos yog HMoob tiag tiag" or "this daughter is really really HMong". Their comments emphasized how HMong I looked, and sometimes suggest that I have out HMong'd them. The disorientation from seeing a younger HMong person look traditional, forced them to become aware that they are no longer engaging in the wearing of the everyday dress. The everyday dress of our people has died and I do not believe it was given a proper burial nor proper recognition as our people continued to find ways to survive in our respective host nations after the Vietnam War.

I speculate that these comments also suggest other things like how certain generations of HMong people collectively engage at various thresholds in the idea of culture being fixed in the older generation. Fixed notions of culture in our community, for example, means that the older generation creates the culture, and authenticity is based on these creators, therefore later generations of people receive a diluted version of the

HMong culture and are seen as less HMong. However, a reality is that culture is never constant, it is a sociological construction and has always been changing and influenced by geography, and the communities we are surrounded by. The mixing of cultures happens so organically that sometimes it is difficult for any one ethnic group to make claims on who authorized shared designs and aesthetics.

These responses reminded me that our elders have also stopped engaging in paj ntaub, that they are also victims of the times, of the lack of space to reconnect with land and bodies of water, and to re-engage in the practices that were once a part of our everyday life. Although the pacing of society today feels faster and instant, for me, wearing ris tsho HMoob slowed down time and allowed for much needed observation and reflection about how our people looked and how we have moved throughout human history. Through the making and wearing of paj ntaub, I understand today that at one point, we saw ourselves as kin to the land and the living things around us. Embedded in the fibers are the collective memories and archival evidence that perhaps our ancestors have done everything that they can to create the possibility that the future will be a better place. Our ancestor's struggle to survive is a reason why I wanted to better understand how to properly grieve the death of the everyday HMong dress. The wearing of ris tsho HMoob is precisely sacred because I believe it is our ancestor's labor of love and sacrifice, and collectively it communicates across generations without a written language system.

Yet when learning how to create paj ntaub, the process is not as rosy and romantic compared to the theories about its beautiful aesthetic. For example, today HMong women and girls that are still making paj ntaub and ris tsho HMoob, however their voices are often rendered invisible in the patriarchal society. People often say that it takes patience to create paj ntaub, but as one engages in the making, it has little to do with patience. Paj ntaub involves small repetitive gestures, and for some it can take several weeks to one month to complete, paj ntaub is more like an endurance and requires dedication to the craft. The craft however is not dead, and is very much alive in the diaspora. On the internet it is easy to find gatherings of HMong people on social media sharing and exchanging knowledge about paj ntaub and other cultural practices. Similarly, today it is more common to see HMong clothing sold via online and on social media through the Facebook live streaming option, where HMong women and men stream and record online shopping sessions.

During these sessions, the seller dresses in the clothing they are advertising, they measure, describe and communicate directly to their HMong audiences or buyers in real-time. It can be entertaining and addictive to watch and for the HMong living in the Western hemisphere, the internet provides instant access to buying cultural materials that otherwise would have been difficult to obtain. These sellers live all over the world, but the majority of materials and labor utilized to create their products are sourced from Laos, Vietnam, Thailand and China. It is noticeable that the majority of ris tsho HMoob today is no longer made from natural fibers like hemp and cotton. They have been replaced by plastic fabrics and additionally machine printed paj ntaub are produced more quickly than the laborious needle work typically found on HMong clothes. My project engages in these tensions in how the commoditizing of paj ntaub has expanded on the practice. In relation to the consumption of paj ntaub, I am also interested in observing what becomes of these materials and clothing. Considering the fast pace at which ris tsho HMoob is being created today, will ris tsho HMoob become less sacred and be treated like fast fashion? Who really benefits from the demand of ris tsho HMoob in the global textile market? What does it mean to wear ris tsho HMoob today?

In reflection it took me roughly two years before I was able to arrive at more nuanced questions about paj ntaub. Throughout this project I noticed consistently how there has been little pause given to the large changes in how our people engage in culture materials and practices. Another reason why I created the project *Hnav HMoob, Wear HMong* is because I grew up hearing that paj ntaub practices are dying. For me this statement creates fear within the community and adds to the generational trauma and loss that our people have been carrying since the 17th century when they were persecuted and forced to migrate from China. What I think has been overlooked in the statement 'paj ntaub practices are dying' is that in the general HMong community, the desire to commoditize, capitalize and consume paj ntaub is more urgent and easier to access than engaging in the practice itself. Assimilation, trauma, and surviving makes it difficult to learn and maintain paj ntaub practices because of the lack of access to teachers and mentors and general exposure to ancestral cultural practices.

Additionally, collectively in the HMong diaspora, there has been little effort and support to hold space to engage HMong identifying people intergenerationally in paj ntaub and other cultural practices like basket weaving. I often question how active and involved we all are in our culture's erasure? We all collectively feel ownership of paj ntaub and other cultural practices, however not all will feel the obligation and need to organize to teach the youth about traditional practices. As historically stateless people, people without a national identity, who has the ability to authorize what is and is not HMong culture? What is it that we need to do to shift the language of fear in the changes that we see in paj ntaub and other cultural practices to arrive at a place where these conversations are included in the scholarship about our people?

Hnav HMong, Wear HMong centers women's knowledges, and recognizes that paj ntaub as something that is still a gendered expectation of women and girls in some HMong societies. It recognizes that HMong women have been at the forefront of creating records of our people's relationship to land and the natural materials that we give and take from. This project does not seek to test theories or find answers about who our ancestors are or what a specific article of clothing and stitch symbolizes, but instead encourage speculation, and questioning.

I originally created *Hnav HMoob, Wear HMong* with the intentions of inviting and involving various HMong identifying people, yet at the beginning I was not able to foresee what kinds of situations people will experience. Especially as the body is dressed differently from the norm, anyone who engages in *Hnav HMoob, Wear HMong* will not be protected. Therefore I proceeded with the project alone and overall it has been an alienating experience. Although I have the advantage of living in the Twin Cities, Minnesota where it is densely populated with HMong people, no one here looks like me.

With that said, to all HMong identifying people who encounter this letter, I am inviting you to participate in *Hnav HMoob, Wear HMong.* I want you to know that this project is guided by rules that you get to create, that centers your own unique experiences of culture and identity (see the attached guiding performative text). I cannot guarantee that you will be safe as you engage in the wearing of HMong in the public, however, I encourage you to take small steps to build confidence and find meaning for why you are interested in ris tsho HMoob? For example, instead of walking outside in ris tsho HMoob right away, for a few hours simply wear it indoors in the safety of your home or a controlled space. This will allow your body to feel the weight of the clothing, and to practice seeing yourself in the mirror. When you feel like you can move forward, make adjustments, perhaps walk outside for a few minutes, then try wearing ris tsho HMoob for a whole day.

At the beginning of the project I was not able to anticipate what would become of my life because I was not able to imagine a future with paj ntaub. I wanted to find a different way of communicating to the general HMong community beyond the classroom and gallery walls, while also reaching our ancestors, our peers, and the future HMong. Now, I am at a point in the project where I am no longer anticipating how people will see me or how they think about what I am wearing. I no longer have to brace myself for the way people gawk, sexualize and stare from curiosity. Their gazes however, still remind me that looking stereotypically HMong, feminine, and different from how the majority of people are dressed today, is unsafe; but there is much to learn and much to gain from the disorientation, and that is a risk that I am willing to take. I believe that sometimes people need to see what I am wearing to see the question that I am asking, what I am trying to say is that for me, the best way to imagine a different future and create new language around the complexity of our personhood, we need to breathe new ideas into existence. I still feel new with wearing ris tso HMoob as my everyday fashion and I will continue to dress myself this way until it no longer serves me. I will continue to leave as much information behind as this project progresses and I hope that you consider challenging yourself by participating.

With much love,
Dej Txiaj Ntsim/Kuab Maiv Yaj/Koua Mai Yang

HNAV HMOOB, WEAR HMONG PERFORMATIVE TEXT

1. Wear ris tsho HMoob or HMong clothing everyday:
    a. How did you arrive at this project? What is your understanding of ris tsho HMoob?
        i. these can be clothing that you create
        ii. gifted to you
        iii. ones that were purchased
2. What needs to happen to center self-exploration? How do you want to experience self?
    a. try not to anticipate how others will react
        i. unless reaction is what you seek to understand yourself
3. Document the experience everyday
    a. documenting the experiences become a material of time and history
        i. examples of documentation are:
            1. Photographs
            2. sound recordings
                a. songs, speech
            3. Drawings
            4. Paintings
            5. Writings
            6. Textiles
    b. If adjustments are made where one decides not to document, take note of why that is
4. Reflection
    a. Write, record your experiences, thoughts, ideas and questions that arise from the performance
        i. to consider what has happened, to slow down the experience
        ii. to make meaning of the performance and images
5. Allow yourself to make adjustments the rules:
    a. adjusting the functions of the rules are needed to protect the self from being overwhelmed by new and old experiences

6. Repeat 1-6
    a. or decide when the performance ends

PUBLICATION NOTE

This work was published online in 2021 by the *Journal of Southeast Asian American Education and Advancement* in Volume 16, Issue 1. Minor edits have been made here. The original can be found at http://doi.org/10.7771/2153-8999.1227.

33

#34 Luk Lao

VICTORIA GILL

"Mung ouk jak hee Lao, mung thong vao Lao"
 You came out of a Lao pussy, you have to speak Lao
"Maa Lao, luk Lao thuoa"
 Lao mother means a Lao child, of course
These were my mother's battle cries
 We not only survive, we toil to thrive

School is where the head is
 Keep your Lao aside
Home is where the heart is
 Keep your English outside
Knowing when to use which words where
 Keeps us alive

I am of her blood and bones
 survival warriors of the unknown
of refugee camps, of clashing thrones
 of the Khmer genocide
 there's nothing for me to decide
I embrace her unwillingness to hide
 dutifully I abide

Khoun Maa, Lao Isaan
 Fought for her life and now
We fight for her language
 for I am luk Lao

I hold on to it tight—this legacy
    it is the air I need to breathe
In this way, we, she, and our ancestors
    Remain in existence—in immortality

PUBLICATION NOTE

This work was published online in 2022 by the *Journal of Southeast Asian American Education and Advancement* in Volume 17, Issue 1. Minor edits have been made here. The original can be found at http://doi.org/10.7771/2153-8999.1247.

34

Lai mi ka si (I am lai mi); Kan i ton tthan lai (We will meet again); Kan lam tti lai (Let us dance together); Thihnak Mei (Death Fire); and The dead had names

THANG C. LIAN

LAI MI KA SI (I AM LAI MI)

I strolled to my grandfather's house each day, excitedly waiting by the door as he stretched out his sore muscles and drank warm tea. After what seemed like an eternity, he would put on his boots and a scarf. With his rough, calloused hands grasping mine, we would slowly creep up the hills like ants as the morning settled. My grandfather was a quiet but happy man; he laughed more than he spoke. When he did say something, I listened attentively: "You are *lai mi*, do not forget."

I am *lai mi*, I will not forget.

When I was not with my grandfather, I was with my grandmother. I would wait for her by our door as Mother cooked, igniting embers by blowing into a bamboo pipe. My grandmother— carrying a basket using a tumpline—traveling down the hills was like God descending from the mountain's peak. Often, my grandmother would bring succulent fruits like guava. Where my grandmother went, I would follow behind; I was her shadow.

The night before we left, my grandmother slept with my mother and me: three generations closing the gap before physical separation would forever push us apart. I remember my mother and I getting on the bus in the morning. I remember my grandmother standing outside. For the first time, I was no longer her shadow. My grandmother wept, hot tears that streamed down painfully. I didn't want to cry; I wanted to show my grandmother that I was strong.

As the bus' engines revved, grandmother wailed. No words were said between us. No one had to. I was leaving, and my grandmother was not coming with us.

I am lai mi, I thought. *This is my home.*

When the bus began to move, grandmother waved goodbye. Hollow cries banged my eardrums. A funeral was taking place, but it wasn't for the dead: it was for the spirits of the living. Once we left the mountain and disappeared into the fog, we would never return. My grandmother wept for our *lai mi* spirit, forced to leave its ancestral homeland.

I am lai mi, I thought. *This is my home.*

The bus croaked down the dirt roads of *Hakha*, and the cries grew distant. Then, turning my face away from the window, I felt my spirit cry.

I am lai mi. I have no home.

I consoled my spirit. *Don't cry, spirit, don't cry.*

KAN I TON TTHAN LAI (WE WILL MEET AGAIN)

When I think of Burma, I envision myself crawling up the hills, Grandmother slowly walking behind me, supported by a sturdy stick I found somewhere along the way. The air is sticky, the clouds rise high above me, and on that hill, I turn around. "Grandmother, come on! You're so slow!" *Chuckle.* I don't think of my sandals, held together by rubber bands. I think only of my grandmother, her petite frame, like a caterpillar, inching up the mountain's shoulders. We lived. We cried. We were human.

It has been fifteen years now. Sometimes, it is easy to forget. Sometimes, I think really hard, and nothing appears in my mind: Burma is quietly fading. It scares me. I embarked on this journey of remembering, of relearning to love, because I am scared of forgetting. There are pictures of Burma without sound, scent, or flavor in my head. Often, people's faces are empty, their humanness blank. Thus, speaking with my grandmother, father, and mother is my attempt to make the pictures move—to hear, to smell, to taste Burma. To once again reach the hills, to be a child once more.

In those fifteen years, much has happened. On February 1, 2021, a military coup d'etat swept across Burma. I was in my room in America when it happened. I was safe. My family and the other *lai mi* in Burma continued living; they continued resisting. Hundreds of thousands of people, like in 1988, marched: a deluge of anger, sadness, tiredness. Thousands, like in 1988, have perished.

When I called my grandmother, I asked her if she was scared. She laughed. She told me that she's never once known life without the military in her lifetime. Then she cried. She cried because she missed me, she cried because she is now weak, she cried because she can't sleep at night when the gunshots don't stop. Then she prayed. She prayed for her grandson, she prayed for her children, she prayed for her country.

Fourteen months later, the people of Burma continue living. They continue fighting. When I ask my father and my mother if they have hope for Burma, they nod without hesitation. My mother says, "*Lai mi* means family. We stand by each other, protect one another, and care for each other. We are strong. When you graduate from college, our people will have won this fight."

I immortalize her words on paper because I believe them to be true.

Since our escape from Burma in 2007, our family has yet to come home. For my father, it has been twenty years. When I call my grandmother and my grandfather, they tell me they are holding on—they will not die. "*Aathang*," my grandfather says, "Until you finish college and return back to us, we will hold onto the living world."

For us *lai mi*, rarely do we show affection with words. Maybe it is because spoken words lose life the moment they've left your body, while action moves the spirit with care and intention. And so, through the movement of my fingers and the words I carefully and intentionally place onto paper, I say and act out my love: for my grandfather, grandmother, father, and mother.

To my grandmother and my grandfather, may these words reach you safely. When we meet again, it'll be atop the hills of *Hakha*: *kan i ton tthan lai.*

We will meet again.

KAN LAM TTI LAI (LET US DANCE TOGETHER)

Some say the body dances when it mourns, contorting itself into broken figures—the dance of sorrow, a ritual of grief, the loss of something warm, something familiar, and maybe familial. We dance until our bodies crumble to the floor, heaving from the shock and the hurt and the loss. We empty the ocean inside, and wonder where this river will carry us. We pray and hope and desire that the soul find its way home. In case it doesn't, we scream and clap and trample the earth. *If the spirit becomes lost and hears us, maybe then it'll return.* My love, in this ritual dance for the dead, may the trails of our tears guide you towards rest. Now is the time to wail—
now is the time to cry. Our spirit is mourning, our spirit is breaking. Grief is the language of the living to love a little bit longer, to hold onto the passing soul. Grief is the way my body moves to the rhythm of absence, the way my soul says, "I love and care for you, so may your soul find the grace this bitter earth dared not give to you." I don't know if the dead speak the language of grief, or if all they see is a dance—
bodies moving, contorting, grieving. So watch as I dance for you. Pass on gently, my love: you were loved, you were loving, you are love.

for my uncle who died fighting for his people and family

THIHNAK MEI (DEATH FIRE)

In the silence
The gaps are filled with bones
Grey and white and cracked
Terror rattled where they sat—
Ash and dust and tears Tearing at the seams
Breath doesn't exhale here
It stays trapped

Freedom twists and entangles
The femur, the tibia, the fibula
No longer with leg or feet
Black soot—the fire ritual of pigs
Rattle and hiss and cry and mourn
In the silence
The gaps are filled with bones
And families must decide
Which one is mine?

THE DEAD HAD NAMES

The day the war
Reached our doors
It swung our world
Wide open.

The bitterness
Of loss
Lingered like heavy
fog And dared not
dissipate No matter
how hard We prayed.

Days became numbers
Too heavy
Too big
To even count.

Instead we counted
The number of the dead
And whispered their names
For we feared of forgetting
That the dead had names.

The day the war
Reached our door
It left a hole
In families

That were once
Whole.

This war that's invaded
This war that's pervaded
How much longer
Until we shut the door?

PUBLICATION NOTE

This work was published online in 2024 by the *Journal of Southeast Asian American Education and Advancement* in Volume 19, Issue 1. Minor edits have been made here. The original can be found at http://doi.org/10.7771/2153-8999.1298.

Contributors

VIKRANT CHAP is a doctoral candidate of Literacy and Language Education in the Purdue University College of Education. He is the Editorial Assistant and Journal Manager of the *Journal of Southeast Asian American Education and Advancement.*

VICHET CHHUON, PhD, is an Associate Professor of Culture and Teaching in the University of Minnesota Twin Cities College of Education and Human Development. He is the Book Review Editor of the *Journal of Southeast Asian American Education and Advancement.*

BAO DIEP at the time of his original publication in JSAAEA, Bao was a PhD candidate in the Culture and Teaching program at the University of Minnesota–Twin Cities. He earned his BA in Sociology and his MSW in Social Work, also from the University of Minnesota–Twin Cities. His research interests include Southeast Asian American students' experiences in higher education; Vietnamese American students' experiences, and how their identities, particularly queer identities, impact their experiences in higher education in the United States.

MOZZIE DOSALMAS (They/He) is a Senior Researcher and Curriculum Developer for an Oakland, CA education nonprofit, Co-Lead of the Research Justice at the Intersections program for the Mills Institute, and an adjunct professor. Mozz's work focuses on the teaching and learning needs of youth traditionally underserved by educational institutions and in STEM fields. They aim to broaden access to these fields by bringing a critical women of color feminisms and queer theory lens to curriculum development, educational research, and educational leadership.

VICTORIA GILL is a first-generation, Lao Punjabi American poet, practitioner-scholar, and Assistant Professor at Lesley University. She obtained her doctorate in Reading, Writing, and Literacy from the University of Pennsylvania. Having long been passionate about issues of power and identity, she investigates their intersections and how they relate to language, literacies, and pedagogies in ways that create pathways for teachers to build inclusive classrooms that center historically excluded perspectives, knowledges, and voices. Her current research examines how teaching can be impacted by understanding and using the theory of intersectionality with aims for equity and agency, with a focus on Children's and Young Adult Literature and Southeast Asian representation in secondary English Language Arts classes. Dr. Gill's research has been published in *The English Journal*, the *Assembly on Literature for Adolescents of NCTE, LEARNing Landscapes, Writing & Pedagogy, in:cite, Journal of Southeast Asian American Education and Advancement*, and the *Urban Education* journal.

TRANGĐÀI GLASSEY-TRẦNGUYỄN, PhD (trangdai.net) is an award-winning bilingual author and multidisciplinary scholar. She has worked to foster world peace, racial equity, cross-cultural understanding, and social justice. She has been honored with more than 50 awards and recognitions for her creativity, scholarship, leadership, and advocacy, including an exceptional ranking Fulbright grant.

DARYL GORDON is a professor in Adelphi University's Bilingual/TESOL Program. She earned her doctorate in Educational Linguistics at the University of Pennsylvania. She has taught and designed curricula for ESL learners in the United States, Mexico, and the Lao PDR. She currently teaches classes in Sociolinguistics, TESOL pedagogy, and ELL assessment. Her research interests include gendered second language socialization, the impact of trauma on refugee second language acquisition, and civic engagement and belonging for adult immigrants.

QUAN MANH HA is Professor of American literature and ethnic studies at the University of Montana. He is the co-translator of *Other Moons: Vietnamese Stories of the American War and Its Aftermath*, Bao Ninh's *Hanoi at Midnight: Stories*, Ta Duy Anh's *The Termite Queen*, *Longings: Contemporary Fiction by Vietnamese Women Writers*, and *Light Out and Modern Vietnamese Stories, 1930–1954*.

SARAH HANSEN leads Open Education and Strategic Initiatives at MIT OpenCourseWare. Dr. Hansen and her team at the Massachusetts Institute of Technology build relationships across institutions to promote innovative and equitable learning opportunities for teachers and learners on a global scale. At the time of the original publication of this work in JSAAEA, she was a doctoral student at the University of Minnesota.

EZEKIEL JOUBERT III is an Associate Professor of Educational Foundations in the Division of Advanced and Applied Studies at California State University–Los Angeles. His research, scholarship, and writing focus on the intersections of racial capitalism and Black education, educational inequality in Black rural communities in the Midwest, Black mobilities, organic intellectual thought and activism, and ethnic studies pedagogies. At the time of the original publication of this work in JSAAEA, Ezekiel Joubert III was a PhD student at the University of Minnesota.

SUNEETA KERCOOD is a tenured full professor in the College of Education at Butler University (Indianapolis, IN), with a doctorate from Purdue in special education (cognate of Education Psychology), master's in Psychology, and bachelor's degree specializing in intellectual disabilities from India, and is a Board Certified Behavior Analyst (BCBA-D). Dr. Kercood is also a practicing paramedic, EMT and Paramedic educator, and an active longtime volunteer for American Red Cross Disaster Health services. Dr. Kercood's research interests and agenda include interdisciplinary projects that study teaching and learning methodologies, and equity-access issues in education and health of individuals with disabilities and other special/vulnerable populations including refugees, immigrants, and tribal communities. Dr. Kercood was selected as the first non-medical recipient of a disaster medical fellowship with the IU School of Emergency medicine, a Fulbright scholarship, and received the Distinguished Faculty for Research and Scholarship at Butler University.

KEVIN D. LAM is Associate Professor of Urban and Diversity Education in the Dept. of Teaching and Learning at Drake University. Lam is the author of *Youth Gangs, Racism, and Schooling: Vietnamese American Youth in a Postcolonial Context* (Palgrave) and co-editor of *The Critical Pedagogy Reader*, 4th ed. (Routledge) and *The Selected Works of Antonia Darder: On Theory and Struggle* (Bloomsbury, forthcoming). His research and teaching interests include Asian American youth violence, critical theory of racism, Vietnamese diaspora, critical pedagogy, urban education, and political economy.

RAVY S. LAO is a lecturer and virtual simulation coordinator in the College of Education (COE) at California State University, Los Angeles, where she instructs education courses for preservice teachers at both the elementary and secondary levels. In addition to teaching, she is a project director of a three-year National Science Foundation (NSF) funded study, Simulation for Minority Interactive Learning Environments (SMILE): A Design and Development Project, at the COE to research the integration of mixed-reality virtual simulations in STEM teacher preparation. Dr. Lao's research focuses on preservice teachers' development of teacher identity and discourse and the integration of technology in teacher preparation.

JIN SOOK LEE is Professor of Education in the Department of Education and an affiliated faculty member in the Departments of Linguistics and Asian American Studies at the University of California, Santa Barbara. She also serves as the Associate Dean of the Graduate Division at her institution. Her research examines sociocultural factors that shape the learning and teaching processes of culturally and linguistically diverse students, particularly in the development and maintenance of their dual language capacity. She co-edited *The Education of Language Minority Immigrants in the*

United States (Multilingual Matters, 2009) and *Feeling It: Language, Race and Affect in Latinx Youth Learning* (Routledge, 2018) and serves on numerous editorial boards of prominent journals in her field. She is a former Fulbright Senior Scholar of Applied Linguistics.

STACEY J. LEE is the Vilas Research Professor & Frederick Erickson WARF Professor of Educational Policy Studies at the University of Wisconsin–Madison. She is the author of *Unraveling the Model Minority Stereotype: Listening to Asian American Youth*, *Up Against Whiteness: Race, School, and Immigrant Youth*, and *Resisting Asian American Invisibility: The Politics of Race and Education.*

THANG C. LIAN Thang was a student at Duke University studying history and international comparative studies with research interests in Asian American community and political formations, specifically focused on Chin refugees from Myanmar.

JIA "GRACE" LIANG is an Associate Professor of Educational Leadership at Kansas State University. She holds a PhD in Educational Administration and Policy along with a master's in educational psychology from the University of Georgia. Her research and professional work focus on educational leadership and equity, particularly related to Asian Americans and Pacific Islanders, community engagement, capacity building and leadership development, and intersectionality and women leadership. She has served as the Chair of the Research on the Education and Asian and Pacific Americans Special Interest Group of the American Educational Research Association and the President of the Eastern Educational Research Association. She has been a co- or lead PI for National Science Foundation grants that focus on minoritized student populations on university campuses. Her work has appeared in leading journals and book chapters such as *Educational Administration Quarterly*, *Journal of School Leadership*, *Gender and Education*, *International Journal of Mentoring and Coaching in Education*, *Journal of Cases in Educational Leadership*, *Best Practices and Programming Approaches for Mentoring Educational Leaders*, and *Handbook of Urban Educational Leadership*.

PACYINZ LYFOUNG is a French-born, Minnesota-grown, Hmong/Asian American poet, attorney and activist. She emerged as a poet as part of the Hmong American literary movement and the Asian American Renaissance in Minnesota. She has published in many journals such as *Paj Ntaub Voice*, *The Journal of Southeast Asian American Education and Advancement*, Split This Rock's *The Quarry: A Database of Social Justice Poetry*, *The Stonecoast Review*, and *Cultural Daily*. Her work has been anthologized in *Bamboo Among the Oaks: Contemporary Writing by Hmong Americans*, *To Sing Along the Way: Minnesota Women Poets from Pre-Territorial Days to the Present, The Forgotten River: An Anacostia Swim Club Member Anthology*, and *They Rise Like a Wave: An Anthology of Asian American Women Poets.*

MAI NGUYEN DO (ĐỖ NGUYÊN MAI) is a Vietnamese American poet from Santa Clarita, California. Her debut poetry collection, *Ghosts Still Walking*, is available from Platypus Press, and her second poetry collection, *Battlefield Blooming*, is available from Sahtu Press. At the time of her original publication in JSAAEA, Mai was pursuing a PhD in the Department of Political Science at the University of California, Riverside, where she studied Southeast Asian refugee communities in the United States and the school-to-prison-to-deportation pipeline.

TRISH MORITA-MULLANEY is an Associate Professor at Purdue and holds a courtesy appointment in the Asian American Studies program. Her research focuses on the intersections between language learning, gender, and race and how this informs the identity acts of educators of multilingual communities. Guided by critical and feminist thought, she examines how these overlapping identities inform the logics of educational decision making for multilingual families. She has studied the Lau case and how it was developed, experienced, and implemented by the Chinese American community of San Francisco, representing the original history and voice of Lau, documented in her book with Multilingual Matters entitled *Lau v. Nichols and Chinese American Language Rights: The Sunrise and Sunset of Bilingual Education.*

MIKE HOA NGUYEN, PhD, is Assistant Professor of Education at New York University. His research examines the benefits and consequences of public policy instruments in expanding and constraining the academic operations of colleges and universities, with a specific focus on federal diversity initiatives. He is the principal investigator of the Minority-Serving Institutions (MSI) Data Project. An extension of this work explores Asian American & Native American Pacific Islander Serving Institutions (AANAPISI) and their role in building capacity to serve Asian American, Native Hawaiian, and Pacific Islander (AA and NHPI) students, staff, faculty, and administrators. Prior to earning his doctorate, Nguyen served as a senior staff member in the United States Congress.

ANCHALEE PANIGABUTRA-ROBERTS, with the Thai nickname "Joy," was born and raised in Thailand. She currently works in an academic library and lives in Knoxville, Tennessee. Her poems are influenced by different languages and cultures she has learned over the years. They are her testament to our shared humanity.

GILBERT C. PARK is an Associate Professor of Social Foundations and Multicultural Education at Ball State University. His research focuses on school experiences of Asian immigrants and the potential for multicultural education to be used as a tool for advancing social justice. Specifically, he has been interested in the process of segmented assimilation for immigrants from Asia in American public schools. His other research looked at the limitations and possibilities of Korean multicultural education for the children of immigrant mothers and North Korean refugees in rural Korean schools as a U.S. Fulbright Scholar to Korea. As the president of the Korean American Educational Researchers Association, he sought to build solidarity with other Asian American scholarly organizations against Anti-Asian American Hate Crimes during the recent pandemic.

LINDA M. PHENG is an Assistant Professor of Education at the University of Pennsylvania's Graduate School of Education. Dr. Pheng is an expert in community-engaged scholarship and civic and political youth work with Asian immigrant and refugee students and communities. As an interdisciplinary scholar, her scholarship draws on theories of race and racialization and critical refugee studies to unpack the ways in which diverse Asian immigrant and refugee students navigate race, class, and immigrant/refugee identities in and out of schools. At the time of the original publication of this work in JSAAEA, Dr. Pheng was a doctoral student in Educational Policy Studies at the University of Wisconsin–Madison.

MALAPHONE PHOMMASA is the Assistant Dean of Academic Success Initiatives in the Office of Teaching & Learning at the University of California, Santa Barbara. She is a proud daughter of Lao refugees and first-generation college graduate. She earned her BA in Sociology at the University of California, Irvine, and her MA and PhD in Education at the University of California, Santa Barbara. At the time of the original publication of this work in JSAAEA, Dr. Phommasa was a PhD candidate at UCSB and an Assistant Professor, Minority Faculty Fellow at Marshall University.

CHANG PU is an Associate Professor of TESOL and director of the ESOL Endorsement program at Berry College. Her research focuses on TESOL, bilingual education, heritage language education, teacher education, virtual exchange, and global learning. She has published empirical studies in peer-reviewed journals such as *Bilingual Research Journal* and *Educational Forum*. Dr. Pu was named a Longview Foundation Global Teacher Educator fellow.

JAI ARUN RAVINE is a trans-identified, multidisciplinary writer, dancer, visual and performing artist of mixed Thai and white American heritage. Jai received an MFA in Writing & Poetics from Naropa University and a BA in Interdisciplinary Asian Studies from Hollins University. A Kundiman Fellow, Jai's first chapbook, *IS THIS JANUARY*, is available from Corollary Press.

NIDA RINTHAPOL received her PhD in Educational Psychology with an emphasis in Cultural Perspectives and Comparative Education from UC Santa Barbara. She worked as an Associate Director for Data Resources at UCLA, then transitioned into teaching at various California State Universities. After the pandemic, she shifted her focus to fighting homelessness.

JALISA SANG is a Cambodian American from Minnesota. She graduated from the University of Minnesota Twin Cities in 2024 where she earned a Bachelor of Science in Family Social Science & Youth Studies with a minor in Public Health. Her research interests include Southeast Asian American immigrants/refugees, Cambodian history, immigration policies, detention and deportation, education, and early childhood education disparities. Currently, she is working as a Paraprofessional at an elementary school. Her next plans are to attend graduate school and earn a Master of Social Work.

CHHANY SAK-HUMPHRY, PhD, is an Associate Professor of Cambodian (Khmer) Language at the University of Hawaii at Mānoa College of Arts, Languages, & Letters. She is the founding Associate Editor of the *Journal of Southeast Asian American Education and Advancement* and a past president of the National Association for the Education and Advancement of Cambodian, Laotian, and Vietnamese Americans.

SOKUNTHARY SVAY is a Cambodian writer from the Bronx, New York. A founding member of the Cambodian American Literary Arts Association (CALAA), she has received fellowships from the American Opera Project, Poets House, and Willow Books, as well as commissions from Washington National Opera, the Asian American Writers' Workshop, the Chautauqua Institution, and ISSUE Project Room. In addition to publishing a poetry collection, *Apsara in New York* (Willow Books, 2017), Svay has had her writing anthologized and performed by actors and singers. Svay's first opera, *Woman of Letters*, set by composer Liliya Ugay, received its world premiere at the Kennedy Center in January 2020 as part of the American Opera Initiative. A recipient of the OPERA America IDEA grant, her second opera with Ugay, *Chhlong Tonle*, received its premiere in March 2022. She is a PhD candidate in English at the CUNY Graduate Center and a Lecturer at the City College of New York in Harlem. Her hybrid memoir *Put It On Record: A Memoir-Archive* is out now from Willow Books.

QUAN TUE TRAN is Senior Lecturer in Ethnicity, Race, and Migration at Yale University. Her book manuscript, *Anchoring Boat People's History and Memory*, examines transnational processes of memory and history making in the contemporary Vietnamese refugee diaspora by documenting and analyzing boat refugee burial sites, memorials, archives, and cultural productions in Southeast Asia, Western Europe, and North America. Her teaching and research interests include critical refugee studies, Asian American studies, and Vietnamese diaspora studies. Her scholarly publications appear in *Journal of Southeast Asian American Education and Advancement*, *Journal of Vietnamese Studies*, *Memory Studies*, *Amerasia Journal*, and in anthologies such as *Toward a Framework for Vietnamese American Studies: History, Community, and Memory*; *Refugee Crises, 1945–2000*; *Looking Back on the Vietnam War: Twenty-First-Century Perspectives*. Dr. Tran is also a poet and translator.

BUNKONG TUON is a Cambodian American writer, Pushcart Prize–winning poet, and professor who teaches at Union College in Schenectady, NY. He is the author of several poetry collections. In 2024, he published *What Is Left*, a Greatest Hits chapbook from Jacar Press, and *Koan Khmer*, his debut novel from Northwestern UP/Curbstone Books. He lives with his wife and children in Upstate New York.

PHITSAMAY S. UY is an Associate Professor of Leadership in Schooling and Co-Director of the Center for Asian American Studies at the University of Massachusetts Lowell School of Education. She is the Associate Editor of the *Journal of Southeast Asian American Education and Advancement* and a past president of the National Association for the Education and Advancement of Cambodian, Laotian, and Vietnamese Americans.

MAI DER VANG is a Hmong American writer/poet who lives in Fresno, California. Her poems have been published in *Paj Ntaub Voice*. In September 2009, she completed a residency at Hedgebrook, a program for women writers. She is also a member of the Hmong American Writers' Circle (HAWC) and currently serves on the editorial board for an upcoming Hmong literary anthology with HAWC for Heyday Books.

MAI NENG VANG At the time of her original publication in JSAAEA, Mai was a graduate student in the Educational Policy Studies program at the University of Wisconsin–Madison. She has a broad research interest in the educational experiences of immigrant and refugee students. More specifically, she is interested in understanding how race, ethnicity, gender, and class intersect to inform the lives and experiences of Hmong American students and their families.

THONG VANG is a PhD candidate in the Culture and Teaching program at the University of Minnesota–Twin Cities. His research involves uncovering the teaching and learning practices within and identity development of diasporic communities. More specifically, he examines how teaching and learning occur within HMoob American communities and how they combat deficit models of academic identities. Thong is a recipient of the University of Minnesota's 2023–2024 Doctoral Dissertation Fellowship and a Lub Zej Zog Critical and Indigenizing HMoob Educational Studies Writing Fellow. He is actively engaged as a researcher and curriculum writer for the California H[Moob] History and Cultural Studies Model Curriculum.

SENGARONE PETER VETSMANY pursued a Master of Fine Arts in Creative Writing with an emphasis in poetry at Minnesota State University, Mankato. He expected to finish in 2020, just in time for the 45th anniversary of the Lao Diaspora. Born and raised in Boise, Idaho, he is a graduate of the University of Idaho with a BS in philosophy. His work has appeared in *Little Laos on the Prairie* and the *Asian American Writers' Workshop*. He is the Graduate Assistant for Asian American Affairs at Minnesota State University, Mankato, and resides in Minnesota.

BRYAN THAO WORRA is a writer and poet. He is the first Laotian American to receive a Fellowship in Literature from the National Endowment for the Arts. He is the Creative Works Editor of the *Journal of Southeast Asian American Education and Advancement.*

WAYNE E. WRIGHT is the Associate Dean for Research, Graduate Programs, and Faculty Development, and Professor and Barbara I. Cook Chair of Literacy and Language in the Purdue University College of Education. He is the Founding Editor of the *Journal of Southeast Asian American Education and Advancement.* Wright was a Khmer bilingual teacher in the Long Beach Unified School District in California, and was a Fulbright Scholar in Cambodia. He is the author of *Foundations for Teaching English Language Learners: Research, Theory, Policy, and Practice* (4th ed., Brookes Publishing) and co-author of *Foundations of Bilingual Education and Bilingualism* (8th ed., Multilingual Matters).

CHOUA P. XIONG is an Assistant Professor of Hmong Studies in the Department of Anthropology, Global Religions, and Cultures at the University of Wisconsin–Oshkosh. She teaches a range of courses in Hmong Studies and Educational Studies that examine displacement, race, gender, and community building. Choua's research approach is informed by her activism as an educator in Southeast Asian community-based educational spaces, schools, and higher education. She had led various collaborative and community-based participatory action research (CBPAR) projects that center the perspectives of minoritized youth. Her work highlights the roles communities of color play in educating youth about schooling, political participation, belonging, and healing. At the time of the original publication of this work in JSAAEA, Dr. Xiong was a graduate student at the University of Wisconsin–Madison.

YANG SAO XIONG is an assistant professor in the Department of Anthropology and the Asian American Studies Program at CSU Fresno. He received his PhD in sociology from UCLA. He studies post-1965 non-White immigrant groups' social movements and their political incorporation in the United States. He is the author of *Immigrant Agency: Hmong American Movements and the Politics of Racialized Incorporation* (Rutgers University Press, 2022). His work has been published by the *AAPI Nexus*, *Amerasia Journal*, *ANNALS of the American Academy of Political and Social Science*, *Contexts*, *Ethnic and Racial Studies*, *Ethnicities*, *Hmong Studies Journal*, *Journal of Southeast Asian American Education and Advancement*, *Urban Science*, and elsewhere. At the time of the original publication of this work in JSAAEA, he was a doctoral student at UCLA.

AHMAY YA is a bilingual Adult Mental Health Case Manager in Wilder's Southeast Asian Services. She is earning a social work degree at Metropolitan State University. Her goal is to become a licensed clinical social worker in order to serve families and her Karen refugee community and other ethnic groups from Burma. She will be one of the first social workers fluent in the Karen and Burmese languages and cultures, and this will help her in helping others to become better community members and citizens. She is interested in understanding mental health needs for the Karen community, currently an unmet need. Her hope is to increase knowledge and insight into this population. She hopes to do work that is not only culturally competent but also culturally responsive to her community.

DEJ TXIAJ NTSIM, KUAB MAIV YAJ, KOUA MAI YANG received her Bachelor of Fine Arts from the University of Wisconsin, Milwaukee, in 2012 and her Master of Fine Arts from the University of Minnesota–Twin Cities in 2020. Working in multiple media such as drawing, painting, paj ntaub, photography, performance, and installation, Yaj's artistic practice interrogates recurring themes in the HMong imagination. Her current project, HNav HMoob, Wear HMong, engages in HMong ancestral dress through making paj ntaub, performance, installation, and photography to raise questions about HMong materiality, aesthetics, culture, and femme invisibility. Her practice moves slowly and lingers on the complications of HMong participation in capitalism—in the selling and consumption of HMong bodies and knowledge. She was a 2020/2021 MCAD-Jerome Early Career fellow, a 2023 Art Matters: Artist2Artist Fellow, and currently resides in West Saint Paul, Minnesota.

Index

Page numbers in italics indicate Figures or Tables.

www.ingramcontent.com/pod-product-compliance
Lightning Source LLC
Chambersburg PA
CBHW071541031225
36158CB00013B/571